Strategic Consequences of India's Economic Performance

...a collection of Baru's journalistic greatest hits... brilliant scene-setting essays analysing the strategic choices that have faced India since it started to open its economy 15 years ago... make it required reading for anyone interested in the interplay between domestic economic strategy and global power politics.

Financial Times
LONDON

Today it is easy to talk about India as a rising great power... But a decade-and-a-half ago, it needed a lot of insight as well as intellectual courage to stand up and propose new directions for India's economic and foreign policies. It is that bold vision and conviction about a new India which was being forged in the 1990s and the early 2000s, that comes through in this collection of Baru's essays and columns... As India continues to march forward to acquire "comprehensive national power", that brings together all the elements that constitute the strength of nations, the analytical path opened by Baru will remain an important one to emulate.

The Indian Express
NEW DELHI

Sanjaya Baru is perhaps one of the first mainstream economic commentators in the country to look at the intersection of economics and national security. ...Baru's essays and columns collected in this book are a vital contribution towards initiating a contemporary debate that will help shape a future policy.

Hindustan Times
NEW DELHI

...stimulating collection...
Baru's book deserves to be prescribed reading for policymakers.

Outlook
NEW DELHI

strategic
consequences of
India's
economic performance

essays & columns

sanjaya baru

ACADEMIC FOUNDATION
NEW DELHI

Published in 2006

by : ACADEMIC FOUNDATION
    4772-73 / 23 Bharat Ram Road, (23 Ansari Road),
    Darya Ganj, New Delhi - 110 002 (India).
    Tel : 23245001 / 02 / 03 / 04.
    Fax : +91-11-23245005.
    E-mail : academic@vsnl.com
    www.academicfoundation.com

Cataloging-in-Publication Data--DK
    Courtesy: D.K. Agencies (P) Ltd. <docinfo@dkagencies.com>

Baru, Sanjaya, 1954-
    Strategic consequences of India's economic
    performance : essays & columns / SanjayaBaru.
        p.   cm.
    Includes bibliographical references (p.   )
    Includes index.
    ISBN-13: 978-81-7188-558-6
    ISBN-10: 81-7188-558-6

        1. National security--Economic aspects--
    India. 2. India--Economic policy--1991-
    3. India--Foreign relations--1984-   4. Security,
    International.   I. Title.

DDC 338.473 550 095 4   22

Designed and typeset by Italics India, New Delhi.
Printed and bound in India.

10 9 8 7 6 5 4 3 2

For
Rama and Tanvika

CONTENTS

Foreword

THIS volume of collection of seminar presentations and articles written for journals and newspapers over a period of eight years (1996-2004) is a very timely contribution by Sanjaya Baru to the ongoing debate in the country on the choice of strategy to enhance India's economic growth and development and international security. Today one often hears a demand for the formulation of a consensus on this issue. It is not, however, recognised that this country is in fact having its fourth debate on such a choice. The first one was even before Independence when Gandhiji and Jawaharlal Nehru debated the options for post independence development. While the former pressed for a decentralised rural economy and opposed industrialism (and not industrialisation) the latter was for speedy industrialisation.

The second round came with the setting up of the Planning Commission and India embarking on centralised planning. Nehru explained in his famous essay on the 'Middle Path' the need for India adopting a mixed economy. He was criticised on the one side by the Communists (who then commanded some 11 per cent of votes) for not going far enough on the Socialist path and by the Swatantra Party, on the other side, for going too far! The licence permit quota *raj*, which got entrenched after Nehru, was partly the result of the then prevailing international strategic environment and partly the beginning of organised corruption in our electoral politics and top down control of our political parties.

Then came the third round of debate. Faced with threats of international payments default India launched on economic liberalisation, in 1991. There was no dearth of critics. There were prophets of doom who predicted that the country would be flooded with foreign goods, our country could not face international competition, and it would lead to increased unemployment. None of these forebodings came to be fulfilled. The Indian economic growth accelerated, trade expanded and foreign exchange reserves rose. India got recognition as an IT power. Outsourcing of BPO to this country expanded and increasing number of multinationals started to set up R&D centres in India.

Now there is yet another debate on how India should respond to the US-led global interaction with India. As happened earlier there are those who are for taking advantage of this chance and exploiting it for India's benefit and others who are cautious about venturing on this new path. It is in this context that Sanjaya Baru, a strong protagonist of change, is offering his perspective on the nature of transformation in international economic order, as well as, in the strategic environment. I do not pretend to be unbiased on this issue. I am for India adapting itself to the emerging global balance of power and economic globalisation. Both Baru and myself subscribe to the view propounded by Prime Minister Manmohan Singh that globalisation is irreversible and India has no alternative but to adapt itself to it. Those who are arguing that as a continental sized country India can isolate itself from globalisation should do well to bear in mind the fate of the experiment of building socialism in isolation in continental sized economies such as Soviet Union and China.

The merit of Sanjaya Baru's compilation is in his development of a holistic view of the symbiotic relationship between international economics and international strategic developments. A globalised economy, with this degree of interdependence among nations, and in a balance of power strategic system, has not existed before; at least not in the industrial age. The world did not have nuclear weapons and missiles that deterred outbreak of war among major powers. Nor have we a precedent to a world where knowledge will be the currency of power. The opposition to India's enhancement of its relationship with the US comes largely from people who are risk averse. Sanjaya Baru has done well to highlight in his writings the Chinese example. Mao Tse-tung and his colleagues had far more justification to suspect US bonafides in 1971 than India has in 2005. Yet the Chinese leadership took the risk and did very well.

The Indian political establishment is totally absorbed in domestic politics and does not have much familiarity with international politics and economics. There is no institutionalised long-term strategic assessment, very few think tanks and no university centres for research on foreign policy. The indifference of our legislators to foreign policy and strategic issues is notorious. During the era of Non-alignment we got isolated from international strategic developments. The Non-aligned declarations were a compilation of platitudes and there were very few attempts at analysis of current realities.

In the early years of the Cold War, alliance with the US did not yield very tangible results as was seen in the case of Pakistan, Iran and Turkey. The Indian strategy of autarchic development was justified in those circumstances. But once the rebuilding of Europe and Japan got completed the development of friendly nations was accelerated by strategic considerations by market economies. The East Asian Tigers and China were the principal beneficiaries of this phenomenon. Now the international system has progressed into the new phase of six-nation balance of power, in which, the major nations face no prospect of war but compete peacefully in an evolving rule-bound globalised order.

A correct understanding of this evolution is essential for India to make right policy choices to maximise its advantages. In his Independence Day Address on 15th August, 2005, at New Delhi's Red Fort, Prime Minister Manmohan Singh said: "There comes a time in the history of a nation when it can be said that the time has come to make history. We are today at the threshold of such an era. The world wants us to do well and take our rightful place on the world stage. There are no external constraints on our development. If there are any hurdles they are internal." This compilation is a valuable contribution to promote an understanding of the relevance of overcoming these internal hurdles and its consequence for India's place in the world. For this Dr. Sanjaya Baru deserves our congratulations.

K. Subrahmanyam

New Delhi

K. Subrahmanyam is India's leading defence analyst and former convenor, National Security Advisory Board. He has also been consulting editor of *The Times of India,* and *The Economic Times.*

Acknowledgements

IN writing these essays and columns, in the decade 1994 to 2004, I have incurred several intellectual and personal debts. I must, however, first record my gratitude to the publishers of the various publications from which these essays and columns have been re-printed, for permitting me to include them in this volume. The 'Sources' have been duly acknowledged at the end of this volume.

My most important intellectual debt, in writing on the subjects covered in this book, is to Mr. K. Subrahmanyam, to whom I am also indebted for the valuable *Foreword* he has so graciously written. My second intellectual debt is to Dr. Manmohan Singh, who shaped my thinking on economic policy and globalisation during the 1990s. This book could not have been written but for the paradigmatic change that Dr. Singh helped bring about in India's economic policies and performance. In recent history nothing has defined India's place in the world more importantly than the new profile India's economy has acquired.

I would like to thank my former colleagues at *The Times of India, The Economic Times, The Indian Express* and *The Financial Express* for the stimulating discussions we had on many of these issues. I am also grateful to the faculties of the Research and Information System for Non-Aligned and Other Developing Countries (RIS) and the Indian Council for Research in International Economic Relations (ICRIER); participants at various seminars where some of these papers were presented; and members of the National Security

Advisory Board, where many of my ideas on the economics of national security were shaped, for comments on earlier drafts of some of these essays, and for stimulating many of the ideas contained in the columns published here.

I am grateful to the Prime Minister for permitting me to publish these essays and columns. All these essays were written and published before I joined the Prime Minister's Office. They do not reflect the thinking of the Government of India or the Prime Minister. This book does not contain any information made available to me in my present position. I am grateful to the Kapila family and the editors at Academic Foundation for the high degree of professionalism they brought to bear on the printing and publishing of this volume.

One incurs many debts of gratitude over a period of a decade, but none more important than the debt one owes to our loved ones. I dedicate this book to the two people who gave me their unquestioned love and support and made it possible for me to write these essays and columns—my daughter Tanvika and my wife Rama.

Introduction

WHEN Thomas C. Schelling was awarded the Nobel Prize in economics in 2005, the economics profession had finally come to recognise the value of a strand of economics that still has few practitioners in India. The economics of national security. Schelling's seminal work on the strategy of conflict and the 'nuclear game' took economics beyond the more mundane pre-occupation with the economics of war and national security that grabbed the attention of many Western economists during and after the Second World War. John Maynard Keynes and Nicholas Kaldor, in Britain, and John Kenneth Galbraith and Charles P. Kindleberger, in the United States, were intensely engaged, as professional economists, in studying the financial aspects of war and its economic consequences. Galbraith and Kindleberger were in fact on the staff of the US Office of Strategic Services during the War. Professional economists continue to be hired both by the US Defence and State Departments and by the British Foreign and Commonwealth Office.

Even in China, the collapse of the Soviet Union seemed to encourage greater respect among strategic policy makers for the views of professional economists in shaping strategic and foreign policy choices. It was at a defence establishment think tank that Chinese strategists developed the notion of Comprehensive National Power (CNP), that gave a higher weight to economic and social aspects of national security over the purely military.

Economists have not had the same profile in India's foreign policy and defence establishments, nor in shaping Indian strategic thought. In Government, there has been an institutional disconnect between economic planners and strategic policy makers. Outside Government, a think tank like the Institute of Defence Studies and Analyses has never hired an economist to study the economic and fiscal aspects of defence and national security. Professional economists have rarely considered the economic costs and benefits of India's strategic and foreign policy choices. Thus, a combination of professional disinterest, on the part of economists, and institutional neglect, on the part of Government and think tanks, has contributed to the relative neglect of the economic dimensions of our foreign policy and strategic choices, and the economic consequences of those choices.

My own interest in these issues was not stimulated when I was still a professional economist. It is as a journalist that I came to educate myself on the economic dimensions of India's foreign policy and strategic options. It was in 1995, when I took charge as the Editorial Page Editor of *The Times of India*, that I was called upon to take a view on India's stance on the permanent extension of the Nuclear Non-proliferation Treaty (NPT) and the vote on a Comprehensive Test Ban Treaty (CTBT). I had informed colleagues in the TOI's editorial team to whom I first turned, like senior editors Manoj Joshi, Monu Nalapat and Ramesh Chandran. Soon the editorial team expanded and I had other colleagues like Vidya Subrahmanyam, Shastri Ramachandran and Siddharth Vardarajan joining me. The morning editorial meetings had become seminars on India's nuclear policy with diverse views being expressed. I realised I had to educate myself to be able to guide the raucous debate. I turned to the *Bhishmapithamaha* of Indian strategic policy thinking, K. Subrahmanyam, for guidance!

Subrahmanyam had joined *The Times of India* as its strategic affairs editor. He gave me long tutorials on India's nuclear policy, its history and geography, its economics and politics. I began reading books on foreign affairs and strategic policy and would regularly attend seminars at the Institute of Defence Studies and

Analyses (IDSA) and the India International Centre (IIC). By the time *The Times of India* was required to take a view on India's vote on CTBT, in 1996, I was clear in my mind that we should stand firm against India signing up on CTBT, till the required round of nuclear tests were completed.

My interest in the economics of India's foreign and strategic policy was further stimulated during my stint at the Research and Information System for Non-Aligned and Developing Countries (RIS) and the Indian Council for Research on International Economic Relations (ICRIER). Most of the essays published here were written when I was on the faculty of these two institutions. Some of these essays have come out of working papers I had prepared for the National Security Advisory Board (NSAB), of which I was a member in 1998-2001, and was nominated the convenor of its sub-group on Economic Security.

My first published essay on the economics of Indian foreign policy was, in fact, inspired by an interview that Dr. Manmohan Singh had given to the editors of *World Affairs*, a foreign affairs journal published from New Delhi, for their first issue in early 1997. Looking back at the geopolitical context of the early post-Cold War world in which he had introduced economic reforms in India, Manmohan Singh spoke at length about how China and other Asian economies had used economic openness and links with the West as a strategic instrument of development and foreign policy.

Taking off from these views of Dr. Manmohan Singh, I wrote an essay for *World Affairs* on "The Economics of India's Foreign Policy" (Chapter 2). In writing this essay my thinking was shaped by Jawaharlal Nehru's speech on foreign policy, delivered as early as in December 1947 in the Constituent Assembly (Appendix). I was struck by a statement in Nehru's speech that I felt had acquired a new resonance in the post-Cold War world. Nehru had said, "Talking about foreign policies, the House must remember that these are not just empty struggles on a chess board. Behind them lie all manner of things. Ultimately, foreign policy is the outcome of economic policy."

Surely, I thought, Nehru must have had good economic reasons for his various foreign policy initiatives. The popular myth about our post-Independence foreign policy was that it was based on 'universal principles' and not on 'narrow' national interest. But if economics is the basis, how can one deny the role of self-interest? I came across a fascinating essay by the Polish economist, Michal Kalecki, the co-founder of the Keynesian Revolution in macro-economics, who likened the economics of a 'mixed economy' and the foreign policy of 'non-alignment' to a 'clever calf sucking two cows'! Given Kalecki's impeccable left-wing and anti-imperialist credentials, I figured he was not maligning non-alignment, merely characterising it.

It became clear to me that Manmohan Singh's views, as articulated in the *World Affairs* journal had brought back the relevance of economics into our foreign policy debates. The end of the Cold War after the collapse of the Soviet Union, the growing salience of international trade in international relations, thanks to China's mercantilism and the creation of the World Trade Organization (WTO), and our own increasing economic engagement of our neighbours were all pointers to the renewed relevance of Nehru's dictum on the economics of our foreign policy.

It was, however, the nuclear tests of 1998 that brought out in sharp relief the link between foreign policy and strategic policy options and economic choices. The Pokhran-II nuclear tests in May 1998 sparked a debate among economists and economic journalists on the financial and economic implications of going nuclear and on the cost of sanctions imposed on India by the United States, Japan and some other countries. In an alarmist page one news report *The Economic Times* claimed that Pokhran-II would cost the economy upto $20 billion in terms of sanctions and reduced market access. This claim was very competently challenged by G. Balachandran and T.C.A. Srinivasa Raghavan in a study, *Sanctions: A Indo-US Perspective.*[1] Balachandran and Srinivasa Raghavan showed convincingly that "the sanctions imposed by the US and others,

---

1. Asian Institute of Transport Development, New Delhi, 1998.

though nationally irksome, are unlikely to have any serious effect on our economic development."

Their view received professional endorsement from a highly regarded American analyst, Fred Bergsten, chairman of the International Institute of Economics, Washington DC, who showed that India's experience with US sanctions was consistent with the global experience, as IIE's extensive research had shown. A country as large as India could not be negatively impacted by sanctions imposed by just one country or a small group of countries. IIE's monumental work on sanctions showed why a large country like India could not be easily disciplined by external sanctions. Visiting India after the Pokhran-II tests, Bergsten told an audience at ICRIER that his own estimate of the net impact of post-May 1998 US sanctions on India would be around US\$ 500 million, far from *ET's* alarmist \$20 billion!

While being comforted by this optimistic view, the Government of the day did not want to take chances. It launched several economic initiatives, to mop up dollars, and launched a massive diplomatic offensive, sending teams of Indian analysts and journalists to different countries to explain why India declared itself a nuclear weapons power and why the world should appreciate India's benign intent. I was drafted into this exercise by the IDSA and the IIC and travelled to many capitals with K. Subrahmanyam, N.N. Vohra, Jasjit Singh, Raja Mohan and others to convince the world that a nuclear India is no threat to the rest of the world.

In fact, I argued, a more self-confident and secure India and a stronger Indian economy should be welcomed by the world. Many of my newspaper columns, published in this volume, came out of those travels to distant capitals, ranging from Tokyo and Beijing to Paris and Washington DC. My interest in the economics of India's foreign policy and the strategic implications of India's economic development was stirred by this experience.

It was in early 2002 that I was invited by the Olin Institute of Strategic Studies at Harvard University, Boston, to read a paper at a monthly seminar on Economic Security. I chose to put my random thoughts on the matter, as expressed in a clutch of essays and columns, in a paper that I entitled *Strategic Consequences of India's Economic Performance*. I was delighted by the response I got to this paper from a variety of experts including Henry Kissinger and Martin Feldstein.

The first section of this book also contains an analytical piece I wrote for the *National Security Annual Review* published for the National Security Council Secretariat, on the concept of 'economic security' and a paper that Amit Mitra of the Federation of Indian Chambers of Commerce and Industry (FICCI) invited me to write as a background paper for a FICCI Annual General Meeting that focussed on national security.

The second section of the book contains essays on India and Asia. Here again my interest was first stimulated by a paper I wrote at RIS on India and ASEAN. Extensive travel in East and South-East Asia generated many newspaper columns and an essay that the editor of the Italian journal, *Heartland* asked me to write on the question, that he posed to me, "How Asian is India?" My research on India's trade relations with East and South-East Asian economies at ICRIER yielded a paper on India and China's trade relations with Asian economies. Analysing the so-called 'Asian financial crisis' of 1997 for ICRA's journal *Money & Finance*, I found that what began as a financial crisis became, in some countries, a wider economic crisis and, in some others, evolved into a major political crisis. The strategic consequences for Asia of the economic and financial crisis were all too visible in Indonesia. China's influence increased in the region, while that of the United States had waned.

Spending a summer at the East-West Center, Hawaii, as the First J. Watamull Fellow in 2000, I wrote a paper on the impact of the information technology boom in India on India-US relations. In my essay on India-ASEAN relations I offered the rationale for a 'Bay of Bengal Community', explaining the geo-economic logic of BIMSTEC (Bangladesh, India, Myanmar, Sri Lanka, Thailand Economic Cooperation). India's frustration with SAARC (South Asian Association for Regional Cooperation) made the idea of BIMSTEC popular at that time. However, I viewed BIMSTEC as a bridge to East Asia rather than as a rival to SAARC.

My enthusiasm for regional trade blocs had little to do with the purely economic rationale that trade economists were concerned with. Economists wedded to the idea of free trade viewed regional trade blocs as a diversion from their preferred agenda of unilateral and multilateral trade liberalisation. They viewed regionalism as an escape route from the WTO process. Protectionists, on the other hand, viewed regional trade blocs as the 'back door' of multilateralism. What was politically difficult to accomplish through the WTO, they felt, was being sought to be ensured through regional blocs that appeared politically less threatening. I share the view of those who see regionalism as a stepping stone, a building block, of multilateralism. More importantly, I also viewed regional preferential and free trade agreements as instruments of foreign policy. As trade economist Richard Cooper once put it, "trade policy is foreign policy" and more so with regional trade arrangements. Rather than view trade as a means of creating 'dependencies', *a la* the Latin American school of thought in trade policy, I shared the view that international trade creates relationships of 'mutual inter-dependence'. Consider what China did with the United States? It used trade to lock the US middle class into a mutually beneficial relationship that has acquired a political dimension and has shaped US-China relations over the past decade.

My analysis of the economics of Indian foreign policy and the strategic implications of India's economic development also pointed to the fact that for the first time after Independence, India's superior economic performance was becoming a differentiator as far as India's relations with Pakistan were concerned. I was able to see that Pakistan would pay a bigger economic price for Kargil than India. Pakistan's economy was in a tailspin after 1998 and this was reversed only after 2001, thanks to 9/11. Pakistan had not drawn the appropriate lessons from the collapse of the Soviet Union. The Soviets had armed themselves to their teeth to fight NATO on every possible battlefield. Yet, they lost the Cold War in the market place. The collapse of the Russian economy was a reminder for all nations that attempted to pursue power through the barrel of a gun. India drew the correct lesson and turned its attention inwards in the first half of the 1990s to repair its economy and make it more globally competitive. China's economic success also pointed in this direction. Power in the modern world was based as much on economic competitiveness and political resilience of a country as it was on military capability.

In some ways this debate has not ended. There are still the votaries of military power who see a large military programme in the nuclear field as a necessary requirement of power. There are others who believe that India's influence in world affairs will be shaped as much by its military potential and political profile as by its economic performance. This latter view is what informs China's notion of 'Comprehensive National Power' (CNP), that I have discussed in one essay and a couple of columns.

Apart from the 'hard power' dimensions of India's economic performance and strategic capability, India's emergence as a major power has also been shaped by her 'soft power' capabilities. The growth of India's 'knowledge economy', India's entertainment and news industry and the people-to-people links established by the so-called 'Indian diaspora', the people of Indian origin worldwide, have also shaped our global profile and prospect. Many of my newspaper columns were devoted to these issues and have been published here.

The central argument of this book is captured by the title of a TOI column, published here, "walking on two legs". It is an argument elaborated in Chapter 1, the Harvard lecture. The argument is simple. India is destined to regain its pre-eminent place in the global arena. To do so at a faster pace India must ensure faster paced economic growth, that is more efficient and equitable, and generates the revenues required to sustain a level-headed strategic policy. Equitable growth, within a framework of an open society, will enhance internal security and assure political stability; more efficient growth within a framework of an open economy will boost external security.

In the pre-colonial world, India, China and Europe were the three poles of equal power. European colonisation weakened India and China. The history of the 20th century has been the history of reversing this process. In the 21st century India and China will regain their place in a new 'multipolar', or 'poly-centric' world in which the United States will continue to be the pre-eminent power but will have to accommodate the aspirations of many other nations, including India. For India, the process of recovering the lost space in the global arena will, as it has been for others like China, require economic development and a strengthening of national capabilities. Unless the Indian economy becomes more competitive and is more globally engaged, unless the economic well-being of all Indians is assured, unless the financial health of the Government improves, India will not be able to sustain itself as a major power, nor acquire the other attributes, `hard' as well as `soft', of Comprehensive National Power.

Hence, India's rise and re-emergence on the world stage is a function of her economic and strategic capabilities. India's improved economic performance will perforce have strategic consequences. It will enable India to better engage the world economically. It will help build new relationships of economic inter-dependence that can have benign consequences for international relations. It will fiscally empower the Government to invest in strategic capabilities. It will reduce social and economic tensions at home as Government finds resources to invest in social and economic infrastructure. It will enable a more equitable and efficient growth process that will reduce domestic social and political tensions.

The new turn in India's economic policies and performance in the last decade of the 20th century—the success of Indian enterprise in the post-WTO world; the emergence of a confident professional middle-class; a demonstrated nuclear capability; and, the resilience of an open society and an open economy, in the face of multiple and complex challenges—these have all shaped India's response to the tectonic shifts in the global balance of power in the post-Cold War era. These essays and columns, written over a decade and for different audiences, offer a perspective on the economic and strategic dimensions of India's re-emergence on the world stage.

All these essays were written and published before I joined the Prime Minister's Office. They do not reflect the thinking of the

Government of India or the Prime Minister. This book does not contain any information made available to me in my present position.

The strategic consequences of India's economic performance

AT a time when the world was still coming to grips with the implications of the end of the Cold War for the global balance of power, for the role and relevance of different nations in the emergent global system, and, before there was as yet any considered appreciation of the impact of the turnaround of the Indian economy on the global and Asian balance of power, one of Harvard's most distinguished strategic thinkers made an interesting forecast about the nature of the post-Cold War international system that resonates to this day among strategic policy analysts in India. Prefacing his study of western diplomacy with a reflection on the 'New World Order', Henry Kissinger (*Diplomacy*, 1994), hypothesised that:

"The international system of the twenty-first century will be marked by a seeming contradiction—on the one hand, fragmentation; on the other, growing globalisation. On the level of the relations among states, the new order will be more like the European State system of the 18th and 19th centuries than the rigid patterns of the cold war. It will contain at least six major powers—the United States, Europe, China, Japan, Russia, and probably India—as well as a multiplicity of medium-sized and smaller countries" (p. 23).

Admittedly, the US remains the dominant military power but it has come to accept the emergence of other centres of economic power. Reiterating his earlier formulation more recently Kissinger (2000) has again spoken of India's 'potential' as a major power underscoring the importance of its economic performance. In 1994 India had neither convincingly demonstrated its ability to generate the kind of economic growth that it did in the period 1992-98, nor had it as yet declared itself a nuclear weapons power. Was Kissinger prescient in 1994 or was he drawing our attention to historical factors and underlying strengths in classifying India as a nation *en route* to 'major power' status? As a student of power and *realpolitik* Kissinger may well have come to understand by then that not only was India capable of sustaining the acceleration of economic growth it had already initiated in the 1980s but that its economic policies would be marked by a greater degree of realism, as in fact was the case by then with respect to its foreign policy, a fact that Kissinger readily acknowledges. However, if Kissinger, like so many other analysts, continues to only see the 'potential' of an as yet unarticulated Indian power, the question is what must India do to translate that potential into reality?

The analysts of power may suggest that notwithstanding India's declared nuclear power status there is still a credibility and a capability gap that has to be bridged before India can truly be viewed as a military and nuclear power with relevance to the world beyond her immediate neighbourhood. Nothing can be more important in bridging this gap between 'potential' and 'reality', between 'promise' and 'performance' than the sustained growth of the Indian economy. Economic development and growth is fundamental to India's re-emergence as a 'Great Power'. If India succeeds in sustaining a high rate of economic growth and can generate the resources needed not only for its defence and security but to invest in human capabilities and well-being and ensure peace and security in its neighbourhood, Kissinger's qualification can finally be dropped.

Emerging perceptions

Whatever western, and in particular American, perceptions of India during the Cold War, by the end of the 20th century two dominant factors seem to have shaped a new thinking about India in the western hemisphere—first, India's economic performance in the last decade of the century and the shift in economic policy and thinking in India; and, second, India's declared nuclear weapons status. Both these elements are factors endogenous to economic and political developments in India to which the US has had to respond. There are two other elements shaping US perceptions about India more recently, which are 'exogenous' to India but have a bearing on India-US relations. These are the rise of *jehadi* terrorism in the Muslim world and China's rising profile within Asia. Together, these factors, namely, India's economic empowerment, her military and technological capability and her role as a liberal and secular democracy in the fight against sectarianism and terrorism will shape the bilateral relationship with the US and the western world in the 21st century and, in turn, this will define American perceptions of India's global role in decades to come.

The challenge for India is to be able to deal with each one of these elements—economic growth and development, national security, *jehadi* terrorism and China's growing power and influence in a manner which will enhance national security and ensure national well-being in the foreseeable future. How India deals with each of these challenges will define the extent and nature of India's power in the 21st century and its national security.

Economic imperative

In a recent classic, the Oxford historian, Neil Ferguson (2001) while rejecting the more simplistic recent theories of the economic foundation of national power, has argued:

"Tolstoy's question was: 'What is the power that *moves* nations?' Substitute the word 'mobilise' and the question is perhaps easier to answer. Clearly, it is something more than purchasing power. Economic resources are important, of course, but they are not the sole determinant of power. A state's means of destruction consist of more than the output of its steel industry. As we have seen, a state can defeat an economically superior foe if it has better strategic, operational and tactical ability. Nor is the effectiveness of military mobilisation sufficient. We also need to take into account a state's financial sophistication: its ability to appropriate resources from taxpayers and to borrow from investors. And in major conflicts a state must also be able to mobilise civilians optimally. The right balance must be struck between the different sectors of the economy in order to maximise war-making resources without undermining domestic well-being. The quality of bureaucratic organisation in both the state and the private sector can therefore be as important as the quality of military organisation" (p. 418).

Ferguson draws attention to what he regards as the four key institutional pillars of financial strength, constituting the economic 'square of power', namely, a tax-collecting bureaucracy; a representative parliament; a national debt; and a central bank. Admittedly, Ferguson shies away from an economic deterministic theory of state power and says as much:

"No matter how efficient the tax system, no matter how representative the parliament, no matter how liquid the bond market and no matter how well managed the currency, in the end the legitimacy of a state is bound up with such intangibles as tradition (the memory of past benefits), charisma (the appeal of present leaders), popular belief (faith in future rewards, material and spiritual) and propaganda (the state's use of available media to bolster all these). Though Carlyle feared that modernity would turn all human relations into economic relations, the true 'homo economicus'—constantly aiming to maximise his utility with every transaction—remains a rarity, and to most of us rather a monstrous one. Every day, men and women subordinate their economic self-interest to some other motive, be it the urge to play, to idle, to copulate or to wreck" (p. 422).

Thus, states can pursue power and increase their strategic relevance even without the economic wherewithal, but in the long run sustainable power is built on the foundations of sustainable development.

For India, there is no doubt that the first and most important challenge is that of accelerating the rate of economic growth and development. Economic performance and capability certainly constitute the foundation of national security and power even more so for a developing nation like India. It will define the limits to military capability and alter the relationship between India and its neighbourhood, especially its two major adversaries, namely, China and Pakistan. India has the military capability to defend her territorial integrity and security, however, it will have to sustain higher rates of economic growth to be able to alter the strategic balance in Asia, and globally, to her developmental advantage. For this reason, her enemies will act to keep her economically weak. This only underscores the economic imperative and the strategic consequences of sustained economic development.

In his survey of the 'potential and promise' of Indian power, Stephen Cohen (2001) offers a balanced appreciation of both economic and military strengths in the making of a major power, posing the question: "Can India develop the technological, logistic, and military capacity to be more than a south Asian power in years to come?" However, Cohen focuses far too much on India's military, diplomatic and political capabilities, treating economic capability only cursorily. Cohen correctly draws attention to the disjunction between the 'worldview' and 'self-image' of Indian elites, and India's real capabilities. But in defining the latter he shows inadequate appreciation of the centrality of economic performance. A robust performance on the economic front is critical to the full realisation of India's strategic potential and national security.

The economic dimension was introduced more directly into the calculus of evolving strategic power equations in Asia in a RAND study (Yeh and Zycher, 2000) that says that if India can sustain into the period 2000-2015 the economic growth performance it recorded in 1992-1998, then there would be a major reordering of Asian power equations. Following this argument, Ashley Tellis (2001) analysed the many strategic consequences of India's improved economic performance.

"The moral of the story," says Tellis, is that "If India can sustain an average growth rate of even 5.5 per cent or thereabouts for the next two decades or so, it will become a significant actor on the Asian stage. If it can accelerate its growth rates to levels beyond this 5.5 per cent band, then its significance for Asian geopolitics only increases further." Tellis then defines a new marker, "A realisation of a growth rate consistently 7 per cent or higher, an economic performance that inexorably transforms India into a great power, positions it as an effective pole in the Asian geopolitical balance, and compels international attention to itself as a strategic entity with continentwide significance" (p. 240).

These ideas also find reflection in Teresita Schaffer's *Rising India and US Policy Options in Asia* in which the robustness of economic growth and governance are seen as key variables determining the nature of Indian power. Says Schaffer, "The extent of India's rise as an economy and as an international actor will be determined primarily by factors internal to India. Two factors emerged as central drivers in our scenario analysis. The first is economic change, which will profoundly affect the political climate, the leadership contests, and India's international behaviour...The second driver,... is the quality of political leadership,...."

The idea that economic performance and capability is a necessary, though by no means a sufficient, foundation of political and diplomatic influence and military power is now widely acknowledged, more so after the implosion of the Soviet Union under the burden of its economic weightlessness, and the role that rapid economic development has played in China's emergence as a major power.

Having said this, it will be our contention that it is not economic growth in itself that holds the key to India's global profile and power, its strategic role and relevance and its national security, but the nature of that growth process and the manner in which the economic challenges it faces today are addressed. By 'nature' we mean the distributional aspects of growth, the impact of growth on global competitiveness and integration with the global economy and the sectoral composition of that growth, that is the extent of industrialisation, and its fiscal sustainability. This is relevant because India's bigger security challenge, in its journey to major power status, is largely internal both economic and political. The threat to, what more recently has come to be defined as 'homeland security', is posed by social and economic backwardness, the inequalities and the political uncertainty this generates, and the quality of economic development.

India's primary external security challenge, that posed by cross-border terrorism in the north-western region bordering Pakistan, cannot be addressed without dealing with its domestic counterpart which feeds on social and economic backwardness of minorities, and communal and caste tensions. Inegalitarian growth can only feed such threats to national security. Equally, economic backwardness holds the Indian economy back from competing globally and thereby limits the range of her global engagement. Sustained and sustainable economic growth and development are, therefore, the foundation of India's power and security.

I : India's past economic performance and contemporary power

If accelerated economic growth holds the key to realising India's strategic potential, the question arises how has India done and what exactly is the gap between performance and potential.

It is useful to acknowledge at this point that several factors, other than economic growth, contribute to India's self-image as a major power—her civilisational history, her contribution to religion and philosophy, her intellectual, especially scientific and mathematical achievements, her demographic size and composition, her geographical size and location, her military strength and capability. As John Garver (2001) notes in the opening line of his study of the rivalry between India and China "Two of the most brilliant civilisations yet produced by humanity, those of China and India, lie side by side on the continent of Eurasia. The peoples that have produced these civilisations are both rightly proud of their histories and achievements, and determined that their nations will play a major role in the modern world" (p. 3).

A recent statistical enterprise of the Organisation of Economic Cooperation and Development (OECD) captures this notion of historic potential through striking economic numbers. Angus Maddison's (1998) study of China's economic performance has thrown up a set of numbers on world income for the period 1700-1995 that draws attention to India's and China's dominant position in the world economy in the pre-industrial and pre-colonial era, and their more recent journey to regain this lost share. In 1700 China and India accounted for 45.7 per cent of world's national income. (Table 1.1) By the end of the 19th century this share had fallen to 24.2 per cent and by the middle of the 20th century to a lowly 9 per cent. The decline in the share of these two Asian giants in world income was matched by the dramatic increase in the share of the US and subsequently Japan. Europe saw its share increase to a peak of over 40 per cent by the end of the 19th century and a subsequent decline to levels enjoyed before the colonial era. These numbers feed the *hubris* of the Indian strategic and economic policymaking community that India is destined to regain its pre-eminent status as a major actor on the world stage. Equally, they draw attention to the centrality of economic performance in shaping a country's strategic power and relevance.

Table 1.1

Distribution of World Income: 1700-1995

	1700	1820	1890	1952	1978	1995
China	23.1	32.4	13.2	5.2	5.0	10.9
India	22.6	15.7	11.0	3.8	3.4	4.6
Japan	4.5	3.0	2.5	3.4	7.7	8.4
Europe	23.3	26.6	40.3	29.7	27.9	23.8
US	-	1.8	13.8	21.8	21.8	20.9
Russia	3.2	4.8	6.3	9.3	9.2	2.2

Source: Angus Maddison, *Chinese Economic Performance in the Long Run*, OECD, Paris, 1998.

Admittedly, the dramatic story of the second half of the 20th century is China's economic performance, though the jury is still out on the authenticity of the statistical claims. China set itself on a high growth trajectory before India and has succeeded in doubling its share of world income within a span of a quarter century, going up from 5.2 per cent in 1978 to 10.9 per cent in 1995. China's economic growth performance parallels its emergence as a mercantilist trading power, with its share of world trade increasing from around 1 per cent in the late 1970s to 4.5 per cent in 2000. By contrast, India was a slow starter. However, there has been a consistent acceleration in India's economic growth in the 20th century (Table 1.2).

Table 1.2

Macroeconomic Trends in Indian Economy, 1900-2001

	Trend Growth Rates of GDP by Sectors@						
	1900-01 to 1946-47	1950-51 to 1959-60	1960-61 to 1969-70	1970-71 to 1979-80	1980-81 to 1998-90	1990-91 to 1999-00	1997-98 to 2001-02$
Primary	0.46	2.8	1.4	1.8	3.0	2.9	2.1
Secondary	1.82	6.1	5.4	4.7	6.9	7.2	4.5
Tertiary	1.65	4.0	4.5	4.5	6.4	7.7	7.8
Total GDP	1.05	3.7	3.3	3.5	5.4	6.2	5.4
Per Capita	0.22	1.8	1.0	1.2	3.1	4.3	-

Source: S. Sivasubramonian, *The National Income of Indian in the Twentieth Century,* Oxford, 2001.
Notes: Average annual growth rates of GDP based on end values, at 1938-39 prices.
@ At 1948-49 prices.
$ Ninth Five Year Plan, 1997-2002.

What exactly has been India's more recent growth performance and what is the extent of the gap between performance and potential? While India has been slow to start, if a long view is taken of the growth process then we do see a steady acceleration of growth. After recording virtually no growth in the first half of the 20th century, the economy grew at an annual average rate of 3.5 per cent in 1950-80 and 5.4 per cent in 1980-1990 and 6.2 per cent in 1990-2000. In the mid-1990s, 1992-1998 the economy recorded over 7 per cent growth, however in 1998-2002 there has been a marginal deceleration, largely on account of slow industrial growth. This raises some questions about the medium-term growth potential. If the NBAR-CSIS view is accepted, then an average rate of growth of 5.8 per cent, which is the long-term rate registered during

1980-2002, is inadequate to enable India to not only deal with the challenge of development in a poor, populous country but also acquire the diplomatic and military profile of a major power. Indian planners recognise that the elimination of mass poverty and the challenge of human development can only be fully addressed if the economy delivers at least 7 per cent to 8 per cent growth over the next decade. Strategic analysts also believe that such a rate of growth of income is necessary for the government to raise the resources required for the modernisation of the conventional armed forces and the operationalisation of a command and control system relevant to a credible nuclear deterrent.

Notwithstanding these caveats, the acceleration of growth over the past two decades has already had its strategic consequences. If there is further acceleration to a medium-term average of 7 per cent, then there will be further consequences. It is to these issues which we now turn.

II : Strategic consequence of what has been achieved

India's accelerated economic growth and, more importantly, the policy of trade and investment liberalisation has already impacted upon its political and diplomatic relations with nations near and far, ranging from the US and European Union to ASEAN and Taiwan. Nowhere is the impact more dramatic from a strategic perspective than on the relations with her two immediate neighbours and strategic competitors.

India and Pakistan

From the time of partition and independence, India's immediate strategic challenge has been the relationship with Pakistan and, in turn, Pakistan's relationship with the US and China. Pakistan's relatively better economic performance in the period 1950 to 1980 only made matters difficult for India, notwithstanding the fact that Pakistan was defeated in every single battlefield confrontation with India. On its own India could have neutralised the Pakistan challenge, but big power support during the Cold War and the relationship with China helped Pakistan neutralise India's advantages to a considerable extent. While Pakistan's nuclear capability has further reduced the structural imbalance between the two south Asian neighbours, the differential economic performance of the two neighbours has begun to turn the balance once again in India's favour.

Consider the fact that while in 1960-80, Pakistan's GDP growth rate was closer to 6 per cent per annum compared to India's 3.5 per cent, in the 1990s India's growth rate was closer to 6 per cent while Pakistan's had slipped to below 4 per cent per annum. This has had an impact on a variety of economic indicators. For example, India improved its ranking in the Human Development Index (HDI) (compiled annually by the United Nations Development Programme) while Pakistan's ranking has actually slipped. India has moved up in the 1990s from being classified in the 'low HDI' category to the 'medium HDI' category. On another front, India has moved up from being classified as 'moderately indebted country' (external debt classification of the World Bank) to now being regarded a 'low indebted' country. Pakistan, on the other hand, has experienced a deterioration in its external debt profile during the 1990s and has had to seek debt rescheduling after coming close to default.

These and similar divergent economic trends have encouraged strategic analysts to increasingly 'de-hyphenate' the two south Asian neighbours in any strategic assessment of the region. As early as in 1997 an analyst at the National Defense University, Washington DC, (Clawson, 1997) observed:

"The changed GDP ratios (between India and Pakistan) would have military implications. Given that India spends 2.5 per cent of its GDP on its military and that Pakistan's economy is 19 per cent the size of India's, Pakistan would have to spend 13 per cent of GDP to match the Indian military budget in absolute size. In fact, Pakistan cannot afford to spend that much. Pakistan can only afford military spending that is little more than half the size of India's. That is, Pakistan can only afford to dedicate 6.5 per cent of its GDP to the military, because to do more would drain away the resources needed for the investment that sustains future growth. Already, Pakistan faces the same quandary as the former USSR—the military spending necessary to keep pace with the historic foe would drain off so many resources that the economy would fall further behind that of the adversary. The problem will get much worse (when)...Pakistan's GDP slips relative to that of India. As India becomes richer, it will be able to afford to fund its military more generously. The ratio between the Pakistani military budget and that of India could easily become one to three, rather than one to two. At that point, it would become less and less plausible to see Pakistan as in any way comparable in national power to India.

"In short, the gap between Indian and Pakistani economic prospects could lead to a shift in the balance of power in the region. On present trends, India is likely to become the clearly pre-eminent regional power. Indeed, as the difference in economic growth rates becomes clearer, the trends in India's favour will affect perceptions—India will be seen as the power of the future, and that will in turn multiply its power in the present."

Given that economic trends have indeed moved in the expected direction, notwithstanding India's recent growth deceleration, the 'de-hyphenation' of the two south Asian neighbours has already started. This has prompted Tellis to argue that:

"When the economic, political, and strategic fortunes of India and Pakistan are considered synoptically, the opposing trend lines appear in sharp relief. India's grand strategic trajectory appears ascendant, while Pakistan, remaining trapped in the mire of stagnation, appears at risk of collapse. If these trend lines continue, the stage will be set for a consequential geopolitical transformation within south Asia itself. That is, India will steadily acquire the economic, political, and strategic capabilities that set it along the path to great-power status, thus enabling it to break out of the limiting confines of the Indian subcontinent (where it has been since at least 1962) and take its place as one of the major centres of power in Asia writ large" (p. 238).

Even though Pakistan has tried to neutralise the impact of this differential economic performance by, one, going nuclear, and, two, imposing a non-conventional security threat on India, through what has come to be known as 'cross-border' terrorism, in the long run if Pakistan does not reverse the process of economic decline, it will be unable to continue to 'hold India back', one of its most persistently pursued strategic objectives. Indeed, in order to make economics work for it in a positive manner Pakistan will have to seek *modus vivendi* with India and normalise its political relations so that it can turn its attention to economic development.

Their differential economic performance has already impacted upon the economic and business relations between developed industrial economies, including China, and the two south Asian neighbours. Neither the US nor China would like to hurt their business prospects in India. Indeed, China has in the past year delinked its growing business relationship with India from persisting differences on the political and diplomatic front. This partly explains China's equivocal stance on an increasing number of India-Pakistan bilateral disputes like the Kargil War and the campaign against terrorism.

Pakistan will also come under regional pressure from other south Asian countries to cooperate with India when they realise that Pakistan's thwarting of the process of regional economic integration is hurting the region as a whole. India has already delinked the process of regional integration by pursuing bilateral liberal trade agreements with Sri Lanka, Nepal and Bangladesh. India's desire to seek closer economic relations with its eastern neighbours, the members of ASEAN, along with some of the other south Asian countries like Sri Lanka and Bangladesh, will further reduce Pakistan's economic relevance for south Asia. India's Dialogue Partner status in ASEAN, its membership of the ASEAN regional Forum and the India-ASEAN summit scheduled for later this year suggest that ASEAN member countries, including Muslim-majority nations like Indonesia and Malaysia, have decided to place business above politics and religion and pursue closer relations with India. India's 'Look East Policy', its increasing strategic interaction with ASEAN, Australia and Japan and the attempts to create a new regional group around the Bay of Bengal, excluding Pakistan, symbolise a willingness on the part of India's other neighbours to 'de-hyphenate' their relations in south Asia. This proces is largely driven by the emerging economic and business links between India and her wider 'southern Asian' neighbourhood.

India and China

For centuries India and China have been neighbours and at comparable levels of development. China moved ahead of India in the 18th century (Table 1.1), but slid back to level with it by the end of the 19th century. In the period 1950-80 the two economies remained at similar levels of development, even though China had started moving ahead of India by the early 1960s. When China launched the post-Mao modernisation programme it was already ahead of India on most economic and military indicators save one, namely, its extent of integration with the world economy. India and China had comparable levels of share of world trade, around 0.8 per cent each in the 1970s. The period 1980-2000 has made all the difference. China not only sustained a very high rate of growth compared to India during this period, even if China's growth figures are vastly exaggerated, but more to the point China increased its share of world trade four-fold, to around 4.0 per cent by 2000, compared to India's still lowly share of 0.7 per cent.

China's rapid economic growth, its emergence as a major trading nation and the phenomenal increase in foreign direct investment have combined to widen the gap between the strategic power and potential of the two Asian giants. China has used its economic and trading power to build strategic relationships with all major powers and, equally importantly, with each one of her Asian neighbours from the central Asian republics in the west to Japan and Korea in the east and ASEAN in the south. For India to be able to restore the balance within Asia it will not only have to pursue faster economic growth and domestic economic modernisation, but also increase its share of world trade and widen its economic links with the Eurasian landmass as well as with the trans-Atlantic and Asia-Pacific economies.

China has leveraged its economic power in the strategic arena in a variety of ways. At the time of the Asian economic crisis, it played a stabilising role thereby increasing its relevance and role in the region. This has helped impart momentum to projects like an Asian Monetary Fund, and the ASEAN-plus-3 group, which China has pursued. By investing in central Asian oil and gas projects and giving the latter access to the east and South-East Asian markets *via* land-based pipelines through China, its has been able to impact on energy security in the region as well as increase its economic influence in central Asia. Finally, China has emerged as a major market as well as a competitor for all east and South-East Asian economies. In short, it has increased its political influence both in South Asia and South-East Asia by leveraging its economic potential. Indeed, India-China relations have also improved in recent months riding on the back of increased trade and investment flows. China (including Hong Kong) has emerged as India's second largest trade partner next only to the US.

The strategic consequences of the economic competition with China are, therefore, fundamental to India's future role within Asia and the global system. If India can sustain above average growth (over 7 per cent per annum in the next decade) and if China experiences a deceleration of growth, coupled with domestic political uncertainty, the widening gap between the two civilisational neighbours can be reversed to an extent. If not, China will emerge as the pre-eminent Asian power and force India into accepting its strategic leadership even within south Asia. The key to this strategic rivalry will be the relative economic performance of the two countries. The main strategic challenge for India in the medium term is, therefore, its relative economic performance *vis-à-vis* China. Tellis has summed this up admirably:

"They (Indian policy-makers) believe that the best antidote to the persisting competitive, and even threatening, dimensions of Chinese power is the complete and permanent revitalisation of the Indian economy. The pursuit of this objective implies that Indian security managers believe that the best insurance against assertive Chinese power lies not in participating in any evolving anti-China alliance but rather by emerging as a strong and independent power on China's periphery... Within the subcontinental setting, India has focused entirely on economic renewal in order to secure the great power capabilities that eluded it during the cold war" (p. 257).

If India has to realise its power potential, it must address important challenges on the economic front with a direct bearing on her strategic capability. However, successive governments in India, at the centre and in the states, have not been able to devote single-minded attention to economic reforms. Political uncertainty, the vagaries of democratic politics and social tensions have constantly diverted governmental attention away from the economic reform programme. The two areas where the link between economic policy and performance and strategic capability and political influence are most direct are fiscal policy, which limits the economic power of the state, and trade policy, which defines the manner in which a country can utilise its economic power as an instrument of diplomacy, building relationships of inter-dependence between nations and shaping the institutions of multilateralism and the process of globalisation.

III : Economic impediments to national security

If India has to bridge the gap between performance and potential and leverage her economic size for strategic advantage then it must address at least two major economic policy challenges to make economic policy work more effectively to its strategic advantage. We are not considering here the larger challenge of human development and poverty eradication, which are obvious and manifest economic challenges facing India.

The meaningful resolution of these constraints is fundamental to securing strategic capability commensurate with her economic size and civilisational attributes. However, here we consider two limited macroeconomic policy challenges whose resolution is of equal significance to India's strategic capability. The term 'strategic capability' refers to the ability of a nation to deploy its economic, political, intellectual, cultural and military capability in the defence of its national interest and the well-being of its people, and influence the course of events within its strategic environment.

The fiscal empowerment of the state

In Ferguson's model of strategic power, the "square of power" as he dubs it comprises—the tax bureaucracy, the parliament, the national debt and the central bank. It is these four institutions of fiscal empowerment of the state which enable the projection of national power by creating the institutional framework for the mobilisation and deployment of financial resources. In Ferguson's view, "(these) institutions that initially existed to serve the (British) state by financing war also fostered the development of the economy as a whole. Better secondary and higher education, the rule of law (especially with respect to property), the expansion of financial markets and the stabilisation of the credit system: these were vital institutional preconditions for the industrial revolution" (p. 17).

Not surprisingly India inherited these British institutions of war financing and industrial development and managed to put them to good use in the post-independence period. The Indian finance ministry and the central bank by and large pursued a conservative policy of fiscal empowerment that enabled India to avoid many of the fiscal pitfalls of development, like hyperinflation, excessive external debt and exchange rate volatility, that marked the experience of many developing countries. As two distinguished analysts of Indian fiscal policy observed (Joshi and Little, 1994):

"The British created in the Indian Civil Service a small, high-minded, highly elitist bureaucracy with a Gladstonian fiscal outlook; its successor, the Indian Administrative Service, preserved—at least initially—the same traditions... (p. 8). The 'fiscal conservatism' of the civil service manifested itself in a low tolerance for inflation, in the search for exchange rate stability and in a dislike for high budgetary deficits. This paradigm, however, began to shift in the 1970s. Since then India has witnessed a deterioration in its fiscal profile. While this initially contributed to high inflation and high deficits, it finally precipitated a balance of payments crisis in 1990-91, with far-reaching consequences for Indian strategic policy. The

1990s witnessed a gradual improvement in the external profile of the Indian economy. India's current account deficit has been kept within the manageable limit of 1 per cent to 2 per cent of GDP. India's external debt to GDP ratio has declined ovei the 1990s and the debt service ratio has improved as well" (Table 1.3).

ıable 1.3

External Debt Indicators

Year	Debt-Stock GDP Ratio	Debt-Service Ratio	Debt-Exports Ratio	Short-Term Debt/Total Debt	Short-Term Debt/Foreign Currency Reserves
1990-91	28.7	35.3	491.7	10.3	382.3
1995-96	27.1	24.3	295.,	5.2	28.5
1999-00	22.0	16.0	258.6	4.1	11.5

Source: Ministry of Finance, Government of India.

While the external financial profile of ᴛ.ᴇ economy has improved, there has been a deterioration of the government's fiscal profile. The tax to GDP ratio has declined from over 11 per cent in the 1980s to around 9 per cent by the end of the 1990s. The combined fiscal deficit of the central and state governments remains at around 10 per cent of GDP after a decade of fiscal correction. The persistence of the fiscal problem prompted the Reserve Bank of India to urge the government to fiscally 'empower' itself through a Fiscal Responsibility Act which seeks to place mandatory legislative curbs on the fiscal and revenue deficits of the central government. From a national security perspective, sound macroeconomic management entails:

- elimination of the revenue deficit, a manageable fiscal deficit, elimination of wasteful subsidies not targeted to the poor;

- low and manageable current account deficit;

- low internal and external debt, low short-term debt in overall external debt;

- profit-generation by public enterprises; privatisation of non-strategic public enterprises;

- self-financing public utilities like power, irrigation, water and public transport; and
- an increase in the tax/GDP ratio to levels reached by rapidly industrialising developing countries of around 15 per cent of GDP from the current low of 9 per cent of GDP.

The medium-term fiscal threats facing the economy arise from an inability to finance essential development expenditure and the inability to ensure a truly efficient financial system. Productive investment is being held back by the inability to reduce unproductive subsidies, mobilise adequate direct tax revenues and generate returns to existing public investment. These systemic weaknesses increase the vulnerability to external economic pressures, especially from multilateral and bilateral aid agencies and donors. In making the transition to 'major power' status India will have to find the resources for national defence and military capacity building. Higher economic growth as well as political and military

Table 1.4

Structure of Central Government Expenditure (percentages)

Item	1980-85	1985-90	1990-95	1995-00	2001-02	2002-03
Non-plan expenditure	59.90	65.52	71.02	75.00	73.00	72.33
Interest payments	13.07	16.52	24.59	30.00	29.00	28.60
Defence	16.72	16.35	14.70	15.00	15.60	15.80
Subsidies	8.35	9.52	9.86	8.50	8.40	9.70
Police	1.24	1.35	1.65	2.00	2.00	2.03
Pensions	1.60	2.04	2.25	3.40	4.00	3.67
Loans and advances to States and Union Territories	2.86	6.03	5.31	6.80	-	-
Grants to states and UT	2.58	2.76	2.52	2.40	4.66	4.67
Other non-plan expenditure	13.48	10.95	10.14	9.00	-	-
Plan expenditure	40.10	34.48	28.98	25.00	27.00	27.67
Total	100	100	100	100	100	100

Source: Economic Survey (various years), Ministry of Finance, Government of India.

strength cannot be achieved without a major programme of fiscal regeneration at both the state and central levels.

In the 1980s growth acceleration was fuelled by fiscal profligacy and imprudence which in turn contributed to the balance of payments crisis in 1990-91. The non-sustainability of such fiscal expansion is demonstrated by the sustained increase in interest payments from 2.2 per cent of GDP in the early 1980s to 4.7 per cent of GDP by the late 1990s. The increasing pre-emption of public finances by non-productive interest payments and subsidies has left little for productive investment, on the one hand, and for defence, on the other. Unless the growth process is fiscally sustainable, India will not be able to translate her economic gains into military and strategic capability.

Fiscal empowerment and public investment

In the current phase of privatisation inadequate attention is being paid to necessary public investment and to making existing public investment more productive. This will remain a challenge even after all public enterprises have been privatised. There are at least two areas in which public investment will remain relevant and important—one, social and economic infrastructure; two, defence and strategic industries (including aerospace, space, shipbuilding and nuclear energy). The central and state governments will have to find the financial resources for increased investment in health, education, urban services and utilities.

There are also important governance issues in each of these areas. Fiscal empowerment is both a function of revenue mobilisation and improved productivity and profitability of public investment. This is a necessary pre-condition of accelerated economic growth of 7.0 per cent and above. The experience of China once again suggests that even as the space for private enterprise and market forces is increased, public investment must not only continue but must become increasingly productive if economic growth is to translate into strategic capability.

Fiscal empowerment and defence spending

India's national security concerns, especially arising out of *jehadi* terrorism, and her long-term nuclear capability building will undoubtedly impose a financial burden on the government. Equally, the acceleration of economic growth will increase concerns about the security of energy supplies. This will also require India to bolster her strategic capability within the Indian Ocean region. India is a modest spender on defence and the 'guns *versus* butter' issue has never been a major point of political contention. A Regional Security Assessment by Jane's Information Group (1997) observed, "India's defence spending remains modest compared to other countries with major security concerns." Through the 1990s India's defex has remained in step with world averages, at around 2.5 per cent of national income, compared to over 5.0 per cent for Pakistan and China. In the last two years, after the Kargil war, there has been a steep increase in defence spending but this remains below the peak of 3.5 per cent of GDP reached in the mid-1980s. India's frontline role in the campaign against terrorism will imply that the government will have to find the resources for defence and national security. The burden of this effort is directly related to economic growth and the fiscal empowerment of the government. The relationship between economic performance and strategic capability is direct in this case.

In a large continental economy like India public investment in strategic industries has economic externalities going beyond power projection. India's investment in defence related industries, as indeed in the case of the US and China, has helped develop domestic technical capabilities with spin off benefits for the civilian sector. The fiscal pressures on the defence budget have in fact meant a reduction in capital expenditure, hurting the development of domestic scientific and technical capabilities, which in turn hurt economic development.

The 'fiscal empowerment' of the state is, therefore, a vital step in the realisation of the economic potential, which in turn will enable India to bridge the gap between her current strategic capability and her potential as a major power.

IV : Globalisation and trade diplomacy

It is not a coincidence that the turn in India's external economic policies after 1991 coincided with the end of the Cold War. The re-engagement of the global economy, in particular re-building economic relations with the US, on the one hand, and with the wider Asian neighbourhood, on the other, have been important planks of India's economic policy in the 1990s. The strategic consequence of this new policy of outward-orientation is obvious. Among developing countries India was late in shifting gears from inward-oriented industrial development to outward-oriented development. The end of the Cold War, coinciding with a balance of payments crisis in 1990-91, forced the pace of this change.

Table 1.5

Trends in Combined Fiscal Deficit and Contingent Liabilities of Central and State Governments (As Percentage of GDP)

Year	Gross Fiscal deficit	Government Guarantees
1990-91	9.4	-
1995-96	6.5	9.9
1999-00	9.4	10.7
2000-01	10.0	-

Source: Annual Report (various years), Reserve Bank of India.

However, India remains on the margins of the process of globalisation, still accounting for a mere 0.7 per cent of world trade, compared to China's share of over 4.0 per cent, and with as yet modest foreign direct investment inflows (Table 1.6). This compares with a 2 per cent share of world trade that India had in the 1950s compared to China's share at that time of less than 1 per cent. China has used a 'mercantilist trade policy', based on a cheap currency, as a strategic instrument of international engagement, which India is yet to even begin doing. As a result of its overall trade expansion, China is today a larger trade partner of every single country in Asia, with the exception of Nepal and Sri Lanka, than India. Her increased penetration of Asian and western markets has given China a strategic profile which India has yet to acquire.

Table 1.6

Changing Profile of Foreign Trade

Period	Foreign Trade as a Percentage of GDP	Share of India in World Exports (per cent)
1985-86	10.99	0.5
1990-91	13.32	0.5
1995-96	19.28	0.6
2000-01	21.80	0.7

Source: Medium Term Export Strategy, 2002-07, Ministry of Commerce, India.

The arena of trade diplomacy, now including the World Trade Organization, will play an increasingly important role in shaping the external profile of China and India and their bilateral relationship. Interestingly, 'Greater China', that is the People's Republic and Hong Kong taken together, has emerged as India's second largest export destination next only to the United States. The US market accounts for around 22 per cent of India's exports followed by China and Hong Kong with a combined share of over 8 per cent. Countries like the UK, Germany and Japan have a share of around 5 per cent each. India's trade with China is likely to increase in the near term with both countries using business to build a bridge over troubled political waters.

India's tariffs remain high by Asian standards, though they are set on a downward course, and the weakness of trade-related infrastructure hurts the competitiveness of Indian exports and adds to import cost. Altogether this is an area for further reform. If India sustains 6.0 per cent and above growth it will be able to secure a larger share of world trade. This will alter the strategic equations within south Asia and impact on India's relations with other Asian nations. India has been able to improve her trade relations with Sri Lanka, Nepal and Bangladesh, even as Pakistan has continued to drag its feet in the creation of a South Asian Free Trade Area (SAFTA). India has pursued a dual track policy of seeking improved bilateral trade relations with major trading partners, particularly the US, ASEAN and some of her immediate neighbours; on the one hand, while maintaining an aggressive stance in multilateral trade negotiations. However, there is much ground waiting to be covered both in terms of policy and infrastructure building if India has to match China's trade power in the region.

Interestingly, China has emerged as India's second largest trade partner (PRC and Hong Kong taken together), next only to the US (if European Union is not viewed as a single entity) India and China are seeking to use trade and business relations as a means of improving their bilateral relations, even as differences on the delineation of their common border are kept on the back-burner. China's willingness to allow trade relations to improve, even as political differences remain, is exerting pressure on Pakistan to similarly enable progress on the business front and not make this hostage to differences on Kashmir. China's membership of the WTO poses a major diplomatic challenge for India both at the regional and multilateral level. Further, China's aggressive campaign for an Asian Free Trade Area (AFTA) and an Asian currency unit will exert pressure on India. Increasing India's trade competitiveness will, therefore, remain a strategic policy challenge with far-reaching consequences for how India can translate her improved economic performance into a foreign policy asset.

As a traditional trading nation with historic trading relations with all of Asia, India can make external trade relations work as an effective instrument of international engagement by creating relationships of mutual inter-dependence with key countries. India's growing trade relations with some member countries of ASEAN have helped strengthen the political relationship with the regional grouping. Sub-regional preferential trading arrangements and joint infrastructure projects have also gathered momentum around the rim of the Bay of Bengal. New trading opportunities will come India's way, as it becomes more hospitable to FDI and foreign trade. How effectively India can do this will depend on the pace of domestic economic reform. However, the relatively low share of world trade and domestic fears regarding the competitiveness of Indian manufacturing exports have made India a defensive player in multilateral trade negotiations, as most recently exemplified at the Doha Ministerial Meeting of the World Trade Organization. A steady acceleration of exports and perhaps the recent success in information technology and software services exports will help change attitudes and policies that in turn will enable India to regain her share of world trade and income.

While domestic industry remains wary of globalisation, as in most countries, India has the potential of making globalisation work for it in a more positive way than would be the case with many other developing countries. The large and diverse Indian 'diaspora' has emerged as a new network of overseas business and can, as in the case of China, work to India's advantage in the global economy. If domestic policies are more attuned to external trade and capital flows in general they will also enable India to tap the resources of the 'people of Indian origin' worldwide.

V : Economy and power–emerging challenges

A strategy of 'inward-oriented' industrialisation and the political choices India made during the Cold War reduced India's global economic and strategic engagement during the half century after Independence. However, the steady acceleration of economic growth in the last two decades and the shift in economic policy towards a more open, outward-oriented economy in the 1990s has helped India seek new relationships of economic engagement with her neighbours in Asia as well as with major powers. Two unrelated but parallel events have propelled this process in the 1990s—first, the end of the Cold War; and, second, the IT and software 'revolution' at home. These events have enabled India to impart a strategic relevance to her economic policies.

India's sustained economic growth within the framework of an open economy and the new capabilities in information technology have helped create new relationships of economic inter-dependence with other growing economies, especially in North America, east and South-East Asia and Europe. India's economic performance in the 1990s has helped redefine her political relations with such diverse nations as the US, China, Korea, Israel, Russia, Singapore, Thailand, Australia, European Union and her own neighbours. More to the point, it has helped India graduate from the so-called 'south Asian' box, into a 'southern Asian' power, with economic and strategic links spreading from the energy rich west Asia to the growing markets of east Asia. To sustain this growth process, however, India will have to ensure the security of energy supplies and access to foreign markets. Together these needs will continue to give an economic edge to India's external relations, with its own strategic implications.

The importance of IT and software in India's growth process has contributed to a strengthening of India's links with the 'Anglo-Saxon' world, namely the US, Canada, UK, and Australia, which are the largest markets for Indian software service personnel. Equally, it is helping in redefining India's relations with China and Japan. The growing importance of each of these relationships is altering India's erstwhile global profile as a poor, developing country in south Asia hobbled by an irritant called Pakistan.

However, to be able to make a decisive break from the past and from the constraints imposed by Pakistan's diabolic agenda of keeping her boxed in the confines of south Asia and held back by divisive social tensions, India will have to move faster on the path of economic modernisation and improved human development. If it falters on this economic front, its wider political quest will be impaired.

It is on the foundation of sustained economic growth that India will be able to address what can be dubbed the 4-D challenge of development, defence, diplomacy and the diaspora. Economic development within the framework of a 'decentralised democracy' (the two other Ds) is the biggest challenge facing India. India's 'strategic capability' would be seriously impaired by the prevalence of mass poverty, high illiteracy and economic backwardness. The growth process of the past two decades has enabled India to address many of the challenges of development. The poverty rate has gone down from 50 per cent in the 1970s to below 30 per cent in the 1990s, the literacy rate has gone up to over 60 per cent, and per capita income growth of over 4 per cent per annum in the 1990s has been the highest in living memory. This has enabled India to move up the HDI ladder from being classified under 'low HDI' to now being classified as 'medium HDI'.

The second challenge of defence is critical to India's national integrity and development as it is to ensuring peace and stability in the wider southern Asian region, as events of the past few months have dramatically shown. India's ability to play the role of a regional peace keeper and stabiliser, ensuring the security of the Indian Ocean and the free flow of energy from the region to the global markets beyond, policing piracy on the high seas and facing the threat of non-state actors and terrorist organisation critically depends on her ability to generate the resources required for the requisite defence capability. India is currently agonising on the question whether it can afford to buy an aircraft carrier from Russia. Many countries in the region would like India to be more pro-active in dealing with piracy on the high seas and the US, Australia and Japan have welcomed India's active participation in Indian Ocean security. However, India will not be able to take on this role which today others would like it to, unless it can generate the fiscal resources required. This is a function both of the 'fiscal empowerment of the state' and of generating tradable products and services to raise the hard currency resources required.

The third challenge of diplomacy is even more directly related to economic performance because international relations have increasingly come to be shaped by economic relations. The phenomenon of globalisation, the growing importance of regional economic groups and free trade associations and China's aggressive mercantilism have all given an edge to economic diplomacy which India can not effectively deploy unless it emerges a larger trading nation and a more open economy. To enable this, without hurting domestic business interests, India will have to sustain a higher rate of economic growth. India has set itself the target of doubling its share of world exports in the next five years. It is also pursuing closer economic relations with the wider southern Asian neighbourhood and with Africa, Latin America and Russia, apart from the continuing economic relationship with the US, India's largest trade partner, and the EU.

Finally, in making globalisation work for India, it can make productive use of the diverse and talented community of 'people of Indian origin' worldwide, of over 25 million, the so-called Indian 'Diaspora'. This community has emerged as an important strategic asset in India's relations with the US, and the Anglo-Saxon world as a whole, as well as with South-East Asia. However, India's ability to draw on the skills and capital of this community will depend to a large extent on its domestic economic performance and the opportunities for business it throws up at home.

Clearly then, it is India's economic performance which will shape the manner in which each of these strategic assets can be deployed in the projection of Indian power and influence worldwide. The sustained, if gradual, acceleration of economic growth and its translation in to all-round development, defence capability, diplomatic influence and the process of globalisation, mediated by the diaspora, will shape the nature and extent of India's strategic capability.

References

Cohen, Stephen (2001). *India: Emerging Power*, Oxford University Press.

Ferguson, Neil (2001). *The Cash Nexus: Money and Power in the Modern World, 1700-2000*, Allen Lane, The Penguin Press.

Garver, John (2001). *Protracted Contest, Sino-Indian Rivalry in the Twentieth Century*, Oxford.

Haas, Richard and Gideon Rose (1997). *A New US Policy toward India and Pakistan*, Council on Foreign Relations Press.

Joshi, Vijay and I M D Little (1994). *India: Macroeconomics and Political Economy, 1964-91*, Oxford.

Yeh, K.C. and Benjamin Zycher (2000). *Asian Economic Trends and Their Security Implications*, RAND.

Maddison, Angus (1998). *Chinese Economic Performance in the Long Run*, OECD, Paris.

Clawson, Patrick (1997). "The Relationship between Security and Economics in South Asia", NDU, Washington, DC (*mimeo*), December.

Schaffer, Teresita (2002). *Rising India and US Policy Options in Asia*, CSIS, January.

Tellis, Ashley (2001). *'South Asia' in Strategic Asia*, National Bureau of Asian Research.

Wolf, Charles, Anil Bamezai, K.C. Yeh and Benjamin Zycher (2000). *Asian Economic Trends and their Security Implications*, RAND.

This paper was read at the Economics and National Security Seminar, John M. Olin Institute of Strategic Studies, Weatherhead Centre for International Affairs, Harvard University, Cambridge MA, USA, April 11, 2002. I am grateful to K. Subrahmanyam, Teresita Schaffer, Devesh Kapur and the participants at the Olin Seminar, especially Martin Feldstein, for their comments on an earlier draft.

2 ESSAY

The economic dimension of India's foreign policy

THE last decade has witnessed a vibrant and wide-ranging debate on India's economic policy regime. There have been fundamental changes in the direction and priorities of its economic policy. An important aspect of this transformation is the change in India's external economic relations. A change that has dramatically altered India's trade and investment regimes as it moves from an inward-oriented economy to a moderately outward-oriented one. These systematic changes in economic policy have occurred at a time when global economic and political relations have also altered in fundamental ways—the end of the Cold War, the collapse of the so-called 'centrally planned economies', the emergence of East and South-East Asia, including China, as the new engine of growth in the world economy, the globalisation of economic activity, the regional integration of major industrial economies as well as of newly industrialising countries, the emergence of new communications and information technologies, and so on. All of these new factors have altered the external environment in which the Indian economy, like any other, operates.

Economic policy makers in government have been alive to these changes and have tried, with varying degrees of success, to explicitly reorient domestic economic policies in order to meet the emerging challenges. While several policy documents have now defined the government's economic policy agenda fairly clearly, there has rarely been any explicit articulation of the implications of these changes for India's foreign policy, even if there is now growing awareness of the positive fallout of economic liberalisation on foreign relations. Admittedly, foreign policy makers have come to recognise the fact that the heart of diplomacy in the nineties is economics.

In the inaugural volume of this journal, former Indian finance minister, Manmohan Singh, alluded to the favourable foreign policy implications of his economic policies.[1] An example of how this link can work positively for India is provided by the pro-India vote in the US Congress in early September 1997, on the amendment proposed to the US Foreign Aid Bill seeking to reduce foreign aid to India by 25 per cent, as a punishment for its alleged human rights violations. The amendment proposed by Congressman Dan Burton was defeated by a margin of 19 votes in 1995, 169 votes in 1996 and 260 votes in 1997. Several commentators have made the point that effective lobbying by US companies investing in India has helped to increase support for India in the US Congress.

Economic foundations of foreign policy

The link between foreign policy and economic policy was clearly recognised by Jawaharlal Nehru, the architect of India's post-Independence foreign policy and external economic relations. He told the Constituent Assembly in December 1947:[2]

"Talking about foreign policies, the House must remember that these are not just empty struggles on a chessboard. Behind them lie all manner of things. Ultimately, foreign policy is the outcome of economic policy, and until India has properly evolved her economic policy, her foreign policy will be rather vague, rather inchoate, and will be groping. It is well for us to say that we stand for peace and freedom and yet that does not convey much to anybody, except a pious hope. We stand for peace and freedom. I think there is something to be said for it. There is some meaning when we say that we stand for the freedom of Asian countries and

---

1. Manmohan Singh, "Liberalisation and Globalisation: Where is India Heading?" *World Affairs,* Vol I, No.1, January-March 1997.

2. Jawaharlal Nehru, Speech in the Constituent Assembly (Legislative), New Delhi, December 4, 1947.

for the elimination of imperialistic control over them. There is some meaning in that.

"Undoubtedly it has some substance, but a vague statement that we stand for peace and freedom by itself has no particular meaning, because every country is prepared to say the same thing, whether it means it or not. What then do we stand for? Well, you have to develop this argument in the economic field. As it happens today, in spite of the fact that we have been for some time in authority as a Government, I regret that we have not produced any constructive economic scheme or economic policy so far...When we do so, that will govern our foreign policy more than all the speeches in this house." Nehru then adds:

"To come to grips with the subject in its economic, political and various other aspects, to try to understand it, is what ultimately matters. Whatever policy we may lay down, the art of conducting the foreign affairs of a country lies in finding out what is most advantageous to the country. We may talk about international goodwill and mean what we say. We may talk about peace and freedom and earnestly mean what we say. But in the ultimate analysis, a Government functions for the good of the country it governs and no Government dare do anything which in the short or long run is manifestly to the disadvantage of that country."

While the foreign policy of a country may from time to time be influenced by specific non-economic, purely strategic or political or geopolitical priorities, Nehru's emphasis on the ramifications of economic policy on the long-term foreign policy framework of a country can be well appreciated in the context of the then existing post-colonial, bipolar world. Clearly, however, Nehru's worldview is even more valid in the contemporary post-Cold War world of pragmatism and business-orientation in foreign policy. What is advantageous to a country can no longer be defined purely or even primarily in political or strategic terms, but must be fundamentally defined in economic terms.

One of the lessons of the Cold War era is that, sooner or later, the success of a country's foreign policy is circumscribed by the efficacy of its economic policy. Successful economies have greater degrees of freedom in shaping an independent foreign policy than failed or weak economies. More importantly, economic policy can itself be an instrument of foreign policy if it enables a country to win friends and influence people.

Admittedly, in the era of decolonisation and at the height of the East-West confrontation, some countries in the South, especially India, could afford to pursue a foreign policy that had a higher profile than was warranted by the strength of the economy. In the post-Cold War period, pragmatic rather than ideological considerations have come to the fore in relations between nations. This was evident even in the 1970s after the oil shock of 1973 when strategic policy analysts recognised the importance of geoeconomics over geopolitics. Control over high technology is clearly even more critical to political power today than the control over economic and natural resources. Since such control is increasingly exercised by non-sovereign, extra-national corporate entities, the ability of nation states to deal with such multinational corporations is central to the success of a country's foreign policy. Equally, with the spread of regional economic groups and regional integration of economies, India's external economic relations with her neighbours are critical to the success of her wider foreign policy goals.

Non-alignment and mixed economy

In India there is a misplaced popular belief, both, among politicians and academic analysts, that Indian foreign policy in the immediate post-Independence period was shaped more by a commitment to 'universal principles' than national 'self-interest'. Notwithstanding Nehru's recognition of the link between economic policy and foreign policy, as quoted above, a popular view has persisted that the policy of non-alignment, the principles of *Pancha Shila,* the anti-colonial and anti-racist stance and the commitment to peace and disarmament, were all pillars of Indian foreign policy because they were universal principles worth defending in their own right.

A more critical and realistic view of foreign policy in the fifties suggests that national interest was very much the defining feature of foreign policy even in the 1950s. Indeed, whatever may have been the initial 'universalist' motivation for non-alignment, a major plank of Indian foreign policy at the time evolved as the foreign policy counterpart of a domestic 'mixed economy' model, which was undoubtedly a pragmatic response to India's current development needs. The strategy of a 'mixed economy' was espoused even by Indian businessmen who demanded public investment to come in. This was articulated in the famous "Bombay Plan" written by six eminent Bombay-based businessmen, including J.R.D. Tata, G.D. Birla and Purshottamdas Thakurdas.[3]

This instrumentalist view of 'non-alignment', as a manifestation of the requirements of a particular domestic economic policy at the time, was aptly summed up by the Polish economist Michal Kalecki. He suggested that the foreign policy of non-alignment of the intermediate regimes was in a sense a counterpart to their internal set up. He argued that, "On the international scene, the internal position of the ruling lower-middle class finds its counterpart in the policy of neutrality between the two blocs; an alliance with any of the blocs would strengthen the corresponding antagonist at home ... The intermediate regimes are the proverbial clever calves that suck two cows; each bloc gives them financial aid competing with the other. This has been made possible, the 'miracle' of getting out of the USA some credits with no strings attached as to internal economic policy."[4]

Kalecki characterised the newly independent countries of the post War period like India, Egypt, Indonesia and so on, as "intermediate regimes," that were placed between the imperialist and the socialist blocs but which were at the same time ranged equally against a domestic working class, the feudal class, and the imperialists. It may be argued that the end of the Cold War created the kind of situation that Kalecki prognosticates, with 'imperialism' seen to be reasserting itself. However, it is important to note that a bipolar Cold War world is being replaced by a multipolar balance

---

3. John Mathai *et al. A Plan For The Economic Development of India,* Bombay, 1944.

4. J. Osiatynski (edited), *Collected Works of Michel Kalecki,* Oxford: Clarendon Press, 1993.

of power rather than a hegemonistic, unipolar world. Moreover, the dynamic of capitalist development in India is more integrally linked with internal economic processes, the development of capitalism in agriculture, the emergence of indigenous business enterprise and so on, and is not influenced by external factors to the extent that smaller developing, outward-oriented economies are.

The 'instrumentalist' or 'strategic' view of non-alignment is different from the alternative view that sees non-alignment as a 'universal' principle of developing economies in a post-colonial world. It will be no exaggeration to suggest that in the 1950s non-alignment was indeed a strategy, a way of 'sucking two cows' but that in the 1970s and 1980s, especially after the Algiers conference of the Non-Aligned Movement (NAM) in 1972, non-alignment became a 'movement' of the developing countries against the developed, and the distinction between non-alignment as 'national' strategy and non-alignment as an 'international movement' was not adequately appreciated by policy makers.

It was because Nehru viewed non-alignment as a national strategy, rather than as an ideological campaign against imperialism, or against India participating in the international division of labour, that he was able to combine his commitment to it with an equally zealous commitment to keeping India open to foreign investment. Diluting his party's anti-imperialist rhetoric Nehru set out in 1949 to win US support for India's development effort. In April 1949, Nehru set the tone with his famous statement on foreign capital, in direct response to a US demand for 'national treatment' of foreign firms (a phrase that is central to the recently launched OECD initiative for a Multilateral Agreement on Investment). Nehru stated, "As regards the existing foreign interests, the Government does not intend to place any restrictions or impose any conditions which are not applicable to similar Indian enterprise. The Government would also so frame its policy as to enable further foreign capital to be invested in India on terms and conditions that are mutually advantageous. Foreign interests would be permitted to earn profits subject only to regulations common to all. We do not foresee any difficulty in continuing existing facilities for the remittance of profits, and the Government has no intention to place any restriction on the withdrawal of foreign capital investment, but the remittance facilities would naturally depend on foreign exchange considerations. If, however, any foreign concerns come to be compulsorily acquired, compensation will be paid on a fair and equitable basis."[5]

Nehru conceded yet another demand of US business, put forth by the India-America Conference of leading businessmen, when he reversed the policy of not permitting majority share holding by foreign partners in joint ventures. The ministry of industry announced in August 1949, that, "With the exception of about half a dozen key industries, India will not object to majority control by Indians, Britons or Americans. There is almost a free zone outside the 'key industries reserve'...The participation of foreigners even in the 'reserve' field may be considered."

Finally, in September 1949, on the eve of Nehru's visit to the US the Government of India issued a statement which said: "The policy of the Government of India was to allow foreign capital to come in to operate freely in the industrial field... every attempt must be made to secure the maximum possible influx of foreign capital in the shortest possible time. The Government of India categorically declared that permission to retain a majority of non-Indian interest in the ownership and effective control in some cases could not *ipso facto* be considered as detrimental to the interests of the country."[6]

After providing all these assurances and urging greater US investment in India, Nehru travelled to the US in October 1949 in search of food aid and more investment. A famine in large parts of the country forced the government to import foodgrains, especially wheat, and Nehru hoped the US would oblige. But the US did not. Neither was food aid forthcoming nor more US investment. US outward investment in this period was all headed towards western Europe. The reconstruction of post-War Europe and the need to

---

5. D.C. Vohra, *Economic Relevance of Non-Alignment*, Delhi: ABC Publishing House, 1983.

6. Sanjaya Baru, "Change and Choice in Indian Industrial Policy", in T.V. Satyamurthy (Ed.) *Industry and Agriculture in India Since Independence*, Oxford University Press, 1995.

build new alliances in East Asia kept US investment away from countries like India, which tried their best to attract it. India was neither a strategic partner, like Pakistan, nor was it an attractive enough place like western Europe for US investors.

In 1949, US President Harry Truman asked the National Industrial Conference Board to poll US companies with investments abroad on their views about India as a destination for US investment. Of the 25 companies which replied, 17 had problems with India's export and import quotas. Other common problems were—control of capital movements; lack of adequate transportation or storage facilities; limitations on remittance of profits; lack of trained native personnel; inability to recruit personnel in the United States; and inadequacy of facilities for employees. From October 1949 till June 1950 the US administration and the Congress discussed in detail the Indian request for a wheat loan. Both mentioned several conditions that would have to be met by India if US wheat had to be exported. India then approached China and the Soviet Union and both agreed to provide the grains sought. It was only when China and the USSR stepped in that the US government agreed to sell wheat to India. It is this experience that must have convinced that 'non-alignment' was a useful development strategy.

Through the fifties and the sixties, in the negotiations involving the setting up of major public sector plants, especially steel plants, the Indian government tried to get the best deal it could by bargaining with the East and the West.

This approach was adopted on several occasions. In 1961-62, G.D. Birla travelled to the US canvassing support for US aid for the Bokaro steel plant. He told members of the US Congress, that such assistance to a public sector steel plant at Bokaro would encourage private enterprise. A view shared even by the World Bank. The US refusal to support Bokaro, notwithstanding the fact that Germany and Britain helped in setting up the Durgapur and Rourkela plants, forced India to seek Soviet help. This has been the most important economic aspect of non-alignment. Each time India was pushed by one side, mostly the US, it would approach the other and in the process strike a bargain with both.

Through the fifties and the sixties, in the negotiations involving the setting up of major public sector plants, especially the steel plants, the Indian government tried to get the best deal it could by bargaining with the East and the West. The last time India successfully adopted this approach was in 1981 when the government approached the International Monetary Fund (IMF) for support under its extended fund facility (EFF). The US government initially blocked the Indian request. But when India suggested that this might force it to approach the USSR for financial support and also entail making defence purchases from there, the US administration directed its executive director to abstain from the vote on India's request for a loan.

What is important to note here is that the policy of 'non-alignment' did not come in the way of Nehru pursuing a conciliatory policy towards foreign capital, in particular towards US business, in the period, 1947-50. However, when India's gestures were regarded inadequate by the US administration and US was unwilling to assist India in a major way, it had no option but to pursue a more inward-looking economic policy and a 'non-aligned' foreign policy. It is perhaps this experience, more than any ideology, that affirmed Nehru's and the Indian political establishment's commitment to a mixed economy and to non-alignment. The policy of a mixed economy in fact became a corollary to the policy of non-alignment and *vice versa*. With a change in the economic policy regime in the 1990s, it is pertinent to ask what implications this has for foreign policy.

Moreover, over the last decade NAM has demonstrated its inability to project any common position on global and multilateral economic or security issues. Indeed, the proclivity of the so-called 'non-aligned' to become aligned even during the Cold War period, to one power bloc or another is well documented. In the post-Cold War period also this capitulationist tendency manifested itself in the manner in which the entire non-aligned movement refused to endorse India's stance on the Comprehensive Test Ban Treaty (CTBT). In approaching CTBT, India interpreted non-alignment to mean the right to take an independent view and to resist what some have termed "nuclear apartheid". However, the Non-aligned Movement did not accept this view. Admittedly, many developing countries felt they were taking a genuinely principled position on CTBT ratification, some others saw no reason to fight the nuclear 'haves' on behalf of the nuclear 'want-to-haves' or 'will-haves'. Whatever the motivation, the CTBT experience exposed the hollowness of NAM solidarity on the political front.

On the economic front, the manner in which the Uruguay Round agreement was wrapped up showed that NAM's economic radicalism, discovered at the Algiers meeting, has also been given a quiet burial. The end of the Cold War along with the processes of globalisation and regional economic integration have marginalised the NAM platform. It is time to re-examine the economic and political relevance of non-alignment both in the light of India's present level of development and her external economic and strategic relations, and in the context of the relationship between nations in the post-Cold War era.

Economic policy in the post-Cold War world

The emerging structure of power in the post-Cold War world has been described by many analysts as being 'multipolar'. US strategic policy analyst, Henry Kissinger, being the most prominent exponent of this view, has suggested that:

"International relations have become truly global for the first time. Communications are instantaneous; the world economy operates on all continents simultaneously. A whole set of issues has surfaced that can only be dealt with on a worldwide basis.

"The international system of the twenty-first century will be marked by a seeming contradiction: on the one hand, fragmentation; on the other, growing globalisation. On the level of the relations among states, the new order will be more like the European state system of the 18th and 19th centuries than the rigid patterns of the Cold War. It will contain at least six major powers—the United States, Europe, China, Japan, Russia, and probably India—as well as a multiplicity of medium-sized smaller countries. At the same time, international relations have become truly global for the first time. Communications are instantaneous; the world economy operates on all continents simultaneously. A whole set of issues has surfaced that can only be dealt with on a worldwide basis, such as nuclear proliferation, the environment, the population explosion, and economic interdependence."[7]

While it is premature to regard India as a major power today, it is necessary to recognise that it is capable of becoming one within the first half of the next century. Indian policy makers, especially politicians, have not yet adequately appreciated the wider policy implications of such a status for India. The Chinese leadership seems to have a better appreciation both of the opportunities and the responsibilities that a 'major power' status brings with it. For instance, no Indian prime minister or foreign minister has so far been able to conceptualise the post-Cold War world in quite the way that China's former foreign minister Wu Xueqian did in an essay on the post-Cold War era, published in this journal. Developing Kissinger's perspective of a 'multipolar' world, Wu Xueqian concedes that the United States will continue to be the strongest economic and military power, but adds that other major powers will be Japan and the European Union, Russia and 'a number of developing countries including China and India'. He goes on to say, "The multipolar evolution—even though in a transitional stage—has become so irreversible that even the existing superpower has to take into account the possible reaction of other countries when taking important decisions on foreign affairs...The emergence of the developing countries is also a major event in contemporary international relations."[8]

What are the implications of such a worldview for India and her foreign and economic policy? Clearly, the non-aligned nations no longer have the bargaining power that the Cold War had given them. The smaller, less developed, non-aligned countries with more outward-oriented economies discovered this fairly quickly. The Uruguay Round of GATT talks showed that the postures adopted

---

7.   Henry Kissinger, *Diplomacy,* New York: Simon and Schuster, 1994.

8.   Wu Xueqian, "The Post-Cold War Era: A Chinese Perspective", *World Affairs,* January-March, 1997.

in the 1986-1989 period were quickly abandoned after 1990 with most developing economies choosing to fall in line with developed industrial economies, especially the US, by the time the Marrakesh agreement was signed in December 1994. Despite the more reassuring assessment of the global power balance by Kissinger, most Third World leaders believed that the bipolar world had been replaced by a unipolar world. The quick and resolute conclusion of the Uruguay Round after the Dunkel Draft was circulated in 1992 reflected this assessment.

With the passage of time it is now clear that the Kissinger view had greater credibility and the world is indeed likely to see the emergence of competing centres of power. The next decade or two will witness constant competition circumscribed by structured cooperation between 'major' and 'minor' powers. The 'multipolar' power structure is going to influence the manner in which the forces of competition and the mechanisms of cooperation are going to operate. Whether it is the functioning of the WTO or the outcome of discussions on MAI (Multilateral Agreement on Investment), whether it is transfer of technology or the movement of people, nothing is going to be shaped by the power structures of the Cold War era, in which superpower rivalry and ideological conflict defined the outcome of any given competition or attempt at cooperation. Nor will the United States always be able to unilaterally dictate the terms of resolution, and will be required to look to other major powers for support on an increasing number of global issues. In the coming years multilateral negotiations can have wholly unpredictable outcomes since the forces of competition and cooperation will remain in a state of flux, until the six major powers are able to define a new equilibrium. China's increasingly high profile presence in multilateral forums can only add to the flux. India cannot still take its position within the multipolar structure defined by Kissinger for granted, and will have to work hard at it—both on the foreign and strategic policy front, as well as on the domestic and external economic policy front. This is by no means an easy task.

The imperatives of economic diplomacy

What does this mean in operational terms for Indian diplomacy? First and foremost, Indian politicians and policy makers must realise that with the status of a 'major power' come obligations, to the world in general and to smaller nations in particular. It is easier to pursue big power status in foreign policy, be it in NPT (Non-Proliferation Treaty) and CTBT negotiations or in the campaign for a Security Council membership, but more difficult to pursue the domestic economic policy that is necessitated by such a status.

India must be a major trading nation in the world, its share of world trade and investment flows must increase. Its trade and investment regime must encourage freer flow of goods, services and capital, and become more open to the smaller economies in her own neighbourhood. In order to ensure this without suffering the pain of destruction of the sub-optimal structures built during the decades of protected, inward-looking development, India must quickly invest in improving the economic and social infrastructure and the skills of its people. Investment in health and education—basic, technical, professional and higher—is an imperative as is new investment in power, irrigation, communications and transportation, both in the public and private sectors.

The public sector, especially in defence-related industries, must be rejuvenated as an instrument of advanced research and development of new technologies. All the other major powers, especially USA, Russia and China, invest heavily in defence-related industries and seek to exploit technological externalities. Indian industry has rarely viewed public investment in defence, space and nuclear, programmes in these terms. Public procurement and major business deals must be linked with explicit foreign policy objectives, as China has done systematically. Compare the manner in which the Chinese have used foreign investment as a means of leveraging foreign policy, best exemplified by the use of the Boeing deal to ensure continuation of MFN status by the US, and the inability of the Indian political system to view foreign investment policy within a wider foreign and strategic policy perspective.

Equally, India must improve its 'bargaining skills' in global forums and give a sharper edge to economic diplomacy, both in its relations with the developed industrial economies of the 'North', as well as in its relations with the countries of the 'South', particularly her neighbours. The focus of policy formulation as well as public debate in the area of foreign policy has for long remained obsessed with political and security issues, so much so that economic diplomacy has till recently not acquired the primacy it should.

Even the policy and the public debate on India's relations with her neighbours has not fully integrated political and economic diplomacy on this front. India's shabby response to the Sri Lankan proposal for a bilateral free trade agreement, reflecting the power of domestic lobbies, and the slow pace of development of the idea of a South Asian Free Trade Agreement (SAFTA), where India can even now easily make unilateral trade concessions provided the government is willing to face up to domestic lobbies, is a telling example.

While the Indian government, especially the ministry of external affairs, has been alive to the beneficial potential of such initiatives, there has been knee-jerk resistance from domestic lobbies and local politicians in some parts of India to proposals like, for example, the BBNI (Bangladesh, Bhutan, Nepal, India) trade grouping, where local vested interests in Bengal have been lobbying against freer trade with Nepal and Bangladesh. Despite official Indian enthusiasm for ideas like BIST-EC (Bangladesh, India, Sri Lanka and Thailand Economic Cooperation) and IOR-ARC (Indian Ocean Rim Agreement for Regional Cooperation), domestic business response has so far been lukewarm. The lack of genuine enthusiasm within the Indian business community for a more liberal trade and investment regime underscores the limits of effective foreign economic diplomacy. Since the MEA and the finance ministry seem to have a better appreciation of its potential they must communicate their policies more effectively to political leaders, businessmen and academia.

Unless India is willing to pursue a 'liberal' outward-oriented, foreign economic policy, which enables it to improve bilateral relations with other major powers and other developed and developing countries, it will find it difficult to pursue a nationalist defence and security policy. Moreover, it should also be understood by those who advocate a more inward-oriented trade and investment policy that an India which is insular with respect to the developed industrial economies, cannot be open and expansive towards the economies of the South Asian region. Acquiring economic and political leadership within the South Asian, or even the Indian Ocean region carries with it the obligation of being more open to global investment and trade flows. Indeed, a more liberal trade and investment regime with respect to her neighbours, through a South Asian Free Trade Agreement (SAFTA) should be the first step in reaching out to the world, first to other developing economies, especially in Asia (through closer links with ASEAN and membership of APEC), and then to the developed industrial economies.

It should also be recognised by our policy makers that sustained high growth is as much a politically and strategically necessary objective as it is an economically desirable one. Indeed, a pro-growth and liberal economic policy is a necessary element of a strategic policy commensurate with India's status as an emerging power. Economic growth has improved the profile of Chinese diplomacy just as the lack of growth and economic crisis has reduced Russia's.

Elsewhere, we have termed the strategy we advocate as "walking on two legs".[9] A nationalist security strategy, and a liberal, outward-oriented economic policy which would widen the network of support for India on an entirely new basis, as opposed to the platform India sought during the era of decolonisation and Cold War confrontation. In the post-Cold War world, India can no longer take for granted the support of such large international groups as NAM, G-77, or any other forum, while advancing its foreign policy goals. Equally, there should be no illusion that membership of a

---

9.   Sanjaya Baru, "India and the World: Walking on Two Legs", *The Times of India,* December 25, 1995.

multiplicity of regional fora, like SAARC, IOR-ARC, BIST-EC, ASEAN and so on, is a solution in itself. These must all be various elements of a comprehensive arsenal, and we must undoubtedly remain active in each forum but cease to view them as principal instruments of economic diplomacy.

Nor should the Indian response be one of aligning with one or another power. Rather, the path we adopt must reflect the understanding that we are in a world of 'competition' and 'cooperation', and accordingly reorient our economic diplomacy to meet this challenge. The key element will have to be the ability to deal with major powers on a one-on-one basis.

Economic and foreign policy coordination

We now come to the practical, albeit administrative, aspects of the problem. India is probably the only country among the so called six 'major powers' that has no overall mechanism for coordinating economic and foreign policy.

In the 1950s, Nehru was undoubtedly the fountainhead of all strategic policy thinking on both the economic and foreign policy fronts. However, he never let the process remain informal. The Secretary-General in the foreign office presided over meetings which involved the foreign secretary, finance secretary and the commerce secretary. Till the early 1960s, the S-G's office functioned effectively as a policymaking link between the two ends of the North and South Block, as well as Udyog Bhavan and the South Block. The last S-G, N.R. Pillai, in fact, came to MEA from the commerce ministry. Another commerce ministry official who played a key role in economic diplomacy in the 1960s and 1970s was K.B. Lall. Other high profile 'economic' diplomats have all been from key economic ministries and, with the singular exception of Muchkund Dubey, who increased the profile of economic diplomacy in the early 1990s, an 'economic diplomat' has never become the foreign secretary. Till recently the passport to power in the MEA was specialisation in political diplomacy, mainly relating to India's neighbours, security issues and UN diplomacy. This is reportedly changing and economics has acquired precedence over politics in foreign policy.

The earlier relative neglect of economic diplomacy within the MEA did not matter so much during the period when the Prime Minister's Office (PMO) was all powerful, and became the centre of both economic and foreign policy formulation. However, with coalition governments in place, and with policy incoherence between ministries, the MEA should be more proactive in external, economic policymaking.

While there has been an increased interaction between the foreign and key economic ministries in recent years, the formal structures for such interaction are not fully in place. For economic policy to be used more effectively as an instrument of foreign policy, that is, if India's foreign economic diplomacy has to be strengthened, then we need both a policy perspective on this as well as institutional mechanisms by which internal talent is identified, created, trained and put in place.

Finally, the MEA should also make better use of outside talent and strengthen interaction with 'think tanks' in the area of economic, strategic and foreign policy. This is also important to strengthen 'track two' diplomacy, within Asia as well as with 'major powers'. All the major powers, especially the US, use non-governmental institutions as effective instruments of both — economic and political diplomacy. Here India's record so far is patchy. While institutions like the Research and Information System for the Non-Aligned and Other Developing Countries (RIS), Indian Council for Research on International Relations (ICRIER), Centre for Policy Research (CPR), Institute of Defence Studies & Analyses (IDSA), Rajiv Gandhi Foundation (RGF) and so on, have been interacting with the MEA, the level, quality and range of such interaction can easily be improved and made more meaningful for policy makers as well as researchers.

To sum up, with the end of the Cold War and with the replacement of a bipolar 'ideologically' divided world by a 'multipolar' economically integrated world in the nineties, economic diplomacy has acquired centre-stage in foreign policy. India's record at coping with this challenge has been patchy, mainly because there is still no internal political consensus on how this should be done. Equally, the institutional mechanisms required to operationalise this are also not in place. Not only must we formulate a coherent worldview on how best we can make use of economic diplomacy, but we must also examine what the implications of this would be for the Indian economy in an increasingly integrated world economy.

3 | ESSAY

Conceptualising economic security

THERE is, as yet, no established concept of 'economic security' in mainstream economics, much less a framework of analysis to define the elements that contribute to it. In the absence of a 'theory' of 'national economic security', there are no quantitative indicators and hence no official database. Economists have more recently tried to develop the concept of 'human security', based on the concept of 'human development', drawing attention to access to basic needs and access to 'entitlements' and provision of 'capabilities', all of which go to enhance the security of life for all people.[1] There are other, more focused concepts of economic security pertaining to energy security, environmental security, financial security and so on. Yet, economic theory has not yet come forward with a comprehensive view of what exactly constitutes economic security of nations. The matter is further complicated by the increased 'globalisation' of all national economies in recent years, with more open trade and capital flows. Thus, the concept of 'economic security' is in flux.

In the absence of an established and widely understood and accepted conceptual framework, it is not surprising that there is no official data available on what may be regarded as indicators of

---

1. See Mahbub ul Haq, *Reflections on Human Development,* New York: Oxford University Press, 1995 and S. Fukuda-Parr & A.K. Shiva Kumar, *Readings in Human Development,* Delhi: Oxford University Press, 2003.

economic security, either at the national level or at the international level. Neither national governments nor multilateral organisations like the United Nations, the International Monetary Fund or the World Bank put out any estimates of trends in economic security or the economic security status of countries. The UNDP's Human Development Report tries to capture trends in 'human security' through measurement of human development.

More recently, however, security and strategic policy analysts have tried to estimate national economic security through the prism of national power, with power expressed and estimated in terms of economic and non-economic national capabilities.[2] Developing the idea of economic power as national power, Tellis has constructed a framework for the measurement of trends.[3] From such studies and estimates analysts in China, the United States and India have constructed an index of 'national security'.[4] It is a moot point whether it can be presumed that there is in fact a positive correlation between economic 'power' and economic 'security'. The assumption that 'power' guarantees 'security' can be questioned for a variety of reasons. Hence, an index of national power need not be relevant to measuring national security. Yet, this is what has been attempted by analysts in the US, China and India.

Analysts at the China Academy of Military Sciences have attempted a measurement of Comprehensive National Power (CNP), defining it as weighted sum of military, economic, scientific and technological power. The eight variables used are natural resources (with a weight of 0.08), domestic economic capability (0.28), external economic capability (0.13), scientific and technological capability (0.15), social development level (0.10), military capability (0.10), government capability (0.08) and foreign affairs capability (0.08).[5]

2. See Michael Pillsbury, *Chinese Views of Future Warfare,* Washington DC: National Defense University, 1997; Indian Edition, Lancer, 1998.

3. Ashley J. Tellis *et al. Measuring National Power in the Postindustrial Age,* Rand-Arroyo Centre, 2000.

4. See Satish Kumar, "National Security Index", in S. Kumar (Edited), *India's National Security Annual Review, 2003,* Delhi: India Research Press, 2004.

5. Michael Pillsbury, *China Debates the Future Security Environment,* Washington DC: National Defense University Press, 2000.

It is possible to collect quantitative data for each variable and try and measure year-to-year changes in CNP and extrapolate from that changes in the level of economic security of a country. Note the fact that purely economic indicators as well as indicators with a high economic content have a high share in the CNP index, of more than 50 per cent.

Based on such concepts, the INSAR's National Security Index (NSI) for India is an attempt to construct a simpler index based on five variables, namely, defence capability, gross domestic product, human development levels, research and development levels, and the quantity and quality of population. Regrettably, however, annual and up to date statistical information is not available on all the components that go into the construction of this index for us to as yet measure changes from year to year in national security. The leads and lags in data, especially with respect to human development, demographic trends and even R&D capability make it difficult to come up with accurate year-to-year estimates of index of national security. However, it is possible, on the basis of available data to come to some tentative conclusions in a medium-term framework.

For India, the improvement in the economy's performance in 2003-04, with acceleration in the rate of growth of national income should have enabled a marked improvement in the GDP indicators in the NSI. Similarly, a good monsoon, a moderation in rates of inflation, and increased budgetary allocations for education and defence should normally suggest an improvement in NSI.

The economics of economic security

However, the NSI does not capture other dimensions of 'economic security' that may be equally important for a large continental economy like India in a globalised world. What could these be? This question was discussed within the Economic Security sub-group of the National Security Advisory Board of India in 1999-2001. A paper prepared for the sub-group defined 'economic security' thus:

"The concept of economic security is wide-ranging and comprehensive. It implies political and economic sovereignty and autonomy of decision making, albeit in an increasingly inter-dependent world characterised by the 'globalisation' of economic activity. It implies the assurance of economic well-being and social justice as reflected in particular by generalised access to food, clothing, shelter, education and employment. It implies the acquisition of skills and knowledge aimed at acquiring technical and technological capabilities required for sustained and self-reliant economic development and the assurance of defence capability."

There are 'external' and 'internal' dimensions to economic security. Internal economic security requires a sustained growth of per capita income, based on a higher investment and savings ratio and productivity; general economic well-being of all people, assurance of minimum economic needs; stable macroeconomic policy, sustainable fiscal and monetary policy and moderate inflation; economic viability of domestic business, particularly in the financial sector, competitiveness of domestic firms; and, a reduction in inter-regional, inter-sectoral (urban/rural and industry/agriculture), inter-class, inter-communal and inter-caste inequalities in development.

External economic security entails viability of the balance of payments, manageable current account deficit, reasonable stock of foreign exchange reserves, growing external trade, manageable external debt with minimum dependence on short-term debt, prudent management of foreign assets and a market-based exchange rate policy within the parameters of an open trade and investment regime, with active participation in multilateral, regional and bilateral trade agreements. The NSAB paper observed that:

"The economic security challenge for India is to pursue above average national income growth at the annual rate of at least 7.0 per cent to 8.0 per cent so that India's share of world GDP is commensurate with her population size, and a larger economic base can more truly reflect India's status in the global arena. Increasing the size of India's national income will enable the country to better address the aspirations of the mass of the people, and also generate resources required to address the external and internal security challenges confronting the nation. While the assurance of peace and security is necessary to pursue higher economic growth, the pursuit of economic growth is also a means of ensuring peace and security."

This conceptual framework should enable one to construct a more comprehensive index of external and internal economic security, if the required data is available. Much of the macroeconomic data is now readily available, though there are inordinate time lags in data availability and the quality of data is uneven. This framework allows us to list the economic variables that would define and determine changes in 'economic security' for India. These could be divided into (a) indicators of internal economic security; and (b) indicators of external economic security.

Indicators of internal economic security:

- per capita income growth,
- GDP growth,
- employment generation,
- rate of inflation,
- foodgrain production and per capita availability,
- foodgrain stocks,
- revenue and fiscal deficits,
- investment and savings rate,
- literacy, especially female literacy, and
- per capita consumption of electricity and steel.

Indicators of external economic security:

- foreign exchange reserves,
- trade deficit,
- current account deficit,
- exchange rate stability,
- real effective exchange rate, and
- external debt and debt service indicators.

Trends in economic security, 2003

After five years of close to 7.0 per cent economic growth, between 1992-1997, the rate of growth of the Indian economy slipped to closer to 5.0 per cent in the subsequent five years of 1998-2003.

This deceleration of growth was partly on account of the preceding 'overheating' of the economy in the period 1995-1997, and the decision of the authorities to pursue a deflationary monetary policy in 1996-1998. This was compounded by a clutch of external problems like the Asian financial crisis, the global economic slowdown, the increase in oil prices and so on. Finally, a weak monsoon in 2002 made matters worse and further reduced the growth rate to a low of 4.0 per cent. In the absence of data on employment it is difficult to gauge how this impacted on employment but it is likely that there has been no major increase in employment in 2003 either in the organised or unorganised sectors.

The slowdown did contribute to a worsening of fiscal indicators and the fiscal and revenue deficit of the states and the centre increased to over 10.0 per cent, a level earlier reached in the early 1990s at the time of the external payments crisis. Table 3.1 gives trends in major macroeconomic variables and tells us the story that the domestic economy did become weaker in 2003. The weak monsoon also exerted pressure on prices and the rate of inflation went up from such lows as 1.0 per cent and 3.0 per cent to over 5.0 per cent in 2004. The weak monsoon also contributed to a drawing down of food stocks and a consequent increase in food prices. Industrial production did begin to pick up after nearly five years of virtual standstill, but gross capital formation continued to be limited at around 23 per cent of GDP. The continued lack of political consensus on price reform in the power sector remained a barrier to new investment in the private sector, even though some new power projects were taken up in the public sector to augment supply.

Persistently weak government budgets, notwithstanding the reassurance provided by the enactment of the Fiscal Responsibility and Budget Management Bill, high fiscal deficits, slow progress on power sector reforms, slow pace of employment generation and persistent inter-regional inequalities in economic development and growth remain areas of concern with respect to internal economic security.

There are other summary measures of domestic economic performance that capture a country's developmental status and thereby mirror its national power, capability and security. Consumption of steel or electricity is one such, just as literacy, especially female literacy. On both counts India fares poorly, even by comparison with China, and has a considerable distance to travel. India's per capita steel consumption was only 29 kilogrammes per capita in 2002 compared to a world average of 150. China improved its steel consumption per capita remarkably from 103 in 1999 to 163 kilogrammes per capita in 2002. On indicators such as per capita electricity consumption and female literacy also the gradual

Table 3.1

Macroeconomic Trends, 2000-04

	2000-01	2001-02	2002-03	2003-04
1. GDP at factor cost (constant prices)	4.4	5.8	4.0	8.7
2. GDP per capita (constant prices)	2.1	3.4	2.8	-
3. Gross Domestic Savings (per cent of GDP)	23.7	23.5	24.2	-
4. Gross Domestic Capital Formation (per cent GDP)	24.3	23.1	23.3	-
5. Private Capital Formation (per cent GDP)	17.9	17.3	17.6	-
6. Public Sector Capital Formation (per cent GDP)	6.4	5.8	5.7	-
7. Index of Industrial Production	5.1	2.6	5.8	7.0
8. Index of Agricultural Production	-6.4	6.8	-15.1	19.6
9. Per Cap availability of foodgrains (kg/yr)	151.1	-	-	-
10. Wholesale Price Index (per cent change)	7.1	3.7	3.4	5.4
11. CPI Ind. Workers (per cent change)	3.8	4.3	4.0	-
12. Exports as per cent GDP	10.4	10.0	11.1	10.0
13. Imports as per cent GDP	11.8	11.7	13.8	12.9
14. Current Account Balance per cent GDP	-0.8	0.2	0.8	0.1
15. Debt Service Ratio	16.2	13.6	-	-
16. Foreign Exchange Reserves (US$ bn)	42.28	54.11	74.81	110.32
17. Combined Fiscal Deficit (per cent of GDP)	9.4	10.0	10.0	9.0
18. Combined Domestic Liabilities (per cent of GDP)	64.1	67.6	75.5	76.9

Source: Economic Survey (various years), Ministry of Finance, Government of India.

improvement in recent years takes India nowhere near East Asian levels, as yet.

While such domestic economic challenges remain and act as a constraint on internal economic security, India's external economic security is today more robust. Indian economic policy has always been mindful of 'external economic security' and many elements of the *regime* in economic policy that go under the rubric 'inward oriented' industrialisation were based on the paramount need for such external security. These policies were framed within the political paradigm of 'self-reliance'. The importance of such external self-reliance was underscored by the 1991 payments crisis and the experience with economic sanctions imposed by some developed industrial economies in 1998 in response to India's decision to conduct nuclear tests. The need to reduce dependence on aid, to minimise the risk of external default and the need to approach multilateral and bilateral donors for financial assistance and the need to steer clear of global economic shocks transmitted through open capital markets led to the pursuit of a set of economic policies on the external front that in fact increased India's economic security in the 1990s and early 2000s.

The continued accretion to foreign exchange reserves, with almost a 50 per cent increase in reserves in 2003-04, albeit with implied costs of sterilisation of reserves to limit their monetary impact in the home economy, a stable exchange rate regime and reduced dependence on debt and aid flows with increased capital inflows and earnings from invisibles exports contributed to a more robust external economic profile, even though India continued to be a laggard on foreign direct investment.

Thus, in 2003 India's external economic security was better assured than its internal economic security. In 2004, the government will have to pay more attention to employment generation, assuring stability of prices and improving the fiscal health of the central and state governments. The reform of the public sector, in areas where privatisation is not likely to happen or is unwarranted, as in health care, education and urban transportation, is also an area of vital importance.

Table 3.2

Sectoral Growth Rates, 2002-03

	Fiscal Year	
	2002-03*	2003-04**
GDP at factor cost	4	8.1
Agriculture, forestry and fishing	-5.2	9.1
Mining and Quarrying	8.8	4
Manufacturing	6.2	7.1
Electricity, gas and water supply	3.8	5.4
Construction	7.3	6
Trade, hotels, transport and communication	7	10.9
Finance, insurance, real estate, business services	8.8	6.4
Community, social and personal services	5.8	5.9

Source: Same as Table 3.1.

Note: *Quick Estimates; **Advance Estimates.

Fortunately the rate of inflation remained subdued in 2003 at levels below 5.0 per cent. However, indicators are that in 2004-05 new inflationary pressures may develop both on account of an increase in commodity prices, especially oil prices, and also on account of increased demand. The Indian economy has moved to a new 'inflationary threshold' of around 5.0 per cent from the long-term average 'threshold' rate of around 8.0 per cent. Reduced inflation tolerance is a global phenomenon and policy makers in India must remain alive to the fact that world inflation rates are still below India's current levels. Hence, any increase in inflation rates is likely to erode the competitiveness of Indian industry.

According to a study prepared by economists at the Delhi School of Economics,[6] the growth rates for 2003-04 and 2004-05 would be 7.6 per cent and 6.6 per cent respectively. This forecast is based on assumptions relating to the performance of the economy set out in Table 3.3. What this forecast shows is that while the growth rate of the economy over the next two years is likely to be above the long-term average of 5.8 per cent for the period 1980 to 2002, it

---

6.   *Economic Outlook India 2004-2006,* Prepared by Centre for Development Economics and Delhi School of Economics Research Team, University of Delhi, 2004.

Table 3.3

Forecasts for Major Economic Indicators

Variable	Level		Forecast Y-O-Y Increase (per cent)		
	2002-03	2002-03	2003-04	2004-05	2005-06
Real GDP: Rs. Billion (at 1993-94 Prices)	13183.21	13045.48	7.59	6.56	6.80
Value Added in Industry Rs. Billion (at 1993-94 Prices)	4783.77	4687.88	6.55	7.44	7.70
Real Private Consumption: Rs. Billion (at 1993-94 Prices)	8972.43	8931.64	5.37	5.31	5.52
Real Government Consumption Expenditure: Rs. Billion (at 1993-94 Prices)	N.A	1825.73	6.36	7.01	6.98
Real Private Corporate Investment: Rs. Billion (at 1993-94 Prices)	840.92	822.80	5.06	11.74	11.87
Wholesale Price Index (at 1993-94 Prices)	166.8	166.22	5.54	5.07	5.1
Wholesale Price Non-fuel (at 1993-94 Prices)	154.96	154.04	5.23	4.96	5.14
Consumer Price Index (at 1993-94=100)	186.8	186.66	3.77	3.30	3.0
Exports:DGCI & S (Billion US Dollars)	52.72	52.46	17.73	14.73	14.80
Imports: DGCI & S (Billion US Dollars)	61.41	62.70	25.01	19.93	20.73
C/A Balance: RBI*	4.14	4.21	4.88	4.16	3.24

Source: Economic Outlook India, 2004-06, Centre for Development Economics, University of Delhi, 2004 (*mimeo*).

Note: * *Levels in billion US Dollars.*

will not as yet touch the Tenth Plan target rate of 8.0 per cent in the next two years. This will require domestic economic reforms aimed at increasing the productivity of investment at home and increasing gross capital formation.

The industry break up of the aggregate GDP shows that agricultural sector, estimated to grow at 8.6 per cent during

2003-04, is forecast to grow at 2.5 per cent in 2004-05 and 2.66 per cent in 2005-06 on the assumption that normal weather conditions would prevail in both years. However, without new investment in agriculture and infrastructure it will be difficult to sustain an acceleration of growth, nor can the required employment be created in urban, semi-urban and rural areas. The recent decline in food stocks on account of drought also necessitates replenishment of stock to ensure price stability and food security. In recent years food prices have remained under check thanks to huge stocks and lower tariffs. However, if growth acceleration continues the demand for food may well increase, exerting pressure on food prices.

Finally, an important economic security challenge for India is the uneven levels of economic development between regions and the sharp differences in inter-regional trends in economic growth. (Table 3.4). Recent trends do not point to a reduction in this

Table 3.4

*State-wise Per Capita Gross Domestic Product
and Rate of Growth of GSDP*

State	Per Capita GSDP (Constant Rs.), 2001-02	Rate of Growth of Per Capita GSDP, 1980-98 (per cent)
Punjab	17326	3.0
Maharashtra	17029	4.5
Gujarat	16923	4.3
Haryana	16263	3.1
Tamil Nadu	14911	4.3
Karnataka	13294	3.6
Kerala	12338	3.1
Andhra Pradesh	11549	2.9
West Bengal	11386	3.3
Rajasthan	10008	3.8
Madhya Pradesh	8704	2.5
Uttar Pradesh	6829	2.0
Orissa	7039	1.7
Bihar	3757	1.0
All India	13305	-

Source: National Income Statistics, 2004. Centre for Monitoring Indian Economy.

differential. Unless the laggard states invest in human development, infrastructure and urbanisation they will continue to lag behind the rest of the country creating major economic distortions and posing a challenge to political management of the country. The central government has to develop a roadmap for reduced regional imbalances, but much of the effort will remain at the level of the state government. Unless governments in the backward regions embrace economic reforms, assure better governance and raise the resources for development they will be faced with an insurmountable development challenge that can pose a threat to national security. The problem also has an intra-state dimension in large states where the development problems of backward districts require urgent attention to prevent deterioration of the security environment. Breaking up states in to smaller states may not always address the problem. Rather, good governance and institutional mechanisms to deal with agrarian and social backwardness of regions must be evolved.

Conclusion

While there are conceptual imponderables in analysing year to year changes in a country's economic security, recent trends in the Indian economy suggest that challenges relating to India's external economic security, in terms of the sustainability of balance of payments, quantum of foreign exchange reserves, exchange rate stability and external debt flows, have been more convincingly addressed than internal economic security challenges in terms of capital formation, employment, food security, inter-regional imbalances in growth and infrastructure development.

Clearly, public policy must address the domestic economic security challenge as convincingly as it has tried to address the external economic security challenge.

4 | ESSAY

National security in an open economy

ECONOMIC power is the cornerstone of a nation's power in the contemporary world. The economic size of a nation matters and is an important element of national security. Low economic growth, low productivity of capital and labour, inadequate investment in human capital and human capability and a reduced share of world trade have contributed to the marginalisation of the Indian economy in the world economy. The economic security challenge for India is to pursue above average national income growth at the annual rate of at least 7.0 per cent to 8.0 per cent so that India's share of world income is commensurate with her population size and a larger economic base can more truly reflect India's status in the global arena. The critical importance of stepping up growth bears repetition this year when the economy has slowed down and the industrial sector remains in the grip of a recession.

China's sustained economic growth of the past quarter century has increased its economic, political and strategic profile in Asia and in many other parts of the world. If the Indian economy does not catch up with China, in terms of economic growth and human development indicators, its wider security and global profile may be seriously challenged. It is in our national security interest to improve our economic performance, both quantitatively and qualitatively, not just *vis-á-vis* China but with respect to the global economy.

India has registered an average rate of economic growth of 5.5 per cent in the period 1980-2001. If this rate slips below 5.0 per cent in the next five years it would pose a serious challenge to national well-being and security. Maintaining 5.5 per cent growth over the next decade may address the challenge of population growth and India's external security but will not address the overall challenge of national well-being and economic security. It is only if we are able to register upwards of 6.0 to 7.0 per cent growth over the next decade can we emerge as a major power and ensure national well-being, eradicate poverty and address the challenge of national security.

The economy has undoubtedly experienced an acceleration of economic growth as well as of growth of per capita income over the past two decades (Table 4.1).

However, in the last two years there has been a disturbing deceleration in growth, particularly industrial growth. The Indian economy can not sustain overall GDP growth of 7.0 per cent to 8.0 per cent purely on the basis of services sector and export growth. There has to be a further acceleration of growth of agricultural production, mainly through productivity increases, and of manufacturing growth. Improved capacity utilisation and productivity of existing investment must be accompanied by investment in new capacity. Moreover, given the trends in population growth the economy will have to sustain a much higher rate of growth of at least 7.0 per cent to 8.0 per cent over the next decade in order to address the basic needs of over a billion people.

A strategy to stimulate capital formation in agriculture and industrial sectors and widen the domestic manufacturing base is required to ensure further acceleration of growth. Along with pursuing policies that accelerate economic growth, the government must urgently address distributional issues and poverty eradication. Key distributional issues with national security implications include regional, social and economic imbalances and inequities in the growth process.

If these economic challenges are not addressed immediately, and time-bound action plans drafted with widest possible political support cutting across party lines, national integrity and security can be threatened with the spread of disaffection and increasing political influence of anti-national, separatist, ethnic and chauvinistic and communal political organisations among economically and politically marginalised groups. Well-being is the ultimate security all individuals seek. Human well-being may be defined and measured in terms of income, employment, health, educational attainment, housing and social security. Social scientists have come to define the notion of a minimum acceptable level of well-being as the assurance of 'human security'.[1] Clearly, all modern, liberal democratic societies must ensure the human security of all citizens. Going beyond the needs of an individual and socially acceptable standards of human well-being, a sovereign, democratic government must also ensure 'national security'.

The international environment is no longer as favourable to developing countries as it used to be during the Cold War. The policy autonomy enjoyed by India has been substantially curtailed both, due to the end of the Cold War and due to the processes of globalisation. With the end of the Cold War the developed world is no longer willing to extend 'special and differential' treatment to developing countries. Given the increasingly hostile nature of India to regain its share of world income and emerge as a major global power.

There are several dimensions to 'national security'. Clearly, national security encompasses more than national defence and internal security and its foundation must rest on the social and economic well-being of the people. A socially fractious, economically backward and politically divided nation is unlikely to be militarily secure. Military security is a necessary, not a sufficient condition for national security. Equally, human and economic security is also a necessary and not sufficient condition of national security. It is only when both are assured can national security be ensured. However, the foundation of national security for a developing

---

1. *See Human Development Report*, UNDP, Various Issues, for a discussion of the notion of human security. Also, see Mahbub ul Haq, *Reflections on Human Development*, Oxford University Press, 1995.

country like ours will remain rapid and equitable economic progress based on the development of domestic capabilities and international competitiveness.

With far-reaching changes taking place in the world economic and security environment and with India becoming increasingly open to global economic forces, it is important to examine afresh the notion of 'economic security', self-reliance and national interest. As a nation of nearly one billion people India can not afford to remain a marginal player in the global economy, as measured for instance by our share of world trade or income. Commensurate with her size and civilisational characteristics India must assume a greater role in global affairs and the world economy. This will be possible only when the economy grows rapidly so that each citizen has a decent standard of living and the Indian economy emerges as an important participant in the global economy.

Historical perspective

Barely 300 years ago India accounted for nearly 23 per cent of world income, being the world's second largest economy next only to China. Three hundred years of colonialism and unequal trade, combined with the differential impact of the industrial revolution on living standards across the world, greatly weakened the Indian economy. India's share of world income was reduced to less than 4.0 per cent by the middle of the 20th century (Table 1.1, Ch.1). It is only in the past two decades that India has been able to reverse this decline and increase its share to nearly 5.0 per cent of world income.

India's recent growth acceleration compares favourably with its historical record. In the first half of the 20th century, from 1890 to 1940, the territories of British India recorded less than 1.0 per cent growth of national income. This is an average with high growth, close to 5.0 per cent, in regions such as the Punjab, the Bombay Presidency and the Madras Presidency. In central and north-eastern India growth was negative, largely on account of the collapse of the agrarian economy.

However, after Independence the growth rate of GDP was 3.5 per cent in 1950-80, and 5.5 per cent in 1980-90 and over 6.0 per cent in 1992-2001. During this entire post-Independence period, however, India's share of world trade went down from 2.0 per cent in the 1950s to 0.5 per cent by end-1980s. At the turn of the century it was marginally up at around 0.6 per cent (Table 4.1).

Table 4.1
Macroeconomic Trends in Indian Economy

	1980-1992	1992-2001	1993-1994	1994-1995	1995-1996	1996-1997	1997-1998	1998-1999	1999-2000	2000-2001
Agriculture	3.9	3.3	4.1	5.0	0.9	9.6	2.4	7.1	0.7	0.9
Industry	6.3	6.5	5.2	10.2	11.6	7.1	4.3	3.4	6.4	6.6
Services	6.4	8.2	7.6	7.1	10.5	7.2	9.8	8.2	9.6	8.3
Total GDP	5.4	6.4	5.9	7.3	7.3	7.8	4.8	6.6	6.4	6.0

Source: Economic Survey, 2000-01, Ministry of Finance, Government of India.

Both national security, in particular economic security but also military security, and the attendant assurance of the status of a Major Power, can only be built on the firm foundation of sustained economic growth, aimed at doubling per capita income within a generation and of our share of world trade within a decade. This goal subsumes the process of investing in and building human capabilities, increasing the share of investment in national income and stepping up capital and labour productivity.

Redefining self-reliance

It is this perspective which must now inform our concept of 'self-reliance'. The notion of national security, in particular economic security, formed the basis of the definition of 'self-reliance' in economic matters that informed the thinking of nationalist leaders through this century. Indeed, at an early stage in our struggle for Independence, nationalist writers like Ranade, Gokhale and Naoroji identified 'self-reliance' as an important goal of 'free India'. In the immediate post-Independence period, beginning with the First Five Year Plan, India has recognised 'self-reliance' as a cornerstone of her economic policies. In its essence 'self-reliance' has meant the ability to pursue an independent national policy without becoming critically dependent on external support and resources. This notion of self-reliance emphasised autonomy of decision-making. In the post-Independence period, the key areas in which self-reliance was identified as vital to national security interest were food production, core industrial sectors, energy and defence capability.

It is relevant to recall here that during the 1950s, self-reliance in food production was not given the importance it required and the focus of the First and Second Five Year Plans was almost entirely on the industrial sector. The relative backwardness of Indian industry and the desire to build an indigenous capital goods industry remained a dominant concern of the planners, while a series of good monsoons and relatively good agricultural production generated complacency on the agricultural front. It was the drought of the mid-1960s, the excessive dependence on imported foodgrains resulting in what was termed a 'ship-to-mouth' existence, which forced the government to pay attention to the food situation and launch the 'Green Revolution' programme. Since then food self-sufficiency has been an important element of public policy.

Much as on the food front, a generous availability of foreign exchange in the 1950s fostered complacency on the external trade and payments front as well. A combination of 'export pessimism' and 'forex optimism' encouraged planners to pursue 'closed models' of economic development in which external trade and foreign direct investment were not regarded as important options for the economy. Just as the drought of the mid-1960s forced the government to launch the 'Green Revolution' programme, the forex crisis in the late 1950s, the drain on reserves following the food crisis of the 1960s as well as the wars with China and Pakistan and the subsequent denial of foreign assistance to India in the late 1960s encouraged the government to pursue even more inward-looking models of development towards the end of the 1960s.

During this period, that is the mid-1950s to the mid-1970s, more than in the 1950s, 'self-reliance' came to be increasingly defined in terms of greater 'inward-orientation' of economic activity and the protection of domestic enterprise.[2] Rather than pursue export growth, the focus was on import substitution. Admittedly, this created an indigenous base in many industries and this was a major gain for the economy, but it also reduced India's engagement with the world economy. Through this entire period India's share in world trade systematically declined from around 2.0 per cent at the time of Independence to less than 0.5 per cent in the early 1990s.

This decline in export share not only reduced India's ability to finance imports through the current account, but also forced it to increasingly rely on external debt to finance the current account deficit. While higher export growth and a steep increase in inward remittances eased the external economic situation in the 1970s, notwithstanding the oil shocks, India's external indebtedness increased steeply during the 1980s. A deterioration in the internal fiscal situation in late-80s, combined with a sharp increase in short-term external debt triggered a balance-of-payments crisis in 1990-91.

Since 1991, India has pursued a dual strategy of, one, increasing access to foreign exchange resources through increased trade, foreign direct investment and foreign portfolio investment; and, two, of reducing external indebtedness, especially exposure to short-term debt. Given the need to finance vital imports, especially of energy, capital goods and agricultural commodities, and the need to service external debt as well as facilitate repatriation of profits on foreign equity, India must continue to ensure uninterrupted supply of forex resources.[3] Higher export trade as well as increased access to external capital flows, especially long-term investment, is necessary to deal

---

2. The change in India's attitude towards foreign investment, from a relatively liberal outlook in the 1950s to a more inward-looking perspective in the 1960s is recorded in Sanjaya Baru, "Continuity and Change in Indian Industrial Policy", in T.V. Satyamurthy (Edited), *Industry and Agriculture in India since Independence,* Vol 2, Oxford University Press, New Delhi, 1995; and in Sanjaya Baru, "The Economics of India Foreign Policy", *World Affairs* (New Delhi-Geneva) April-June, 1998.

3. The basic approach to external economic policy in the light of the 1990-91 balance of payments crisis has been clearly spelt out in the *Report of the High Level Committee on Balance of Payments,* (Rangarajan Committee) Government of India, April 1993.

with such pressures on the external account.[4] Hence, the pursuit of 'self reliance' in the present context requires, on the one hand, reduced dependence on external debt flows, and, on the other, increased sourcing of forex through external trade and investment.

In the past India, like South Korea, has preferred the debt route to access forex rather than the equity route. Even today, domestic business may favour external debt to foreign equity. There is nothing wrong in opting for debt over equity provided the funds are productively utilised and debt servicing does not become a problem. The fact is that in the 1980s and early 1990s, there was an unsustainable increase in external debt and India did not do enough before 1991 to pursue the equity route, as did China. Secondly, as the Latin American and East Asian crises have shown, from the perspective of 'protecting' domestic markets against entry of or competition from multinational firms, excessive dependence on external debt, on the part of the government, banks and financial institutions or private corporations is no guarantee against external pressures to open up the domestic market.

This is because a financial crisis triggered by such excessive debt exposure can end up forcing a country to go to the International Monetary Fund and accept its aid conditionality that, in turn, involves liberalising trade and investment policies. The issue is not debt *versus* equity but is one of ensuring a proper balance between the two. Equity often entails debt. The key goal must be to ensure the sustainability of debt. In this context it is the structure of debt that is more important than total quantum. India has traditionally relied more on low-cost multilateral debt rather than higher cost commercial debt. Here the policies being pursued by the government since 1991, and the policies articulated in the report of the High Powered Committee on Balance of Payments and External Debt,

---

4. The Rangarajan Committee quoted Union Finance Minister Manmohan Singh as saying: "Our vision of a self-reliant economy should be an economy which can meet all its import requirements through exports, without undue dependence on artificial external props such as foreign aid." The Committee itself believed that "over the medium term, ... an atmosphere of liberal trade regime with a self-correcting exchange rate and a gradual movement towards international competitiveness would have to be the basic objective."

have served India well. The policy of minimising dependence on short-term debt has played an important role in shielding India from the full impact of the Asian financial crisis in 1997-99.

Furthermore, given the increasing 'globalisation' of industrial activity and the link between trade and foreign direct investment, the increased 'outward-orientation' of the economy will perforce entail new relationships of 'inter-dependence' with global markets and firms, and the need to adhere to existing and new multilateral economic regimes.

Given the inevitability of globalisation and its ramifications for a large economy like India, it is necessary that we equip ourselves to deal with both the opportunities and the threats this process entails. Intelligent integration is the answer to the challenge of globalisation. Intelligent integration also helps create new webs of inter-relationships that creates 'inter-dependence' rather than 'dependence'.

Self-reliance in the contemporary world, therefore, has to be defined as the ability to ensure inter-dependency so that other countries, big and small, near and afar, benefit from India's economic growth and prosperity and are hurt by any economic crisis or stagnation here. Just as the world economy benefits from the prosperity of the economies of the United States, China or Japan, and is hurt by any crisis in these economies, India must also construct relationships of interdependence with other countries so that enough number of countries have a stake in India's growth and well-being and are hurt by its decline.

The concept of 'self-reliance', in the traditional sense, has implied complete autonomy of decision making of national governments. In the increasingly globalising world, few countries enjoy such complete autonomy. Rather, the new paradigm of self-reliance is defined in terms of creating relationships of inter-dependence that increase the room for manoeuvre of sovereign entities. The key words are 'interdependence' and 'economic engagement'. In the past 'self-reliance' was defined as liberation from external 'dependence', henceforth it will have to be viewed in terms of ensuring 'interdependence' through economic engagement.

Economic liberalisation and national security

It is clear now that the principal architects of India's 'new economic policies' of the early 1990s had an appreciation of the external political context within which external economic liberalisation was pursued. This external factor was the end of the Cold War and the dominant influence of the United States. India had resisted US pressures to liberalise her trade and investment policies till the early 1990s. India joined Brazil and several other developing economies to block progress on further trade liberalisation through the Uruguay Round of trade negotiations in GATT.

However, India was forced to change its stance in 1991 because it realised that 'economic engagement', especially with the US, was the new post-Cold War paradigm of international economic relations within which developing countries had to operate. While India's economic policies in the 1990s were publicly never so articulated or defended, the fact remains that the altered external political environment had an important role in shaping India's economic policies in the 1990s.

The Chinese model of external economic liberalisation in the 1990s drew India's attention to the foreign policy and external security potential of increased FDI flows. China utilised its open FDI policy to secure for itself a constituency of support within the United States. What the Chinese did was not new. Indeed, most of East and South-East Asia pursued this policy during the Cold War period to ensure a 'balance of power' in the region between China, USSR, United States and subsequently Japan. China neutralised US hostility by opening up its economy to American multinationals. India was slow in adapting to this changed environment, but when it did the opening of the Indian economy to external trade and investment flows in the 1990s can be viewed as a 'strategic' response to a new, potentially more hostile, external political environment.

The political leadership never articulated its policies in this manner. Hence, rather than be viewed as a 'pro-active' strategic response to an altered external environment, the 'new economic policies' were largely viewed, not just by the political opposition but also within the government at that time, as being pursued at the behest of the IMF, the World Bank and the G-7 economies, in particular the United States. It is only more recently, especially in the aftermath of the Pokhran-II tests and the imposition of sanctions by the US and Japan, that there is now wider political appreciation in India that external economic liberalisation can be an important element of a national security strategy.

This relationship manifests itself in two ways—first, increased foreign trade and investment creates benign webs of inter-dependence and mutual benefit with the outside world; second, it increases the cost of a crisis in India to the rest of the world. While trade economists generally emphasise the purely economic and 'rational' reasons for trade liberalisation, political economists and strategic policy analysts must also appreciate the 'foreign policy' and 'strategic' dimension of external liberalisation. It has long been recognised that 'trade policy is foreign policy' (Richard Cooper, *Foreign Policy*, 1972). However, while in the colonial era it is 'trade that followed the flag', as suggested by many historians, in the contemporary world, particularly in the post-Cold War era, and in the case of the newly-industrialising economies, it can be argued that it is often the 'flag which follows trade'. In other words, newly industrialising economies, including large economies like China, have been able to increase their political leverage in international affairs, both in bilateral relations and in multilateral forums; by increasing their share of world trade, particularly their trade relationship with the United States and other major OECD economies.

Economic relations have acquired a new political dimension in the age of pragmatism in foreign policy. No country has demonstrated the power of commerce in diplomacy better than Dengist China. India has been slow to adapt to this age of pragmatism in international relations. It is pertinent to state here that in India's wider 'southern Asian' neighbourhood, from Iran and Central Asia to our west to the ASEAN economies in the east, India's share of the total trade of each of these countries is way below China's share, with the exception of only three countries, namely, Bangladesh, Nepal and Sri Lanka, with each of whom China is rapidly increasing its trade relationship. China has succeeded in increasing its bilateral trade with each of the countries in Asia. While India has managed to increase her trade with other South Asian economies as well as some ASEAN economies, it lags far behind China in its ability to build political and strategic bridges through trade and investment flows.

While trade and investment liberalisation is, therefore, well advised from an economic security perspective, we must guard against the danger of de-industrialisation and of a loss of competitive advantage of our own industry. The persistent economic slowdown over the past four years, particularly the sluggishness in the growth of investment and output in the industrial sector must be reversed. The threat of de-industrialisation is real and the decline in the investment ratio and in capital expenditure is alarming. If allowed to drift, this situation can hurt India's economic security.

A large nation of one billion people must build its own domestic capability in modern manufacturing and create the industrial and technological base required to ensure sustained and stable economic growth and the required defence capability. This can not be ensured if the threat of de-industrialisation and the take-over of domestic companies by foreign companies becomes larger and persistent. External investment liberalisation must be focused on greenfield projects and infrastructure development and not pursued at the cost of building indigenous capabilities, companies and brands.

Trade and technology

Apart from such external economic and political advantages, trade and investment liberalisation must also be viewed as an increasingly important means of accessing new technologies. In the past it was possible for firms in developing countries to buy technology. Today technology comes embodied as capital or as goods. Without allowing open trade and investment regimes and conforming to global regimes on intellectual property protection it is becoming difficult to acquire new technologies. This does not mean that new technologies are available for the asking. Indeed, if anything, it is becoming increasingly difficult to access new technologies, especially in 'sunrise industries'. Hence, even as we seek new technology through more liberal trade and investment regimes, in the interests of economic self-reliance and security, national investment, public and private, in technology development and modern industrialisation remains critical, even as developing economies become more open to external trade and investment flows.

A large economy like India must foster an efficient and competitive domestic manufacturing base even as it becomes more open to external trade flows. India can not afford to pursue higher macroeconomic growth only through the expansion of incomes in the agricultural and services sectors. It must also invest in the growth of a more competitive domestic industrial sector. Both these goals require sustained public and private investment in new technologies and frontier areas of research and development. India has built up an infrastructure for research in space, nuclear energy, biotechnology and drugs and pharmaceuticals. This base must be constantly renewed and widened. Unless we invest in science and technology we can not ensure economic security and retain sovereignty. Even as we do this, we must fight hard to ensure global regimes that enable us to develop this indigenous capability. The fight against unequal obligations such as TRIPs in the WTO is part of this campaign.

I: Internal economic policies and economic security

Human security and human development

National security is built on the foundation of a prosperous and free economy where 'human security' is assured. Where individual freedoms are denied, where individual well-being and the security of life and property is not assured, national security can not be ensured. Hence, the primary requirement of economic security is 'human security', that is, the well-being of the people defined in terms of their longevity, access to education and other skills that enable them to seek gainful employment and access to food, energy, housing, clothing and other necessities of a civilised life. A nation can not regard itself economically secure if its people are not assured of such bare necessities. Going beyond these essentials, a poor nation's economic and political security rests on the pursuit of a balanced and sustained economic growth.

While such balance will have to be sought in inter-class, inter-caste, inter-regional, inter-communal and other such social, economic and political terms, in the short-run what will have to be ensured is that everyone is better off as a result of economic growth, even if some are more better off than others. A democratic society can live with an increase in relative inequality but not with an increase in absolute inequality. Political stability in the face of wide-ranging social change is a key element of economic security. As stated at the beginning of the previous section, the notion of 'self- reliance' *vis-à-vis* the external world has undergone a change in India and it is no longer viewed as the pursuit of an 'autarchic' model of development. Rather, 'self-reliance' is now defined as the ability to ensure such 'inter-relationships, with the outside world that national interests are better served. Hence, to the extent imports of technology, energy, defence equipment, food and such like are required, a self-reliant economy will be one which is capable of trading with the outside world. To ensure this it is necessary that the economy is internationally 'competitive' so that there is a sizeable 'tradable' sector and is open to external trade and investment flows. This has been elaborated in the previous section.

What this entails as far as the domestic economy is concerned is investment in people—in social and economic infrastructure and higher productivity or all factors of production, in line with international standards and at least of our competitors. Investment in universal education, the creation of a domestic skill, resource and technology base that makes the economy competitive and enables constant engagement with the outside world is essential. It is instructive to remember that no modern industrial economy in the world, not a single one, has less than 80 per cent literacy.

Without a sound educational base, a self-reliant and modern economy can not be built. Without the latter, no economic security can be assured to a large economy like India. Further, in a labour-abundant country any strategy of development that seeks political stability and economic security will have to ensure adequate growth of employment.

Political stability and economic security also require that regional inequalities are minimised and backward regions are offered incentives to invest in productivity improvement and investment. A sound macroeconomic policy, moderate rates of inflation and public investment in social and physical infrastructure are all essential building blocks of economic security in a developing economy. Going beyond such 'fundamentals', national security also requires the assurance of economic security in critical areas such as food, energy, technology and capital.

Food security

The importance of 'food security' to national security was brought home to the political leadership of our country in the mid-1960s. The severe drought of 1965-67 sharply reduced food availability and increased dependence on imported foodgrains. As often noted, India led a 'ship to mouth' existence. This vulnerability on the food front was exploited by foreign powers and the United States used its food aid to India to push through its own foreign policy objectives in the region, particularly with respect to Pakistan claims over Kashmir. The 'Green Revolution' was launched in the context of such a national crisis. The record of food production and availability since then is creditable, though not laudable. While India has never faced a shortage of food since the mid-1960s and has been able to bridge any periodic gap with imported foodgrains, the fact is that productivity gains in agriculture have been minimal and, with population crossing the one billion mark this year, per capita food consumption of the bottom half of India's population is sub-optimal. Calorie deficiency, malnutrition and lack of access to potable water remain major problems for more than a third of our population. Pressure is again mounting on India to re-invest in productivity growth and infrastructure development in agriculture. Neglect of these priorities can generate serious threats to national well-being and security. According to official estimates, the annual foodgrain production increased from 55 million tonnes in 1950 to over 195 m.t. by the end-90s. Most of this expansion has come from higher yields, especially in the 'green revolution' districts, owing to improved seeds and increased irrigation. While per capita consumption of food has increased over this half century by a modest 0.5 per cent per year, the interclass distribution of this growth is highly skewed. Consequently, there are serious inter-regional, inter-class/caste and inter-gender imbalances in food consumption. Food and energy malnutrition is widespread and protein malnutrition is a serious problem. Assuming that foodgrain production will continue to increase at 2.7 per cent per year, as in the past, the projected foodgrain output for year 2020 is estimated to be 290 m.t. and by 2050 it may go up to 410 m.t. Based on population growth projections it is estimated that by 2020 India's population may be 1.4 billion and by 2050 it may be 1.6 billion. This implies a food demand of 310 m.t. and 425 m.t. in 2020 and 2050 respectively, based on current levels of per capita consumption, leaving a gap of about 20 million tonnes. Alternative scenarios of food production and population growth can be worked out showing more optimistic and pessimistic outcome. It is clear that even the most optimistic projections would suggest that for the next half century ensuring sustained food production and availability and improving the nutritional status of the people without becoming critically dependent on external support will remain a key priority for national security.

To ensure sustained and sustainable growth of food production and elimination of malnutrition forward-looking policies will have to be pursued in infrastructure development, agricultural research and trade policy. Public investment in agriculture, especially productive investment in irrigation and new seed technology, has been neglected over the last decade. Distorted pricing and trade, internal and external, have also discouraged productivity growth and have repressed rural incomes. In order to meet the target of

310 m.t. foodgrain production by 2020 and 425 m.t. by 2050, average foodgrain productivity will have to increase from the present level of 1.7 tonnes per hectare to 3.0 tonnes/ha by 2020 and 4.2 tonnes/ha by 2050. This is a stupendous task and requires both massive public investment in irrigation, rural infrastructure and bio-technology as well as the pursuit of economic policies that shift resources from wasteful subsidies into productive investment and encourage greater trade in agricultural commodities, both internal and internationally.

Energy security

India will face a serious shortage of energy resources if economic growth is sustained at over 6 per cent over the next decade. India's energy consumption has increased from 84.5 million tonnes of oil equivalent (mtoe) in 1953-54 to 290.4 mtoe in 1996-97, growing at a rate of 2.91 per cent per year. With a growing population size and, more importantly, with per capita income expected to increase at a faster pace than in the past five decades, energy demand will accelerate. India faces a resource deficit in per capita terms and the energy deficit is expected to increase, given existing rates of growth of demand and supply. While indigenous energy sources like hydro and thermal electricity are being exploited, the dependence on imported oil and natural gas has been increasing and will continue to increase. In order to fully utilise the hydro potential in the region India should pursue bilateral projects with Nepal, Bangladesh, Myanmar and China. India must also invest diplomatic energy in pursuing the oil and natural gas pipeline option from Iran and Central Asia. Here again improved external relations, especially with Pakistan, are vital to any long-term and meaningful exploitation of the available options.

Equally, we must pursue alternative energy sources. Two major sources which are currently under-exploited and which deserve increased investment are nuclear energy and biomass. Nuclear energy contributes to just about 3 per cent of our current energy requirements. This share can easily by trebled. An important source of renewable energy is bio-residues or biomass. This can be obtained from three sources — agro-residues, plantation residues and waste land utilisation. All these sources can be used for power generation. While various options are available, unless consumers pay for what they consume it will not be possible to sustain the rates of investment required to meet the expected demand. Indeed, the greater challenge in the energy sector is to improve the political 'management' of energy policy rather than ensure energy security through increased investment. If governments and State Electricity Boards (SEBS) can get consumers to pay for power, half the problem of managing energy demand will be dealt with. It is the financial bankruptcy of existing utilities, due to non-collection of user charges, rather than a shortage of new investment, which has contributed to power shortages in all sectors of the economy.

The problem of energy security goes beyond that of the rising oil and gas prices, with its attendant impact on the public exchequer, and the need to increase user charges for power, kerosene, LPG and water. Ensuring economic viability of the domestic energy sector is the most important energy security issue for India. Rising oil prices have had a serious negative impact on economic growth worldwide. They have also hurt Indian economic growth in 2000-01 and impacted on the balance of payments as well as on domestic inflation and industrial growth. While there has been a moderation in oil prices recently, India can not afford to be complacent and must be prepared for price volatility. Given India's rising growth rates and increasing per capita consumption of energy, we need a long term energy strategy to deal with the pressures generated by excess demand and inadequate domestic investment and availability.

Power shortages will continue to constrain economic growth and reduce the efficiency of resource utilisation unless power sector reforms are vigorously pursued and new investment, both private and public, is enabled. The annual losses of SEBS have totalled up to over Rs. 15,000 crore by the end of the 1990s. Public utilities are facing bankruptcy across the country. Private investment has been slow in coming into the power sector for a variety of reasons. More importantly, the strategy of first privatising power generation without privatising distribution has discouraged new private investment. The first priority for the government, both at the centre and in states, must be to reform SEBs and ensure that all consumers pay for power. Along with implementation of universal user charges, the government must also tackle the problem of power theft on a war footing. In the national capital alone half of the power generated is stolen.

Power sector requires fresh infusion of public investment in generation. This should be accompanied by privatisation of power distribution. There should be a political consensus cutting across all parties in favour of universal user charges for power, even if there is differential pricing in favour of weaker sections of society.

The prospect of increasing import dependence in energy supply is a matter of concern for India too and to that extent western models of energy security remain relevant for India also. However, in a developing economy with a fractious democracy like India, a third dimension will have to be added to the concept of energy security. This relates to the 'efficiency' of the domestic supply side, the production and distribution infrastructure, and the economics of the demand side, mainly pricing.

Technological self-reliance

At a higher level of development, economic security is critically dependent on investment in science and technology and domestic research and development. Such technological 'self-reliance' is required, from the viewpoint of economic security in areas such as food production (particularly biotechnology), energy (including nuclear energy), defence, space and information technology. In these areas India can certainly benefit from greater 'engagement' with the outside world and the paradigm of 'inter-dependence' is relevant up to a point. However, these are areas where indigenous technology development is vital to ensure economic security. This is because in the first place new technologies are not easily available even on payment. In each of these areas, even private companies are not willing to make new technologies available.

Going beyond such 'market-based' intellectual property protection, there has been technology denial for a quarter century now and these sanctions have been intensified after Pokhran-II tests. India will have to assume that such technology denial will continue for a long time, perhaps forever, and act accordingly. Domestic R&D and public investment in new technologies is critical to the assurance of economic security in a technology-driven global economy. The technologies concerned range from defence-related technologies (including space and nuclear) to biotechnology, information technology and such like. Both in order to access new technologies from abroad and to encourage domestic attempts at technology development India must conform to multilateral agreements on intellectual property protection and strengthen her machinery for awarding and tracking patents.

The record of the private sector in investment in R&D and promoting indigenous technology has so far been dismal. Indian business communities continue to be characterised by their merchant and trading class origins. In a captive home market of limited scale they were under no pressure to innovate and compete on the basis of new technologies. Most technology is imported and most scales of production remain sub-optimal. After 1991 there has been an attitudinal change and the pressure of competition and threat of cheaper imports is finally forcing some of them to invest in new technology development. This pressure must be maintained. Public policy must endeavour to bring together the professional community which possesses the 'skills' and the business community which possesses the 'funds' to encourage skill-based industrial development. India lags behind all major industrial countries in new product development and patented technologies. This must change if economic security has to be assured.

An important pre-requisite for technological self-reliance is investment in basic and technical education and incentive systems for excellence and innovation. Apart from the challenge of eradicating illiteracy and making India fully literate, there is an equally important challenge of making the existing educational system, at all levels, both modern and relevant to the needs of the time. While the apex of the educational pyramid meets global standards, the rest of the system is below world standards and is rapidly deteriorating both in terms of curricula and quality of teaching as well as physical infrastructure.

Finally, the educational system lacks an appropriate incentive system and does not adequately reward merit. This has contributed to some extent to the problem of 'brain drain'. Converting the notion of 'brain drain' into that of a 'brain tank' is also an important route to technological self-reliance and the assurance of economic security. In this regard, India must make better use of the pool of talent available outside India, especially in the United States. Simpler rules and regulations for inward investment by non-resident Indians and 'people of Indian origin' (PIOs), special finance windows and venture capital support for professionals. Easier systems for granting of patents to Indian scientists and technologists, and overall support for creative activity is critical. The disincentives to pursue research and work in India must be reduced, the reward for contributing to the national effort must be increased and there must be greater recognition of the role of market forces and merit in remuneration for professionals working even within publicly funded R&D institutions.

Infrastructure

Over the last five decades there has been a slow acceleration of economic growth. From a zero rate of growth of national income in the first 50 years of Independence, real GDP growth increased to an average of 3.5 per cent during 1950-80 and to 5.5 per cent in 1980-1998. As against 5.5 per cent growth during the 1980s, in the post-reform period of 1992-97 GDP growth was around 6.0 per cent. However, the limits to growth acceleration may have been reached due to infrastructural constraints. Unless there is a new spurt in infrastructural investment in all sectors it is unlikely that India can sustain 6.0 per cent growth, not to talk of a further acceleration. Such investment is required in irrigation, roads (national highways and rural roads), internal waterways, telecommunications, power and drinking water and sanitation.

Private investment, local and foreign, can only bridge the gap up to a point and only when a project is commercially viable. Much of the required investment in infrastructure will have to come from public investment. Even in developed market economies like the United States, Germany and Japan investment in infrastructure, especially highways, power and telecommunications initially came from the public sector. Public investment in infrastructure will continue to be an important priority both from a developmental and a security perspective.

Apart from new investment, public policy must also ensure viability of existing investment. This requires economic pricing of utilities, especially power, telecommunications and irrigation water. Unless public investment in infrastructure can generate a minimum rate of return so as to pay for itself it will not be possible for government to maintain the level of investment required by the country. In the interests of national security and development, apart from the interests of consumers, the government must levy user charges and ensure economic viability of public investment. This in itself can largely help bridge the gap between supply and demand if public utilities and enterprises can generate resources to ensure full utilisation of existing capacity. Improving the productivity of investment, particularly public investment, is a national security requirement given the dangers of a loss of competitiveness of domestic industry on this count.

Macroeconomic policy

A stable and sustainable macroeconomic policy is a corner-stone of economic security. Even from a purely national security perspective, strategic analysts have come to increasingly recognise the importance of sustained economic growth, high factor productivity, a high domestic savings and investment rate along with a liberal trade and investment regime. The old dichotomy between 'outward-orientation' and 'inward-orientation' is increasingly viewed as a superficial, perhaps a purely ideological, debate. Large economies like the US, China and India must be both inward and outward oriented at the same time. Indeed, most developed industrial economies are. The bottomline is not the extent of trade-openness but competitiveness and growth. India must move to a higher growth path at higher levels of factor productivity. Clearly, the two are linked. The East Asian economic crisis once again draws attention to the fact that in the increasingly globalised world economy it is difficult for individual nations, howsoever stable and sustainable their internal macroeconomic policies, to insulate themselves from global economic and financial crises. While countries like China and India have escaped the full impact of the Asian financial crisis, partly because neither of them has implemented full capital account convertibility, the fact remains that both have been affected by the crisis and remain vulnerable to the aftershocks.

The deceleration in India's external trade is partly on account of the loss of competitiveness and of markets following the Asian crisis. India can not remain unmindful of actions taken by other countries in responding to internal and external crises. China's exchange rate policy, the depreciation of the Renminbi, for example, has had serious implications for economic competitiveness of many Asian economies, including India. Such economic actions can challenge a country's economic security and thereby its national security. The key message from the Asian crisis is that individual countries must follow sound and transparent macroeconomic policies to secure themselves against externally triggered crises. As the Korean crisis shows, sound monetary and fiscal policy alone are not adequate. A globalised economy must also pursue sound foreign trade and payments policies and ensure transparency in international financial transactions. A healthy and efficient financial sector is also an important prerequisite.

An economic crisis always constitutes a potential threat to national security. In developing economies, a mere shortage of food can pose a threat to security. The Asian economic crisis has shown, however, that even at higher stages of development an economic crisis triggered by a crisis in the stock market, banking sector, in external trade and payments and so on, can quickly pose a serious challenge to national sovereignty and the very survival of governments. Indeed, it can even be argued that systemic economic crisis or chaos can challenge even the very existence of a nation as indeed was the case with the erstwhile Soviet Union. Economic problems left unaddressed can also create social tensions with serious consequences for national survival and sovereignty. The economic and financial crisis in East and South-East Asia has so far only destabilised national governments, as in Indonesia, but has not yet broken up a nation in this region.

Whether it was the Mexican or the Korean crisis, even large economies and members of the OECD have accepted an erosion of sovereignty in dealing with the consequences of crisis and in restoring normalcy. What India must remember, however, is that the United States is unlikely to bail it out of an external payments crisis as it did in the case of Mexico and South Korea. India has no godfathers, it must fend for itself. Even Thailand was disappointed at the limited assistance it secured from the US. Russia has been left to fend for itself. Indeed, not only can the US not be expected to bail-out India directly, but it's support in securing an IMF loan can not also be taken for granted considering that currently it has extended its economic sanctions against India to cover the lending policies of multilateral financial institutions. Given the political nature of decision making in the IMF and World Bank, and their record on this count whether in response to Pokhran-II or the Asian economic crisis, India will have to be doubly careful about falling into an external economic crisis which necessitates seeking multilateral assistance.

Hence, the key message as far as macroeconomic and financial sector management is concerned is that the government must pursue sound policies and ensure good economic governance for national interest. The link between economic and financial crises and loss of national sovereignty has been clearly established in the Latin American and East and South-East Asian cases. Indeed, even in Eastern Europe, poor economic management gave the West the opening to intervene in national politics and shape policies.[5]

---

5. On the strategic policy implications of the Asian economic crisis for India, see Sanjaya Baru, "The Asian Economic Crisis and India's External Economic Relations", *Money & Finance*, Issue No. 7, Oct-Dec, 1998, reprinted as a chapter in this volume.

In the modern world, it is not possible for India to insulate herself from global forces. Rather, she must integrate intelligently and be prepared to deal with any contingency. Above all, the domestic economy is in need of reform and continuous modernisation. The financial sector, in particular, has to be reformed to cope with the challenge of integration into the global economy. Equally important, key macroeconomic indicators like the exchange rate of the rupee must reflect market realities and ensure export competitiveness even if the central bank chooses to intervene to moderate fluctuations and deal with speculative attacks. This is the other lesson of the Asian crisis—fixed exchange rates can not be sustained without risking an economic crisis. The key parameters to be constantly monitored and kept within reasonable limits, from the viewpoint of ensuring economic security, are the fiscal and revenue deficits, the current account deficit, external and internal debt, and so on.

Fiscal management and national security

While the external economic indicators have been improving in recent years for India, particularly the CAD/GDP ratio, debt servicing ratio and external debt indicators, the internal fiscal situation, particularly the revenue deficit and the internal debt, remain alarmingly high. The medium-term fiscal threats facing the economy arise from an inability to finance essential developmental expenditure and the inability to ensure a truly efficient banking system. Productive investment is being held back by the inability to reduce unproductive subsidies, mobilise adequate direct tax revenues and generate returns to existing public investment.

In its latest Annual Report, the Reserve Bank of India has drawn our attention to the notion of 'fiscal empowerment' and of its relevance for economic security. "The path of durable fiscal consolidation is through fiscal empowerment, *i.e.*, by expanding the scope and size of revenue flows into the budget. A fiscal strategy based on revenue maximisation would also provide the necessary flexibility to shift the pattern of expenditures and redirect them productively; on the other land, fiscal adjustments based predominantly on expenditure reduction involve welfare losses and risk the danger of triggering a downturn of overall economic activity."

Revenue maximisation covers not only taxes but also non-tax revenues, especially cost recovery in respect of commercial services and utilities provided by government or quasi-government entities. The RBI report also draws attention to the danger of fiscal laxity at the State level and, while recognising the many demands made by civil society on the exchequer, observes: "The strategy of fiscal empowerment is of special significance for States since the bedrocks of socio-economic welfare, *i.e.* law and order and social services are in the State sector. There is considerable merit in emphasising the quality aspects of fiscal adjustment in the process of reduction in the fiscal deficit and this means fiscal empowerment rather than fiscal enfeeblement as an appropriate strategy."

A major and sovereign economic and political entity such as India can ill afford to be caught in the whirlpool of fiscal and financial crisis. The consequences of such a crisis entail a compromise in the autonomy of decision making and can have far-reaching political, diplomatic, strategic and social consequences beyond the obvious economic consequences. The Asian financial crisis, as much as the fiscal crisis in Russia, demonstrated quite clearly the political risks attached with weak fiscal-and financial management. In a democracy, politicians in power and in opposition rarely look beyond the next elections. Such myopia encourages fiscal irresponsibility. Unless governments remain firmly committed to prudent fiscal management they can compromise economic and national security. Hence, prudent fiscal management and responsible economic governance in the public sector is in the interests of national security. An important step in this direction would be the adoption of the proposed Fiscal Responsibility and Budget Management Bill. The draft bill recognises that such a law should not come in the way of ensuring financial support for national security.

Defence spending and fiscal management

Finally, we come to an economic policy question directly linked to national security, namely, defence spending. There is a widespread perception among economists in India, encouraged by many western analysts, that India spends far too much on defence and if this could only be reduced it would be possible to address the development challenge. From our analysis above it should be clear that in our view India, like any big nation, is destined to stand alone and defend itself in the face of any external or internal threat to its economic and national security, sovereignty and integrity. India is not and has never been a member of any military alliance. It is not protected by any external umbrella. Hence, it must at all times be prepared to deal on its own with any crisis—political, economic, social or military. On occasions, and for limited purposes, other countries or groups of countries or multilateral organisations may be willing to help India. Such external support will always be welcome and can be sought. But, in the final analysis, India must be ready to defend itself on its own. Hence, any defence planning for India must be based on the assumption of the need for complete self-reliance. The defence budget is defined by this broad principle. Since India has opted to declare itself a nuclear power in the interests of her security, it will have to generate the resources required to sustain a minimum, credible nuclear deterrent.

Having said this, it must be emphasised that India's defence spending is broadly in line with the global trend and is definitely on the conservative side compared to the defence budgets of her two immediate neighbours whose defence postures matter most to the assurance of India's security. In the second half of the 1990s, India's defence spending has come down to less than 2.5 per cent of GDP. The world average (for 174 countries listed in the UNDP's *Human Development Report)* is also around 2.5 per cent in the late 1990s. However, China (which has a bigger GDP) still allocates over 4 per cent of its GDP to defence, having brought this down only recently from a long-standing high figure of over 6 per cent of GDP. Pakistan also allocates over 5 per cent of its GDP to defence. India's long-term average of defence to GDP ratio (1965-85) was around 3.0 per cent. In the late-1980s it was stepped up to over 3.5 per cent and since 1990 there has been a secular decline in this ratio. In the aftermath of the Kargil conflict, and given the need to modernise

India's armed forces, a realistic long-term defence to GDP ratio for India would be in the range of 2.6 per cent to 2.9 per cent, if India can sustain a GDP growth rate of around 7 per cent over the next decade. While there may be an immediate step jump in the defence/ GDP ratio in 1999-2000 and 2000-01 to over 3.00/0 of GDP, the government must aim to keep defence spending down to around 2.5 per cent of GDP in the long-run, with the growing size of GDP enabling modernisation and defence-preparedness.

India must learn from the Soviet example and never allow its defence and police budgets to sink its larger economy. A large nation like ours can acquire regional leadership and a global standing through our economic potential, emerging as the largest, most dynamic and vibrant economy in Asia functioning within the framework of parliamentary democracy. A free and prosperous people are the ultimate guarantee of national security.

Imbalances in development

Finally, from the perspective of economic and national security, we must remain concerned about persistent inequalities and imbalances in the development process. While our democratic system of governance gives full freedom and play for the voicing of all grievances and forces government to respond to a range of demands, policy must remain focused on reducing these inequalities and imbalances. While all societies, including in the developed world, are characterised by social and economic disparities, in a large continental country like ours regional inequalities can have a negative impact on political stability and economic security. It is in recognition of this that our political leadership put in place federal institutions such as the Planning Commission to enable planned regional development. However, after half a century of planned development regional disparities in development, many a heritage of two centuries of colonial rule, persist.

Economic liberalisation in the 1990s has accentuated the problem by increasing the disparity in investment flows between developed and backward states. According to a recent study, nearly 75 per cent of capital expenditure planned in 2000-01 is to go to four states of

Maharashtra, Gujarat, Tamil Nadu and Andhra Pradesh. Both the central and north Indian states as well as eastern and north-eastern states remain low recipients of both private and public investment. The problem of low investment in industry and the services sector is a function of low investment in literacy and education, inadequate growth of the middle class and poor infrastructure development. The weak progress of agrarian development has also hurt the backward regions. Many reasons can be found for the backwardness of backward areas. The real challenge is for the government to find ways to redress these imbalances.

If such imbalances in development remain, they can weaken national integrity and pose a challenge to both national and economic security. The economic and political development of backward regions is a national security requirement.

II: External economic policies and economic security

India effected a strategic shift in its economic policies in the 1990s by moving from an inward-oriented economy to becoming a more outward-oriented economy, emphasising the importance of external trade and investment liberalisation. Increased openness of the economy, it is hoped, will make domestic enterprise globally competitive and speed up the modernisation of the economy. It is also hoped that this process will encourage Indian producers to access the world market and enable development of skills to world standards. The strategic policy thinking that underlies this shift is based on the realisation that external economic relations create relations of economic inter-dependence that contribute to a more stable global economic and political order.

While recognising the strategic importance of greater external trade and investment liberalisation, the policy makers were equally alive to the critical importance of reducing external debt exposure. Indeed, the policy, the trade and investment liberalisation was in part aimed at shifting the burden of external financing away from debt flows to trade and investment flows. Consequently, after 1991 India pursued a systematic policy of reducing its external debt exposure, particularly in the case of short-term debt, and improving its debt service ratio.

An important element of government policy since 1991 has been to reduce tariffs. Prior to 1991 India had some tariff rates around 300 per cent. The maximum tariff rate was brought down to 45 per cent in 1997-98 and recently to 35 per cent. The government has declared its intention to bring this down further to 20 per cent by 2005. The average trade-weighted tariff rate was estimated to be around 30 per cent, with the highest rates in the case of consumer goods and lower rates for agricultural and capital goods. Apart from reducing tariffs the government has also reduced quantitative restrictions (QRs) on imports and by April 2001 all QRs are slated to go.

Apart from trade liberalisation the government has also liberalised foreign currency transactions on the current and capital accounts. While current account transactions have been fully liberalised, the capital account has been gradually liberalised, encouraging Indian professionals and corporates to increase their transactions with the rest of the world. India has always been open to foreign investment but foreign-owned enterprises were highly regulated. Foreign companies are now treated on par with domestic enterprise and India has entered into bilateral investment protection agreements with many capital-exporting countries. India offers full post-establishment national treatment to foreign enterprises.

Going beyond FDI, the capital market has also been opened up to foreign institutional and portfolio investors. Foreign investors are allowed to buy into stocks and mutual funds and Indian companies have been permitted to list on stock markets abroad, including NYSE and NASDAQ. The external commercial borrowing limits for Indian companies have been eased, after the highly restrictive regime put in place at the time of the balance of payments crisis in 1990-91, and Indian companies have been permitted to raise funds through global depository receipts (GDRs) and american depository receipts (ADRs). Within a span of a decade, the Indian economy's integration with the world economy has considerably increased. Only a few minimal restrictions still apply to economic transactions with the outside world, particularly with respect to capital account transactions of Indian nationals.

The critics of the external liberalisation policies have been concerned both about the growth implications of trade openness, particularly the danger of domestic de-industrialisation, as well as the impact of foreign capital on indigenous enterprise. Clearly the Indian economy is still passing through a phase of transition and it is too early to hazard a guess on the long-term impact of external liberalisation on manufacturing growth and domestic enterprise. The experience of the decade 1991-2001 is so far mixed. While the period 1992-1997 saw an expansion in investment and of industrial growth, there has since been a deceleration in investment and growth. Fears of de-industrialisation are increasingly expressed. This may in part have been caused by an increased degree of external competition, however it may largely be on account of an inadequate growth of the home market for industrial goods. Unless there is an increase in domestic savings and investment as well as in foreign direct investment, contributing to an overall increase in the rate of investment and employment generation, the economy will not be able to ensure a higher rate of growth.

Overall national income growth accelerated from an average of 5.4 per cent in 1980-81 to 1991-92 to 6.4 per cent in 1992-93 to 2000-2001. In 1994-97, GDP growth hit a record annual average of 7.5 per cent. Manufacturing growth was as high as 12.0 per cent and 14.9 per cent respectively in 1994-95 and 1995-96, with the average rate of growth for the period 1992-93 to 2000-01 being 7.4 per cent. Decadal averages do not, however, tell the full story. The first five years, 1992-97, did undoubtedly see an acceleration of growth compared to the five years before the 1991 crisis. However, the second half of the 1990s experienced a slowdown in GDP growth, mainly on account of a deceleration in industrial growth (Table 4.1).

While growth trends in the agricultural sector have been erratic, the services sector has performed consistently well during the entire decade. It is in the case of the manufacturing sector that we see a marked deceleration of growth in the second half of the 1990s.

Analysts believe that at least one reason for this is the increased exposure to external trade. While there is no doubt that there has been an acceleration of export and import growth in the 1990s compared to the previous decade, there is no evidence of trade acting as a disincentive to domestic production in the second half of the 1990s. Rather, it would appear that the major factor responsible for the deceleration in industrial growth in this period is the decline in the overall rate of capital formation and the consequent fall in investment demand.

The policy of shifting the balance in external support of the economy from debt flows to trade and investment flows is reflected in the improvement in external debt indicators and the increasing share of trade in national income (Table 4.2). While India has been more open to foreign investment, FDI and portfolio flows into India are still modest both by comparison to our needs and the flows into other countries, particularly China. According to the *World Investment Report*, inward FDI accounted for 27.6 per cent of China's GDP in 1998 (up from 7.0 per cent in 1990) compared to a mere 3.4 per cent in the case of India (up from 0.5 per cent in 1990). India's share in world FDI stocks remains a mere 0.25 per cent, compared to China's share of 4.7 per cent in 1999 (Table 4.3).

Table 4.2

External Economic Indicators

	1980-81 to 1991-92	1992-93 to 1999-00	1999-00 to 1991-92
Export growth (per cent)	7.6	10.0	11.6
Import growth (per cent)	8.5	13.4	16.5
Exports as percentage of GDP	5.1	8.4	8.5
Imports as percentage of GDP	8.2	11.5	12.3
Short-term debt/Forex reserves per cent	137.5	23.8	10.6
Debt service/Current receipts per cent	31.8	22.2	16.0
External debt as per cent GDP	31.4	27.9	21.9
Months of imports covered by forex	3.8	7.2	8.2
Current account balance as per cent GDP	-1.9	-1.2	-0.9

Source: Economic Survey, 2000-01, Ministry of Finance, Government of India.

Table 4.3

Global FDI Flows (Millions of US dollars)

	1988-1993	1999
India	234 (0.12)	2,168 (0.25)
China	8,852 (4.6)	40,400 (4.7)
World	190,629	865,487
Developing Countries	46,919	207,619

Source: *World Investment Report,* UNCTAD, 2000.

Note: Figures in parentheses are percentage of total.

In short, the 1990s have seen a greater degree of outward orientation of the Indian economy but the change has been modest, particularly by international comparison. This relative insulation of the Indian economy has its positive aspect, as for instance the fact that India was not very adversely affected by the Asian economic crisis and slowdown. India's principal economic management has also been superior in the 1990s, compared to the 1980s, as a result of which it has been able to reduce its external debt exposure, avoid any requirement to take recourse to exceptional financial support from multilateral or bilateral lenders, notwithstanding the fact that India came under G-7 economic sanctions in the aftermath of its nuclear tests in May 1998.

The extant global economic environment

Apart from the efficacy of domestic policy reform, a favourable external environment also helped in improving India's overall external economic profile in the 1990s. The sustained boom in the US economy, India's principle export market, the decline in oil prices and increased global trade and capital flows, dampened only partly by the Asian economic crisis, helped keep India more than afloat in this period. However, the first few years of the 21st century may end up causing some concern for India.

The most important cause for concern in the extant global economic environment is the slowdown of the United States and Japanese economies. Both the US and Japan are important trade partners for India. The US is also an important investor in India and a source of employment for skilled Indian professionals, especially in the information technology sector. A slowdown of the US economy is potentially hurtful for India. It can hurt Indian exports, encourage the US to be tougher on trade liberalisation in India and rekindle protectionist hopes in the US. It can also slowdown the growth of the Indian software industry and of the employment opportunities thereof.

A disturbing feature of the current scenario is that for the first time in post-War history, both the US and Japanese economies are slowing down at the same time. In the past whenever one of the two slowed down the other was able to step in and act as the engine of growth of the world economy. When Asia slipped into a crisis in 1997, the strong US growth performance helped Asian economies recover from the crisis. This year, both the US and Japan are slowing down and no other economy is able to sustain global growth. There is, therefore, growing concern about a general global economic slowdown and a potential recession in 2001.

A second cause for concern has acquired a lower profile more recently, namely the downward rigidity in world oil prices. India benefited from the decline in oil prices in the 1990s and was hurt by the spurt in prices till recently. Sustained high oil prices can hurt the economy in many ways. It will most definitely manifest itself in a worsening of the current account deficit. It will continue to exert pressure on the balance of trade. It can generate inflationary pressures and constrain fiscal adjustment and deficit management. For all these reasons, medium-term trends in oil prices will remain important determinants of economic growth and external payments stability. While the recent easing up of oil prices is helpful it remains to be seen if this situation will persist.

A third area of concern is the slide in global capital markets and the bursting of the 'tech stock bubble'. This has particularly hurt India because of the increased exposure of Indian investors to global markets. More importantly, the decline in interest in 'emerging markets' has reduced flow of funds into the Indian capital market.

A fourth area of concern is the resurgence of external debt burden. India raised close to $10 billion through the Resurgent India Bonds and the India Millennium Deposit. The external commercial borrowing of Indian companies has also gone up. Consequently, external debt obligations have increased. Unless trade and investment flows pick up in the medium term India will find itself facing a worsening debt service profile.

Finally, there is growing evidence of a slowdown in global FDI flows. Just at a time when India is beginning to become more hospitable to FDI such a slowdown can hurt investment in industry.

The Economic Survey, 2000-01 of the Government of India does not fully reflect these concerns. However, it states (p.127):

"Looking ahead, there is very little that any emerging economy can do to stop these international shocks from occurring. On the contrary, India can minimise or even avert, as in the past, the adverse effects of such shocks in future, by further strengthening the country's economic fundamentals. This requires the strengthening of our policy stances in the areas of fiscal balance, exports, POL imports, tourism earnings, foreign investment flows and domestic monetary and fiscal policies, that have been reiterated and emphasised in the Economic Surveys of the past. This will greatly help India to grow in an environment of a viable BoP, reasonably stable exchange rate, a sustainable external debt profile and an external sector with durable strength and vigour."

The difficult external environment provides the backdrop for stable and sustainable domestic policy regimes. Unless the government remains alive to the critical external environment, it may easily end up pursuing policies that may make the domestic economy more vulnerable to external shocks and constraints. Strict fiscal discipline, sustained growth of exports and FDI flows into India, close monitoring of current account balance and short-term debt and a forward-looking market-oriented exchange rate policy are all critical to the pursuit of a balanced macroeconomic policy in a difficult phase.

India and the World Trade Organization

An important external policy challenge India will have to continue to grapple with will be the policy on a new round of world trade negotiations under the auspices of the World Trade Organization. The WTO ministerial meeting in November 2001 at Qatar has given its imprimatur, though not categorically, to a new round of trade negotiations. India will have to be prepared to take on this challenge. India is right to remain firmly committed to a multilateral framework for international trade. It is in our interest to strengthen the WTO, make it's functioning more transparent and non-discriminatory and its procedures less expensive and cumbersome. India is not well served by the growing trend towards regionalism in trade. If the WTO runs aground and multilateralism is weakened, this can strengthen regional trade blocs and preferential trading arrangements. This is not in India's interests, nor is it a healthy development from the viewpoint of world trade and balanced global development. Hence, it is in India's interest to strengthen the WTO and the multilateral trading regime.

India's share of world trade is a mere 0.6 per cent, compared to close to 4.0 per cent for China. India must pursue a higher share of world trade within the framework of a multilateral trading system. After the failure of the Seattle ministerial meeting of the World Trade Organization, multilateralism has receded and regionalism has once again gained momentum in international trade. This is harmful to India. India is not a member of any major regional trade bloc. It is unlikely to qualify for membership of ASEAN or APEC in the near future. Moreover, the action in Asia is moving onto a new group of 'ASEAN+3 (China, Japan and Korea)'. While it is in India's interests to be in the WTO and to make it a more transparent and development-friendly institution, it can not allow the WTO to become a World Government, expanding its influence into new and largely non-trade areas of national policy.

India must, therefore, pursue a three-track strategy with respect to the WTO of:

(a) seeking revitalisation of multilateralism and strengthening the WTO as a genuinely international system of trade openness, with the developing countries having a voice commensurate with their stake in the global system;

(b) pursue bilateral free trade agreements with major trading partners, especially USA, Singapore, South Korea, European Union, and some of our neighbours; and

(c) strengthen sub-regional economic cooperation around the Bay of Bengal and Indian Ocean regions.

Trade is an important instrument of national security. India's declared strategy of seeking 'implementation' of Uruguay Round agreements before a new round was sound. However, this view has not prevailed at Doha and a new round has received partial endorsement. In the next two years, India must evolve a new strategy to deal with the extant situation. This strategy will have to address the domestic policy agenda as well as external opportunities and challenges. Our strategy in the WTO must be based on the following principles:

First, we must be pro-active, not reactive, in shaping the WTO agenda. We must have an agenda of our own and canvass support for it internationally. We must enter into alliances wherever possible and necessary with both developed and developing countries with a shared perspective on specific issues. We must mount both an intellectual and a diplomatic campaign in support of our interests.

Second, on every issue where our interests are at variance with those of other influential WTO members, we must have a clear negotiating brief, and build alliances based on the principle of 'give and take'.

Apart from trade and investment flows, an important aspect of India's economic interaction with the world is the flow of labour services. Indian labour in the Gulf region of West Asia continues to remain an important source of foreign exchange earnings for the country. More recently, software professionals in the information technology sector have emerged as an important source of hard currency earnings. The US slowdown is likely to slow down the pace of growth of software exports from India, but in the medium term this sector will remain an important source of export earnings and employment opportunities.

While the global slowdown is likely to exert new pressures on the Indian economy, because of its increased external exposure, the government must remain alive to external payments pressures and avoid having to turn to the International Monetary Fund for balance of payments support. India's external economic security thus rests on the pursuit of a more liberal trade and investment policy, making India more attractive to foreign investment and encouraging skilled Indians to secure employment and income-earning opportunities in the developed economies, while at the same time reducing the external debt exposure. While seeking a strengthening of the multilateral trade regime, India must also actively engage her neighbouring economies in the southern Asian region, spanning the region from Iran, West and Central Asia to Japan, Korea and South-East Asia.

Economic diplomacy and economic security

Flowing from this general principle of seeking national security through 'economic engagement', is the more specific idea of utilising regional economic integration as an instrument of regional security. This idea is in fact at least a half-century old. The principle of building political alliances through joint economic ventures was the foundation on which the Iron and Steel Community was formed in Europe between France and Germany. The European Community and the European Union have been created in response to the felt need of the region to pursue 'economic engagement' as an instrument of peace and regional political stability. While no explicit parallel structures exist between economic and security groupings in Europe, the fact that economic integration has aided regional security is quite clear. This link can run both ways. In the case of ASEAN, it is political cooperation, which encouraged economic interaction and integration. In the case of Mercosur, it is economic cooperation that has helped create a regional security relationship.

South Asia is just beginning to explore the political and security potential of regional economic cooperation. The slow progress of a South Asian Free Trade Agreement (SAFTA) and of bilateral free trade agreements is partly because political concerns continue to dominate the region and override economic considerations. However, over the last two years progress has been made in the area of regional economic cooperation and there is growing realisation of the political potential of economic cooperation. When the India-Sri Lanka bilateral free trade agreement was signed, the external affairs minister Mr. Jaswant Singh, explicitly drew attention to the potential of regional economic cooperation increasing regional security. There is no doubt that India's immediate external security environment will vastly improve if India can deepen and widen its economic engagement with her neighbours.

However, in the post-Kargil context it will be unrealistic to expect economic relations to alter the worsened political equation between India and Pakistan. Till Kargil, the logic of the so-called 'Gujral Doctrine' and the 'Lahore Process' was to use improved economic and commercial links as a means of improving political relations. The Kargil aggression by Pakistan has once again brought political issues to centre-stage and unless these issues are addressed it is unlikely that much progress can be made on the economic and business side. At any rate, given the slow progress of economic cooperation within the South Asian Association for Regional Cooperation (SAARC), thanks largely to Pakistani intransigence and the exaggerated impact of the India-Pakistan bilateral relationship on regional cooperation within SAARC, it may be necessary for India to work on parallel tracks in the regional context and see if regional economic cooperation can be pursued at a faster pace in a wider southern Asian context. The framework for such regional cooperation is currently offered by BIMSTEC—the Bangladesh, India, Myanmar, Sri Lanka and Thailand Economic Cooperation group. The defining feature of BIMSTEC is that its members are the rim economies of the Bay of Bengal. Hence, BIMSTEC (with its unwieldy name which requires a change each time a new member joins the group) may in fact be called the "Bay of Bengal Community" (BOBCOM). At some future date, when BIMSTEC (BOBCOM) is willing to consider the idea of expanding its scope it can consider favourably the case of the two landlocked countries in South Asia which are completely dependent on the Bay of Bengal for their national economic needs, namely, Nepal and Bhutan, for the membership of BOBCOM. If these two countries are added, then BIMSTEC or BOBCOM becomes SAARC *minus* Pakistan *plus* Myanmar and Thailand. India can clearly benefit from countries like Bangladesh, Myanmar, Singapore, Sri Lanka and Thailand moving closer to create the Bay of Bengal Community to facilitate speedier trade liberalisation and increased intra-regional capital flows within such a community. The land-locked States of Nepal and Bhutan, directly dependent on this sea, may also be invited to join, If China's south-western provinces, Malaysia and Singapore find it useful they may also establish special links with such a group. It is easy to see why a 'Bay of Bengal Community' (BOBCOM) may end up being a far more dynamic group. BOBCOM's ASEAN component, especially Thailand, can help speed up the pace of trade liberalisation and regional economic cooperation within South Asia at a pace faster than what SAARC has been capable of. Moreover, BOBCOM has the added advantage of emerging as the link between South and South-East Asia.

A closer economic relationship with South-East and East Asia, a desire which informed India's stated 'Look East' policy of the early 1990s, is imperative both from a purely economic viewpoint as well as a security perspective. India's most dynamic and outward-oriented regions, of western and peninsular India, are already linked closely to South-East Asia through maritime trade, air links and other commercial and financial links. Singapore and Mumbai maintain a close link in the financial sector with many banking and financial institutions in the two major financial centres closely linked. Singapore has also been an important media centre for Indian satellite TV channels till recently, though some Indian companies continue to maintain their Singapore links despite India permitting direct uplinking from her soil.

If the next phase of India's outward-orientation has to proceed apace, it is important that India's trade with the APEC economies must increase. The 1990s witnessed a perceptible increase in India's trade and investment relations with South Korea, Singapore, Thailand, Malaysia and Indonesia. The Asian economic crisis' has hurt this process. Nevertheless, there is need for a renewed attempt to increase India's 'economic engagement' of East and South-East Asia. While India's 'Look West' strategy must focus on the United States, European Union, West Asia and Central Asia, its 'Look East' policy must be firmly focused on Singapore, Thailand and Korea. India must also rebuild its links with Myanmar. India-Myanmar economic and political relations have been neglected for far too long. There is potential for the development of India's north-east through greater cooperation with Myanmar, Thailand and Singapore.

India's membership of the ASEAN Regional Forum, a security grouping, enables it to forge the link between economic cooperation and regional security if the India-ASEAN equation is vigorously pursued. However, for India to become a full member of ASEAN and of other groups like APEC, it is necessary that it pursues with greater vigour the policy of external economic liberalisation and greater integration with the economies of the region. Apart from East and South-East Asia, India must also seek greater economic engagement with Central and West Asia. It is useful to emphasise here the fact that in almost all countries around India, ranging from Iran, Pakistan and Central Asia, to India's west, to the ASEAN economies on India's east, China has forged a closer and deeper economic and commercial relationship over the last decade, leaving India far behind. India's bilateral trade exceeds that of China with only three countries in the entire West, Central, South-East and East Asian region. These three countries are Nepal, Sri Lanka and Bangladesh. Every other major Asian country has a larger trade relationship with China than with India. This imbalance must be corrected in the interests of India's economic and national security.

Another regional group with as yet untapped potential is the Indian Ocean Rim Association for Regional Cooperation (IOR-ARC). India is the oldest maritime nation in the Indian Ocean. For centuries, even before the Arabs came to India, Indians sailed the seas. However, in the post-Independence period there has been a relative neglect of India's maritime interests and capabilities. India had a bigger shipbuilding industry than South Korea in 1960 but today it lags far behind Korea. Apart from the neglect of shipbuilding and maritime activity, we have also neglected our ports and inland waterways. This neglect of the economic and strategic potential of the waters surrounding peninsular India must be reversed. An important stimulant to maritime activity will come from increased trade interaction with the countries of the Bay of Bengal, Arabian Sea and Indian Ocean rim. The Indian Ocean Rim Association for Regional Cooperation (IOR-ARC) is an important initiative that seeks to re-build traditional Indian maritime and economic links with the rim countries like West Asia, East Africa, South-East Asia and Australia. The IOR-ARC initiative remains under-explored partly because India's interaction with most of these countries is still very limited.

However, an important security consideration that India must bear in mind is the assurance of peace and security in the Indian Ocean to ensure safety of passage to commercial vessels. India will be increasingly dependent on West Asian oil and Asian markets and so must ensure the security of passage for all vessels through these waters. The Indian Ocean will also provide access to the oil-exporting West and Central Asian region to such imported-energy-dependent economies as China, Japan, Korea and many ASEAN economies. The United States will remain a major factor in the Indian Ocean. Hence, it is in India's interests to secure plurilateral cooperation for the assurance of peace and security in the Indian Ocean with the help of the US, China, Japan, ASEAN and other interested countries.

External economic relations and the challenge of globalisation

A large sub-continental economy like India must maintain good economic relations with all major economies in the world. Hence, while 'regional' economic cooperation within Asia is important, India can not afford to neglect its bilateral economic relations with United States, Russia, European Union and some of the major economies of Latin America and Africa. The bilateral relationship with the United States is a key factor in the pursuit of national security in the immediate future. Apart from being the 'sole superpower' in the post-Cold War world, the United States remains an important source of capital, markets, new technologies and, for the Indian middle class, an important source of employment both in India, thanks to the new information technologies, and abroad, thanks to the opportunities thrown up by globalisation and the IT revolution. Given India's need for sourcing foreign capital, foreign technologies and external markets, it can not afford to neglect this vital relationship with the United States. Moreover, from a security perspective, notwithstanding the differences in perception on a range of political issues and the US decision to impose a range of economic and technological sanctions on India, we must continue to explore avenues for improved interaction with the US. Getting the equation with the US right is central to any security strategy for India. However, India's bilateral economic concerns with both the US and the EU are best addressed within a multilateral framework. There is a fairly widespread consensus in India that multilateral trade and investment regimes are preferable to bilateral agreements, especially with the major industrial powers. Given this understanding, regional economic cooperation should not be seen as an alternative to but a means of participating more effectively in the global economy. The policy obligation India will have to accept in order to facilitate SAFTA or widen the network of regional cooperation to other Asian neighbours will enable India to also conform to her global policy commitments, especially in the World Trade Organization.

Given domestic resistance within India to external liberalisation, it will be politically easier for India to make concessions to its smaller economic neighbours, which in turn will enable India to conform to multilateral commitments. For instance, India's willingness to eliminate quantitative restrictions (QRs) on imports within the framework of SAFTA will also help India meet her obligations to WTO. In short, trade and investment liberalisation can be on a 'fast track' in regional groups where India feels more secure, while it is pursued on a relatively slow track with respect to the developed world through the WTO commitments. But, it is important to recognise that regional economic cooperation can only run parallel to multilateralism in trade and investment policies and can not be a substitute for it. Regionalism is a stepping stone to globalisation not an escape route from it.

Conclusion

The 'revolution of rising expectations' constitutes the most important challenge to economic policymaking and political management in our country. The new world order presents its own challenges. If the Indian economy reverts to the low growth syndrome of the 1950 to 1980 period, India will neither be able to address the domestic social and economic challenges nor meet international opportunities and challenges. If we continue with the 5.5 per cent rate of growth of the past two decades, we will be able to better address our domestic challenges but will remain a 'developing country with a huge potential' for yet another century. If, on the other hand, we are able to step up investment, raise productivity, reduce social and economic disparities and empower people by creating new capabilities, thereby converting the liability of a large population into an asset of a vibrant and creative nation, and can deliver 7.0 per cent to 8.0 per cent annual rate of growth, with moderate inflation, then India will re-emerge a great and secure nation. India's real security will be built on such foundations.

Stewing in our own juice

REVIEWING the current economic situation at a recent meeting of the Prime Minister's Economic Advisory Council, the advisor to the finance minister, Rakesh Mohan, showed a series of charts tracing the roots of this year's economic slowdown in India all the way to 1998. I admired his courage in patiently explaining to the prime minister, his key economic ministers and officials, and the other economists present at the meeting, the bare fact that it was the acts of omission and commission of the last five years in the management of the economy which were primarily responsible for the current slowdown as also the grim fiscal situation confronting many state governments and the central government.

Could it not have occurred to the prime minister and his senior colleagues that Rakesh Mohan was in fact holding their government's inaction on the economic front during their entire tenure in office responsible for the current mess? This knocked the bottom out of finance minister Yashwant Sinha's argument that it was the global economic slowdown, particularly the US recession, which was responsible for the weak performance of the Indian economy in the current fiscal.

Taking off from the presentation, I urged the prime minister and the finance minister not to exaggerate the negative impact of the global slowdown on the Indian economy. Foreign trade accounts for barely 10 per cent of our national income. Foreign direct investment hardly counts for anything in total investment in the country. The only significant impact that external events have had on the economy has been through the stock market, where foreign institutional investors have become bearish and are not bringing in money, and on the IT sector, where software business may have been slightly affected.

There is a basic lesson of Keynesianism which has remained relevant despite the intellectual marginalisation of Keynes in western economic thinking. Simply stated it is that in a market economy characterised by uncertainty and atomisation of decision making by a multitude of actors and where so much is predicated upon sentiment, expectations have a way of being fulfilled. Negative expectations can have a real negative impact on sentiment while positive expectations can alter the mood in favour of a resumption of economic activity.

So, I urged the political leadership around the table, "Please do not talk the economy down." Talking up may not work unless the talkers carry conviction, but talking down certainly has an infectious quality about it irrespective of who starts the process.

All this happened on 10 September 2001. On 11 September the world entered a new phase of history. Recovering from the initial shock, the prime minister went on prime time television and addressed the nation. The terrorist attacks in the United States have had a serious impact on peace and security worldwide, he said, warning that hard times were ahead of us. The government will have to take tough economic decisions. It may even have to hike energy prices. People must be prepared for sacrifice and difficult times. The prime minister was grim-faced. Even the most cheerful TV viewer would not have slept easily that night.

A few days later US President George Bush urged Americans to stop watching the TV and go out and have a good time. There was a sudden decline in demand as people stopped having fun, stopped travelling, stopped shopping and stopped spending. Spend, was Bush's message. Sacrifice, was Vajpayee's. President Bush was talking up the economy; Prime Minister Vajpayee was talking it down further.

Even though the prime minister listened intently to what I said at the EAC meeting, and even chuckled when I pulled Omkar Goswami's leg apropos of something Omkar had said, he had not internalised my message. A full month later, Finance Minister Yashwant Sinha came to the annual conference of economic editors and repeated the 'scenario is grim' theme. He was talking down sentiment further.

For a country which is hardly anywhere near the action, not even hosting US planes on its airfields, for an economy which is hardly globalised and barely exposed to the negative impact of the US slowdown, we are getting a bit too worked up about the negative consequences for us of global political and economic events. Big deal! Look at China.

China, like India and indeed the United States, is a continental economy which is largely inward-oriented, notwithstanding its much higher share of world trade than India's. The Chinese economy continues to be driven by domestic economic growth and while it no longer posts 10 per cent growth, it has not done badly over the past two years, staying globally at the top with 7.0 per cent to 8.0 per cent growth.

Even as the western world worried about a recession and worried even more about the negative economic consequences of the 11 September attacks, the Chinese political and economic leadership continuously talked their economy up. China put in place counter-cyclical policies and aggressively pursued politico-diplomatic initiatives that ensure beneficial economic possibilities. Consider, for instance, China's success in securing the right to host the 2008 Olympics in Beijing. This news was followed up by a decision to bolster China's airlines with the purchase of new aircraft that sounded like music to Boeing's ears in the US.

China has acted thoughtfully in projecting itself as a secure and safe place for foreigners and foreign investors at a time when the western world is terribly nervous about terrorism. It will not be surprising if many Americans feel safer in China today than at home! What do we do? As if the current tension in our neighbourhood is not enough, the Vishwa Hindu Parishad goes and forcibly enters the cordoned-off area in Ayodhya. There is palpable increase in communal tension across the country. The government correctly bans the Students Islamic Movement of India (SIMI) but does not ban similar communal outfits advocating violence owing allegiance to other religions, particularly the Bajrang Dal. We pursue internal politics that is likely to heighten global concerns about domestic peace and security.

It is important to appreciate that neither the United States nor India is in fact battling 'terrorism'. Terrorism is only the means adopted, the manifestation of a cause and that cause is religious fundamentalism, monotheism, exclusivism, mono-culturalism. Both the US and India are plural, multicultural and democratic societies. The terrorists who challenge us are challenging our 'way of life, our way of thinking'. The fight against terrorism is, therefore, a fight against chauvinism of all kinds and a struggle for pluralism. Strengthening India's secular and plural traditions is in the interest of our national integrity and security. Anyone who challenges secularism and pluralism is in fact challenging the Indian Constitution and is therefore anti-national, irrespective of religious affiliation.

So what's the message? Be it the slowdown in the Indian economy or perceptions relating to a heightened security threat to India, the roots of our problems are internal. Don't blame the outside world too much. If we cannot get our act together, we will have to stew in our own juice.

The talk about India's globalisation over the past decade has resulted in an exaggerated view of our external dependence and exposure. I believe this is largely on account of the excessive visibility of the superficial symbols of our westernisation. Be it the neighbourhood McDonalds or the many satellite TV channels accessible in our living rooms, or indeed the Americanisation of the print media, the fact remains that outside of the software sector, the Indian economy remains largely inward-oriented even by Asian standards, not to speak of European ones.

This had proved to be a weakness when the world economy was growing faster than ours and a blessing when it grew slower than ours, or was caught in the maelstrom of financial liberalisation. If India did not enjoy the benefits of the post-War boom in the United States, as East and South-East Asia did, it did not suffer the pain of a financial crisis engineered by fast-paced financial sector liberalisation.

Admittedly, few countries that had globalised 'intelligently', that is with a focus on building domestic capabilities, have fared worse than India in the post-War period. Those that globalised without any attention to domestic capabilities, like many African and Latin American ones, have indeed become worse off. The lesson for India is that globalisation is not an alternative to building domestic capabilities; it is a complementary process, as China has shown.

The main economic challenge for India is internal. However, for us the lesson of the last half century is that the home economy cannot remain isolated from the global economy and, indeed, that it should not. Building globally competitive capabilities and structures is essential for growth and survival in the new world. That is India's challenge. There will be political, social, economic and technological obstacles and challenges along the way and these have to be addressed, if possible anticipated.

Terrorism, communalism, big power bossism, neo-colonial non-market interventionism and so on will challenge us and we must intelligently and rationally plan to address them, rather than approach each challenge as a crisis. India has the capabilities to deal with such challenges. The task of the government and of corporate leadership is to be able to identify and harness this talent in the national interest so that India may be a better place to live in and we may matter more in the world.

India and the world

Learning to walk on two legs

IN the recent past nothing has confused our intelligentsia more that India's relationship with the world. Emerging out of the Cold War cocoon India has spent the better part of the past four years redefining her economic, political and strategic links with the developed and developing worlds, examining old assumptions and discovering new opportunities and challenges. In many ways an ill-articulated debate of the last four years has come into sharper focus in 1995 and as the year draws to a close an unexpected series of events have helped clarify many issues.

As we approach the end of the 20th century, and before we enter the next millennium, we have to urgently deal with the two challenges of this century that are still with us. First, the internal challenge of mass poverty and degradation; and, second the external challenge of defining our status in the global economy and society.

Since the end of the Cold War and the disintegration of the Soviet Union coincided with a political and economic crisis in India, policy makers and the Indian elite have remained largely preoccupied with domestic, mainly economic, issues in the last four years. The nervous turnaround in economic policy, in the aftermath of the balance of payments crisis of the early 1990s, has perforce brought India's economic ties with the world into sharper focus than her more enduring and complex cultural, political and strategic relationships. As a result, the debate on 'globalisation' has been preoccupied with economic, and even more narrowly trade and investment, relations with the developed industrial economies to the neglect of more enduring links between India and the world.

In a rather timid and myopic response to external economic pressures, some have argued that India must rapidly shed its inhibitions in dealing with global economic forces and must pursue an 'open-door' economic policy. Reacting to this 'capitulationist' view others have demanded a return to the more 'inward-looking' policy of 'swadeshi'. The western response to this superficial debate within the Indian elite has been equally facile, admonishing the government for not 'opening up' to the world fast enough, and for remaining a 'marginal' player in the global 'marketplace'.

Such black and white assessments of the challenge and opportunity facing India can only generate simplistic policy responses. It can be nobody's case that India should limit its economic relationship with the world nor can it be anybody's case that Indian economic policy can only be accommodative of external pressures and process without an autonomous basis. Equally, as the experience of China in recent years has demonstrated most graphically, the pursuit of economic opportunities in the world cannot remain unmindful of the strategic challenges that face India.

Unfortunately, thus far the popular debate on India's relationship with the world has remained preoccupied with economics and business. Both the proponents and critics of 'globalisation' to use an unsatisfactory catch-all phrase, have been obsessed with trade and investment flows to the neglect of the more complex cultural and strategic links India has with the rest of the world. Echoing this 'economistic' view at home, western observers have also looked at India's global role in purely business terms. "India matters now", said a senior official in the European Commission's directorate-general for external economic relations in Brussels, in a recent conversation, "because it figures on my computer". The reference was to a chart on EC's trade and investment links with the rest of the world.

The proponents of trade and investment liberalisation have often advocated an 'open-door' policy almost as an end in itself. This is the 'TINA' thesis—'there is no alternative' for India but to fall in line with what the developed nations demand. Even the most liberal economies of the west do not quite see their economic links with the world in such terms. Strategic interests impinge on economic relations in a variety of ways and the two have always gone together. When the United States denies high technology or Japan refuses to import rice they are mixing business with politics and not crafting economic policy in a strategic policy vacuum. India's external trade and investment policy regime has to be shaped in the context of both her strategic policy perspectives and domestic priorities, like increasing the rate of savings, investment and productivity, and improving the standard of living of its people. At the same time, it must also enable her to win friends and influence people in her neighbourhood as well as in the emerging global power centres, linking her growth process to the new 'engines of growth', especially in Asia.

Equally important is the need to reach out to the vast Indian diaspora worldwide, whose potential India has largely ignored. What distinguishes India from the smaller East Asian and South-East Asian economies, on the one hand, and from the other developing economies is not just her continental economic dimension but her civilisational cultural attributes. In this respect India and China have a similarity in that both are capable of drawing on the economic and technological potential of the diaspora.

China has been able to do this quite effectively despite her 'Middle Kingdom' syndrome, a delusion from which India has never suffered. Rather, Indians have been able to deal self-confidently with other races and cultures even after migrating to settle down in diverse lands in Africa, Europe, East Asia and North America.

It is not surprising, therefore, that a strategic policy thinker like Mr. Henry Kissinger should regard India as one of the six great powers of the post-Cold War 'polycentric' world along with United States, Russia, China, Japan and the European Union led by

Germany. However, while India has the potential to be a part of this league it would be rash to surmise that we are already in it. In order to take on the obligations that such a status imposes India must not only ensure the economic well-being of its people, and maintain internal social stability, but it must learn to walk on two legs in dealing with the world. On the one hand, it must be an active member of the global economic community, participating in a partaking of trade and investment flows, like China; and, on the other hand, it must demonstrate its ability to defend her sovereignty and territorial integrity, again like China.

This implies that a policy of economic liberalisation must be accompanied by a resolute security strategy. India's policy of nuclear ambiguity, by which it retains the right to equip her armed forces with nuclear weapons as long as other nuclear powers retain this right, it can be seen, will form one leg on which India walks into the next century. If compelled, India must be prepared to move from ambiguity to clarity. Her liberalised economic policy must be the energetic second leg.

7 | COLUMN

The economics of national security

THE political and strategic fallout of the Asian economic crisis has brought economic policy concerns to the centre-stage of security policy debates across the world. In the early 1990s, the 21st century was hailed as the Asian or Asia-Pacific century and the newly industrialising economies of East and South-East Asia, beginning with Japan and then including China, were viewed as the new engine of world economic growth. The financial and economic crisis in the region has clouded that optimism. Equally, the travails of a large economy like Japan and the growing clout of China have alerted strategic policy analysts to the political consequences of economic crisis in the region.

There is now growing appreciation of the fact that the United States has emerged stronger in the region not just because of its victory in the Cold War, but also because of its ability to insulate itself to a considerable extent from the negative fallout of the Asian crisis and enter into a *modus vivendi* with China. This has emboldened the US to be more aggressive in its dealings with Japan and South Korea.

That an economic crisis in any major global economy or economic region has political and strategic consequences is well known. The 'Great Crash' of 1929 and the Great Depression of the 1930s profoundly influenced the course of political and strategic events across Europe, culminating in a World War and a reordering of the global balance of power. It does not require too much foresight to see that the Asian economic crisis, coming in the wake of the end of the Cold War, is going to alter the balance of power in the region well into the next decade. While the US and China have emerged more influential, Japan remains nervous about its influence and the two Koreas worry about the immediate prospects for their unification. The region is in a political flux and it is still not clear how the chips will fall.

What does all this mean for India? Clearly, India must carefully study the Asian experience and learn from both the success stories and the problems in the region. The growth experience of the region has much to offer Indian policy makers as much as its recent crisis. India can hardly afford to remain either uninvolved or smug. Several commentators have already made the point that India must adopt many of the key elements of the model of development pursued by the big and small economies of the region, in terms of a higher investment in human development (education, health and general well-being), deepening the home market through agrarian reform and improved asset and income distribution, openness to global trade and investment flows and global competitiveness, ability to adapt and induct new technologies, and so on.

Indian policy makers must also pay greater attention to the political consequences of the crisis and respond to the region's desire, more latent than stated, to see India play a larger economic and political role in Asia. India can hardly afford to remain a mute witness to the changing balance of power in Asia. A more open Indian economy is a necessary condition for acquiring a higher profile in the region. Unless India's economic involvement with the region increases, it is unlikely to match the influence of the three Big Powers in the region, namely, the United States, China and Japan. The decline in Russia's influence in Asia as a result of its own domestic economic crisis is a clear pointer.

The pursuit of sound macroeconomic policies, a liberal trade and investment regime, increased investment in the well-being of the people as well as in new infrastructure are not only the necessary pre-conditions for higher growth but also for a higher global profile for India. What is more, these are also the building blocks of enhanced national security. An India that is economically stable and prosperous and is increasingly involved in global economic flows is more likely to build webs of economic inter-dependence which offer it greater political security. An inward-looking economy, a navel-gazing polity and a people that will not give but only ask, are unlikely to be a secure nation. Given this perspective, it should be clear that the key economic determinants of national security for India, at this stage of her development, are a higher and more balanced economic growth combined with a more open and liberal economic regime.

Three traditional economic concerns for security analysts have been, and remain, food security, energy security and access to new technologies. Food security is less of a concern today than in the 1960s, but the other two have gained in importance. A recent addition to this list would be financial stability. This cannot be ensured through economic isolationism but calls for intelligent regulation and supervision. Finally, increased global economic engagement that builds bridges of support for India's political stability and economic prosperity. Such webs of inter-dependence have to be built not just with the Big Powers, but with our neighbours, each and every one, with smaller powers in the region and with the major players in the world economy—the big corporations and banks.

In the past, the traditional view of economic security encouraged Indian policy makers to pursue an inward-oriented model of self-sufficiency. What India needs today is an outward-looking model of self-reliance that guarantees national security by giving the world a stake in India's stability and prosperity.

The Bombay plea

THEN it was a bang, now it is a whimper. Then it was the trumpeting of an unshackled elephant, now it is the plaint of a wounded tiger. Then it was a plan, now it is a plea. How else can one compare the grand vision, the strategic thinking of the authors of the famous 'Bombay Plan' of 1944 (and 1946) with the modest charter of demands of the so-called 'Bombay Club'—a group of businessmen who have been discussing India's new economic policy and its implications for domestic business.

In 1944, some of India's most ambitious, enterprising and energetic businessmen came together to author a 15-year macro-economic perspective plan for India, setting the agenda for post Independence economic development. It had a strategic intent as well as the basis of how to implement the plan across sectors and over time. It was called the 'Bombay Plan' because its authors were all from that vibrant centre of Indian enterprise—Mr. G. D. Birla, Mr. J.R.D. Tata, Mr. Ardeshir Dalal and Sir Purushotamdas Thakurdas. They were assisted by Mr. John Mathai who later became a Union finance minister.

So, when a group of businessmen from Bombay, Delhi and Madras met in Bombay recently to discuss the P.V. Narasimha Rao government's agenda for economic liberalisation and fiscal adjustment and decided to draw up a statement of concerns of Indian businessmen, they were immediately dubbed the "Bombay Club". It includes Mr. M. V. Arunachalam, Mr. Rahul Bajaj, Mr. C.

K. Birla, Mr. Jamshed Godrej, Mr. B.K. Modi, Mr. Bharat Ram, Mr. Hari Shankar Singhania and Mr. L.M. Thapar. The club met twice, once in Bombay and a second time in New Delhi and drew up a list of demands which it presented to the Union finance minister, Dr. Manmohan Singh. Some other industrialists were present at the first meeting in Bombay but were not in Delhi to meet the finance minister.

The creation of the club received much media attention since this was the first time after the launching of the Rao government's new economic policies that such a ginger group of corporate leaders had met to lobby their case with the government. The demand for a 'level playing field' in the drive towards the 'globalisation' of the Indian economy, the fears stirred up by the capitulation, as some viewed it, of Indian brands to multinational companies—most dramatically illustrated by the Coca-Cola-Thums Up deal—and the concerns generated by the course which the Uruguay Round of GATT negotiations had taken offered the backdrop to what was correctly perceived by many analysts as an important corporate event.

Perhaps some of the media hype was exaggerated. Perhaps this was why many invitees to the club chose to underplay the significance of the event. Understandably, some did it because they did not want Indian business to be seen as chickening out of a fight by friends at home and abroad. They did not want to appear as if they were running scared of external competition, even if that was true. They did not want to strengthen the domestic anti-liberalisation forces since there was much in the programme of liberalisation that they wanted pursued. They did not want critics to allege that they were once again 'lobbying' with government, in the tired old ways, to secure concessions and preferential treatment. Rather, they preferred to be viewed as supporters of the finance ministry's agenda, but only concerned about the 'sequencing' of the liberalisation programme, and worried about the unfair advantage that foreign investors had secured from a government that was trying to replace external debt flows with external equity flows.

Admittedly, their initial agenda was narrowly defined. Yet, given the circumstance and given the fact that their meeting had created such national and international interest in what the club was up to, it would have been only appropriate for them to have widened that narrow agenda and come up with a broader vision of India's economic policy, of the challenges facing Indian business, and the tasks ahead.

Instead, they presented the finance minister with a modest 'pre-budget' list of demands, with only a couple of requests that will have a significant impact on the way in which Indian industry is organised. There was no assurance that meeting such demands will make Indian industry more competitive and ready to take on the global challenge.

For decades macroeconomic planning has been the business of government. In recent years it has become the preoccupation of multilateral financial institutions, so much so that the only places where one meets professionals concerned about India's long-term development prospects, about the next decade if not the next century, are institutions like the Planning Commission and the International Monetary Fund and the World Bank. Government ministries, including the finance ministry, are far too preoccupied with next week and next month to have any time left for even next year, not to mention the next decade or century.

Most developed economies have think tanks, both within and outside the government, doing this job. When the Uruguay Round of GATT negotiations began, South Korea created an entire research institute to study and prepare its case for GATT. Economists in universities and research institutions in India are far too involved either with microeconomic processes or with offering critiques of existing or past policies. Few have the interest, the stamina and the imagination to create alternative strategic visions for the future, fill the policy skeletons with the meat and blood of concrete microeconomic tasks, and define the possibilities and limits for a developing, democratic polity of close to 900 million people.

In normal times, it is unfair to expect businessmen who are naturally more concerned about corporate balance sheets than national finances, about market shares than national visions, to produce anything better than a pre-budget memorandum when they meet the finance minister. But pre-budget memorandum are written every year, supplications to the finance minister are made every season, fiscal concessions are demanded every quarter. Strategic visions are offered once in a generation or two.

Admittedly, the generation that wrote the Bombay Plan was unique in many ways. No society has seen within the span of one century two generations that have offered it new visions of how to live and conduct one's economic and social life. India's turn this century is over. Perhaps this is not the era of grand visions and not the hour for strategic thinking. Perhaps this is the interregnum of good housekeeping. If so, it is just as well that we do modest tinkering with the plumbing and the wiring, provide a coat of good paint — to the exterior and learn to live within our means — our economic and intellectual means.

But for those who will not be satisfied with such modesty, the challenge of rebuilding a new house is there to be grabbed and acted upon. Indian business must aspire for such a challenge and show that it has the means and the urge to think and act big.

Competitive advantage

Merit, markets and the middle class

THE epithet commonly used when referring to the Indian middle class is 'vocal'. Politicians consider them a nuisance, businessmen view them as a market, but few recognise the more enduring qualities of the urban middle class, that of enterprise and a competitive spirit.

The peculiar circumstances of colonial rule and the relative underdevelopment of both the peasant and working class, on the one hand, and of the feudal and business class, on the other, has shaped the role of the middle class in post-colonial India. From taking the lead in the national movement and heading powerful institutions of governance, to creating world-class higher education and research institutions and nurturing among the best and brightest in the corporate and financial sectors, the Indian middle class has been a powerhouse of talent and enterprise for the greater part of this century.

Yet, surprisingly, of all the social classes, the middle class is the least researched and understood. Scholars of middle class origin have written reams about the feudal, peasant, industrial and commercial classes, but have rarely studied their own class. Exceptions like Mr. B.B. Misra have made tentative forays into this complex world while some perceptive European scholars have spun some analytical threads which need to be weaved into a more comprehensive theory.

One must recognise that the middle class is neither a homogenous nor static group. Over the last century, especially the latter half, it has undergone fundamental change with new entrants from subordinate social classes and castes. Upward social mobility in democratic India has widened and altered the caste composition of the middle class.

This heterogeneity also has geographical dimensions since both economic development and the economic and social power of various castes and classes has varied significantly across the subcontinent. The middle class had greater opportunities for growth and empowerment in certain regions of British India like the presidencies of Bengal, Madras and Bombay and after Independence its growth was more pronounced in western and southern India and in the Punjab. The largely feudal regions of central and northern India have lagged behind in generating and sustaining a self-confident middle class.

The heterogeneity of the middle class is most evident in the fact that most social conflicts in India are fought within the class rather than between the rich (landlord and capitalist) and the poor (workers and small peasants). Conflicts between communities and within them, between communal and secular forces, over language, economic rights and ethnic identity are often internal to the class. Given the role that education has played in the empowerment of the middle class, ideology often divides it against itself.

Since the earliest opportunities for upward mobility of the middle class were found in higher education and the civil service, thanks to the establishment of a meritocracy, these became its main bastions. Partly due to the *brahmanical* appreciation of knowledge as power and partly due to the role played by British liberalism in creating the institutions of 'meritocracy', with competitive examinations determining entry into the civil service, the middle class quickly grasped the importance of building excellence into education. Since the middle class was not rich, it ensured access to the system at a low cost and placed greater value on merit than on money, wisely recognising the role of reservations for the disadvantaged as a political necessity.

Today when India's ability to produce world class managers, doctors, scientists, engineers, computer scientists, diplomats, banker, social scientists, linguists, artists and so on is recognised, it is this investment in higher education that is being celebrated. The quality may have suffered with increased quantity, but the best in the top bracket are comparable to the best in the world. Those who wish to reform India's ailing educational system must first recognise that it is this very system, now in need of repair, which gave a vibrant middle class its wings. Any agenda for reform must strengthen the foundations of meritocracy, ensuring equal opportunity to the middle class, even as new structures based on market principles are erected simultaneously.

It is rarely recognised that the middle class took on the challenge of global competition much before the protection—seeking business class, the socially interwoven merchant community and the servile feudal gentry were willing to do so. A merit-based entrance examination to professional institutions and the civil services gave access to knowledge and power, and by seeking to establish a world-class professional educational system the middle class produced professionals for the world market. Despite the weak appeal of the 'Made in India' label in the manufacturing sector, 'made in India professionals' have been in demand the world over. It is not surprising, therefore, that even as the old business oligarchy of the 'Bombay Club' variety feels threatened by global competition, the more self-assured professional middle class has welcomed this.

After winning spurs in the civil service and the educational sector, the middle class has lately demonstrated its capabilities in the corporate and commercial world as well. Take the case of the public sector. It remains a testimonial to middle class managerial ability despite all its faults. Indeed, it is political interference and the demands of a protected domestic business class, from outside the ranks of the meritocracy, that has weakened the public sector more than managerial incompetence. Where managerial autonomy was assured the professional middle class has been able to deliver— the defence, space and nuclear industry being examples.

Even in the private corporate sector, the best-run companies are the professionally managed ones and the best managers come from the meritocracy rather than the plutocracy. Companies like ITC, ACC, L&T, SAIL, Maruti, BHEL, Hindustan Levers, and a clutch of multinationals are all run by managers of middle class origin with world class competence. The replacement of family-run companies with professionally managed ones on the lists of the best run companies is a testimony to middle class ability.

The heroes of the corporate and financial world in the 1980s and 1990s have largely been first generation businessmen and managers from the middle class, many of whom have earned their reputation in the global market before returning to India to take on the established feudal and business oligarchy. Not surprisingly, most of the companies that have not shied away from competing in the global marketplace are professionally managed ones, even if family-owned. Traditional Indian business has not demonstrated the enterprise and courage that middle class professionals, be it in the public or private sector, have.

Recently, when Mr. Rajat Gupta, a middle class non-resident Indian aged 45, became international chief executive of McKinsey & Company, the globally reputed consultancy firm, he was asked by a business magazine what role his 'Indian-ness' played in his selection. "I can safely say," said Mr. Gupta, as if no other explanation were required, "this is one place which is truly a meritocracy." Merit recognised in the marketplace, Mr. Gupta clearly thought, was the secret of his success. Policy makers and businessmen must ensure that the educational system and the corporate environment reward professionalism. This is the only way the Indian economy can make the most of the competitive advantages of its middle class.

The fruits of economic diplomacy

THE value of economic diplomacy came through very clearly this week at Manila and Colombo. Much of the nail-biting by foreign policy analysts, waiting to read the final draft of the statement by the Chairman of the ASEAN Regional Forum (ARF) on India's nuclear tests, could have been avoided if they had a better grasp of the emerging relationship between India and ASEAN.

While in Manila, Jaswant Singh was largely cashing in on existing economic relations with the region, in Colombo, Prime Minister A.B. Vajpayee took a historic step forward with unilateral trade liberalisation. By focussing clearly on the growing economic relations with her Asian neighbours, India has been able to limit the damage inflicted by the nuclear tests. Clearly, Indian diplomacy has moved positively along the learning curve.

However, India can ill-afford to rest on the laurels won at Manila, nor remain content with promises made in Colombo. Concrete and meaningful action will have to be taken and projects got off the ground if diplomacy has to be encashed. The fact is that Indian initiative in deepening the content of business and economic relations with both the ASEAN and SAARC members remains inadequate and hobbled by red tape and resistance from lobbies at home.

While the recent financial crisis in the region has also contributed to a slowing down of India-ASEAN trade and investment relationship, the slow progress of specific projects, especially those involving the more influential ASEAN members like Singapore and Malaysia, has hurt this process. After Manila and Colombo, the Vajpayee government will hopefully give greater attention to trade and investment deals involving ASEAN and SAARC countries.

It is no secret that India's 'Look East' policy took a knocking in the aftermath of the financial crisis in the region. Hence, one must welcome Mr. Singh's reinterpretation of the 'Look East' policy in the context of the financial crisis, underlining India's intent to be 'supportive of the economic recovery' in the region and the recognition of the fact that the crisis is transitory and that the ASEAN economies are capable of bouncing back.

Mr. Vajpayee's announcement in Colombo lifting quantitative restrictions (QRs) in intra-SAARC trade is also significant both because he has been able to clinch an issue on which there has been much domestic resistance and because this decision signals to the world that Mr. Vajpayee's government will stay the course on external economic liberalisation. India cannot remain open to South Asia for very long without becoming open to the rest of the world. The QR elimination within SAARC can only be the first step towards a more generalised policy on QRs.

While economic diplomacy undoubtedly played a part in shaping the outcome at Manila, it is also important to appreciate the changing nature of India's political relations with several key ASEAN countries. It is useful to recall, in this context, the contents of a dispatch from the Singapore correspondent of *The Hindu*, (May 12, 1998) sent on the very day Pokhran-II had occurred. The report stated that, "Defence officials in the region (South-East Asia) are not too worried about India's reluctance to get on board the CTBT or its determination to exercise the nuclear option if it is warranted. They realise the security implications of that decision and concede that India's track record makes it clear that it will not go to war on its own."

The correspondent also quoted a scholar at Kuala Lumpur's Institute of Strategic Studies saying that he regretted India's delay in taking some 'substantial steps' to make its presence felt in the region. "We know of India's capabilities," the Malaysian strategic analyst reportedly told the correspondent, "but it may be time to stand up and be counted. Perhaps India needs to demonstrate its potential and step up its presence on all sides of the India Ocean."

The Hindu despatch also quoted anonymous South-East Asian defence officials saying that they would like to see "India reach its full economic and defence potential before the next five years so that it can effectively balance a resurgent China which seeks to emerge as a regional and global superpower." The link between economic and defence potential is the key to appreciating India's relationship with many of the ASEAN countries. What is important to appreciate is the fact that both are potentially benign for the region and the world.

Closer home, India bears a greater responsibility to yield space on the economic front to her smaller neighbours to assuage their security concerns. Mr. Vajpayee's announcement on QR elimination within SAARC and bilateral free trade agreements must be viewed in this light. It is useful to recall that the former Prime Minister, I.K. Gujral, had proposed these steps but claimed he was facing resistance from within the government. If Mr. Vajpayee has been able to go ahead, it is both a testimony to his leadership skills and to the pressure that nuclear tests have exerted on the government to think anew on such matters.

A word of caution. India's business relations with some ASEAN countries have already come under a cloud for lack of transparency. While yielding economic space in pursuit of strategic policy goals is in the national interest, underhand deals between Indian politicians and their counterparts, or their extended families, in the ASEAN region can only hurt the process of India-ASEAN friendship. Already some of the infrastructure projects involving relatives of the Malaysian Prime Minister, Mahathir Mohammed, have attracted criticism for lack of transparency. Myopic and cash-hungry politicians should not be allowed to damage what is clearly an important strategic relationship for India.

11 | COLUMN

The Madrid impasse

India and G-9 stand up to be counted

THERE was a moment of stunned silence in the 'Londres' room of the Palacio Municipal de Congresos when the US treasury secretary, Mr. Lloyd Bentsen, asked his fellow governors on the interim committee (IC) of the International Monetary Fund, in his characteristic Texan accent, "Does anyone object to the proposal?"

After waiting the entire day for a compromise proposal to emerge from the closed door deliberations of the finance ministers of the group of major industrial nations, the G-7, the interim committee was now being asked to vote on the individual items of what was all along regarded as a 'package', the extension of the systemic transition facility (STF), a financing window created to help the former socialist economies of Europe, beyond the existing expiry date of December 31, 1991, and a fresh allocation of special drawing rights (SDR), the Fund's reserve currency and non-conditionality finance, available to all members.

Even at lunch, when the IC adjourned, the consensus view was that the SDR-STF package would be retained even if the SDR allocation would be scaled down well below the target of SDR 36 billion ($ 50 billion) set by the managing director of the IMF, Mr. Michel Camdessus. Now the G-7 had done a *volte-face* and were proposing a 'vote', a rare event in the proceedings of the committee, on individual items of the package.

For an embarrassingly long half a minute there was tense silence in the room as eyes moved around the table. Then the soft voice of a diminutive man broke the silence. "I do," said India's finance minister, Mr. Manmohan Singh, thereby creating history. As chairman of the group of developing country representatives on the IC, the G-9, for the month of October, Mr. Singh voiced a consensus view.

For the first time in the Fund's 50-year history, a proposal jointly brought forward by the world's most powerful economies, those who have run the Fund as their personal fiefdom, using it when it was useful, ignoring it when it was embarrassing, discarding it when it became its policies, was being rejected by those who counted for so little in the organisation's management.

Never before has a G-7 proposal been blocked in the Fund's 24-member IC, its highest policymaking body. The G-9, comprising Algeria, Argentina, Brazil, Gabon, India, Malaysia, Mozambique, Saudi Arabia and United Arab Emirates, finally chose to dig in their heels and signal to the world the emerging change in the balance of economic power in almost all multilateral institutions. The voice of the developing economies has gained in strength with the growing assertiveness of the newly industrialising economies and the inability of the G-7 to orchestrate a common perspective on how to deal with global economic problems.

The roots of this revolt lie in the hidden anger of the developing countries with the two-faced policy of the G-7 towards the IMF and the Bank. On the one hand, the G-7 have increasingly neglected these multilateral forums, preferring to coordinate macroeconomic policy through the G-7 and dealing with developing countries bilaterally. On the other hand, they have forced the Fund to foot the bill of economic restructuring and reconstruction in the former socialist economies of Europe, the so-called "economies in transition"(EIT), even as they have refused to loosen the purse strings for the developing economies.

The SDR was created in 1969 in order to supplement existing international reserves, at a time when the dollar was in crisis, and with the intention that it would become the principal reserve asset in the global monetary system. There have been two SDR allocations since then, the 1970-72 and in 1978-81, amounting to a sum of SDR 21.4 billion. Since 1981 there has been no further allocation with the G-7 resisting the idea arguing that there was no 'global need'. The G-7 economies have preferred to meet the hard currency needs of the developing world through their own currencies rather than allow the IMF to augment its reserve currency.

This had created a peculiar anomaly within the Fund in the early 1990s since none of the Fund's 37 new members, who had joined after 1981, had any SDRs allocated to them. With another 36 countries which had not fully participated in the SDR system in 1981, as many as 73 of the Fund's 179 members stand to benefit from a fresh allocation. In augmenting SDRs in order to cater to the needs of the new members, 21 of whom are EIT, there is an additional problem of maintaining the existing parity in SDR allocation between nations and, in fact, altering this parity in order to reflect the changes in the relative economic power of the Fund's members.

The countries of East Asia have a disproportionately low share of SDRs which does not take account of their increased economic importance in the 1980s. For all these reasons, the IMF had itself proposed an allocation of SDR 36 billion. Some of this as a general allocation to all members and some as a 'special' allocation to the new ones. In the run-up to the Madrid meetings, the G-9 took the view in the Fund's executive board (where India is represented by the former Union finance secretary, Mr. K.P. Geethakrishnan) that SDR allocation, STF extension and an increase in the limit on the access to SDR (which was limited 68 per cent of a member's quota) should all be part of a 'package'. The G-9 unity on the issue was unprecedented and significant because together the G-9 have almost 30 per cent of the vote in the Fund and any resolution requires an 85 per cent vote in its favour to be adopted.

Responding to the G-9 solidarity, and the German intransigence on SDR allocation (Germany was unique in its total rejection of the G-9 view), the US and the UK came forward with a compromise formula which visualised an allocation of SDR 16 billion. The hitch with this formula was that it tied up a uniform general allocation of SDRs to all members, which is permitted under the articles of agreement of the Fund, with a special allocation to only some members, which requires an amendment of the Fund's articles of agreement. This, in turn, has to be ratified by all the parliaments of the member countries. Since this is a cumbersome process, the G-9 urged an upfront 'general allocation' to be delinked from a subsequent 'special' allocation. The US-UK formula did not address this issue and was, therefore, rejected by the G-9.

The French offered another proposal by which the IC would agree in principle to a general allocation of SDR, but would first clear a special allocation. The G-9 rejected this as well stating, "What is wanted is not changes in wording but a will to go ahead with the general allocation and the G-9 would like the industrialised countries to signal their willingness by agreeing to a general allocation now."

The G-7 did just the opposite. A day before the IC met, G-7 finance ministers issued a statement rejecting a general allocation. This act of arrogance made the historic confrontation inevitable. Even the uncertain Mr. Singh, who was uncomfortable playing the role of David against the G-7 Goliath, and has been since advised by some of his colleagues to ensure that India's brave multilateral stance does not harm her bilateral relations with the G-7, was emboldened to stand firm.

The G-7 was taken by complete surprise when the G-9 vetoed any compromise that did not include a general allocation. It was an unprecedented stand-off. How the IC and Mr. Camdessus will resolve this impasse remains to be seen. Whatever the final compromise and however fragile the unity of G-9, with Saudi Arabia being most vulnerable to pressure from the US, the developing countries have made their point and can no longer be taken for granted in the management of the Fund.

Intimations of greatness

The challenge of realising India's potential

WHEN Spiderman's uncle Ben realises that his nephew has acquired supernatural powers he has a word of sage advice for his energetic and eager nephew, "With great power comes great responsibility." Spiderman's guiding principle has become a *leitmotif* of strategic policy thinking in the United States, particularly after 9/11, and may come to haunt the Bush administration as it grapples with the challenge posed by Saddam Hussein.

Trying to articulate the responsibilities of a 'great power' in the post-9/11 world, US President George Bush Jr. published last week a policy document under presidential seal entitled "The National Security Strategy of the United States of America". The document sets out a new policy paradigm of 'pre-emption', as opposed to deterrence, which is to guide US security strategy in the near term.

Unlike the fate of a similar document prepared in India by the National Security Advisory Board that must be gathering dust in some governmental *almirah* marked 'secret', the US president's strategy paper is available free for anyone who wants to read it on the internet at www.globalsecurity.org.

Apart from offering an overview of US international strategy, especially in the campaign against terrorism and the use of weapons of mass destruction, and apart from enunciating important principles with respect to the defence of democracy and of free markets and free trade, the presidential paper also paints a picture of the world today as the US sees it.

The interesting novelty here for Indian readers is the fact that for the first time a US presidential paper gives its imprimatur to the Henry Kissinger's view of India as a 'potential' Great Power. Kissinger expressed the view in 1994 that the 21st century would have five or six great powers: The US, European Union, Russia, China, Japan, and 'probably India'.

Years later, in a more recent book on US foreign policy, Kissinger repeated this formulation without removing the prefix, even though India had become a declared nuclear power in 1998. When asked what in his view it would take even nuclear India to rid itself of his prefix, his answer was categorical—a larger economy and greater economic engagement with the world and the ability to realise the strategic potential of that economic power.

A competitive economy is the foundation of power in the modern world. India has not yet completed the task of building that foundation. Hence there is considerable distance to be covered before we can claim 'great power' status, even of the kind China now enjoys as a trading power. The Bush paper, therefore, quite understandably still refers to India, in fact along with China, as a 'potential great power'.

While the first reference to India in the Bush strategy document is in the context of South Asia wherein the US underscores the need for India and Pakistan to 'resolve their disputes', and the Bush administration draws attention to the fact that it has 'invested time and resources building strong bilateral relations with India and Pakistan', the only other reference to Pakistan is in the context of the 'war against terror'. India finds further mention on its own, with no further reference to the P-word! That is a message we have to internalise. To be able to view ourselves in the world without reference to our adversaries.

India figures in the chapter on cooperative action with 'other main centres of global power'. "We are attentive to the possible renewal of old patterns of great power competition," says the strategy paper, "Several potential great powers are now in the midst of internal transition—most importantly Russia, India, and China. In all three cases, recent developments have encouraged our hope that a truly global consensus about basic principles is slowly taking shape." Listing out common areas of interest between the US and India, including the "free flow of commerce through the vital sea lanes of the Indian Ocean", the fight against terrorism, defence of democracy and "creating a strategically stable Asia", the paper admits to differences on India's nuclear programme and the 'pace of economic reforms'. However, the paper says, "While in the past these concerns may have dominated our thinking about India, today we start with a view of India as a growing world power with which we have common strategic interests. Through a strong partnership with India, we can best address any differences and shape a dynamic future."

One area of difference which is going to engage the two countries in the near term is multilateral trade policy. The Union commerce ministry is holding on to the fiction that a new round of trade negotiations has not yet been launched. Bush's strategy paper, on the other hand, not only refers to the "new global trade negotiations... (launched) at Doha... " but says that its 'ambitious agenda' covering trade liberalisation in manufacturing, services and agriculture is scheduled for completion by 2005.

Going beyond multilateral trade liberalisation, the Bush doctrine is pushing for greater action in regional free trade agreements and bilateral free trade agreements. Apart from a Free Trade Association of the Americas, an Asian Free Trade Area, including China, Japan, Korea and ASEAN is taking shape. What about India?

Unless we come to terms with the political challenge of globalisation and the challenge of sustained economic growth, the Kissingerian prefix of our 'probably' being a Great Power will linger longer than even our ill-wishers presume. Sustained high rates of more equitable economic growth and domestic political and social stability are essential requirements of national power. If growth falters, if political and social divisiveness becomes pronounced, not even our most ardent well-wishers will be able to help us.

For precisely this reason, those who do not wish to see India regain its glory will do their best to disrupt the social and political stability that is required for our economic progress. Must we help them with our acts of omission and commission?

Diplomatic business

Trade and flag in today's world

THE South Korean conglomerate, Hyundai, has done it again. Taken its corporate flag where its home country's national flag does not fly. Recently, the 83-years old founder chairman of the Hyundai group of companies, Mr. Chung Ju Yung, called on the North Korean leader, Mr. Kim Jong II to mix business with diplomacy, and returned home with a multi-billion dollar deal.

Reportedly, Mr. Chung was pursuing the South Korean President Kim Dae Jung's 'sunshine policy' towards the country's arch-rival, of using business and cultural contacts as a cementing factor in the troubled relationship between the two Koreas. Mr. Chung's visit has enabled his company to bag lucrative deals which will bring in revenues for Hyundai of up to $ 3 billion till 2007. For its part, North Korea gets investment of $ 906 million from Hyundai spread six years for a range of projects. The Hyundai chairman has spoken of joint oil exploration, development of tourist resorts in North Korea and such like. All this is good news both for the still grounded South Korean economy and the crisis-ridden North. More importantly, Hyundai is enabling a thaw. The point is, it is Hyundai's brand name which is helping unfurl the South Korean flag in what has been enemy territory for an entire generation. Hyundai, incidentally, has used its corporate flag in national interest before.

In 1990, when Iraq invaded Kuwait, several South Korean nationals working with various companies were stuck in Kuwait and had to retreat from their homes to their embassy for shelter. When the South Korean government wanted to fly them out, Kuwaiti authorities could not guarantee their safety in the transit from embassy to airport because Iraqi troops were already on the streets. Hyundai's executives came up with an idea. "Our company logo is very popular in Iraq", they told the embassy staff, "we will drive in Hyundai buses, flying the Hyundai flag with the corporate logo. The Iraqis will not hurt us." Sure they didn't. In fact, according to a senior Hyundai executive, they waved at all the convoys shouting "Hyundai, Hyundai", as they sped to the airport to catch the last flight home.

Indian corporates do not have many such *filmi* stories to tell about the role of business in diplomacy, but there are some worthy of recollection. At the height of the last episode of India-Pakistan bonhomie a couple of years ago, when economics and business had overshadowed Kashmir on the subcontinent's diplomatic menu card, a group of senior Indian corporate leaders travelled to Islamabad. Their flight from New Delhi to Lahore, the first hop, was delayed so they missed their flight from Lahore to Islamabad and had to spend a night in Lahore. The secretary-general of the Federation of Indian Chambers of Commerce and Industry (FICCI), Mr. Amit Mitra, suggested they drive overnight to Islamabad so as not to miss their engagements next morning. *En route*, the convoy of the captains of Indian industry stopped at roadside *dhabas* for tea. Everywhere, curious Pakistanis gathered to express their friendship and warmth and showed-off their familiarity with Indian brands. The Indian film and music industry has done more to promote the prospect of peace in the subcontinent than all the diplomats and politicians put together.

India's foreign service leadership is slowly beginning to recognise the importance of business diplomacy in the pursuit of national interest, but is still way behind the current practice in the western world. Last month, the British government placed an advertisement in *The Economist* (London) calling for applications from corporate leaders for a senior position in foreign service—the post of British Consul-General of Trade and Investment Promotion, the applicant being sought is someone who has held, says the ad— "senior management positions in business or government, preferably including exporting or international investment experience. An ability to represent UK interests at the highest levels of US business and government in this high profile appointment is essential. Previous experience of work in USA and with the media would be advantageous." The job description states that this person will report directly to the Ambassador, supervise staff in all British consular offices across the US, deal with government departments in London, and project British policies to potential US investors. The advertisement also adds that the New York Consul-General's office deals with the states of New York, New Jersey, Pennsylvania and Connecticut which is an area with a "GDI equivalent to that of the UK".

Such stories are increasingly more the rule than the exception. Such direct involvement of business in diplomacy is still lacking in India even if there is a much greater degree of interaction between the two especially in the 1990s. Regrettably, however, the Vajpayee government has not been as aggressive involving business in diplomacy as the Narasimha Rao and even the United Front governments were willing to do. The Indian equivalent of the Hyundai example could be getting Mr. Rahul Bajaj and Mr. Nusli Wadia (a relative of the late Jinnah) to travel to Islamabad in pursuit of business opportunities. Indeed, Mr. Wadia could well be sent as India's High Commissioner to Pakistan. A businessman with a good track record in Africa may have been better for the High Commissioner's job in South Africa than a moralising Gandhian. Admittedly the caveat 'good track record' is important with respect to Indian businessmen because more often than not they have created a negative image of India in many parts of the world.

The Hyundai story shows that a precondition for successful business diplomacy is a strong brand name. When produce does not find markets because of the negative image of the nation, (the argument that the 'Made in India' label does not sell), then the least one should ensure in the marketing of a nation is the strength of the brand being used to win friends. How many Indian brands can do for India what Hyundai has done for South Korea? This shortcoming of Indian enterprise also acts as a barrier to the effective deployment of business in diplomacy. The time, however, has come when trade must fly the flag than just follow it.

14 | COLUMN

The strategic imperative

NEVER since the early days of the Rajiv Gandhi government has the Prime Minister's Office (PMO) occupied centre stage in economic policymaking as it seems to be doing now. Prime Minister Vajpayee has not only sought out the advice of economists and industrialists through the PM's Economic Advisory Council and the Council on Trade and Industry, but he has more recently constituted a Strategic Management Group (SMG) in the PMO to oversee economic policy implementation issues. Next week he is scheduled to convene a meeting of his senior most cabinet ministers, the ministers of finance, home, human resource development, external affairs and industry and commerce to discuss the government's economic policy agenda.

Both Indira Gandhi and Rajiv Gandhi had economists working out of the Prime Minister's Office. Subsequent PMs allowed, by design or default, their finance ministers to become the focal point of most economic policy initiatives. It can be argued that the finance ministry is normally preoccupied with annual budgetary and macroeconomic policy issues of a more short-term nature and that someone with a wider policymaking ambit should take direct charge of major structural changes in the economy.

That was the thinking in the Gandhi family PMOs, but Prime Minister Narasimha Rao changed that by allowing his finance minister, Manmohan Singh, to become the fountainhead of all economic policy reform. That situation has now changed, though the PMO still does not have any professional economists on its staff, in the manner in which Indira Gandhi had P.N. Dhar and subsequently Arjun Sengupta and Rajiv Gandhi had Montek Singh Ahluwalia.

It is surprising, however, that the PMO has dubbed a group responsible for policy implementation as the "strategic management group". Implementation of policy, getting sanctioned projects off the ground and speeding up reforms are important aspects of governance. Indeed, it is just as well that the system is made aware that the PMO has its eagle eye open and is keeping track of policy implementation. However, policy implementation is different from managing 'strategy' or, indeed, even strategic management.

The Planning Commission was used both by Nehru and, in the early years, by Indira Gandhi as the PM's 'strategic management group' for economic policy. If the deputy chairman of the Planning Commission is a P.C. Mahalanobis or a Sukhamoy Chakravarty, the Commission can indeed play the role of the PM's SMG. However, over time, the Commission has been devalued as a think tank and is today not in the inner loop on policymaking.

Who, then, does the job of linking the imperatives of short-term economic policy management with those of long-term strategy? Who is able to identify the interface and visualise synergy between economic policy, foreign policy, internal security policy, and so on? Is there a need for coordinated thinking on economic policy from a national security perspective? If so, which of the many expert groups is responsible for this?

When US President-elect George Bush and his National Security Advisor Condoleezza Rice take charge, one of the policy papers they will be considering is a proposal from the Brookings Institution to increase the profile of strategic economic policy management in the US National Security Council (NSC). Titled *A New NSC for a New Administration*, the Brookings Policy Brief (No. 68, November 2000), by Ivo H. Daalder and I.M. Destler, calls for the elevation of strategic thinking on economic policy in the NSC.

The paper proposes a major change in past practice, namely, "...adding a second deputy with powers equal to those of the first.

This second person, an economic specialist, would be dual-hatted—reporting both to the national security advisor (NSA) and the head of the National Economic Council (NEC)."

In India, the equivalent institution to the NEC could be the Planning Commission, or the office of the Chief Economic Advisor, which can easily be delinked from the finance ministry and made part of the PMO. Whether this is done or not would depend entirely on the conception the prime minister has of the role of the finance ministry. Is it the equivalent of the US Treasury, managing the fisc and keeping the markets happy, or is it an economic policymaking organisation with policy influence over other economic ministries as well as the external affairs ministry?

In the US case, with its presidential form of government, the Brookings proposal sees the new "deputy for international economics and national security" as a person who "would have overall responsibility for international economic affairs and serve as the government's sherpa to the G-8 economic summits. This person would also oversee the NSC's multilateral portfolio as well as the transnational and economic issues that flow through the regional directorates ...." His counterpart deputy would be dealing with non-proliferation, defence, transnational threats and other security issues.

The reason why India needs coordinated 'strategic' thinking on economic policy is no different from the reason why the US has thought this necessary. Economic policy and business interests have become central to national security and foreign policy interests of most major economies. The US administration has always recognised that 'trade policy is an aspect of national security'. It is a view of foreign trade which China has also pursued, using trade as an instrument of building relations with nations.

Economic growth and development are also recognised as the foundation on which both internal and external security and the well-being of a nation are built. Misplaced economic policies, shaped by sectional and vested interests and lobbies, can have a damaging impact on national well-being and security. Given the diverse dimensions to economic policy, major powers like the US and China, not to mention the European nations, have created the institutional structures to coordinate economic and strategic policy and link economic policy to larger national security goals.

It is this job, a strategic management group in the PMO should be doing. It should be a link between the finance, commerce, industry, agriculture and other economic ministries, as well as the home, human resource development and external affairs ministry, alerting them to the national security dimension to economic policy. Hopefully this will enable the PM to then stop his ministers from hurting national interest by pandering to sectional and vested interests. A caveat, to be effective such a group must itself not become the handmaiden of vested interests.

Brinkmanship blues

Memories of a near forgotten crisis

HOP, skip and jump. Those were the three code words known to just three key actors in the cloak and pen drama of the unprecedented devaluation of the Indian rupee 10 years ago. The date: July 1, 1991. The *dramatis personae*—Union finance minister Manmohan Singh, Reserve Bank of India governor S. Venkitaramanan and RBI deputy governor C. Rangarajan. A day earlier Singh had appraised Prime Minister Narasimha Rao of the balance of payments situation and recommended rupee devaluation. The PM advised him to consult President Venkataraman because his was a minority government.

The three of them decided that the rupee had to be devalued if India was to restore external confidence in the economy and qualify for a balance of payments support from the International Monetary Fund. Singh was asked to communicate the government's decision to the RBI. A nuanced exercise, hop-skip-jump, was to be undertaken so that the impact of such a massive devaluation would get dissipated. The time lag between the first hop and the second jump was not fixed.

It was a bit like Pokharan II. First a signal, second the message. 'Hop' was a teaser, 'step' the interregnum in which to judge the response, 'jump' was the real thing. On July 1, the RBI hopped. Venkitaramanan developed cold feet and conveyed his reservations to the PM. Rao called in Singh and asked him to stop the exercise.

There was already some murmur in the Congress party. Knives were out for Rao. Indira Gandhi had to pay a political price for the devaluation of 1966, does Rao think he is more powerful than her to carry off a devaluation and gain majority support on the floor of the House?

Scared by such scenario building the PM wanted to mark time after the first hop and called off the 'jump'. Singh knew this would be disastrous. If the news leaked no politician would have the courage to take the required jump and the BoP crisis would worsen. He could not say 'No' to his PM, so he depended on the legendary inefficiency of the Indian telephone system to pretend he couldn't get in touch with Rangarajan, who was in charge of rupee management and had the responsibility to announce the next step. This simple device of 'couldn't get through', which so many Indians have used so often to deal with problems big and small, helped. Rangarajan issued the 'jump' command and the rupee was devalued for a second time.

So who says economic policymaking is dull and boring stuff and that economists and bankers are dour men in dark suits? The management of the economic crisis of 1990-91 and the reform Big Bang of June-July 1991, whose 10th anniversary we mark in coming weeks, had its share of drama and thrills. The cliffhanger was the transportation of gold from the vaults of the RBI in Fort, Bombay, to the Bank of England in London. Over 15 tonnes had to be airlifted. The first instalment of five tonnes was to be sent on an Indian Airlines commercial flight.

It was a top secret exercise. A heavily guarded security vehicle left the RBI's vaults and drove in a motorcade of vehicles with armed guards inside. At each street corner between Fort and Santa Cruz security guards were posted to report the motorcade's progress to the RBI governor. Engine trouble, the van stalled, armed gaurds jumped out and surrounded the vehicle and soon word spread through the nation's financial capital. The central bank authorities were worried about the news leak because the aircraft had to fly *via* West Asia and they didn't want any terrorist outfit to know that Indian gold was being airlifted through the region.

Regrettably none of the managers of economic policy in 1990-91 have put pen to paper to write a comprehensive and frank account of what happened at the time. There have been too many academic essays, justifying or criticising the policies put in place, but no authentic account of what happened. A few self-serving accounts have appeared in the media, meant to either highlight or play down the role of various individuals. An honest account of the policies and events that preceded the economic crisis of 1990-91 will be helpful not just for students of public policy and future generations of economists, but also for today's political leaders and policy makers. As it has been said before, those who forget history are condemned to relive it.

The current drift in economic policy in India makes one feel that today's political leaders seem to have forgotten the depths to which India's prestige and self-confidence had plummeted in 1990-91. No one knows this better than the present Union finance minister, Yashwant Sinha, who, as finance minister at the time, went in search of aid to Tokyo in December 1990 and was insulted and had to return home empty handed. The Indian ambassador in Tokyo was unable to secure an appointment for Sinha with any senior Japanese official. Rather than face the humiliation of being received by a lowly joint secretary, Sinha took the next flight back home.

A team of officials, including Rangarajan, chief economic advisor Deepak Nayyar and joint secretary in the finance ministry Y. Venugopal Reddy (at present deputy governor, RBI), went on a secret mission to Washington DC to tap the IMF and the World Bank. They were told the Fund would give money to India if a reform-oriented budget was presented in February 1991. Prime Minister Chandra Shekhar, who now protests loudly against post-1991 policies, and Sinha were ready to do so when the Congress withdrew its support to the Chandra Shekhar government since Rajiv Gandhi wanted to postpone implementing the reform programme until after an election.

In fact, 1991 was growing up time for India. No longer assured of the external warmth of the Cold War era, unable to find any quick-fix solutions to the BoP and fiscal crises, finding itself on the verge of default for the first time, the government refused to blink. Through a combination of clever strategy and hard-headed policy making, with a mix of some bluff and bluster, the government of the day pulled India away from the brink. The rest is history, and yet it seems to have been forgotten. How else can one explain the current drift in economic policymaking?

There is no crisis around the corner, certainly not an external payments crisis. But once again India's lustre is fading, while China forges ahead. The economy is slowing down, the real productive sectors of the economy are not growing. Public focus shifts constantly from politics to more politics, regional, subregional, provincial. Every piece of the jigsaw is so puzzled about its own self, that no one is looking at the shape of the big picture. Like Wajid Ali Shah our leaders play little chess games, when the big forces of globalisation and technological development are sweeping through Asia. So what are today's code words for India—hop, skip and dump?

16 COLUMN

Economic sanctions in war on terror

UNILATERAL economic sanctions are a blunt instrument of diplomacy. They have never worked, according to a comprehensive study of economic sanctions undertaken by the Washington DC based think tank, the Institute of International Economics. For economic sanctions to be effective, they must be truly international, backed by multilateral financial institutions. If a tiny country like Cuba has survived massive economic sanctions imposed over a 40 year period by a neighbour which is an economic superpower, there is pretty little India can do on its own to discipline a country of the size of Pakistan.

If economic sanctions have to be used as an instrument of diplomacy in the campaign against terrorism, to get General Pervez Musharraf's regime to truly wage a comprehensive battle against *jehadi* terrorist groups at home, then such sanctions will have to be imposed multilaterally. The Pakistan economy was pulled back from the brink of crisis last year thanks to a lifeline extended by the International Monetary Fund, the World Bank and many donor countries from the Organization of Economic Co-operation and Development. While some Islamic nations, especially Saudi Arabia, and Pakistan's strategic ally, China, have extended unquestioned economic assistance to Pakistan, with few strings attached, the West has ostensibly secured a promise of good behaviour in exchange for its aid and support to the Pakistan economy.

It is because of Pakistan's critical dependence on Western, Japanese and Chinese economic assistance that it has taken actions against terrorist groups within Pakistan limited to satisfying their concerns. Indeed, in the recent past even this commitment has been openly questioned and the repeated statements emanating from Washington DC and London that "words must be followed by deeds" indicate growing exasperation even in the West with General Musharraf's reluctant campaign against terrorism.

As an exasperated India began stepping up its campaign against Pakistan-based terrorism in this country, in response to an escalation of cross-border terrorist activity in the months of March and April 2002, several analysts have revived arguments in favour of imposing economic sanctions against Pakistan. Among the many actions contemplated the most frequently cited ones are the abrogation of the Indus Water Treaty and withdrawal of the Most Favoured Nation status to Pakistan. The MFN obligation is a basic requirement of the membership of the World Trade Organization which Pakistan has refused to extend to India, while India continues to adhere to its WTO obligation.

Neither of these actions can amount to much since the abrogation of the Indus Water Treaty will have no immediate effect unless India builds dams to withhold the water within Indian territory and terminating MFN is unlikely to impact on Pakistan given the low share of its trade with India in its overall trade.

More to the point, as the IIE study showed, the only real success stories for economic sanctions have been multilateral ones, like the campaign against Apartheid South Africa. As long as multilateral financial institutions and G-7 governments continue to provide economic assistance to Pakistan, offer preferential market access and encourage foreign investment, limited action by India is unlikely to impose unaffordable cost on the Musharraf regime.

Will multilateral sanctions work? Yes, they can. Unlike an Iraq or a North Korea, Pakistan's level of integration into the world economy and the social basis of its market oriented economy are such that Pakistan cannot afford to remain isolated from the global financial system or the world market. If the OECD countries, especially the G-7, and the multilateral financial institutions cut off the financial and trade lifelines to Pakistan, its economy would be seriously hurt. Admittedly, Saudi Arabia and China may yet assist an internationally sanctioned Pakistan, but even they would find it difficult to conduct normal relations if world opinion is convinced that General Musharraf is not doing enough to wage a war against terrorism.

In that lies the key to India's strategic options. India's current problem with Pakistan is not a bilateral dispute about territory or about the status of Jammu and Kashmir, howsoever much Pakistan may claim. In so projecting the problem, General Musharraf has tried to isolate the campaign against terrorism from action against anti-India *jehadi* groups operating from Pakistan, including Pakistan-occupied Kashmir. Growing evidence of the movement of Afghanistani *jehadi* groups, including Al-Qaeda and Taliban, into PoK and J&K show that the battle against *jehadi* terrorism in the region requires comprehensive international action and cannot be waged as a military campaign by India.

Both military and other security operations against terrorist groups operating out of Pakistan, as well as effective economic sanctions aimed at exerting pressure on the Musharraf regime to act, have to be multilateral and international in scope and cannot be effective if they are only unilaterally undertaken by India. This is more so for economic sanctions than military action.

Forcing General Musharraf to act against all *jehadi* terrorists based in Pakistan has to be a global campaign, involving even China. The problem is not India's alone and Pakistan's nuclear blackmail is not just against India. It is an affront to the global campaign against terrorism. If the world views the problem as merely a bilateral dispute between India and Pakistan and as the 'unfinished agenda of the sub-continent's partition' then it will willy-nilly be acquiescing in the Talibanisation of Kashmir. It is the same forces of terror which held unchallenged control of Afghanistan territory for over a decade, and have been forced out by the US-led campaign against terrorism, that are now regrouping in PoK and J&K.

This development does not serve the interests of a modern, democratic Pakistan as much as it does not serve India's interests nor, indeed, that of the rest of the modern, civilised world. Hence, the current stand-off between India and Pakistan is not a bilateral dispute, but is central to the global campaign against terrorism. Indian and world leaders, as well as liberal Pakistanis, must appreciate this to be able to find a lasting solution to the current tension in the sub-continent.

Not an advisable advisory

THE day the United States government decided to launch a military campaign against Al-Qaeda and the Taliban in Afghanistan, an American investor called his fund manager in London and told him, "get my money out of India". The surprised fund manager advised his client not to panic. "Your money is safe in one of India's brightest blue chip companies located in Bangalore several thousand kilometres south of Afghanistan. You don't have to worry."

The client was not convinced, "Look, I don't care about geography. I know something about making money. Right? Now, either you get my money out of the region or I'll send you an atlas!" One more investor had flown out of a 'risky emerging market'. This is a true story, from October 2001. "Sentiment is all in the markets," lamented this fund manager, worrying at the time that "India may be going out of fashion".

His pessimism was not entirely justified. As statistics put out by the Union government's ministry of industry show encouragingly, foreign investment into India increased by over 60 per cent since September 11. Only last week, Japan's Osamu Suzuki flew down to New Delhi with a cheque for a thousand crore to boost his stake in the automobile company, Maruti Udyog Limited. But then, these are uncertain times and the persistence of tension in the region has once again turned market sentiment negative.

Last fortnight, the stock market felt the impact of this uncertainty for days as the sensex slipped with every statement about

India seeking a decisive end to Pakistan's proxy war. This week the market may well react excessively to the news over the weekend that the US government has advised its citizens not to travel to India and has advised those already in India to get out. Is the government ready with its response to this psywar?

It is not clear to what extent the US government travel advisory is motivated by genuine fear of a widespread conflagration in South Asia, including possible terrorist attacks directed against US targets, and to what extent it is aimed at exerting psychological pressure on policy makers in the region to reduce tensions. While the travel advisory is cautiously worded and suggests that American citizens "defer travel to India ... particularly to all border areas between India and Pakistan including the Indian states of Gujarat, Rajasthan and Punjab, and the state of Jammu and Kashmir," it urges "American citizens currently in India to depart the country."

India is a continental country. Asking Americans to get out of border states, given the prospect of a war with Pakistan, is one thing. Asking them to leave India is an exaggerated response. It would be interesting to check out if the US government urged all Americans to leave the European Union when its forces joined the hostilities in the Balkans! If not, the current travel advisory, and reports suggesting that there could be an airlift of all Americans out of India, may be viewed as psychological tactics aimed at influencing policy options in the region. The market must then discount the advisory for what it is intended to be.

The travel advisory was not the first instrument of a possible psywar campaign. The scenario building on a nuclear conflagration in the region appears equally orchestrated. All manner of commentators and analysts have been creeping out of the Washington DC think tank woodwork to paint grim scenarios of Armageddon in South Asia. If Pakistan was unable to resort to nuclear blackmail during Kargil, why does the US take Pakistan's nuclear threat more seriously now, that too when US troops are present on Pakistan soil?

More to the point, the mobilisation of Indian armed forces to exert pressure against cross-border terrorism in the region is being projected as an Indian offensive against Pakistan when in fact it is nothing more than an aspect of the campaign against terrorism, in pursuit of which the United States has also deployed troops in the region. If the Bush administration treats India and Pakistan even-handedly in this confrontation, viewing the problem as a bilateral dispute over Kashmir, it would be missing the wood for the trees.

The attempts at raising the spectre of a nuclear conflict, the travel advisory that is undoubtedly going to hurt market and investor sentiment, which in turn will hurt India rather than help, are counter-productive at a time when both the US and India have the same objective of weakening the forces of *jehadi* terrorism in the region. Indeed, even General Pervez Musharraf says he is committed to this cause.

If this is so, then any attempt at turning Jammu and Kashmir into a Talibanised Afghanistan, a haven for *jehadi* terrorists and mercenaries from across the world, serves neither the interests of India nor of Pakistan, nor indeed any of the other major powers in the region, namely the US, Russia and China. India's current military posture aimed at exerting pressure on the present regime in Pakistan to give up the path of globalised *jehadism* and its immediate manifestation in Jammu and Kashmir should be strengthened by all nations battling terrorism.

To pressure India at this stage with misplaced anxiety about a nuclear conflagration, and excessive nervousness about the safety of American citizens and property in the rest of this sub-continental nation cannot help strengthen the campaign against terrorism. Rather, it would appear as if the US has become a victim of Pakistani nuclear blackmail, retreating under that pressure from the campaign against terrorism. If India and the US were to begin quarrelling today, who in the region will be laughing all the way to the next target of terrorist attack? The US should immediately put an end to its psywar against India and widen the campaign against terrorism. The issue at heart is not the future of Kashmir, it is the future of the world.

18 | COLUMN

Who wants charity?

NOW that Japan has decided to withdraw the 'measures' taken against India and Pakistan, a Japanese euphemism for the sanctions imposed as punishment for the May 1998 nuclear tests, Prime Minister Atal Bihari Vajpayee must make bold to declare when he visits Tokyo that he will not seek any aid or financial assistance from Japan. No grants or aid, please; open markets, inward investment and job opportunities for Indians will do, thank you.

Someone in the finance ministry may say that this is money worth having. Aid and cheap loans help in the short run. There are teams of officials employed to process aid, with opportunities to travel to the aid-giving countries, and politicians like signing bilateral agreements at stately photo-ops. Even the aid-givers like the experience of travelling to distant corners of the world where they are received with decorum and courtesy and they can go home and tell their guilt-ridden liberal constituents that they have done their bit for the poor of the world. It's a conspiracy of convenience that no one likes to expose—neither the recipient nor the donor.

The time, however, has come for India to say no to grants and aid. We did that with a couple of Scandinavian countries which also withdrew aid in 1998 to punish India for going nuclear. After some time when they offered to rescind their notifications and resume aid they were politely told to keep their money. We have learnt to say no to Scandinavia, it's time to say no to Japan, Britain, the US and lesser mortals.

The government's sober and muted response to the decision of the US and Japan to lift sanctions is a welcome departure from earlier practice of expressing exaggerated gratitude for such token gestures. Japan had in fact been told that it could earn some diplomatic brownie points with India if it had voluntarily lifted sanctions before the US. This advice was conveyed to Tokyo but Japanese officials said that its stance on nuclear policy was linked to domestic politics and the strong anti-nuclear sentiment in Japan, the 'only victim of a nuclear attack'.

"We would like to withdraw these measures," many Japanese officials told their Indian interlocutors over the past two years, "but what can we do, domestic political opinion in Japan was alienated by India's tests which provoked poorer Pakistan to also follow suit." Why cannot India at least declare its willingness to sign the Comprehensive Test Ban Treaty (CTBT), ("you don't actually have to do it, just say you will and that can help us ease sanctions", we were told). Mercifully, our political leadership was not easily scared into doing the bidding for now these measures have been removed with no promise on CTBT.

But all that seems to have changed the moment the US decided to withdraw sanctions. The US did so to help Pakistan to enable the latter to help the US in the campaign in Afghanistan. So why has Japan chipped in? Clearly, to help the cause in Afghanistan. Cynics would say don't complain, after all the purpose of getting Japan to lift sanctions has been served. If this means getting some easy money from Japan, why not?

Sorry, our view is that this gift horse is not worth riding. Just say thank you, we don't need this charity. More trade? Yes. More investment? Yes. More jobs in the information technology sector for Indian techies? Yes. Trade, investment and skill flows are fine. Aid is not needed, should not be taken and all aid programmes must be wound up. Not just with Japan, but with all the rich industrial countries. We must learn to live without aid.

It is demeaning that our governments have no problem accepting foreign aid for poverty alleviation, literacy programmes, rural development and now even 'good governance'! Economic assistance can be accepted where it comes with technology that is not locally available. It is useful in areas where Indians secure access to new technologies and managerial practices, but a democratically elected government must spend its own tax payers' money to educate its people, bring succour to the poor and care for the distressed.

It is disturbing to see how even the anti-west Left wing and populist political leadership at home that so readily debunks foreign investment has no compunction in accepting foreign aid. There is righteous indignation against multilateral trade regimes and financial institutions, of which we are in fact members and where we have a voice, but no qualms in accepting aid. Why this condoning of alms-seeking even as we damn deal making?

If India is not prepared to cut deals in the World Trade Organization and if the policy of 'give and take' is unacceptable, what makes aid-receiving politically correct? Indian diplomacy must at all international forums remind the developed industrial nations that they all, with the exception of a few Scandinavian countries, have reneged on their commitment to the UN to set aside a mere 0.7 per cent of their national income for development assistance to the developing countries. Yes, that point must be made. But there is no reason why we must seek a share of that pittance.

Let Pakistan rejoice the lifting of sanctions, a country that has damned its economic future by diverting its wealth to *jehad*, militarism and to foreign banks. Must we be in that category?

We felt elevated the day the government announced a donation of a million dollars worth of ciproflaxicin tablets for US citizens seeking cheap medicines to fight the anthrax scare. When the Gujarat earthquake crumbled so many homes and hopes it was correct to accept foreign help. On such occasions accepting help is a graceful act of gratitude.

One must differentiate between such help and the regular bilateral aid, often tied to unacceptable conditions that continues to come and that is increasingly becoming a means of fiscal balancing by state governments. The only development expenditure incurred by many state governments is now financed by foreign aid. Just as huge bureaucracies and vested interests took root in New Delhi in the aid business, there are now in many state capitals public careers being made by the dispensation of foreign aid.

So huge is this foreign funded developmental activity that the Department for International Development (DFID) of the UK now even employs IAS officers to administer its aid programmes! A new vested interest in the perpetuation of aid may have already come into place. This must end. Equally importantly, even as we stop aid, we must fill the external resources gap with more trade and investment flows and adopt more liberal economic policies and create the domestic infrastructure that enables trade and investment flows to grow. Developed countries will then think twice before they impose sanctions. Sanctions are imposed to hurt others, not one's own. Ironically, they are also lifted to help one's own, not others.

Who is afraid of globalisation?

TURN the clock back to *circa* 1972. The rupee is fixed and stable, the big banks have been nationalised, the licence-permit *raj* is in full sway, foreign companies are packing up and no one is talking of promoting foreign trade. India's share of world trade is 0.5 per cent and foreign trade accounts for about 5 per cent of national income. India is relatively insulated from the world economy. Yet, economists Dandekar and Rath tell us that half the population is living under the poverty line and there is communal strife in Gujarat.

China is just about recovering from the Cultural Revolution and Mao Tse-tung is preparing to meet Henry Kissinger. Its' share of world trade is not vastly different from India's, at around 0.8 per cent, but it is a more closed economy than India ever was. Fast forward to 2002. There is still communal strife in Gujarat, but less than a quarter of the population is under the poverty line. The rupee is in a flexible mode, the share of foreign trade in national income has more than doubled, but India's share of world trade is still around 0.7 per cent, compared to China's share at over 4 per cent. Multinationals are flocking into China, while India worries about terrorism and communalism.

In the intervening period, the world has become familiar with a phenomenon called 'globalisation'. China has expanded its global economic engagement in this period, riding the wave of globalisation, even if it has steered clear of financial globalisation, while India has tread cautiously. There are barely one score McDonalds in the whole of India, while China is host to over 500 outlets. If China has globalised more, why is India complaining more?

It's a question few were willing to grapple with at a one-day 'national dialogue' on the 'social dimensions of globalisation' organised by the World Commission on the Social Dimensions of Globalisation. The Commission is an eminent persons group, with Professor Deepak Nayyar representing India, and is the product of the Seattle impasse, when the attempt of the developed countries to link 'social issues' like labour standards to trade policy agreements of the World Trade Organization was rebuffed by the developing countries.

Inspired by western trade unions who are worried about competition in a more open global economy from the newly industrialising Asian economies, the ILO and western governments put together a global commission that curiously has three Americans in a 21-member body!

What is the 'social dimension' to globalisation? Has globalisation in the current phase been only about the free movement of capital and goods, with little interest in the movement of people? Is globalisation a one-way street with the developed North recolonising the developing South? What is the current state of affairs across the world as far as the social impact of globalisation is concerned and what do we do about it? These questions were posed to a group of persons drawn from various backgrounds— business, labour, parliamentarians, NGO activists, academics, scholars, artists, writers, journalists and government officials at a meeting this week in Delhi.

In the opening session a member of the Commission from China, Mr. Lu Mai, reported that at the end of a similar dialogue in China, it seemed that most participants there took an 'optimistic' and positive view of globalisation, while the main people who were worried were representatives of trade unions. There is concern in China about rising unemployment and inequality, both regional and social, but by and large, China has taken a positive view of the opportunities offered by globalisation.

Mr. Lu's view gained added value when Bill Brett, a British trade union leader and a member of the Commission told the gathering that everyone across the world was complaining about globalisation because the losers were many and the winners few. Who, in his view, were the winners? Multinational corporations (to be expected) and China! A British trade union leader worrying about competition from China in a globalised world economy, with freer trade flows? Not surprising and explains why China takes an optimistic view.

By the same token, should India not be taking a similar view? No—was the majority view at the New Delhi dialogue. The 'optimists' were outnumbered by the pessimists. Many of the pessimists attributed every conceivable ill in our society to globalisation—from unemployment to communalism, from child labour to gender imbalance, from regional inequality to the attack on tribals.

The optimists' view that, like China, India could also benefit from globalisation was drowned by the alarm of naysayers. The most vociferous critics of globalisation seemed to be parliamentarians and academics. Two influential groups in society are not yet convinced about the positive potential of globalisation.

When China's example is mentioned, the typical Indian response is to dismiss it away saying that a non-democratic society like China can better control the negative fallout of globalisation and is therefore less worried. To compete in the global economy, India requires to be more disciplined and efficient, it will have to curtail workers' rights but will not be able to erect barriers against western cultural invasion. China does all this which is why it worries less about globalisation.

Mr. Lu responded to that simplistic view in a very clever Chinese manner. There are winners and losers in China too, he said. Their not being a democracy is not what helps them gain from globalisation. It is just that they are learning to compete, to be more efficient. Globalisation requires countries to be more competitive.

Is the Indian diffidence borne of a conviction that we cannot compete or is it that we find it convenient to blame the new 'foreign hand' of globalisation for all our faults? If we continue to take this ostrich-like attitude, will we ever be ready to compete. Becoming competitive is necessary, both to deal with the threats posed by globalisation as well as to derive the opportunities offered. Is India ready? It seems not.

The Delhi dialogue must worry policy makers. As a nation of a billion people, as the home to a global Indian diaspora, as home to so many global religions and ideas, cuisines and cultures, India is destined to be more globalised. Yet, a representative group of Indian opinion and policy makers seems still afraid of globalisation.

Sizing up the competition

LIKE many Indians who were deeply disappointed at *Lagaan* missing the Oscars so were we at *The Financial Express*. However, a colleague raised a pertinent question at our daily editorial meeting. How many of us were familiar with the competition that *Lagaan* was up against? None of us had the opportunity to view *No Man's Land* or *Amelie*, nor any of the other films nominated for the Best Foreign Feature Film award. So what was our disappointment based on? Sheer patriotism and affection for the likeable Aamir Khan! It was clearly not based on any informed judgement about whether *Lagaan* stood a chance given the quality of the competing movies.

Every 18-year old entering an Indian Institute of Technology starts, from day one, finding out what (s)he must do to prepare for competitive examinations to gain admission to one or another university in the United States. Notes are exchanged about GRE tests, model question papers are attempted and the seniors tell their juniors what the nature of the competition they are up against is like and what it'll take to make it. By the time each student is applying for admission (s)he has a good idea of the competition (s)he's up against and where (s)he stands with respect to it. It is in the nature of such tests of excellence that those competing familiarise themselves with the nature of the competition. When they don't make it, they are of course disappointed as indeed are their families and friends. But at least they knew what they were up against.

Surely Aamir Khan must have done his homework and he must have had an idea of the competition he was up against. There was a telling statement made by one of his team members who was watching the awards ceremony on television in Mumbai. Asked by a reporter why he was in Mumbai and not in the US, the *Lagaan* team member said, "We wanted to go, but Aamir suggested we stay back here. He must have his reasons for advising us so." Clearly Mr. Khan must have known that *Lagaan* was unlikely to make it. Because, like all good professionals he must have sized up the competition and come to a judgement that the odds were not in favour of his film.

But how could any one of us have come to any judgement on that question? No film distributor in India thought it fit to screen the competing films so that Indian viewers could acquire an objective assessment for themselves as to the nature of competition *Lagaan* was up against. Worse still, no one in the media, print or electronic, cared to tell us in advance anything at all about *No Man's Land* or any other foreign feature film. None of our film critics had viewed the competition, none of our media brought home to us international opinion about the competition. Yes, we managed to see some of the Hollywood films competing this year since the commercial circuit saw a market for these, but the non-Hollywood films never made it.

The first step to becoming competitive is to get an objective assessment of the nature of competition. In any given market or industry, firms, producers, individuals are likely to be no more competitive than what is required by competition. This is the central idea behind trade liberalisation. It widens the market and increases competition and forces players in any given product or service line to benchmark themselves against the most competitive player and become more efficient, productive, cost-effective, in short, more competitive. This is as true in the manufacture of a car or a shirt as it is in the cultivation of tea or coconuts as it, indeed, is in artistic endeavours such as film making.

That is why people like Jawaharlal Nehru and Indira Gandhi thought up devices like international trade fairs and film festivals.

Since India was still relatively insulated from external competition and influence, one way of helping Indians benchmark themselves against global competition was to bring that competition home, in controlled doses, so that people saw what the world was doing and learnt to do things as well. International trade fairs and film festivals were the window to the world in an era of inward-oriented development. In the more globalised and open economic system we run today, there are more ways of finding out what kind of competition we are up against. The myopic benchmark themselves only against the immediate competition they face in the market they presently occupy, the foresighted benchmark themselves against potential competition in potential markets. If Aamir Khan had aimed only for Screen or Filmfare awards, his effort would have been so circumscribed. If he had dreamt of an Oscar before making the film, he would have benchmarked his production against what the global market has on offer. The key is benchmarking for future competition, not the existing one. How many Indian companies do that?

Indian professionals have come to do that for many generations now since the Indian middle class has aspired for professional avenues worldwide. Engineers, medical doctors, economists, computer professionals, scientists have sought admission abroad at the world's best universities. They have sought jobs abroad in the world's best institutions and companies. Indian firms have only recently started taking on global competition. This has been true for much of the 20th century. Even during British rule, students were exposed to international competition by having to take European standard examinations to enter certain professions including the upper echelons of governmental service in the British *Raj*. But Indian businesses were granted protection in industries they saw an opportunity in, namely, textiles and sugar. Only the brave entered unprotected businesses and took on European competition on home turf.

After Independence, the middle class professionals continued to seek pastures abroad and test their skills against international standards. But much of Indian business preferred the comfort of sheltered existence, shying away from global competition and markets. Even today, it is in areas like information technology, gems and jewellery and handicrafts that skilled professionals are willing to globally compete and acquire a market share. In manufacturing and commodities we still shy away from the big bad world of global competition.

Doing our own thing

SOMETIME in the mid-nineties, film maker Kumar Shahani came to see me to urge me to write an editorial against an attempt by the United States of America to bring global trade in cinema under the aegis of the World Trade Organization. "I have just returned from Paris," Shahani told me, "and the French are very worried about American cultural hegemony. Free trade in cinema will mean the global domination of Hollywood. India must join France in opposing this."

I reflected on Shahani's concerns and researched the matter and, after a few days, proceeded to write an editorial comment that would not have pleased him. The French film industry may feel threatened by Hollywood, I conceded, but Indian film makers must seek free international trade in cinema. Given the global dispersion of the Indian diaspora and the cross-cultural appeal of Indian cinema in large parts of Africa and Asia, the Indian film industry will benefit from open market access and a multilateral regime in cinema trade.

European arguments against American dominance are always appealing but India, like China or any large civilisational entity, must take an independent view of global developments. Those who lament alleged Indian equivocation on US invasion of Iraq must recall that on similar occasions in the past, be it the Soviet invasion of Hungary (1956), Czechoslovakia (1968) and Afghanistan (1979) or US aggression in Vietnam and Latin America, successive Indian governments have taken ambivalent postures in public, unless

India's vital national interests were involved, as when China invaded Vietnam (1979).

Indian ambivalence, sometimes couched in non-aligned rhetoric, was always on account of the fact that each government of the day gave priority to national interest, seeking diplomatic space to pursue the agenda of national economic development. As so many political economists have written over the years, the bipolarity of the Cold War era gave developing countries like India space in which to focus on national development. Diplomatic postures on international events were less often based on universal principles and more often meant to secure a wider margin for policy manoeuvre.

As much was conceded by non-other than the *guru* of realism Henry Kissinger who told an Indian audience once how he was summoned by US President John Kennedy to the White House to explain a particular Indian position and he told Kennedy that he thought a US president would do exactly what the Indian prime minister was doing, pursuing national interest. Kissinger repeated this analysis to President Clinton when India went nuclear and said the Indian prime minister was doing what he had to, while the US president had to do what he had to!

Grandstanding in the United Nations and empty pulpitry is not going to alter the logic of recent global developments. The US has emerged as the world's most powerful military, economic, scientific, technological and cultural power that is also resource rich and has solved the problem of population size through a skill-based immigration policy aimed at attracting the best and brightest from across the world with a capacity to absorb them socially with a policy of multiculturalism. Europe has been unable to cope on all these counts.

Never before in history has one nation combined all the attributes of power. But my *guru* in strategic policy, K. Subrahmanyam, the Bhishmapithamaha of the Indian strategic policy community, adds a caveat. It is true that the US combines all aspects of power, he says, but it has not and no nation has yet acquired a monopoly on wisdom! What the US lacks is the wisdom to deploy its power, and that is manifest in recent events. In this lies hope for others. Indeed, every empire has crumbled due to a paucity of wisdom within rather than the unity of opposition without.

We may lack many attributes of power but mercifully our political leadership has so far demonstrated wisdom in dealing with external challenges. Even in the present international crisis we have pursued a considered and careful strategy that should serve our national interest well. One often wishes equal wisdom is summoned in dealing with challenges at home.

Wisdom we have, and perhaps more than some others. However, our weakness remains in our inability to as yet acquire the other facets of power, especially economic. Therein lies the challenge for India.

Irrespective of the military and political outcome of the Iraq war, the US will remain the world's most powerful nation for some time to come. The only nations that will be able to challenge its supremacy will be those who are able to acquire these various facets of power. A multipolar world cannot be built on rhetoric at the UN or by sloganeering against the US. The transition from a unipolar world to a multipolar one will be based on the greater regional dispersal of the attributes of modern power. The question for us is what are we doing to acquire these attributes? Economic and human development, scientific and technological capability, industrial competitiveness, cultural liberalism and multicultural politics, an open and internally stable and free society.

It is only when other nations acquire these attributes of American power that US supremacy will be weakened and the world will be truly multipolar. We must stop worrying about whether the world will be unipolar or multipolar as a consequence of US unilateralism today. Irrespective of the global balance of power, India's real challenge and opportunity remains at home.

Accelerated economic development, within the framework of a liberal political system, an open society that fosters the growth of knowledge-based development, and the ability of the government to raise the financial resources needed to invest in economic capabilities and infrastructure and, at the same time, in defence and military power. Such is the foundation on which individual nations can enable the emergence of a multipolar world. Raving and ranting against Pax Americana isn't going to help! Consider why a veto power like China remains so coy abroad and is busy at home pushing for more economic growth!

A Jaswant Singh doctrine on foreign aid

DENMARK'S decision finally did it. It happened five summers ago. India went nuclear and Denmark cut off aid. Of course, so did the United States and Japan. But, Denmark? Hello, can you find it on the map for us? From the adrenalin that was then generated came the decision to reduce dependence on external aid. Five years later a proud Jaswant Singh, Union finance minister, has let it be known that Denmark can now keep its money or give it to someone more in need!

Not just Denmark, but also the Netherlands, France, Canada, Sweden, Norway, Italy, Belgium, Austria, Spain, Switzerland, Saudi Arabia, Australia, Czech and Slovak republics. Not all of them had imposed sanctions in 1998, hence it would be wrong to suggest that there is a common diplomatic message to everyone. There is, of course, a common economic message. India does not need aid in driblets. Not worth the diplomatic and administrative cost. So if the sums are not large enough, then may be there are other more needy countries that can be helped, thank you.

A sensible policy, implemented ham-handedly by officials who seemed to have a chip on their shoulder when dealing with donors. Some Europeans are also upset that smaller donors like the US and Russia have not been touched, because they are bigger powers, while smaller nations that are bigger donors have been shown the door. But this avoidable diplomatic *faux pas* should not divert our attention from the significance of what has happened this week.

India has implemented a new policy on external aid first articulated by Mr. Jaswant Singh in his budget speech this year.

Mr. Singh had then said, "While being grateful to all our development partners of the past, I wish to announce that the Government of India would now prefer to provide relief to certain bilateral partners, with smaller assistance packages, so that their resources can be transferred to specified non-governmental organisations (NGOs) in greater need of official development assistance. The current agreed programmes will, however, continue and reach their completion. Of course, there will be no more 'tied aid' any longer."

India did expect the US and Japan to impose economic sanctions in response to nuclear tests. The homework had been done even in 1995 as to what nuclear tests would cost in economic terms. So when the US and Japan imposed sanctions in May 1998 in response to Pokhran-II, nobody was really surprised. But Denmark? And that too some paltry $28 million? Surely, national security was worth more than that.

And so the decision was taken that India must reduce its dependence on aid. For over four decades accepting foreign aid had become a habit. Plan models had been built to show why we needed aid. Accelerated economic growth required investment which required financial resources. There were two 'gaps' that had to be bridged, a domestic savings gap and an external foreign exchange gap. Aid was needed to bridge this gap.

Aid never comes easy. It always comes with conditionalities and the sufferance it entails is never liked. Sometimes, some countries are brazen in pushing their own agendas along with aid; it is tied to policy, it is tied to imports, to sermons and to the use of favoured consultants. Yet, aid is useful because it is low cost assistance.

The habit had its pleasures. Officials negotiating aid agreements would have to travel to cooler capitals in summer. The Aid India Consortium met annually in Paris when Delhi was hell on earth. Sometime in the mid-1990s, the French lost interest and the consortium, after renaming itself as the India Development Forum to indulge a newly liberalising India, moved to Tokyo.

As Montek Singh Ahluwalia once put it to this writer explaining the relevance of aid, "after accounting for trade and investment flows, we still have a financing gap and aid helps bridge that gap." Indeed, even today there is a resource gap that multilateral and bilateral assistance helps bridge. However, since the money comes at a cost and still comes with advice and entreaties to consent, a view has been taken that if one has to suck there better be enough juice!

While winding up small aid programmes and diverting such sums to NGOs, who often do better work than government agencies, is good policy, India cannot still afford to completely stop aid. Home to the world's largest number of poor people, it will attract aid flows from richer countries and can make use of low cost resources. Moreover, several state governments find aid funds bring in the extra cash required to keep development programmes going when government revenues get used up just paying salaries.

The downside of this is that donor-funded projects secure precedence over locally-funded projects simply because aid money is readily available. The government's cash compulsions then come to drive its development agenda. To deal with this bias some donors are beginning to define their programmes within the perspective of the UN's Millennium Development Goals, working in tandem with local governments.

Thus, just as the government of India is reviewing its aid policy, even donors are reviewing their's. Britain's Department for International Development (DFID) has been reviewing its 'country assistance strategy' for India and asking questions about aid effectiveness. Should aid funds go to a central kitty and be disbursed by the central government or go directly to states or even local bodies? Should aid be given to the most deserving, in terms of their need, or to the most promising, in terms of their capability to benefit from it?

Having made up its mind on small donors *versus* the big, the government will now have to take a view on how the big must dispense their assistance. Whatever the strategy adopted, one thing should be clear to all—India will welcome aid that adequately impacts on development but is in no mood to cling on to funds that are costly to administer and come with sermons, especially on national security! That, in short, is the new Jaswant Singh doctrine on external aid.

23 COLUMN

India launches FTA spree before Cancun

FOLLOWING the laboriously arrived at Free Trade Agreement (FTA) with Sri Lanka three years ago, the Union commerce ministry has announced its intention to negotiate more FTAs and Preferential Trade Agreements (PTAs) with Mercosur (Argentina, Brazil, Paraguay and Uruguay), Egypt, Thailand and eventually the Association of South-East Asian Nations (ASEAN). A Comprehensive Economic Cooperation Agreement (CECA), that would include a PTA or an FTA, is being hammered out with Singapore. Agreements with Afghanistan, Bangladesh, Myanmar and South Africa and the Gulf States are in the pipeline.

A virtual FTA spree has been launched. This should not surprise anyone since the commerce ministry had underscored the relevance of FTAs/PTAs in its Medium Term Export Strategy, 2002-07, (MTES) published last January.

"Careful well thought out FTAs and PTAs are needed," observed the MTES, "Given the propensity observed by other trading nations in this regard. India's inability to create its own web of trade and economic relationships with strategic partners has been a weakness from the standpoint of securing increased export market access for India's goods and services."

According to the MTES, 'strategic FTAs' have to be forged based on certain 'objective' criteria. These are: (i) the possibility and impact of tariff reductions by India and the FTA partner; (ii) India's price competitiveness to export to the FTA partner and scope for exports; (iii) price competitiveness of the FTA partner in Indian market and impact on domestic production; (iv) scope for services exports particularly IT and IT-related; (v) scope for beneficial investment and joint ventures; (vi) complementarity in goods and services between the two countries; (vii) other aspects like political advantage, possibilities of joining a larger regional grouping like say the ASEAN by having an FTA with an ASEAN member country, etc; and (viii) potential exports by looking at the import basket of each country.

While the MTES states candidly that such FTAs will have to be planned taking into consideration both "economic and political interests of India. This also depends on the merits of each case and the extent of give and take that can take place", it is not clear what strategic thinking informs the current FTA spree. Sure, India's first priority have been such neighbours who are willing to enter into FTAs. Apart from Sri Lanka, Nepal and Bangladesh, this category includes trade partners in the wider neighbourhood like Thailand, Singapore and some of the Gulf States.

Further afar India has reached out to friends in the developing world like Brazil, Egypt and South Africa. If more of the Indian Ocean rim countries agree to such bilateral trade agreements, the Indian Ocean regional initiative could gather momentum. Going beyond the wider neighbourhood and the large developing economies, India has not yet reached out to any of the developed economies, even though the idea of an India-United States free trade agreement has been discussed time and again.

Apart from the MTES perspective on FTAs and PTAs, it appears something else may be driving the recent binge. There is a desire on the part of the commerce ministry to tie up with as many influential developing economies as possible in the run up to the World Trade Organization's ministerial meeting at Cancun, Mexico, in September.

The experience of Doha is writ large on the psyche of Indian negotiators. Even though commerce minister Murasoli Maran's brave stand against US and European Union bullying on the Doha Development Agenda won acclaim both at home and within the developing world, India was left standing alone towards the end as one developing country after another succumbed to trans-Atlantic pressure.

By signing up so many FTAs, India is not only ensuring market access in a clutch of developing country markets but is also reaching out to other regional groups like ASEAN, Mercosur, Sadec and so on. One should, however, not exaggerate the importance of such arrangements. While markets like Brazil, Singapore and Thailand are important in as much as they are growing and likely to grow, the prospects for market expansion in some of the other developing countries is rather limited.

Moreover, the US, EU, China and Japan will remain major markets that can only be penetrated through the WTO route. Hence, even as India lines up many FTAs and PTAs, it will need the support of multilateral discipline to retain access to global markets. Active engagement with the WTO is, therefore, essential.

While recognising this basic principle, and being prepared for negotiations at Cancun, there is no need for India to reveal its cards until much later in the game. Unless the EU is willing to concede ground on agricultural subsidies and the US on public health and trade-related intellectual property rights (TRIPs), there is no reason why we should make any concession that we are willing to make, public.

The Indian stance that it is willing to discuss some of the issues of interest to the developed world if they are willing to discuss movement of natural persons and such like issues is a legitimate one. Between now and September, alliances will have to be renewed between India and a range of other countries, both developed and developing, so that the apparent isolation at Doha is not repeated at Cancun.

Of course, there are many in India who really don't care about such isolation. This nationalistic streak in the political and official class has its uses but, in a world of greater inter-dependence, especially even between countries of the South and one's own neighbours, the principle of 'give and take' is an essential feature of trade negotiations.

With its almost exclusive focus on specific markets and products and on bilateral trade, the MTES does not set out a trade strategy within a multilateral perspective. Such a perspective must balance the bilateral and regional initiatives being taken, without diminishing the importance of FTAs and PTAs. This would be a strategy of walking on two legs, both regional/bilateral and multilateral. In both cases there will have to be 'give and take'. FTAs help develop the 'give and take' habit bilaterally so that one can do so multilaterally.

The business of foreign policy

LONG before Bollywood discovered young men from rural Punjab falling in love with 'persons of Indian origin' from London suburbs, Andhra Pradesh's Telugu film industry had made 'America Abbayi' (American Boy), and placed on record the state's 'people-to-people' relationship with the United States of America. Andhra Pradesh's US connection is visible and audible all over coastal Andhra, why even in backward Nalgonda, and not just in Cyberabad!

Walk through the villages of Krishna district when it is vacation time in Houston and San Jose and chances are you'll be hearing a lot of yankee twang and drawl and will be saying 'hi' to Patty Rao (*aka* A.V.V. Lakshmipathy Rao). No prizes for guessing what the foreign policy of Andhra Pradesh would be today. When the tobacco farmers of Guntur district earned in the millions exporting to the former Soviet Union, every tobacco-cultivating Kamma farmer was rushing to join the local communist party, contributing to the jibe that it had become a Kammanist Party! Today the Kammas are in IT and media and the US is second home.

So it was not surprising when a few years back the governor of the US state of California elaborated on a 'foreign policy' for his state and sent out an invitation to Andhra Pradesh chief minister Nara Chandrababu Naidu. The governor of California, he said, had to build relations with the leaders of many Asian nations and regions within nations, given the contribution they make to California's economy. Can the chief minister of Kerala afford to ignore India's relations with the Persian Gulf when the economy of his state is afloat largely on account of the remittances received from his kinsfolk in the region?

Continental economies cannot afford to have over-arching foreign policy objectives that ignore the specific interests of important regions. How regions impact on a national policy is a function of a variety of demographic and political factors. In a democracy, the sheer weight of electoral numbers acquires a relevance that non-democratic societies can afford to neglect. However, even non-democratic societies cannot ignore the weight of economic interests. Can China pursue a foreign policy that ignores the business and economic interests of its dynamic coastal regions? Hardly.

No government in New Delhi can, therefore, afford to pursue a foreign policy that does not take into account the economic interests of the growing regions and the globalising sectors. If the growing regions are also the more populous ones, as is the case with China, then there is a happy coincidence of interest between economic imperatives and political arithmetic. For example, if Andhra Pradesh had as many members in Parliament as Bihar, the Indian Parliament may have been more sensitive to the economic effects of a travel advisory from the United States.

A sharp fall in the number of persons travelling from the US to Andhra Pradesh and Karnataka, as we saw last year after the travel advisories were issued in the wake of fears about a war in the sub-continent, would hurt the regional economy of Hyderabad-Bangalore very differently from the way it would hurt that of Patna or Lucknow. But Patna and Lucknow have a bigger voice in the Indian Parliament than Hyderabad and Bangalore. The dynamics of democratic politics could impact on foreign policy quite differently from those of domestic business, if parliamentary numbers come from backward, inward-oriented economic regions, and globalisation is happening in regions that do not have enough MPs.

A country's strategic and foreign policy must, therefore, be sensitive to the economic interests of growing regions and sectors. How can any government in New Delhi ignore the statistics of foreign trade, investment, skill migration and inward-remittances in making foreign policy choices? If efforts to normalise Sino-Indian relations are finally bearing fruit, it is because both countries have acquired an economic stake in it for the first time. It is not emotion, history and geography alone that are shaping this bilateral relationship, as has been the case in the past, but economics.

It is of course possible to view the economic impact on strategic and foreign policy purely passively, with business interests being viewed as a 'compulsion', an unavoidable constraint. However, it is also possible to view business and economics from an activist perspective and utilise them as instruments of change, as drivers of policy. That is precisely what China did, when it consciously entered into an active trade and investment relationship with the US. It used economics as an instrument of foreign policy. It is entirely possible that it is trying to replicate this model with India by allowing benign bilateral business interests to overpower malign domestic political ones. It's a policy, India is beginning to adopt in dealing with her neighbours.

The Indian strategic and foreign policy establishment has been slow in recognising and then utilising the economic instrument in foreign policy. In the period 1992-98, economic factors came to play a more prominent role, even if they did not overwhelm all strategic policy decisions. For example, the decision not to sign up on the Comprehensive Test Ban Treaty, as indeed the decision on nuclear tests in 1998, was taken on the basis of largely strategic objectives, even though there were fears that there would be an economic price to pay.

The weight of economics in strategic and foreign policy receded with the re-assertion of traditional political concerns after the Kargil war. A pre-occupation with Pakistan and with terrorism has come to overwhelm strategic and foreign policy with economics taking a back-seat. The low point of this phase was the knee-jerk political response to Pakistan-induced terrorism post December 13. Even in the ongoing debate on sending Indian troops to Iraq, traditional political considerations have come to over shadow economic interests.

There is no denying the fact that India must always preserve the freedom to pursue an autonomous foreign policy, that we must have good relations with all our neighbours, with all major powers and with all our economic partners. However, there are times when a nation must make choices. The question is, what must inform that choice? Clearly, one's long-term economic interests must.

Slower track WTO *versus* fast track FTAs

CALLING for some tough talking at the Cancun ministerial meeting of the World Trade Organization a leading ideologue of the Swadeshi Jagran Manch, the protectionist lobby of the Sangh Parivar, S. Gurumurthy said, "India should consider walking out of the WTO and ought to pursue bilateral trade agreements." "China," Mr. Gurumurthy reportedly said, "entered the WTO after years of bilateral trade arrangements with the United States during which period it had emerged strong enough to face the world of multilateralism."

These ideas are so ill-informed that they would not normally merit an editorial response, but for the fact that they have been articulated by none other than Mr. Gurumurthy, a financial advisor who wields considerable influence in business, government and the media.

Consider the options before India. Assume Union commerce minister Arun Jaitley goes to Cancun and rejects all proposals for trade liberalisation on offer and declares India's exit from the WTO and returns home to pursue bilateral trade agreements. With whom would he do that? India's major trade partners, of course. Who are they? The United States, the European Union, People's Republic of China, including Hong Kong, members of the Association of South-East Asian Nations (ASEAN), Republic of Korea, Japan, Brazil, Mexico, South Africa, Israel, Russia and, our neighbours in South Asia. There are, of course the petroleum exporting countries of the Persian Gulf from whom we buy oil and to whom we send our skilled workers.

Together, these constitute the world that India mainly deals with in the sphere of trade in goods and services. Which country in this long list would agree to bilateral free trade arrangements with India that are less onerous in terms of the obligations for trade liberalisation than what India can hope to secure through the multilateral process in WTO? Perhaps Russia and some of our neighbours.

Almost everyone else is willing to move on a faster track, have already moved ahead of India. Moreover, the OECD economies account for almost 50 per cent of India's exports. Will any of them accept an FTA with India that is less demanding than the Doha Development Agenda? Never. More to the point, sustaining India's rapidly growing trade relationship with her Asian neighbours, including China, Japan, Korea and ASEAN members would require bilateral commitments that are more fast-paced than the WTO process.

Consider what is presently happening in the negotiations with Thailand for an FTA. Thailand is seeking tariff free access in the auto components market. Japanese automobile manufacturers with a production base in Thailand would immediately benefit from this since they can export inputs for their auto units in India out of Thailand. Auto companies that have established facilities in India like Tata Motor Co., Hyundai and TVS have objected. They want more time to be ready for zero tariffs. The WTO proposal for zero-for-zero tariffs in auto components proposes a 2015 date, while the India-Thailand FTA could come into effect by 2005. Which is the slow track?

Consider our FTAs closer home. We have an FTA with Sri Lanka, a weaker economy. Sri Lanka has lower tariffs than India and is willing to sign up on all Singapore issues at WTO. We want an FTA with Mercosur. Brazil and Argentina are a step ahead on almost all issues in the WTO. Finally, ASEAN. This week, India is hosting the India-ASEAN Business Summit. We are negotiating a Comprehensive Economic Cooperation Agreement with Singapore and hope to negotiate an FTA with ASEAN. Can that process be slower than WTO?

One of the SJM leaders held up the example of Malaysian President Mahathir Mohammed as a Third World hero in the WTO whom Mr. Jaitley must emulate at Cancun. "Look at Mahathir," the SJM leader reportedly said, "he stands up to the *gore log* (white people)." Really? So is that how the so-called Singapore issues got on to the WTO agenda? It was Malaysia that broke ranks at the Singapore ministerial in 1996 and enabled the Singapore issues to come on board the WTO agenda. Mr. Mahathir may rave and rant against the West but the West invests more in his country than ours. The SJM's racist reference to "gore log" is not only abhorrent and distasteful, it serves no national interest when much of our trade is with the western world.

More importantly, Malaysia is today complaining that India is not doing enough to promote bilateral trade by hurting its edible oil exports to India. Malaysia's trade minister told me at the London meeting of the Commonwealth Business Council in July that India was not doing enough to promote 'South-South' trade. Incidentally, this is a new issue in the WTO discourse. What are large developing economies, like India, doing for less developed and smaller developing economies. It is a question that is asked of us in South Asia by our neighbours. We talk of a South Asia FTA and we are unable to take on the competition from Sri Lanka and Bangladesh? Is this the 'Great Mother India' that SJM leaders and their ilk feel so patriotic about?

Let us not fool ourselves. The alternatives to the WTO are no better, either from an economic or a political viewpoint. They do not serve India's national security interests. The National Security Advisory Board of India considered this issue in great detail in the period 1998-2001 and came to the considered conclusion that a multilateral trade regime under the auspices of the WTO serves India's national interests better than the alternative of quitting the WTO and pursuing bilateral or regional FTAs.

Further, if there are any FTAs we should be aiming for, they should be with USA, EU and ASEAN—our major trade partners with whom a complementary 'win-win' trade relationship is possible. But they are all ahead of us on the WTO curve and are negotiating FTAs that include issues we are presently refusing to talk about in WTO. Hence, those who imagine that bilateral or regional FTAs are a convenient escape route from the obligations of a multilateral agreement at the WTO are living in a make-believe world. Nothing wrong with living in make-believe worlds, as long as national policies are not shaped in them!

Foreign trade is also about imports

WITH a pick up in economic growth, recent months have witnessed a surge in imports. Merchandise exports have, however, not done too well, growing at 10 per cent in the first half of 2003-04, in US dollar terms, compared to 18 per cent in the same period last year. By contrast, for the same period, imports rose faster at 21.4 per cent this year compared to 9.2 per cent last year.

More strikingly, non-oil imports increased by 28 per cent this April-September compared to 7.8 per cent same period last year. As a result, the overall trade deficit in April-September 2003 was twice as much as in the same period last year, that is, $ 7.1 bn compared to $ 3.5 bn. This has pushed the current account of the balance of payments into deficit, according to the Reserve Bank of India's Mid-term Review (MTR). Though this is offset to a large extent by private transfers and capital inflows in the form of foreign investment, NRI deposits and external loans.

While service exports are believed to be growing, there are no reliable estimates of this growth. Moreover, even if service exports are growing, a deceleration of merchandise exports is not good news at a time when expectations are that global oil prices may firm up in coming months and commodity prices are also trending upward. The acceleration of growth in India is bound to further increase both oil and non-oil import demand. Finally, the time has come for India to further reduce import tariffs. While that in itself could fuel import demand, any further appreciation of the rupee could make imports even more attractive. Hence, one cannot be too blasé about export growth deceleration.

Given the trade-off between the interests of exporters and importers and the preference for the extant regime of managed float for the rupee, neither the RBI nor the government is willing to use the exchange rate as an instrument of policy in dealing with either the issue of burgeoning foreign exchange reserves or slow export growth. In an earlier era, policy makers may have been tempted to encourage the depreciation of the rupee both to encourage exports and discourage imports. Those days are behind us.

On the other hand, a compelling case has been made by some corporates that to further stimulate investment demand and fuel industrial growth, the government ought to engineer a steeper appreciation of the rupee. This too the government is unlikely to find an attractive option, especially when export growth has decelerated.

Echoing the MTR's concerns, the Mid-Year Review, 2003-04 (MYR) of the Union finance ministry also observes that, "The turnaround in the current account from a surplus to a deficit, and the deceleration in export growth, in recent months in particular, is a source of concern. Simply trying to relate the export growth deceleration to the real effective appreciation of the rupee misses out on the important issues of productivity growth and the benefits of a market-determined floating exchange rate regime."

MYR has in fact advocated reduction of tariffs as a preferred option to deal with these challenges on the external front. "Reducing import tariffs since 1991 has served the country well in terms of higher growth and greater export vibrancy. Given the comfortable foreign exchange reserves, and the incipient upward pressure on the rupee, there is need to go forward towards the already announced alignment of tariff structure with ASEAN countries. Given the disappointment from the latest round of multilateral trade negotiations, this will also be important for moving towards promising regional trade agreements with ASEAN as well as with SAPTA countries."

Today, catching up with ASEAN is an imperative for both economic and geo-political reasons. To pursue closer economic and strategic engagement with ASEAN and other Asian economies we will require to reduce import tariffs, which are among the highest even in developing Asia and certainly the highest among the industrialising G-20 countries. Both trade and strategic policy makers have come to realise not only that trade is a 'two-way street', but also that imports are even more important than exports in building a strong external profile for the country.

To be a 'major power' today, implies a country must also be a 'trade power'. However, to be a 'trade power' it is not sufficient to be an 'export power'. It is also necessary, indeed imperative, to be an 'import power'. Look at China. Till recently, the world viewed China merely as an 'export power', just because China sucked away the export business of South-East and East Asia with the United States and Europe, using mercantilist policies, and became an export platform for multinational companies.

More recently, however, the world economy has come to recognise the power of China's import demand. According to Nicholas Lardy, a China expert at Washington DC's Institute for International Economics, China's import ratio, imports to national income, has increased from about 15 per cent in 1990 to 25 per cent in 2002. India's import ratio last year was about 13 per cent. Of course, this compares with a ratio of 14 per cent for the US and a mere 8 per cent for Japan.

There is renewed buoyancy in global non-oil commodities trade, after decades of depression, thanks to China's increased import demand for a range of commodities, from food to steel. Several export-oriented economies are locking themselves into China's market where demand is expected to grow in the foreseeable future. India too has benefited from China's import demand and fears of being flooded by cheap Chinese exports have given way to hopes of riding the import demand wave in China.

India will have to become more open to non-oil imports, even if presently there are concerns about a worsening trade deficit, to be able to create relationships of inter-dependence with other developing countries and the developed world. Industry must, therefore, be prepared for tariff cuts in the next budget. Along with tariff cuts, the government must also reduce non-tariff barriers, a bug bear with some of our smaller neighbours. The share of both exports and imports in national income will have to go up as economic growth picks up and India emerges a bigger economic and strategic player on the world stage.

An open market and an open society

OPINION is free. Facts, as we have been taught, are sacred. So, was the United States Trade Representative, Robert Zoellick, factually correct when he alleged that India is among the world's most closed economies? Did the new US ambassador in New Delhi merely echo Mr. Zoellick's opinion or was his opinion based on facts?

There are, of course, different measures of how open or closed an economy is. Trade economists look at tariffs, at specific and *ad valorem* duties, at countervailing duties, at tariff peaks and escalation, at bound and actual rates, at non-tariff barriers, and these come in all shapes and sizes, to determine how open an economy really is.

Consider one simple rule of thumb indicator, the actual duties collected on actual imports as a share of total import value. India's average collection rate (inclusive of all duties like CVD) is now around 16 per cent. This compares quite favourably with countries at India's level of development.

Consider another number. The share of imports in gross domestic product (GDP). This is a number that really comes out of the wash. It tells you how successful foreign exporters of goods and services have been in penetrating all existing tariff and non-tariff barriers and in actually getting into the domestic market.

The data suggests that when compared to the 'big trading powers', the US, European Union and Japan, India is not any more closed. China, with its huge export-based import economy is in a different league altogether. The share of merchandise imports to GDP in 2001 was 11.6 per cent for the US and 8.2 per cent for Japan, compared to 10.6 per cent for India.

In the case of EU-15, the aggregate number is an impressive 27.7 per cent, but if we exclude intra-EU trade, what EU members import from each other, and only look at imports into EU member countries from 'rest of the world', then for the EU-15 this is a lowly number of 10.8 per cent, almost on par with India.

Consider the import trade in goods and commercial services, as reported by the WTO. Here, we were unable to estimate the non-EU services imports into EU because we couldn't get hold of that data, so we only look at aggregate data. Here too, India compares favourably with the big three. Share of import of goods and services in GDP is 15.5 per cent for India, higher than the 13.2 per cent for US. Interestingly, services imports constitute a larger share of imports for India compared to US or China, suggesting our greater openness on the services front.

In fact, the laggard in both goods and services areas is Japan. Japan remains one of the 'most closed' economies of the world, and given its level of development and per capita income, it is shockingly protectionist. India hardly is by comparison. What is more, the import elasticity of growth for India has actually gone up and more than doubled from 0.7 in 1980-90 to 1.6 in 1991-2000.

We are not suggesting that India has no pending agenda of trade liberalisation. Indeed, both the Union finance minister and the Union commerce minister have repeatedly affirmed their commitment to continued trade liberalisation. To reducing India's peak and average tariffs to enable India to reach 'ASEAN levels' of tariffs. There is a commitment to enhance trade facilitation and to conform to all existing WTO obligations. India has been seeking to increase the imports to GDP ratio to be able to also increase its exports to GDP ratio. The central government and the central bank have not halted or reversed the appreciation of the rupee in recent months even though this may be hurting export growth and encouraging imports.

Those who allege India is a 'closed economy', must also consider our openness on a wider front. India is remarkably open in the area of services imports, especially in the import of entertainment and information software, and in the in-migration of labour. As an 'open society' it has pursued an open skies policy in satellite television and allowed foreign media to enter this country.

If there is an area where we have become needlessly defensive and increasingly closed it is the area of research and higher education. And no prizes for naming the villain! Once again it is that 'Stalinist control freak', the Union minister for human resources development Murli Manohar Joshi. All the goodwill India has gained abroad for becoming economically more open is being dissipated by our becoming academically more closed to outsiders.

Even as thousands of Indians flee to foreign universities and Indian researchers win fellowships to pursue advanced research abroad, foreigners wanting to come to India to study or do research are subject to the most humiliating wait by the tedious visa procedure and scrutiny process put in place by the HRD ministry in active collaboration with the Union home ministry.

I was recently told by a US scholar how much easier it is for him to travel to 'communist China' to do research than to travel to 'democratic India'. What is worse, the sentiment was echoed by a visiting Chinese scholar who came to see me this week and told me it took him all of 24 hours to get a visa for research work in the US and Japan, while it took him three months to get a visa to India! Three months! Because Mr. Joshi's thought police have to give their approval! Democratic India deserves better. We are an open economy and an open society, have been so for all known history, and can afford to be more so without being afraid.

How Asian is India?

GEOGRAPHICALLY, the Republic of India lies in the belly of Asia. It is a nation of continental dimensions with civilisational attributes. Its western reaches touch Central Asia and its eastern reaches lie close to China in the north-east and the Malacca Straits in the south-east. India's maritime neighbours include the states of the Persian Gulf and the nations of Indo-China.

India is the place of origin of Asia's most widely practiced religions, Buddhism and Hinduism, and has for centuries also been home to the world's other two great religions, Islam and Christianity. Christianity came to India directly from West Asia, crossing the Arabian Sea, long before Europeans set foot on the subcontinent. Buddhism travelled *via* Afghanistan and Central Asia into China and Mongolia, leaving behind historic monuments in Bamiyan and Bokhara, in Samarkhand and Sinkiang. Hinduism spread across the Himalayan mountains and the plains below and into peninsular India, from where it set sail into Java, Sumatra, Indonesia and the kingdoms of Indo-China. Hindu temples are found even to this day in Vietnam. Islam spread across many parts of South-East Asia from India. India's cultural imprint is visible all over Asia.

So the question in civilisation terms, if one is permitted journalistic licence, is not 'how Asian is India?' but 'how Indian is Asia?' But who cares for history and civilisation? This is the age of economics and of per capita income. Evaluated against the score of economic growth and trade openness, India lies in the penumbra of the Asia that North America discovered after World War II and integrated into its own economic growth process. It is for this reason that 'Asia' for many in the Americas, has come to mean East and South-East Asia.

India has, for the worshippers of the market, been priced out of Asia. Having been woken up by Asia, when Japan bombed Pearl Harbour off its Pacific coast, and finding so many Chinese, Japanese and Koreans on its west coast, the United States quite understandably began its discovery of Asia from the east. Never mind that Europe, in the form of Christopher Columbus, stumbled upon America in search of India. The latter remained a distant land for the Yankee, Europe's 'Far East' was America's 'Near East', its Asia.

Geography

Geography textbooks are quite clear about where India lies. Dudley Stamp, the distinguished Australian geographer, reminds us of what European geographers have suggested for a long time, namely that the world is divided into seven continents—Europe, North and South America, Asia, Australasia (including the islands of the Pacific), Africa and Antarctica. The geographer's Asia begins near Istanbul and ends near Hokkaido. It stretches across West Asia, Central Asia, Eurasia, the Indian sub-continent ('South Asia' is an Americanism, perhaps invented in the US State Department after World War II), through China and 'Indo-China' (mark the concept) all the way to Japan.

The French historian Fernand Braudel refers to the 'Malacca peninsula' (present-day Malaysia, Thailand and Singapore) and the islands of Java and Sumatra as the "centre of gravity of the Far East".[1] Add to this region Vietnam, Laos and Cambodia, and you get what Stamp and many other geographers have for long called "Indo-China". Why Indo-China? Therein lies the answer to the question of the Asianness of India. India and China were the

---

1. F. Braudel, *Civilization and Capitalism, 15th-18th Century: The Perspective of the World,* Collins/Fontana Press, 1988.

dominant civilisation entities of Asia impacting on the culture and life of the people of this region for centuries. Note the origin of the name 'Indonesia' itself. Little wonder then that this region is called Indo-China. It is the heart of Asia, of which China is the expansive chest and India the enormous belly. But the purely geographical basis of India's Asianness is all too evident to anyone who looks at a map.

History and politics

To be sure, though, the geographical aspect of India's Asianness is not purely cartographic. It is both geopolitical and geoeconomic. History bears witness. Consider again Braudel's reflections, "The Far East taken as a whole, consisted of three gigantic world economies—Islam, overlooking the Indian Ocean from the Red Sea and the Persian Gulf, and controlling the endless chain of deserts stretching across Asia from Arabia to China; India, whose influence extended throughout the Indian Ocean, both East and West of Cape Comorin; and China, at once a great territorial power—striking deep into the heart of Asia—and a maritime force, controlling the seas and countries bordering the Pacific. And so it had been for many hundreds of years."

Braudel notes the depth of India's economic integration with Asia and its central position in the history and politics of the continent thus, "The relationship between these huge areas was the result of a series of pendulum movements of greater or lesser strength, either side of the centrally positioned Indian subcontinent. The swing might benefit first the East then the West, redistributing functions, power and political or economic advance. Through all these vicissitudes, however, India maintained her central position— her merchants in Gujarat and on the Malabar or Coromandel coasts prevailed for centuries on end against their many competitors—the Arab traders of the Red Sea, the Persian merchants of the Gulf, or the Chinese merchants familiar with the Indonesian seas."

Having conducted his monumental and comprehensive survey of world capitalism, Braudel had no doubt at all in his mind that India was an integral part of the 'super world economy' of Asia.

However, Braudel also reminds us that it was with the arrival of the Europeans as a maritime force into the waters of the Indian Ocean that India "gradually lost control of the 'country trade' routes throughout Asia".

The conquest of India by Europe started a process that disrupted the links between the sub-continent and the rest of Asia. The bountiful sub-continental economy and its prosperous trade was disconnected from ancient and long-standing links with West and Central Asia, China and Indo-China and linked to Europe and to the wider British Empire. Where India's Asian links were kept alive it was more to destroy Britain's rivals in Asia rather than strengthen India's links with the mother continent. Consider for instance the opium trade with China. Here India was used as a springboard for the conquest of the Chinese market. For centuries India and China had lived as friendly neighbours. There is no recorded history of conflict between any Indian kingdom and the Empire of China. It is the British who sowed the seeds of conflict. The same was the case with Indo-China. Historically, India's links with this region were benign. Even when Hinduism, Buddhism and later Islam spread to this region the process was largely benign, with rarely any conquest and conflict.

However, the colonial control of the 'spice route', the desire to establish entrepots and commercial monopolies, created relationships of inequity in the region that to this day influence Indo-China's attitudes toward India and Indians in the region.

In sum, India's links with Asia to its east were disrupted for the first time in history by the arrival of Europeans in the region. Europe pursues much the same policy by its not-so-subtle policy of 'divide and engage' when the European Union creates a forum with the Association of South-East Asian Nations (ASEAN) and dubs it a "Europe-Asia" forum and India is kept out. How can 'Europe' engage 'Asia' without India's participation? Until even half a century ago this would have been unthinkable—in India, in rest of Asia and the whole of Europe.

The most important factor contributing to this disruption in the second half of the 20th century was the Cold War. Asia to India's east was drawn deeply into the Cold War and India's 'non-aligned' status contributed to a weakening of her political links with Asia. This was not the case to begin with. Indeed, in the 1950s India, under Jawaharlal Nehru's leadership, and Indonesia, under Sukarno's leadership, actively pursued the idea of a new Asia. The Asian Relations Conference was part of this attempt to forge a new post-colonial Asian identity. Nehru was obsessed by India's Asian identity and Indo-China's Indian roots. The politics of the Cold War, on the one hand, and India's own 'inward-looking' model of industrial development, weakened India's interface with much of Asia.

Economics

It is the economic dimension that, in the final analysis, appears overwhelmingly to influence post-World War II perceptions of India's Asianness. Four distinct factors have shaped this perception.

First, after World War II the United States established strategic relations with Japan and South Korea and with some South-East Asian nations such as the Philippines, thereby emerging as an Asian strategic power. Since India was not part of this anti-communist alliance and opted to remain 'non-aligned' in the Cold War, US relations with East and South-East Asia accelerated at a pace that diminished India's profile in North America. Europe's preoccupations with its own post-war reconstruction, its focus on the trans-Atlantic relationship, the impact of the Cold War on Western European relations with Asian nations and the process of de-colonisation together combined to reduce Europe's interest in the Indian subcontinent.

Second, the outward orientation of South-East Asian economies, their decision to pursue an export-oriented growth strategy and their dependence on Western markets increased the interaction between the ASEAN member nations and the trans-Atlantic economies.

Third, the 'new relationship' between China and the United States and the early pursuit of outward-oriented industrial development by China, after 1978, increased the interaction between China and the trans-Atlantic, especially North American nations.

Finally, India's pursuit of an inward-looking model of import-substituting industrialisation reduced its own interaction with the industrial market economies of Western Europe and North America.

It is obvious that the Cold War was an important element influencing the first three factors above, and India's self-imposed isolation was a second element. India's share of world trade was 2 per cent in the 1950s and declined to 0.5 per cent by the 1980s. Indeed, as late as 1975 India and China had similar shares of world trade but by 1995 India had a share of 0.7 per cent while China's share was close to 4 per cent. Asia to India's east witnessed a similar expansion in its share of world trade through the 1980s and 1990s until the Asian financial crisis in the late 1990s.

India's inward orientation and the small share of its exports in world trade, as well as the geopolitical and geoeconomic dimensions of the Cold War, reduced its profile in the West. Little wonder then that a new generation of post-war analysts in the West ask the historically ill-informed question whether India is in fact an Asian power. We are as Asian as China, Japan, Korea, Indonesia, Malaysia and Iran. But it is our economic isolationism of the post-war period that has diminished our visibility until recently.

The 1990s were a turning point. Not only did the Cold War cease to shape Western attitudes about India, but also our own increased outward orientation has helped to reduce our marginalisation. India's 'new economic policies' of the 1990s, emphasising greater trade and investment liberalisation, and the high-profile migration of skilled Indian workers and professionals to the West, especially North America, have helped increase India's economic and cultural profile abroad. In short, India's increased globalisation is shaping Western perceptions about her once again.

Conclusion

We shall be indiscreet and also suggest that another factor has forced the West to rediscover India's Asianness. This is the emergence of China as a strategic competitor to the West. China's impressive economic performance in the 1990s and the momentum its economy has gained have woken up the West to the possibility of a new 'superpower' taking shape in Asia. China has begun to impact on the politics and economics of almost all its neighbours, spread across the length and breadth of the Asian land mass. From Iran, Pakistan and Central Asia to the west, Russia and Mongolia in the north-west, to the countries of ASEAN in the south and Japan and Korea in the east, China is today a major strategic and economic player. Both North America and Western Europe appear concerned by China's relentless pursuit of economic growth and power and its rising military profile.

If the trans-Atlantic nations persist with their myopic post-war and Cold War view of Asia, then it would seem that the whole of Asia has been already linked to the growth engine of the Chinese economy and has come into the shadow of China's power and influence. Perhaps for this reason there is now a willingness to recognise that Asia is larger than China and its southern and eastern neighbours. That Asia includes another nation of a billion people, a nation that has lived as an equal with China for at least 3,000 years of recorded history. India and China have been civilisation entities and peaceful neighbours through all recorded history. Buddhism travelled to China from India and communism travelled from China to India. Today, China stands as a self-confident power, almost a superpower, but through all history we were equals. We were Asian; we were as a civilisation Asian.

India is Asian but is also rediscovering her Asianness. In 1992, the government of P.V. Narasimha Rao launched a policy of greater economic and political engagement with East and South-East Asia dubbed the "Look East Policy". This has unleashed renewed interest in India's historical and civilisational links with Asia, but it has also helped promote greater economic relations today.

The economic links with ASEAN, Japan and South Korea have been on the increase. India's trade with Asia has grown faster than its trade with the rest of the world over the past decade. South Korea emerged as the fastest-growing source of foreign direct investment into India in the late 1990s. India's European links, forged in the era of colonialism, are fading. It is with the United States and with Asia that India is increasingly interacting. Indian software professionals are eager to pursue a professional life in North America or in developed Asia and Australia. There are no takers for continental Europe. Europe must ponder this trend and ask itself why it has allowed this to happen.

India's Asianness is no longer merely historical or geographic— it is increasingly re-acquiring an economic content, restoring the kind of relationship that, according to Braudel, the Europeans encountered when they first arrived in the waters of the Indian Ocean, the only ocean named after a people and which washes the southern shores of Asia.

India and ASEAN

The emerging economic relationship towards a Bay of Bengal community

THE 'Asian economic miracle' of the 1980s and the early 1990s, the impressive performance of South-East Asia both in terms of economic growth and human development, the end of the Cold War, China's emergence as a major military and economic power in Asia, and India's increasingly outward-oriented economic policy have all combined to mark a new phase in India's relations with Asia to her east. India unveiled a 'Look East' policy of befriending her Asian neighbours, particularly the member countries of the Association of South-East Asian Nations (ASEAN) in the early 1990s, after having launched a new phase in its own economic development with a more open trade and investment regime. India's renewed interest in closer economic and political relations with her south-East Asian neighbours was reciprocated by many of them who seemed to be pursuing an unstated 'Look West' policy of increasing their interaction with India. The perceptible increase in two-way trade and the flow of tourist and business traffic between India and ASEAN countries was paralleled by increasing official interaction and India's membership of the ASEAN Regional Forum (ARF) and it securing a 'dialogue partner' status in ASEAN.

Notwithstanding the recent Asian economic crisis, India and ASEAN have tried to restore momentum to this new relationship, which is now reflected in the fact that in 1999 India's trade with

ASEAN has once again increased at a faster pace than her trade with other regions of the world. More recently, India has shown keen interest in the emergence of a new regional association, BIMSTEC (Bangladesh, India, Myanmar, Sri Lanka and Thailand Economic Coalition), which is likely to emerge as a bridge between South-Asia and South-East Asia, between SAARC and ASEAN and, in particular between India and ASEAN. In pursuing its 'Look East' policy with renewed vigour, India is merely 're-discovering' an ancient link with the region.

Historical background and the evolution of India-ASEAN relations

India's links with the member countries of the Association of South-East Asian Nations (ASEAN) is ancient and civilisational. It is well known, for instance, that in Valmiki's *Ramayana* there are references to places identified as China, Java and Sumatra as likely places of Goddess Sita's concealment.[1] Maritime historians have found evidence of Indian interaction with societies spanning the entire Indian Ocean rim well into 1000 B.C. and earlier.[2] The kingdoms of the Andhra and Orissa coasts were active in promoting maritime contact with the people of Indo-China and the interest shown by the Mauryas and Andhras encouraged emigration to the Indonesian Archipelago and other surrounding islands.[3]

It is believed that about 600 A.D. the Saka kings of Gujarat set sail and reached the west coast of Java. According to the distinguished naval historian, Rear Admiral Sridharan, "This was the first wave of emigrants from the west coast of India to have settled in Java and contributed in a large measure towards the spread of Indian art and culture."[4] There is evidence of intimate contacts between the Sailendras, who were the Hindu rulers of Malaya Peninsula and the Indonesian Archipelago, and the Palas of Bengal.

---

1. Quoted in K. Sridharan, *A Maritime History of India*, Publications Division, Ministry of Information and Broadcasting, Government of India, 1982.
2. *ibid.*, Chapters 1 & 2.
3. *ibid.*, p.27-28.
4. *ibid.*, p.31.

Both Dravidian and Aryan people have had contact with the people of the South-East Asian region. Of the many Indian dynasties which made contact with the region, the Kalinga dynasty played the most important role in promoting emigration to the region, particularly to Java and as early as 75 A.D. Historians believe this marks the beginning of 'Hindu' influence in the region. As Sridharan notes, "There is no doubt that from as back as 75 A.D. if not earlier, the Hindus began to make a descent on the Indonesian Archipelago and eventually left the imprint of Hindu civilisation, Indian art and architecture, Hindu and Buddhist religious customs and manners. The island of Bali shows that even to this day there exist visible signs of Hindu culture and civilisation."[5]

Buddhism also had an equal, in some places greater, impact. Indeed, in large parts of East and South-East Asia today it is Buddhism, which has left an even greater impression than Hinduism. It is clear that until the arrival of Arab traders in the Indian Ocean in the second century A.D. the Indian merchants held an unchallenged monopoly of overseas commerce in the Indian Ocean waters. Sridharan notes that:

"The takeover of trade from south Indian merchants by the Arab middlemen apparently came about at the end of the Chola period. So long as the Cholas wielded their naval power, the Arabs do not appear to have eventured to interfere. But the decline of the Chola power and decadence of the Sri Vijaya Empire had created a vacuum in overseas commerce and Arabs stepped in and their trade rivalry effectively kept the Chinese away from the Indian Ocean. With the passing away of the overseas trade to the Arabs there was little or no direct interest taken by Indians in overseas commerce and they were content to trade with the Arab intermediaries and agents who sailed with their wares between the East and the West."

This however did not weaken the enduring civilisational influences and for centuries India and the countries of ASEAN have

5.   *ibid.*, p.37.

retained a strong cultural bond. The well-known Indonesian scholar O. Abdul Rachman notes, for instance:

"From their birth places, in India, the great religions of Hinduism and Buddhism found their way to Indonesia, where they mingled with the indigenous belief systems to become an enduring and integral component of Indonesian culture, Islam also arrived in Indonesia by way of the Indian subcontinent. During their long process of consolidation, adaptation and growth in Indonesia, these great religions came to be seen by comparing, for example, any of a wide range of religio-cultural expressions and artefacts—such as temples, shrines, ceremonies, and classic literature such as the *Mahabharata* and *Ramayana*—in their respective Indian and Indonesian contemporary manifestations."[6]

Another Indonesian scholar, Soedjate Djiwandono, quoted President Sukarno as saying:

"In the veins of every one of my people flows the blood of the Indian ancestors and the culture we possess is steeped through and through with Indian influences. Two thousand years ago, people from your country came to Jawadvipa and Suvarnadvipa in the spirit of brotherly love. They gave the initiative to found powerful kingdoms such as those of Sri Vijaya, Mataram and Majapahit. We then learned to worship the very Gods that you now worship still and we fashioned a culture that even today is largely identical with your own. Later, we turned to Islam; but the religion too was brought to us by people coming from both sides of the Indus."[7]

In his survey of world history, the eminent historian Fernand Braudel refers to India and East Asia as the 'greatest of all world economies' of the pre-industrial, pre-capitalist era. Braudel talks of the 'Far East' as comprising 'three gigantic world economies':

---

6. Abdul Rachman O., "India and Indonesia in a Changing World", paper presented to *the First India-Indonesia Seminar*, New Delhi, April 1976 (*mimeo*).

7. Quoted in S. Djiwandono, "India's Relations with East Asia: New Partners?" paper presented at the IISS conference on *Rethinking India's Role in the World*, Neemrana Fort, India, September 1997, (*mimeo*).

"Islam, overlooking the Indian Ocean from the Red Sea and the Persian Gulf, and controlling the endless chain of deserts stretching across Asia from Arabia to China; India, whose influence extended throughout the Indian Ocean, both east and west of Cape Comorin; and China, at once a great territorial power–striking deep into the heart of Asia–and a maritime force, controlling the seas and countries bordering the Pacific. And so it had been for many hundreds of years."[8]

"The relationship between these huge areas," says Braudel, "was the result of a series of pendulum movements of greater or lesser strength, either side of the centrally positioned Indian subcontinent. The swing might benefit first the East and then the West, redistributing functions, power and political or economic advance. Through ɪl these vicissitudes however, India maintained her central position — her merchants in Gujarat and on the Malabar and Coromandel coasts prevailed for centuries on end against their many competitors — the Arab traders of the Red Sea, the Persian merchants of the Gulf, or the Chinese merchants familiar with the Indonesian seas to which their junks were now regular visitors."[9]

Discussing the place of the 'East Indies' in this 'Asian super-world-economy', Braduel adds:

"The logical confluence of trade, the crossroads lying at the centre of this super world — economy could hardly be elsewhere than in the East Indies. Geography placed this region on the edge of Asia, halfway between China and Japan on the one hand, and India and the countries of the Indian Ocean on the other. But if geography proposes, history disposes, and in this instance refusal or acceptance could take innumerable forms depending on the actions of the super powers of the Far East: China and India. At times when both were prosperous, in control of themselves and simultaneously engaged in outside activities, the centre of gravity of the Far East was quite likely to lie, and to remain for a longer or shorter period, somewhere

---

8. Fernand Braudel, *Civilisation and Capitalism, 15th–18th Century*, Volume 3, "The Perspective of the World," Chapter 5, pp.484-535, Collins/Fontana Press, 1984.

9. *ibid.*, p.484.

near the Malacca peninsula and the islands of Java and Sumatra. But the sleeping giants were both slow to arouse and invariably slow to act."

Only at the beginning of the Christian era, that is rather late in history, did India really recognise and start to take an interest in the East Indies. Her sailors, merchants and missionaries exploited, educated and evangelised the archipelago, successfully transferring to it her superior political, economic and religious way of life. The islands were thus converted to Hinduism."[10]

Indian and Chinese traders made the islands of the East Indies a 'busy crossroads of trade' for several centuries, and created, what Braudel calls, the 'super-world economy' of the Far East that had attained levels of economic and social development exceeding those of Europe at the time. Rediscovering this ancient link between India and the countries of the ASEAN, Indian foreign minister, Mr. Inder Kumar Gujral, told the ASEAN Post-Ministerial Conference in Singapore in July 1996:

"ASEAN and India are no awkward strangers. We have been neighbours and friends in time, space and existence for as long back as we can remember. Our habits, customs and social mores, our myths and legends, the clothes we drape, the cuisine we savour, the art, craft and design that is our shared legacy, even the languages we speak—all bear testimony to this good neighbourliness. Then there are the pilgrim trails that wind their way through our diverse lands. Our merchants and traders too linked us together for centuries as they ventured across the Indian Ocean and the Bay of Bengal as well as over land and mountain routes to ply their wares in our thriving *bazaars* and towns. The footprints of South-East Asia are to be seen in every aspect of India's ethos.[11]

---

10. *ibid.*, p.523.

11. Statement by External Affairs Minister, I.K. Gujral at the *Post-Ministerial Conferences of ASEAN (PMC07+1)*, July 24th, 1996, Jakarta, Ministry of External Affairs, Government of India.

European expansion into the Indian Ocean region and colonialism altered the nature and course of India's relations with South-East Asia. As historian K.M. Panikkar notes, "The victory of the Portuguese along the western coast of India in early 16th century laid the firm foundations of the European mastery of the Eastern seas which continued for over 400 years."[12]

Beginning with the Portuguese, followed by the Dutch and then by the British and French, the maritime links between India and the South-East Asian nations was almost completely dominated by Europeans and India's independent links with the region revived only after her Independence and the decline of colonial power in the region. Indian political leadership, especially the first Prime Minister Jawahar Lal Nehru, brought India's relations with the rest of Asia, especially East Asia, to the centre-stage of India's relations with the world immediately after India attained Independence from British colonial rule.

The First Asian Relations Conference at New Delhi in 1947, and the First Asian African Conference at Bandung in 1955, tried to define a new post-colonial relationship between the developing countries of the region. Both these Conferences marked important milestones in India's redefinition of its relations with South-East Asia. However, both proved to be non-starters.[13] The Cold War, tensions between India and China and the Vietnam War combined to draw the nations of this region apart, each looking elsewhere, often outside the region, for friends rather than exploring the prospects for a deeper pan-Asian relationship.

India's second attempt at re-exploring its relations with the countries of the ASEAN, after the unsuccessful attempts made in Nehru's time, came in the late 1970s when India began moving away from its 'inward-looking' import-substituting model of industrialisation and sought an increased share of world trade and

---

12. K.M. Panikkar, *India and Indian Ocean: An Essay on the Influence of Sea Power on Indian History,* London, George Allen & Unwin, 1962.

13. For a comprehensive review of India's relations with South-East Asia in the 1950s and 1960s, See: Eric Gonsalves (edited), *Asian Relations,* Lancer International and India International Centre, New Delhi, 1991.

investment. In a detailed study of this new phase of India-ASEAN relations, Charan Wadhwa concluded that the 1970s saw a significant increase in India-ASEAN trade, but that, still this was very limited in scope and marginal to the corporate plans of Indian industry and trade.[14]

Wadhwa notes that in the 1970s India-ASEAN trade grew rapidly but still, in overall terms, remained a low priority for both, India's trade with the ASEAN countries as a proportion of its world trade was small, a mere 1.5 per cent of her total exports and 0.39 per cent of total imports in 1971-72 (values in Rupees). During the 1970s there was an increase in India-ASEAN trade so that by 1978-1979 these shares had gone up to 4.2 per cent and 5.2 per cent respectively.

Based on a detailed country-wise and commodity-wise study of India-ASEAN trade, Wadhwa concluded that the commodity composition of bilateral trade between India and individual ASEAN member countries pointed to the existence of and increasing tendency towards "complementarities in the trade structure of India and the ASEAN countries in recent years. India can look to ASEAN not only for markets for its exports but also for its much needed imports".[15]

A view from ASEAN has been expressed as follows:

"It has become increasingly clear that the industrial countries in general, and the United States and Japan in particular, will continue with their mercantilistic and self-centred economic policies for some time to come. Therefore, neither ASEAN, in terms of access to markets and technology transfer, nor South Asia, in terms of access to markets and to concessional development finance, can expect much satisfaction from the industrial countries. This development, in conjunction with the continuing balance of trade, payments, and budget deficits in many of the ASEAN and South

14. Charan Wadhwa and Mukul Asher, *ASEAN-South Asia Economic Relations*, ICRIER (New Delhi), Marga Institute (Colombo) and ISEAS (Singapore), Singapore, 1985.

15. *ibid.*, p.291.

Asian countries, has increased the urgency for these countries to expand their economic relations."[16]

If this optimism was not reflected in actual trends during the 1980s, it was both due to the inadequate openness of the Indian economy and the persistent inward-orientation of its corporate sector, and the increasing integration of the ASEAN economies with Japan and the OECD economies and their relative disinterest in South Asia in general and India in particular. ASEAN's 'Look East' policy and the consequent Japan-orientation, as well as Japan's integration with ASEAN through the so-called "flying geese" model of industrial re-location reduced India's appeal to ASEAN. While the ASEAN economies infact became more integrated with the world economy, especially the OECD economies, during the 1970s and 1980s, India's external liberalisation was hesitant and slow till 1991. Indeed, the Postscript quoted above anticipated this outcome when it concluded:

"It should, however, be stressed that various problems indicated in the Overview to this volume are not likely to be resolved in the short term. Moreover, even if political will is exhibited in favour of expanding relations, the nature and structure of the economies of the two groupings would continue to be an important constraint. Therefore, for the foreseeable future, only relatively modest improvement in economic relations between the two regions may be expected, compared with their relations with the industrialised countries."[17]

It was not, however, the inability of increased economic relations that inhibited India-ASEAN relations in the Cold War period as much as the politics of the Cold War which constrained economic relations. India's relations with Vietnam and Cambodia and the conflicts in Indo-China remained a major barrier to improved India-ASEAN relations. As Djiwandono notes, "In the eyes of India, together with China and the US, ASEAN seemed bent on 'bleeding

---

16. *ibid.*, p.375.
17. *ibid.*, p.376.

Vietnam white'. India did not agree with the ASEAN prescription to resolve the Cambodian conflict and expressed sympathies with Vietnam. ASEAN did not appreciate this, and therefore India was viewed a threat to regional stability, projected as a surrogate of the Soviet Union, a destabilising factor in the region."[18]

The end of the Cold War, the dissolution of the Soviet Union, the emergence of China as a regional Super Power, the liberalisation of economic policy in India and ASEAN's desire to find new markets and investment opportunities in India, have combined to improve the environment for India-ASEAN economic relations today. Increased people-to-people contact, now made easier with better transport access demonstrated, for example, by the fact that Indians are the largest number of tourists visiting Singapore, has also helped.

ASEAN's economic miracle

It is fair to say, however, that the new relationship of the 1990s between India and ASEAN was not defined as much by ancient historical and cultural ties as by ASEAN's phenomenal economic success in recent times and India's desire both to learn from this experience as well as participate in the growth process unleashed by the new engine of growth in Asia. The ancient cultural and economic ties offer only a distant background to contemporaneous economic relations. Today ASEAN has as much to offer, perhaps more, to India as India has to offer ASEAN and the relationship is seen as mutually beneficial in largely economic terms. ASEAN's phenomenal success as a group of modern industrial and trading nations has opened new opportunities for renewed India-ASEAN interaction.

Much has been written about the 'East Asian Economic Miracle' and, admittedly, its impact is not even across the region. Indeed, Singapore is the only ASEAN economy which can be classified as belonging to the 'top' rung of Asian economies. Along with South

---

18. Djiwandono, *op. cit.*, p.9.

Korea, Hong Kong and Taiwan, Singapore is undoubtedly among the 'Asian Tigers'. However, Indonesia, Malaysia and Thailand have been classified as the Newly Industrialising Economies (NIEs) and, together, all these countries constitute Asia's 'Highly Performing Economies' (HPAEs).[19] Other ASEAN economies have not done so well. Thus, Philippines, Vietnam, Laos and now Cambodia and Myanmar, remain the laggards.

The magnitude of ASEAN's miraculous growth performance is brought out by such simple economic and social indicators as income per person, literacy and longevity. In 1960, (Table 29.1), real GDP per capita (in Purchasing Power Parity dollar, PPP$, terms) was estimated to PPP$ 1, 783 for Malaysia, $ 985 for Thailand, $1,183 for Philippines and $ 490 for Indonesia; by 1992 the comparable figures were PPP$ 7,790, $ 5,950, $ 2,550 and $ 2,950. India's real GDP per capita in PPP$ was $ 617 in 1960 and went up to $ 1,230 by 1992. Singapore is in a superior league and data are not available

Table 29.1

Human Development Indicators and
Per Capita Income: India and ASEAN, 1960-1997

Country	Life Expectancy at Birth		Infant Mortality/1000 Live Births		Adult Literacy Per Cent		Real GDP Per Capita (PPP$)	
	1960	1997	1960	1997	1960	1997	1960	1997
India	44.0	62.6	165	71	34	54	617	1,670
Indonesia	41.2	65.1	139	45	54	85	490	3,490
Malaysia	53.9	72.0	72	10	60	85.7	1,783	8,140
Philippines	52.8	68.3	79	32	83	94.6	1,183	3,520
Singapore	64.5	77.1	36	4	–	91	2,409	28,460
Thailand	52.3	68.8	103	31	79	94	985	6,690
Vietnam	44.2	67.4	147	32	–	92	–	1,630
Brunei	62.3	74.2	63	9	–	–	–	29,773

Source: Human Development Report, 1999 (UNDP), OUP, 1999.

---

19. World Bank, *The East Asian Miracle: Economic Growth and Public Policy*, Oxford University Press, 1993.

for Laos, Cambodia and Vietnam. Clearly, in 1960 India was on par with countries like Thailand and Indonesia, in per capita income terms, and not too behind Philippines and Malaysia. By 1992, with the exception of Philippines, all the others had increased their per capita income by several-fold leaving India far behind.[20] In terms of GDP per capita valued in US dollars the contrast is even more stark (Table 29.2).

Table 29.2

GDP Per Capita, (US$), India and ASEAN, 1960-1997

Country	1960	1980	1997
India	206	262	465
Indonesia	190	354	785
Malaysia	708	1,678	3387
Philippines	418	680	652
Singapore	1,510	5,581	15,467
Thailand	300	718	1,870
Vietnam	–	–	–
Brunei	–	–	–

Source: *Human Development Report, 1999* (UNDP), OUP, 1999.

The last three decades have been a period of high economic growth and improved human development for most of the ASEAN economies. The Indian economy did not perform very impressively during the 1960s and 1970s, but since 1980 there has been an acceleration of growth.

The 'economic miracle' of East and South-East Asia has been the subject of much intellectual enquiry and debate among economists and other social scientists. Alternative economic and sociological paradigms emphasising either the role of the 'state' or the 'market', or even of cultural and political factors ('Asian values') have been used to explain the truly remarkable growth performance of the region. Notwithstanding the recent economic crisis in the

---

20. *Human Development Report,* 1999 (UNDP), Oxford University Press, 1997.

region (see last section), the fact remains that many of the ASEAN economies have moved to the famous Rostowian 'Take-off ' stage.

Whatever the final consensus on the explanation for the East Asian miracle, two or three factors will remain common to all explanations. First, most of these economies focussed fairly early in their industrialisation process on land reform and investment in agriculture—both of which increased agricultural productivity and agrarian prosperity; second, they all invested in literacy, education and health; and, finally, they exposed their industrial sector to the challenge of global competition.[21]

In a comprehensive study of the East Asian miracle the World Bank has suggested that:

"Common to East Asia's success were policies for macroeconomic stability, human resource investments, and outward orientation quite different from what happened in most other developing regions. Because these economies to a large extent took international prices as an ultimate guide to domestic resource allocation, macroeconomic stability was seen as central to maintenance of competition. In addition, a number of regimes had a strong aversion to inflation, which strengthened the hands of technocrats. In the area of human resources, strong public policies were often augmented with high household investments in education. And in many areas, including export promotion, it was not just the design and selection of policies; it was also efficient implementation. By any standard, implementation of policies was East Asia's forte."[22]

---

21. "Several factors explain East Asia's stunning educational achievements: increased demand for a skilled labour force as a result of the rapid growth of the manufacturing sector; the pressures of competition in an expanding and open global market; a relatively early demographic transition that resulted in a sharp decline in the rate of growth of the school age population; and fairly high budgetary commitments to education by the government. However, the key to the sustained performance of East Asia in the field of education lies in the balance that was engineered between public expenditure on basic and higher education", Mahbub ul Haq, *Human Development in South Asia*, Oxford University Press, Karachi, 1997.

22. Danny Leipziger and Vinod Thomas, *The Lessons of East Asia: An Overview of Country Experience*, World Bank, Washington DC, p.4, 1993.

Economists critical of even this 'revisionist' bank view suggest that greater emphasis must be placed on the role of domestic savings and high investment rates as well as investment in higher, and technical, education rather than literacy alone, in explaining the East Asian miracle. While sharp differences still exist in explaining the success of the ASEAN economies, there is now considerable consensus which emphasises the role of enlightened and development-oriented governance.[23] Where many of the ASEAN countries have lagged behind is in moving towards more democratic systems of governance. This may also explain the fact that while ASEAN's record on poverty eradication has been better than that of South Asia, poverty and unemployment remain a major challenge for the countries of the region.[24] Indeed, weak democratic institutions could well become the Achilles' heel of many strong economies.

The ASEAN economies also benefited from what has come to be called the 'flying geese' pattern of industrial development in Asia. The 'flying geese' paradigm suggests that industrialisation can spread from one country to another if they are linked in such a way that as the more advanced country within a group moves forward, along the technological ladder, it shifts its low technology industries to other countries which come to occupy its hitherto held space in the international division of labour. Economists have suggested that industries vacated by Japan, the industrial superpower in Asia, first moved to countries which emerged as the 'Asian Tigers', namely, Taiwan, South Korea, Singapore and Hong Kong, and subsequently to the 'newly industrialising economies' of South-East Asia. Thus, the process of industrialisation has spanned out from Japan to East Asia to South-East Asia. It is indeed possible that India-ASEAN relations can be strengthened further when this process brings India into its fold, with labour-intensive industries moving out of the higher wage economies of East Asia and ASEAN to lower wage

---

23. Ajit Singh, "How East Asia Grew so Fast? Slow Progress Towards An Analytical Consensus", *RIS Occasional Paper* No. 46, 1995.

24. V. Ahuja *et al.*, "Everyone's Miracle: Revisiting Poverty and Inequality in East Asia", *RBI Bulletin* (forthcoming), Washington DC, 1997.

and larger economies like India. To a large extent this process has already happened with respect to China. China has most definitely been drawn into Asia's 'flying geese' formation. India is still at the periphery of this process.

India looks east, ASEAN looks west

The real turning point in India-ASEAN relations came with economic liberalisation in 1991, the end of the Cold War and the enunciation of India's 'Look East' policy by Prime Minister P.V. Narasimha Rao. As a publication of the Indian ministry of external affairs recently observed, "There was a confluence of interests. A new world order, the economic reforms in India along with its 'Look East' policy, coincided with ASEAN's 'Look West' and regionalisation drive."[25]

Under the 'Look East' policy India pursued increased trade and investment cooperation with South Korea and Singapore. Apart from extending India's enduring relations with Vietnam, the policy also pursued greater economic relations with Malaysia, Thailand and Indonesia. India became a 'Sectoral Dialogue Partner' of ASEAN at the ASEAN's Singapore Summit in 1992, and a 'Full Dialogue Partner' at the Bangkok Summit in 1995.[26] In February 1995, the ASEAN-India Business Council was set up.

India was invited to the meeting of the ASEAN Regional Forum (ARF) in July 1996. At this it was decided that ARF would only admit as participants countries that have a direct influence on the peace and security of the East Asia and Pacific region.

Commenting on these decisions of the ASEAN, Mr. Gujral remarked at the Jakarta PMC, "The ASEAN decision to make India a Full Dialogue Partner is based on your farsighted assessment about the political and strategic convergence, acceleration of economic relations and their future potential, and complementarities

---

25. *Friends and Neighbours: India and ASEAN*, Ministry of External Affairs, Government of India, New Delhi, 1997.

26. V.L. Rao and R. Upendra Das, "India and ASEAN: Issues in Sectoral Dialogue Partnership", *RIS Occasional Paper* No. 41, New Delhi, 1993.

in areas that were hitherto not evident or remained unexploited. A key objective of India and ASEAN to move from derivative to direct relationship so that there are no distortions, no misperceptions, no ignorance and no intermediation."[27]

There has been a doubling of trade between India and ASEAN countries in the 1990s and a marked increase in joint ventures and foreign direct investment between the two. ASEAN has emerged as the third largest foreign investor in India, after the United States and European Union. The recent economic and financial crisis in some of the ASEAN countries has slowed down the momentum of India-ASEAN trade and investment flows. However, once countries like Malaysia and Thailand cross the hump, perhaps by year 2000, this growth momentum is likely to gather pace once again. India has set for itself the ambitious target of increasing India-ASEAN trade to US$ 15 billion by year 2000.

There are two dimensions to India's new relationship with ASEAN. First, the trade and investment dimension (which is documented in subsequent sections of this paper); second, the foreign policy and strategic dimension. Neither of these relations has equal value to all ASEAN countries. Clearly, India's economic relations with some are more developed than with others. Similarly, India's political and strategic relations with some are more developed than with others. Suffice it to say, that in no case is the relationship purely uni-dimensional.

The economic relationship is stronger with countries like Singapore, Malaysia and Thailand—which have emerged as important trading and investment partners for India. Singapore is in many ways the hub of the India-ASEAN relationship and played a key role in ASEAN's decision to designate India as a 'Full Dialogue Partner'. Singapore has major investment plans for Tamil Nadu and Karnataka. There are now direct flights from Singapore to Chennai, Bangalore and Hyderabad, apart from Delhi, Mumbai and Kolkata. Malaysia is expected to invest in road and port development

27. Quoted in *Friends and Neighbours, op.cit.*

in Andhra Pradesh and Orissa. Thailand's relations with India have been further strengthened with the creation of another regional economic grouping, the Bangladesh-India-Myanmar-Sri Lanka-Thailand Economic Cooperation group, BIMSTEC.

On the political side, India has traditionally had very good relations with Vietnam and now this relationship has been deepened with increased Indian investment in Vietnam and growing two-way trade. India's defence relationship with Indonesia and Malaysia has also been an important dimension of her relations with this region. This aspect of India-ASEAN relations has acquired higher profile with the emergence of China as a new global 'superpower' and an Asian economic giant.

China looms large over the region and in the new 'balance of power' which all ASEAN member countries are trying to help shape, India, Japan and the United States will be increasingly viewed as checks and balances against growing Chinese economic and military power in the region. All ASEAN member countries are committed to developing friendly and profitable relations with China, and are equally committed to good relations with other major powers in the region, including India. The Indonesian strategic policy thinker Djiwandono notes, for example, "China and India, despite its bilateral problems, are now both ASEAN dialogue partners and participants of ARF. Indeed, in terms of power politics, the engagement of the two largest nations in the world, along with the US, Japan and Russia, might help create a regional balance of power in East Asia and the Asia-Pacific region as part of the global balance that includes the European Union."[28]

Djiwandono goes on to add, "In fact, with the establishment of ARF, ASEAN strives to engage and bring the major powers into a regional structure. In that way, they may play their proper roles commensurate with their respective potential capabilities so as to maintain regional peace, security and stability." Thus, the comprehensive scope of India-ASEAN relations should not be lost

---

28. Djiwandono, *op. cit.*, p.13.

sight of in any evaluation of purely economic benefits and costs. India-ASEAN dialogue and relationship is wide-ranging and will be long-enduring. It is as much interested in building an economic relationship as in improving political and social understanding.

India and ASEAN after the Asian economic crisis

The Asian economic crisis (1997-98) cast a shadow on India-ASEAN relations, hurting particularly the two-way trade and investment flows. While all ASEAN economies were not equally hurt by the crisis, Thailand and Indonesia being the worst affected, the crisis did divert attention and slowed down the process of regional economic cooperation between India and South-East Asia.

Several hypotheses have been put forward to explain why such an unexpected crisis occurred in so many Asian economies in such quick succession. The two major hypotheses discussed worldwide are those of Lawrence Summers and Paul Krugman respectively. Summers is joined by the dominant view within the International Monetary Fund (IMF) in holding the view that it was the large and unsustainable current account deficits (CADs) of the key Asian economies, particularly Thailand and Indonesia, along with pegged exchange rates which snowballed a payments crisis. Krugman places the blame mainly on the failure of financial intermediation, that is the over-extension of bank loans for speculative purposes, mainly investment in real estate and stock market. In an authoritative survey of the debate, Rakshit has rejected both hypotheses.[29]

To quote Rakshit, "The first hypothesis appears inadequate on the following grounds: (a) all afflicted economies in the region did not run large current account deficits; (b) large inflow of foreign funds following relaxation of controls on capital account constitutes an optimal process of capital stock adjustment in the world economy; (c) in Asian countries foreign capital inflow supplemented rather than replaced domestic saving; and (d) slowdown in export growth

---

29. Mihir Rakshit, "Retracing the Roots of Asian Troubles, 1996-97", *Money and Finance*, No. 5, April, ICRA Ltd., New Delhi, 1998.

in 1996 can not be attributed to pegged exchange rates or to the 1994 Chinese devaluation. The Krugman explanation, though elegant, seems unsatisfactory in view of the fact that: (a) the postulated behaviour of economic agents is based on irrational expectations; (b) a major part of investment was not routed through banks; (c) there was no evidence that investment was concentrated in socially unproductive ventures; and (d) even in the first half of 1997 financial 'experts' had no inkling of the impending troubles."

Rakshit's own explanation focuses attention on the excessive dependence of the concerned economies on the global market and their inability to deal with a cyclical downturn in global demand for their exports. This 'external shock' was compounded by what Rakshit calls a "coordination failure", namely the inability of different agents to react in a planned manner to this sudden shock. It was made worse by the fact that the cash flow problems created by a decline in export demand had a cascading effect with corporates forced to renege on debt payments, adding to the NPAs of banks and to a crisis in the banking system.

There was a steep fall in the exports of four ASEAN economies, Thailand (24.6 percentage points), Malaysia (21.8 points), Philippines (11.9 points) and Indonesia (4.3 points), in 1996. Says Rakshit, "Apart from its immediate impact on the countries' macroeconomic performance in general and balance of payments in particular, the crucial significance of the decline lay in two important features of the miracle economies. First, such sharp deceleration in export growth rates had not occurred for a long time and marked a serious break from the steeply rising trends in export growth these countries had enjoyed since 1990. Second, the shake-up in investors' confidence was due in no small measure to the high degree of openness of these economies."

The external shock delivered by a collapse of export demand had internal repercussions with cutbacks in domestic investment and demand, corporates becoming ill-liquid and reneging on bank loans. A crisis on the trade front was transmitted to the banking sector and thereon to the financial sector. All this raised doubts in the minds of foreign investors whether the Asian 'tigers' had stopped roaring. Negative expectations on the economic front were compounded by political uncertainty in the wake of the end of the Cold War and the new relationship between China and the United States.

The crisis undoubtedly had a direct negative impact on India as well as on Indo-ASEAN trade and investment relations. The ASEAN-5 (Singapore, Malaysia, Thailand, Indonesia, and Philippines) had emerged as important sources of foreign direct investment and export markets in the 1990s. India's 'Look East' policy helped double the share of the ASEAN-5 in total FDI into India in the period 1992-1997. India-ASEAN trade had also increased, and so its disruption during 1997-98 hurt Indian exports as well as capital flows into India. While India's exports to the world declined by 2.8 per cent in April-November 1998, its exports to some ASEAN economies declined by between 40 and 70 per cent (Table 29.5). As the *Economic Survey* of the Ministry of Finance, Government of India, (1999) noted, "The economic contraction in the East Asian countries resulted in a sharp decline in import demand, ... Since Asia accounts for about one-fifth of India's exports, India could not escape the fallout from such import compression."

Beyond this, India was largely spared of the so-called 'contagion' effect of the financial crisis. In an analysis of the impact of the Asian economic crisis on India, the deputy governor of the Reserve Bank of India, Y. Venugopal Reddy, claimed that India had been "spared from the 'contagion', and managed to record a GDP growth of 5 per cent and contain inflation at 5 per cent during 1997-1998."[30] While the Rupee took a knock in the last quarter of 1997, and portfolio flows into India dried up for a few months, there was no withdrawal of such funds out of India.[31] Consequently, India's current account deficit remained well within manageable levels at— 1.4 per cent in 1997-98 and 1.0 per cent in 1998-99. The rapid recovery of some of the ASEAN economies rekindled hopes in India of a resumption of the increasing economic relationship with the region.

---

30. Y. Venugopal Reddy, "Asian Crisis: Asking the Right Questions", May 1998, (*mimeo*).

31. Reddy, *ibid*.

As the *Economic Survey*, 1999-00 observed, "The recovery of East Asian economies and improvement in the global trade environment augurs well for Indian exports in the current financial year."

Recent trends in Indo-ASEAN trade relations

India has had trade links, particularly in spices and textiles, with South-East Asian countries for a very long time. However, in the post-Independence period India's trade relations with this region were not particularly significant or encouraging. In part due to the politics of the Cold War era, wherein India and ASEAN found themselves on different sides of the global divide, and in part due to India's 'inward-oriented' development process, because of which India's share in world trade declined from 2.0 per cent in the early 1950s to 0.5 per cent in the 1980s, India-ASEAN trade relations were marginal to both sides. Both India and ASEAN focused much more on their trade with North America and Western Europe than with each other.

Attempts to revive the historic pre-Cold War era trade relations received initial momentum when India was made a Sectoral Dialogue Partner of ASEAN in 1992 and India launched its 'Look East' Policy. As shown in Table 29.3 below, India's trade with

Table 29.3

Rate of Growth of India's Total Trade, 1975-1997

Region	1975-97	1975-90	1991-97
World	8.0	8.48	9.95
Industrial Countries	8.18	8.94	8.3
Indonesia	11.6	3.3	129.07
Malaysia	10.24	14.18	14.91
Philippines	12.17	4.84	26.31
Singapore	13.34	16.79	13.39
Thailand	13.83	11.93	15.24
Vietnam	12.56	-1.6	12.3
Brunei	12.73	20.79	51.92
Myanmar	5.0	9.4	17.15
ASEAN	11.77	12.66	18.15

Source: Economic Survey (various years), Ministry of Finance, Government of India.

ASEAN accelerated at a faster pace than her trade with the rest of the world or even with the industrial economies in the 1990s. The share of India's trade with ASEAN as a percentage of its share with the rest of the world increased from around 4.0 per cent in the 1970s to over 5.0 per cent in the 1980s and to over 8.0 per cent in the 1990s (Table 29.4).

Table 29.4

India–ASEAN Trade in the Global Context

Period	India's Trade with ASEAN as Per Cent of India's Trade with World	ASEAN's Trade with India as Per Cent of ASEAN's Trade with World
1974-79	3.8	1.45
1980-91	5.4	1.78
1992-97	8.0	1.70

Source: Direction of Trade Statistics (various years), WTO.

The economic crisis in South-East Asia hurt this process and India-ASEAN trade declined more sharply than India's trade with the world in the post-crisis year of 1998, but there has since been a recovery in the trade volumes (Table 29.5).

The value of trade between India and seven of the significant trade partners in ASEAN, increased from US$ 243 mn in 1975 to about $ 2.4 bn in 1990, but declined to about $ 1.9 bn in 1991, the year of India's balance of payments crisis. In fact, trade between India and ASEAN-7 grew by 407.4 per cent during 1975-1980, 204.3 per cent in 1981-1990 and by 284.4 per cent in 1991-1996. Interestingly, while there was a slump in India's exports to the region. In the pre-crisis year 1996, as a share of India's exports to the Asian region, exports to Asian-7 stood at over 40 per cent, while the share of imports from ASEAN-7 as a percentage of India's imports from the Asian region was 54 per cent in that year.

ASEAN's significance as a trade partner for India is, therefore, clear. However, India still does not figure prominently as a trade partner for ASEAN (Table 29.6). Even in 1984, when India's share in ASEAN's trade with the world was the highest at 2.54 per cent, only 2 per cent of ASEAN's exports were directed towards India.

Table 29.5

Regional Trends in Indian Exports–1997-1999

Region	Growth Rate (April–November)		
	1997	1998	1999
World	3.5	-2.8	11.7
Asia (excl. M. East)	-1.7	-20.6	18.2
China	0.7	-26.6	24.3
Hong Kong	6.1	-9.6	27.8
Indonesia	5.0	-73.6	91.2
Malaysia	1.5	-44.5	43.9
Philippines	48.3	-60.1	20.6
Singapore	–	38.1	36.5
Thailand	-14.7	-11.1	32.4
Vietnam	1.1	5.5	8.3
Middle East	4.1	20.6	5.9
Russia	13.8	-20.5	37.9
UK	3.6	-13.3	15.7
Japan	-5.1	-16.1	2.4
USA	1.6	8.2	16.5
Europe	4.2	-3.8	9.8

Source: *Direction of Trade Statistics* (various years), WTO.

Table 29.6

India's Share in Total Trade of Some ASEAN Countries, 1991-1997

(Percentage)

Year	Myanmar	Indonesia	Malaysia	Singapore	Thailand	Vietnam
1991	3.19	0.51	0.84	1.13	1.49	0.62
1992	5.78	0.47	0.97	1.08	0.55	0.47
1993	5.85	0.67	0.66	1.02	0.72	0.39
1994	5.60	0.87	0.79	1.02	0.72	0.43
1995	4.95	1.01	0.91	1.15	0.71	0.69
1996	4.99	1.50	1.24	1.20	0.68	0.67
1997	5.67	1.39	1.21	1.29	0.74	0.59

Source: Same as Table 29.5.

Note: *India/China Total Trade (X+M) with Country X/Total (X+M) of Country X.*

In fact, from ASEAN's viewpoint India has not been a significant export market. When compared to the other six countries who have been exporting on an average only less than 1 per cent of their goods to India, (except for Malaysia and Singapore, which were among the major suppliers of imports for India in 1996), the single major exception since 1986 has been Myanmar. India has been the second largest importer from Myanmar, almost 21 per cent of Myanmar's exports were absorbed by the Indian market in 1996, even though India's exports to Myanmar are a small part of Myanmar's total imports.

Recent trends in India-ASEAN investment flows

The 1990s saw some of the ASEAN members emerging as important sources of foreign direct investment in India. In particular, Singapore, Thailand and Malaysia. The period also saw Indian companies investing in some of the ASEAN economies, in particular Thailand, Indonesia and Vietnam. Towards the end of the 1990s and in 2000, the information technology and computer software sector emerged as an important source of outward investment for India, with Indian companies establishing a base in the ASEAN region, in particular in Singapore. As Table 29.7 shows, in 1991-1997 the combined share of ASEAN-5 (Singapore, Thailand, Malaysia, Indonesia and Philippines) in FDI into India was higher, at 5.7 per cent, than of South Korea and Japan, and only marginally below UK's share of FDI in India. This suggests that the region has emerged as an important source of FDI into India.

The type of industries into which ASEAN investments have come remain diversified, but a major sector in which new investment is expected is the infrastructure sector including civil aviation, seaport and airport construction, road development, power and housing. Indian investment into the region has been wide-ranging including steel, textiles, chemicals and petrochemicals, cement, sugar, pharmaceuticals and, increasingly importantly, software services and programming. The financial crisis of 1997-98 hurt this process both ways, but more recent evidence suggests a renewal and rejuvenation of inter-regional investment flows.

Table 29.7

Foreign Direct Investment into India–Country Share (Percentage)

Country	1992-94	1995-97	1991-97
USA	30.4	24.6	25.9
UK	7.6	6.5	6.7
S. Korea	0.7	5.9	4.7
Japan	4.7	3.9	4.2
Germany	3.1	3.5	3.4
Netherlands	2.3	2.6	2.5
France	0.9	2.4	2.3
Singapore	1.5	1.6	1.6
Australia	1.8	2.8	2.5
Italy	2.2	1.5	1.7
Israel	0.0	4.7	3.6
Thailand	1.4	2.3	2.1
Malaysia	0.4	1.7	1.4
ASEAN-5*	3.3	6.4	5.7
China & Hong Kong	1.4	1.7	1.7
Mauritius	2.4	5.7	-
Non-resident Indians	7.3	3.5	-

Note: * ASEAN-5 includes Singapore, Thailand, Indonesia, Malaysia and Philippines. Investment coming in from Mauritius is mainly from offshore companies which operate from offices there because of the tax concessions given to Mauritius based companies in the India–Mauritius bilateral treaty.

Source: India Investment Centre, Government of India, New Delhi.

Towards a Bay of Bengal community

While India remains firmly committed to multilateralism in trade, it has anxiously pursued membership of regional trade blocs given the fact that most of the major trading economies are all members of major trade blocs like EU, NAFTA, and ASEAN. Given India's inability to as yet secure membership of APEC economies, India has been closely watching China's moves to integrate more closely with Asia-Pacific economies and China's increased clout in the region after the Asian economic crisis.

Given the extent of regional integration worldwide, South Asia, India's immediate neighbourhood, remains relatively unintegrated. The slow progress of regional cooperation within South Asia, particularly the inability of SAARC (South Asian Association for Regional Cooperation) to widen economic links within the sub-continent, largely on account of Pakistani intransigence and unwillingness to play by the global rules of the game in trade, has also forced India to 'Look East' for more trade opportunities. While SAARC has progressed from SAPTA 1 to SAPTA 2, creating and widening a preferential trade agreement (PTA), and has placed the creation of a Free Trade Agreement (FTA) on its agenda, the progress on SAFTA has also been slowed down by Pakistani non-cooperation.

Given the slow pace of trade liberalisation within SAARC, India has opted for speedier bilateral trade agreements with Sri Lanka and Bangladesh. Simultaneously, India has also supported the creation of new REGs like the Indian Ocean Rim Association for Regional Cooperation (IOR-ARC) and the Bangladesh, India, Myanmar, Sri Lanka and Thailand Economic Cooperation (BIMST-EC). Regional growth triangles (quadrangles), partly inspired by the example of the Singapore-Malaysia-Thailand triangle, are being tried and if one of these experiments, the BBNI (Bhutan, Nepal and India quadrangle) succeeds, long-term solutions for the development of India's backward north-eastern region can be found.

India's commitment to some of these REGs may increase if the current stand-off between India and Pakistan on the conflict near Kargil further slows down the momentum of economic cooperation within South Asia. SAARC has become hostage to the swings in India-Pakistan bilateral relationship and other SAARC members, including Nepal, Sri Lanka and Bangladesh, have become testy about SAARC's slow progress.

The lukewarm response of SAARC leaders to the report of the SAARC Eminent Persons' Group (1998), which has advocated the creation of a South Asian Customs Union by 2015 and a South Asian Economic Union (SAEU) by 2020, suggests that SAARC may not emerge an important REG for India in the near future.

Given this impasse in SAARC, India may well end up investing more energy in its bilateral relationship with other SAARC members and, at the same time, help create and sustain new forums in which the agenda of trade liberalisation can be pursued. The most promising such forum is BIMSTEC. Its membership includes key SAARC countries as well as two ASEAN members closest to India in geographical terms, namely, Myanmar and Thailand. BIMSTEC is an odd name for an REG. Indeed, there is no REG, anywhere in the world, which is named on the basis of the first letter of the name of each of its member countries. This is an untidy formula, which has forced BIMSTEC to change its name at least once, from BISTEC, when Myanmar joined it.

The defining feature of BIMSTEC is that its members are the rim economies of the Bay of Bengal. If BIMSTEC is in fact, viewed as a 'Bay of Bengal Community' (BOBCOM), there is good reason to include the two land-locked countries in South Asia which are completely dependent on the Bay of Bengal for their national economic needs, namely, Nepal and Bhutan. If these two countries are added, then BIMSTEC or BOBCOM becomes SAARC *minus* Pakistan *plus* Myanmar and Thailand. India, Bangladesh, Myanmar, Singapore, Sri Lanka and Thailand should come closer and create the Bay of Bengal Community to facilitate speedier trade liberalisation and increased intra-regional capital flows within such a community. The land-locked states of Nepal and Bhutan, directly dependent on this sea, may also be invited to join. If China's south-western provinces and Malaysia find it useful they may also establish special links with such a group.

It is easy to see why a 'Bay of Bengal Community' may end up being a far more dynamic group. BOBCOM's ASEAN component, especially Thailand, can help speed up the pace of trade liberalisation and regional economic cooperation within South Asia at a pace faster than what SAARC has been capable of. In the interest of imparting greater dynamism to such a regional economic group, and in recognition of the fact that is the largest hub port serving the entire Bay of Bengal rim ports, Singapore should be invited to join the 'Bay of Bengal Community'.

It is also becoming increasingly clear that the only 'regional' economic links that India can meaningfully forge in the near future, even within South Asia, will be links to her 'East'—the Bay of

Bengal rim, the Himalayan region and eastwards. As long as Pakistan remains a 'rogue' state in the region, sponsoring terrorism and unwilling to restore normal trade relations within the WTO framework, not only will SAARC, SAFTA and SAEU remain hobbled, but even the prospects of regional economic links with Central and West Asia will remain tenuous and limited.

Against this background, a regional economic group based around the Bay of Bengal and linking India, Sri Lanka, Nepal and Bangladesh more closely to the ASEAN economies offers the prospect of widening the network for outward-oriented growth in this part of Asia. BIMSTEC will naturally emerge as the bridge between South Asia, India in particular, and South-East Asia. Through this route India can strengthen its links with ASEAN and reach out beyond South-East Asia to the Asia-Pacific Community, recreating ancient historical links with this region.

The Asia-Pacific community

Barely a decade ago the 21st century was regarded the 'Asia-Pacific Century'. Such *hubris* has been missing since the economic crisis in eastern Asia. However, it is clear now that eastern Asia will be an important engine of growth well into the next century and that the varying dynamic of growth in the region is going to alter the balance of power both within the region and globally. If the next phase of India's outward-orientation has to proceed apace, it is important that India's trade with the APEC (Asia-Pacific Economic community) economies must increase, and that India must in fact become a member of APEC. To enable this, the 'Look East' policy must be firmly focused on Singapore, Thailand and Korea. India must also re-build its links with Myanmar. India-Myanmarese economic and political relations have been neglected for far too long. There is potential for the development of India's north-east through greater cooperation with Myanmar, Thailand and Singapore.

The new regional economic links being forged in the Asia-Pacific region can not be ignored by India. The Manila-initiative to create an ASEAN+3 forum bringing in China, Japan and Korea is one such initiative. Singapore's proposal to create and Asian Free Trade Area (AFTA) is another idea. With the region recovering from the crisis it is easy to see that such initiatives will gather pace. Moreover, with the multilateral trade regime coming under pressure from civil society groups both in the West, particularly in North America, and in other parts of the world, there is the real prospect of regionalism gathering momentum once again. While India should remain committed to multilateralism and should in fact actively campaign against regional trade agreements, even demanding that they be made WTO-incompatible, pragmatism demands that in the interim, India should actively seek membership of the new regional blocs being created in Asia.

So far we have only explained the rationale for India's 'Look East' policy. The question remains as to why Asia to our east must desire to 'Look West' to India. The answer to this question is not very easy. An obvious reason is economic. India's liberal trade and investment policy of the 1990s has opened up the Indian economy and the newly industrialising Asian economies can benefit from this. That is clear. There are strategic factors as well. The end of the Cold War and the emergence of China as a major power has alerted a range of countries in Asia, including Japan, Korea, Singapore, Indonesia, Malaysia and Thailand to consider closer relations with India. What motivates each of these nations is quite different. In Thailand there is a conscious 'Look West' policy of being more actively engaged with South Asia. In Korea, there is a realisation that Japan may have been too slow in responding to market opportunities in India and that Korean brand names have come to stay here and so must be invested in further.

Almost all these countries would like to see a balance of power in Asia in which the United States, China and Japan do not increase their power at the expense of the other. In this context, the emergence of a more economically dynamic and strategically secure India can be a positive factor.

For India, therefore, there is once again an opportunity to relate to Asia to its east. However, so far our diplomacy has been desultory, at best sporadic and episodic. Greater consistency, greater commitment to more open trade and investment relations and a willingness to share in the region's problems and not just in its prosperity will help India move closer. Eastern Asia beckons India once again as we enter a new millenium. While India must 'Look East' with purpose and commitment, the Asia-Pacific community must also accept the fact that its links with this subcontinent, particularly peninsular India, run deep into the foundation of our combined history, and that India is both a factor for peace and stability in Asia as well as a partner in progress.

30 | ESSAY

The Asian economic crisis and India's external economic relations

THE economic and financial crisis in East and South-East Asia has raised two kinds of questions. First, especially in India, it has brought into question, a range of policies with respect to economic globalisation, particularly in the financial sector and more specifically the movement of short-term private capital flows. Second, and equally interestingly, it has raised questions about the economic and political clout of the 'newly industrialising economies' of Asia and the likely change in the balance of power in the region. The role of the United States in 'bailing' out troubled economies, the growing economic and financial clout of China, the contradictions between US, Chinese and Japanese economic interests, the increasing interaction between the two Koreas, the political crisis in Indonesia and, to a lesser extent in Malaysia, and so on.

It is useful to remember that what began essentially as an external payments crisis in South-East Asia soon became a financial and economic crisis in the entire region and, in some cases, even turned into a political and security crisis. The diplomatic fallout of the crisis was all too evident at the recent summit of the Asia Pacific Economic Cooperation (APEC) in Kuala Lumpur in November, where tension between the US and its Asian 'friends' like Japan was all too evident. That the Clinton administration has decided to use the weakening of the regimes in these countries, especially Indonesia and Malaysia, to push through its own diplomatic objectives is also quite evident. The democratic transition in South Korea and Thailand, the collapse of the Suharto regime in Indonesia and the problems that have enveloped President Mahathir Mohammed in Malaysia all have a common genesis. They can be traced to the economic crisis and the varying ability of different governments to deal with the domestic causes and symptoms of the crisis, on the one hand, and external pressures, on the other.

To fully appreciate the economic and political lessons of the Asian economic crisis for India, it is important to understand the changing nature of global political and economic relations, the increased importance of economic relations in defining political equations between nations, and of India's relations with the world economy. Given the primacy of economics in international relations in the post-Cold War world, it would be simplistic to consider issues relating to external economic policy in a political and diplomatic vacuum. Business and political leadership in India must appreciate both the positive and negative role that East Asia's 'growth miracle' and its growing economic clout have played in shaping the global response to the Asian crisis. Economies that have globalised more, like Taiwan and Singapore, have actually been hurt less by the crisis, than those that have globalised less, like Thailand and Indonesia. On the other hand, the kind of global inter-dependence that economies like Japan, China and South Korea have been able to ensure has created a stake in the Western world, especially the United States, forcing the latter to intervene in support of a rescue package for some of these economies. Be it in Mexico in 1995 or South Korea in 1997, US and IMF support has been as much a political response as it has been an economic one.

The politics of the crisis and the rescue effort cannot be delinked from the economics. Hence, countries like India which are beginning to open up their economies to increased foreign trade and financial flows must have a holistic economic and foreign policy which minimises the risks of globalisation and derives both the economic and diplomatic benefits of the increased interaction with the world market.

After all, globalisation is both an opportunity and a threat and a key lesson of recent experience is that globalisation creates both mutual dependencies and vulnerabilities. The increasing integration of a national economy with the global economy is both an insurance against deliberate economic sabotage but it also increases the vulnerability of smaller economies to larger global forces. It is now clear that East and South-East Asia's response to the financial crisis is not going to be a reversal of the process of globalisation, but that national governments are now likely to pay more attention to internal economic systems and policies to ensure that their exposure to global forces of competition does not make them vulnerable to systemic or random shocks. Equally, the role of multilateral institutions in dealing with crises as well as with normal trade and capital flows has come in for renewed scrutiny. The mandate of the International Monetary Fund, in particular, and of the World Trade Organization is being re-examined and new ideas relating to the reform of global institutions are being discussed.

While increased exposure to external trade and capital flows, including short-term capital flows, is viewed less as an option than a necessity by economies big and small, there is now greater attention being paid to establishing appropriate macroeconomic pre-conditions for successful integration with the world economy. In India too it is now recognised that an increased exposure to external private capital flows must be accompanied, if not preceded, by:

(a) sound and stable macroeconomic policies, especially fiscal and exchange rate policy;

(b) transparent code of conduct for government entities, private companies and other market entities;

(c) sound financial and banking system; and

(d) prudent monetary policy.

Second, it must also be recognised that weaving a web of mutually beneficial economic relations with major and minor international economies is in India's interests. External economic liberalisation in the post-Cold War period is, far from being a threat to national security, a means of ensuring economic security in an increasingly inter-dependent world economy. External economic liberalisation has acquired an added diplomatic and political dimension in the 1990s. The Indian economy must not only build bridges with developed G-7 economies but with a range of developing and middle income economies as well. The G-7 economies will surely continue to dominate trade and capital flows into India. But the economies of the ASEAN and APEC groupings as well as the economies of South Asia, Southern Asia (including West Asia) and the Indian Ocean region (including East and Southern African economies) must gain prominence in India's portfolio of traded goods and services and investment flows.

Changing balance of power in Asia

The first signs of an economic crisis in Asia became visible in Thailand in early 1997.[1] Soon other economies in the region, particularly Malaysia, South Korea, Indonesia, Philippines and Hong Kong found themselves drawn into a pattern of problems. A payments crisis, followed by a banking or financial crisis, followed by an industrial crisis culminating in an economic crisis. The economic crisis in these countries has had a profound impact on their politics. In South Korea and Thailand the ruling political parties were trounced and new regimes elected to power. In Indonesia, where General Suharto resisted such a democratic transition public pressure finally forced him to quit. Even in Malaysia, where President Mahathir Mohammed has survived the crisis, his leadership has been challenged and his stature badly dented. In every country the economic crisis has had a profound political impact. Even in Mexico, which escaped relatively unscathed from a financial crisis in 1995-96, thanks to US support, the financial crisis left deep political scars and cemented its close strategic relationship with its powerful neighbour. What has caught the imagination of the strategic policy analysts is the fact that the Asian financial crisis has had a political fallout shaped by the circumstances of the post-Cold War world. At a time when strategic policy analysts

---

1. For a detailed and critical analysis of the course of the Asian crisis see Mihir Rakshit's various articles in previous issues of *Money & Finance*.

were beginning to question the paradigm of a 'unipolar' world and were arguing that the bipolar Cold War equilibrium had been replaced by, in the view of some analysts, a 'multipolar' disequilibrium or, in the view of others, a new 'polycentric' equilibrium, the Asian crisis and the weakening of the Japanese and ASEAN economies, coming in the wake of the collapse of the Russian economy, has once again strengthened the view that at the turn of the century the United States is the sole 'superpower', with China at best a distant second.

The political impact of the crisis has impacted on the 'balance of power' in Asia. In the early months of the crisis, even as late as October 1997, when the annual meeting of the International Monetary Fund and the World Bank was taking place in Hong Kong, Japan was still seen as having escaped the crisis and, more importantly, as a part of the solution. Japan mooted the proposal of setting up an Asian Monetary Fund (AMF) which it would fund handsomely and which would then help in the bailing out of crisis-ridden ASEAN economies. Not only was the AMF idea rejected by the United States, but within months Japan found itself embroiled in a banking and financial crisis which not only resulted in a change of government, but increased US leverage in the region. At least one consequence of this altered scenario was that Japan had to abandon the AMF idea. Admittedly, the timing of the AMF proposal was wrong. A year earlier, when the United States was more concerned about containing the Mexican damage and supporting the Economies in Transition (EIT) in eastern Europe and the erstwhile Soviet Union, and China's own clout was still limited, Japan may have succeeded in pushing the idea through. Even then, Japan's failure to launch the East Asian Economic Caucus (EAEC), courtesy Malaysia's Mahathir Mohammed, showed its limited diplomatic influence in the region. However, Japan's position was further weakened by late 1997 with the US economy in top gear, US-China relations on the mend and the crisis in East and South-East Asia looming over all discussions on international economic relations.

The only major East Asian economies which have so far remained unscathed are Singapore, Taiwan and, of course, China.

China gained in political stature by not only investing over a billion dollars in a rescue package for Thailand but by also resisting pressures for the devaluation of the yuan. Indeed, by repeatedly indicating that it will not devalue the yuan, China has demonstrated to the region and to global financial markets its newly acquired economic stature and an appreciation that is attendant on it.

At a time when no other currency of the region was able to hold its own, and the tribulations of the Indian Rupee was not even news in the global financial media, the global concern about the future of the yuan underscored China's new global economic status. The influence of the yuan is nowhere near that of the yen or the D-mark, not to mention the US Dollar, but through much of 1998 its prospective movement held centre-stage in the global financial media. China's economic eminence had been well established. Clearly, China has emerged more influential in the region after the Asian crisis while Japan's stature has been dented. The United States however, remains the key power in the region.

At the end of the Cold War, when strategic planners in the ASEAN countries were welcoming the new regional 'balance of power', with the US, Japan and China emerging as key players and new institutions like the Asia Pacific Economic Cooperation (APEC) were coming up, a concerned India sought membership of the Association of South-East Asian Nations (ASEAN), the newly created ASEAN Regional Forum (ARF) and APEC to signal its relevance to the region and assert its stake in the emerging balance of power. Indeed, India made considerable headway after the Narasimha Rao government unveiled its 'Look East' policy and forged a special relationship with Singapore and South Korea. The thawing of Indo-China relations and ASEAN's desire to balance China's increasing influence in the region, helped India secure a Dialogue Partner status in ASEAN and full membership of the ARF. The formation of these organisations and the shape they took were itself an outcome of the changing power equations in the post-Cold War period. ASEAN, which had initially been formed as a political grouping, took on a broad economic agenda of regional integration and subsequently pursued a security agenda in which it sought to balance the influence of the US, China and Japan in the region.

The new interest shown by India in increasing its economic links with the region, the liberalisation of trade and investment flows and the special attention given to ASEAN and East Asian economies helped raise India's profile. Strategic analysts in the ASEAN region noted with appreciation the new language of Indian diplomacy in the region in the 1990s. The 1980s had been a period of mutual suspicion and India's growing maritime strength created ripples of concern in countries like Malaysia, Indonesia and Singapore. However, Narasimha Rao's new economic policies and his 'Look East' policy, with the new tone of 'equality' rather than 'superiority' in the Indian approach to the region, received favourable attention in many Asian capitals. It must be emphasised, however, that after the initial forays and the early euphoria, India's 'Look East' policy has run aground. In countries like Singapore, Malaysia, Indonesia and Japan there is great disappointment with the limited progress that has been made by India in increasing her integration with Asian economies. While there has been more action with respect to South Korea and Thailand, even here actual developments have fallen well short of the potential.

It will not be an exaggeration to say that in the early 1990s, in the immediate aftermath of the end of the Cold War and at a time when China's rapid growth had altered western perceptions of Asian economic power, East Asian capitals witnessed intense political lobbying aimed at influencing the emerging new balance of power in the region. The West, especially the US and European Union, was concerned about the growing influence of the newly industrialising economies of the region and Asia's influence in shaping the post-Cold War balance of power. If the West wished to contain Asia's growing global influence, the Asian financial crisis has certainly helped. This is not to suggest that the crisis was a 'conspiracy' *a la* Mahathir's attacks on George Soros, but to recognise the fact that the Asian crisis has added a new dimension to the emerging balance of power in the region by increasing the mediatory role of the United States. The United States has reasserted its status as *primus inter pares*, even as China has so far retained its influence, offering help to bail out Thailand and signalling the yuan's enhanced role in the world economy. These developments have been at the expense of Japan, South Korea and the ASEAN nations.

The new *modus vivendi* between China and the US has also weakened Japan's influence in the region as well as any resistance to US policy intervention in the cleaning up of the financial crisis. Thus, far from being part of the solution through the instrumentality of the AMF, Japan is now increasingly viewed as part of the problem. Even in the Korean peninsula, US policy towards North Korea has put South Korea on tight leash. The ouster of Indonesia's Suharto and the problems enveloping Malaysia's Mahathir, both directly linked to the social and political fallout of the financial and economic crisis, have also increased US influence in the region. The tough talk from US vice president Al Gore at the November APEC Summit in Kuala Lumpur, where he pointedly criticised the authoritarian regimes in Indonesia and Malaysia, show that the US would like to underscore the new reality without mincing words.

One thing has, however, not changed. India still does not figure as an important player in this 'balance of power' game in Asia. Whatever the damage the Asian crisis may have wrought on the 'miracle' economies of the region, and however relatively unscathed India may have emerged, India is yet to reap any advantage from a change in the political balance of power caused by the Asian economic crisis. Apart from the lacklustre manner in which the 'Look East' policy was pursued and India's failure to forge closer links with Singapore and Taiwan where the potential is enormous, India's 'crisis of identity' in terms of its location in the post-Cold War world, its persistent preoccupation with internal, domestic political uncertainty since 1996, the unresolved ideological debate within India on economic liberalisation, and India's inability to prevent the US, China and other major powers from getting her bogged down in the Kashmir imbroglio, have all served to constrain India's profile in the reshaping of the Asian balance of power.

India's stake in Asia

The most important, if obvious, lesson for India in the aftermath of the Asian crisis is that East Asia and ASEAN will remain major players in the global economy in the 21st century. While earlier notions of an 'Asian Century' or a 'Pacific Century' may now appear exaggerated, there is no denying the fact that Asia to India's east will re-emerge as a growth engine early in the next century. India must continue to give Asia its due. The 'Look East' policy requires urgent attention and rejuvenation. While countries like Indonesia, Malaysia and Thailand may now play a lesser role than what Indian strategic and economic policy analysts believed in the mid-1990s, Japan, Singapore, Taiwan and a possibly unified Korea will remain important economies and India's trade and investment relations with these countries should increase.

Korean unification can be a potentially important event for India and for its relations with other Asian countries. At a India-Korea Bilateral Dialogue in Seoul last year, strategic policy analysts at the Seoul Forum for International Affairs were clear in their mind that India must play a larger role in the emerging Asian balance of power. They saw a unified Korea itself assuming a larger role but, given that prospect, were apprehensive about Chinese and Japanese attitudes towards a unified Korea. From India's point of view a unified Korea can be an important Asian partner.

Equally, India must not neglect its relations with Japan, especially at a time when the United States seems to be willing to jeopardise its relationship with Japan in the interests of a stronger relationship with China. The Clinton Administration's China policy, as well as its response to the Asian crisis and to Japan's role in it has weakened the US-Japan relationship. Given India's desire to attract more foreign direct investment, it should aggressively seek to attract investment interest from Japan, Korea, Singapore and Taiwan. This is a necessary precondition for India's participation in the emerging Asian balance of power.

Sub-continental imperatives

The first step in increasing India's involvement with East and South-East Asia will, however, have to be improved relations between India and its neighbours, particularly Pakistan. An India, hamstrung and hobbled by poor relations with its own neighbours is unlikely to make much headway in the rest of Asia. The key to India's participation in ASEAN and APEC will have to be an increased effectiveness of SAARC (South Asian Association for Regional Cooperation). Increased regional trade and greater policy coordination between India and its neighbours will be required. Indeed, India should go along with Sri Lanka and Bangladesh in forging closer links between SAARC and ASEAN. A SAARC-ASEAN link will also strengthen wider regional associations like the Indian Ocean Rim Association for Regional Cooperation (IOR-ARC). Indian strategic policy planners are perhaps correct in feeling that it is precisely for this reason that Pakistan may be loath to allow SAARC to take off on the economic front, because SAARC's success has the clear potential to actually improve India's profile and increase her influence.

While this may be a legitimate concern, India cannot shy away from the necessity of ensuring SAARC's success. What it can and is trying to do, however, is to go beyond SAARC and create new networks of regional economic cooperation like IOR-ARC and BIMSTEC (Bangladesh-India-Myanmar-Sri Lanka-Thailand Economic Cooperation). A Bay of Bengal Community (BOBCOM) can be launched with all these countries plus Singapore, Malaysia, Nepal and Bhutan. BOBCOM can be the basis for the resolution of several bilateral problems within this group relating to the exploitation of natural resources ranging from water and forest produce to natural gas and oil.

The Asian crisis has also thrown up opportunities for India to assist in the monetary and exchange rate policy management of the smaller economies in the region. The governor of the Bank of Sri Lanka has suggested the creation of a common currency in South Asia. Indian companies must be more active in investing in neighbouring countries. India should move quickly, as it has recently begun to do, in eliminating quantitative restrictions for intra-SAARC trade. Increased regional economic cooperation and trade and investment flows within South Asia, Southern Asia and the Indian Ocean Region are important building blocks for India's participation in the larger Asian and global economy as well as in the shaping of the new balance of power in the region.

This suggests that India's response to the Asian crisis should not be to reverse the recent process of external economic liberalisation, but to better manage the transition into a more liberal trade and investment regime. The process of 'calibrated globalisation', as some have preferred to call it, must be consistent with multilateral trading and investment regimes as they have so far evolved. This implies that India must conform to existing WTO rules, even as it gathers support to ensure that new WTO obligations do not hurt the interests of developing economies. Equally, India must build upon the emerging consensus for cautious capital account liberalisation, even as it moves faster in ensuring reform of the financial sector and liberalising existing provisions relating to foreign currency transactions.

Economic policy and national security

An economic crisis always constitutes a potential threat to national security. In developing economies, a mere shortage of food can pose a threat to national security. The Asian economic crisis has shown, however, that even at higher stages of development an economic crisis triggered by a crisis in the stock market, banking sector, in external trade and payments and so on, can quickly pose a serious challenge to national sovereignty and the very survival of governments. Indeed, it can even be argued that systemic economic crisis or chaos can challenge even the very existence of nations as indeed was the case with the erstwhile Soviet Union. Economic problems left unaddressed can also create social tensions with serious consequences for national survival and sovereignty. The economic and financial crisis in East and South-East Asia has so far only destabilised national governments, as in Indonesia, but has not yet brought nationhood into question. Whether it was the Mexican or the Korean crisis, even large economies and members of the OECD have accepted an erosion of sovereignty in dealing with the consequences of crisis and in restoring normalcy.

In the increasingly globalised world economy the answer to such problems is not to close up an economy or even to over-regulate and control economic activity. Rather, the systems of governance must be made more transparent and efficient and regulatory institutions and mechanisms must be made more effective. Better monitoring and regulation is a key to better economic management. Just as military security requires policy planning, early warning systems and first and second strike capabilities, economic security can also be ensured in an increasingly globalised and market-oriented world through improved systems of policy planning and crisis management. The newly proposed National Security Council may help in improving policy coordination on this front.

The most important lesson for India, from the recent Asian experience, is to strengthen the foundations of her economy. India requires to reform her banking and financial sector, to pursue sound and stable macroeconomic policies, ensure transparency in governance, both in government and the corporate sector. India above all, has to increase the level of mutual dependence between India and the world's major economies so that she creates a stake for the world's most powerful economies in her own wellbeing and stable growth. Other economies must wish to stay invested in India's economy. This can only come upon economic interaction of a much larger magnitude than at present.

The United States cannot afford to allow China or Japan to get caught up in the whirlpool of crisis, because what hurts them also hurts the US. The globalisation of the economic pain arising from crises, is one of the consequences of heightened economic inter-dependence. Even if the initial conditions (asymmetrically) tend to determine who hurts the most, the commonality of the concerns— and of its resolution—is unquestioned. India must work towards an outcome where the US and other major economies regard the Indian economy—located in a matrix of inter-dependence and commonality of interests with other Asian and Indian Ocean economies—as one where the size of their stake demands cooperation and assistance. An inward-looking India will not be able to ensure this. A more open India will.

31 COLUMN

South Asian dialogue

Business of peace and security

IT is a regrettable fact that most media coverage of India-Pakistan dialogue sticks to official exchanges while even high level non-official interaction does not get the coverage it deserves. When senior official from Pakistan and India meet, the print and visual media seem quite satisfied to report official versions of what has transpired within closed doors. But when intellectuals, business-persons, retired diplomats and officials, artists and others meet and have frank exchanges, the media does not take adequate notice. Perhaps it is because such discussions take place away from the glare of the media, that they have become increasingly frank and free.

Enlightened participants from both sides speak candidly of the crisis of governance in South Asia, the poor development record of the region; they discuss freely, alternative ways of resolving the so-called Kashmir problem and the threat of terrorism in the region. At a recent South Asian seminar on "Peace, Security and Economic Cooperation: India and South Asia in the 21st Century", organised jointly by the Indian Council for Research on International Economic Relations (ICRIER, New Delhi), the Institute of Defence Studies and Analyses (IDSA, New Delhi) and the Institute of Peace and Conflict Studies (IPCS, New Delhi), participants from all South Asian countries jointly agreed that economic cooperation must take precedence over political issues in the region.

More importantly, mentioning the 'K' word without inhibition, Indian participants emphasised the importance of settling the Kashmir problem within the framework of what was indeed the 'Simla Accord', that is, the conversion of the Line of Control (LOC) into a *de jure* international border. Interestingly, participants from Pakistan, including Pakistan's former foreign secretary, Mr. Shahryar Khan, did not reject this idea. Apart from reiterating the official Pakistani view of conducting a plebiscite in Kashmir under UN auspices, some of them put forward alternative solutions like joint Indo-Pak sovereignty over Pakistan-occupied and Indian Kashmir. Equally importantly, all participants agreed that even if the Kashmir problem is resolved in the near future, all 'Kashmir-related' issues should be settled forthwith. Such dialogues can be path-breaking if they create a climate in both countries in favour of such de-escalation of tensions.

At another similar South Asian dialogue organised last month at the American Studies Research Centre (ASRC), Hyderabad, participants from all SAARC (South Asian Association for Regional Cooperation) countries jointly expressed concern about the growing menace of terrorism and civil conflict in each of their countries. After over a decade of self-destructive and non-productive violence and civil strife, thinking people and governments have begun to realise that force offers no solution to the problems of the region. The fallout of the Afghan conflict has been devastating for Pakistan which has now discovered that it is riding a tiger of fundamentalist terrorism which can easily consume it.

Both at the Hyderabad seminar and the New Delhi one, all South Asian participants emphasised the urgency of increased economic cooperation within the region. A Pakistani businessman said that in his country there was much apprehension about Pakistani markets being flooded by Indian goods. He believed such fears to be exaggerated. If cheaper Chinese goods had not been able to flood Pakistani markets, how could poorer quality and costlier Indian goods pose a threat? However, he conceded that both in India and in Pakistan there would be some restructuring of industry. The Indian steel industry may pose a competitive challenge to Pakistani steel mills. But in other markets, Pakistanis would be able to give their Indian competitors a run for their money.

While Pakistan has been the laggard as far as India-Pakistan economic relations are concerned, with its refusal to yet extend to India the World Trade Organization's mandatory obligation of the 'most favoured nation' (MFN) status, with respect to other South Asian countries, the laggard is India. Former Indian foreign secretary Muchkund Dubey argued that both with Bangladesh and Sri Lanka, India has a trade surplus and unilateral trade liberalising gestures on India's part can help improve bilateral as well as regional economic cooperation. Mr. Dubey has long drawn attention to the fact that India, having the least open economy in the region, has a trade surplus with almost all its neighbours. This must be reversed. ICRIER's Ms. Isher Ahluwalia pointed out that while Indian tariffs were higher than other South Asian economies, excluding Pakistan, India's non-tariff measures were far in excess of other South Asian economies.

Recent attempts by India and Pakistan to present a joint front at the WTO in negotiations relating to *basmati* rice, textiles and intellectual property rights offer some hope that such joint mobilisation at the SAARC level can help all the countries of the region. It is only when SAARC discovers mutual economic benefit in such unit that greater regional economic cooperation and integration would be made possible. As the region's largest and strongest economy, India is obliged to explore more avenues for such cooperation.

The most important areas for greater economic interaction with South Asia are infrastructure and energy. India, Pakistan, Nepal and Bangladesh should jointly be involved in building a trans-sub-continental highway and oil and gas pipeline across the Indo-Gangetic plain linking Central Asia to South-East Asia. The economic benefit of this project for the three Asian sub-regions, Central, South and South-East Asia, can be enormous. This link can branch-off into Nepal, the North-East and into the Deccan. India can assist Sri Lanka develop Trincomalee as a major hub port, competing for business with Singapore, from where trans-oceanic liners can service the smaller ports of the Indian peninsula. The possibilities are enormous.

The heartening news is that an increasing number of informal and unofficial meetings between South Asian policy- and opinion-makers or shapers are willing to discuss these possibilities and state candidly each other's hopes and apprehensions. The time has come to let the region know that some of its best intentioned people want the countries of South Asia to come closer and work together so that through economic cooperation greater political stability and human security is ensured.

Tackling trust, trade and terrorism

THE South Asian Association for Regional Cooperation (SAARC) has managed to breathe new life into its moribund self with the Islamabad declaration on trade and terrorism. It is extremely important that SAARC members take this declaration seriously and run with it so that by the time they meet next year in Dhaka, the region would have acquired a new relevance for its individual member countries. While espousing great ideas about regional cooperation, SAARC members are all guilty of ignoring each other in actual practice and allowing intra-regional trade to remain a fraction of their trade with the rest of the world.

Perhaps one should not expect any dramatic shift in that pattern given the history of the economic structures of each SAARC nation, but the new sense of regional bonhomie witnessed in Islamabad may generate the trust required to encourage greater economic integration. Trust is the key element in the region. There has been a lack of it and the menace of terrorism has dissipated whatever little trust had been generated by the common experience of battling an unfair global environment.

Hence, the significance of the initiatives taken by all leaders in Islamabad, most importantly by the leaders of India and Pakistan, is that they have been able to revive trust in their bilateral and regional perspective. On this basis, a new relationship can indeed be forged within South Asia.

Yet, South Asia will be only one of India's areas of regional focus in the coming year. Within a month, a new regional forum is to hold its first ever summit level meeting. Heads of government from Bangladesh, India, Myanmar, Sri Lanka and Thailand will meet for the BIMSTEC Summit in Phuket in February. Though as yet limited in the scope of its agenda, BIMSTEC (or, in fact the Bay of Bengal Community) can acquire a profile larger than SAARC if it acts as a bridge between the more inward-oriented South Asia and the more outward-oriented South-East and East Asia. India and Thailand must take bold steps in widening the scope and relevance of BIMSTEC for the region.

But going beyond these regional summits, the proposed bilateral visits of Singapore's Prime Minister Goh Chok Tong, in April, and of his proposed successor, the Deputy Prime Minister and Minister of Finance Lee Hsien Loong, the son of the legendary Lee Kuan Yew, next week, would be important from the viewpoint of engaging the region. Singapore has emerged as one of India's more trusted and reliable partners in the Asian region.

Negotiations for a Comprehensive Economic Cooperation Agreement (CECA) between India and Singapore have been followed up by a bilateral defence cooperation agreement. While Prime Minister Goh has long been a friend and supporter of India, his deputy has also reiterated Singapore's commitment to a special relationship with India. Mr. Lee's commitment to India was palpable at a recent forum in distant New Zealand where the two of us were participants and he was addressing an essentially Pacific audience, perhaps even unaware that an Indian was in the audience.

In a wide-ranging speech that set out a realistic perspective on where Asia was headed and its relations with the world's Great Powers, Mr. Lee underscored the relevance of India, given its new record of economic achievements. While recognising China's emergence as a great nation in Asia, Mr Lee said, "But China is not the only emerging economic giant in Asia. India too is opening up, though it is starting later than China. For decades India closed itself off from the world economy, pursued import-substitution policies, and operated a highly regulated and licence-based system.

But in the last few years India has started to change. There is a political consensus in favour of liberalisation, and the business environment is becoming more favourable. More sectors of the Indian economy are being opened up, including ports, airports, telecommunications and financial services."

It is not just this new economic engagement that is defining the India-Singapore relationship, or indeed the India-Thailand relationship, yet another important bilateral relationship in Asia, but also shared strategic concerns, especially with terrorism and perhaps with China's growing influence. While India's relations with Thailand and Singapore are gaining in depth and range, an as yet under-developed relationship that is bound to acquire a new profile in 2004 will be that with Japan.

India and Japan have ignored each other for far too long. That is set to change in 2004. Perhaps the single most important development in the arena of economic diplomacy in 2004 is going to be the renewal of India's relations with Japan. This will be triggered by a possible visit by Japan's Prime Minister Koizumi. But the Koizumi visit will only initial a process already underway. Japan's policy makers have come to the conclusion, it seems, that the time has come for the two countries to think long-term into the future.

What all this means is for India to speed up the process of economic liberalisation and modernisation. Japan is waiting to invest more in India and is looking for opportunities. India's infrastructure development can receive a huge boost if Japanese investment and aid is welcomed more forthrightly and on terms that are mutually acceptable. The fact is that Japan still controls huge investible surpluses. It is not Europe that is sitting on a pot of investible cash surpluses but Japan. The low level of Japanese investment in India is an anomaly that needs to be corrected.

Once developed to their logical level, India's relations with Japan, Thailand and Singapore, apart from ASEAN as a whole, can be the basis of a new condominium in Asia that is developmental in its consequences for India.

To operationalise these relationships, India will have to walk further on the path of economic liberalisation and modernisation.

It must set the pace for South Asia rather than be the laggard in the region. The foreign policy and trade policy initiatives of 2003 have created the foundations on which this more forward-looking agenda can be pursued in 2004.

The visits of Mr. Lee, Mr. Goh and Mr. Koizumi as well as the BIMSTEC Summit should help speed up that process. While re-engaging South Asia is a good beginning, the real challenge and opportunity lies to our East.

A win-win race in South Asia

FOR years after Independence, Pakistan proudly justified partition on economic grounds. Its superior economic performance was proof enough. Notching up rates of growth of over 6 per cent in the 1960s when India was struggling with its so-called "Hindu rate of growth" of 3.5 per cent per annum, Pakistan used good economics to justify a lot of bad politics, including military dictatorship. It faces once again the prospect of some people justifying military rule in the name of good governance. After all, in his indictment of Prime Minister Nawaz Sharif after the military coup of 1999, General Pervez Musharraf pointed specifically to Mr. Sharif's record of economic mis-governance as a justification for military rule.

Last week Pakistan's finance minister Shaukat Aziz claimed for his country the distinction of being South Asia's 'fastest growing economy'. Number crunching economists may want to quarrel, and certainly the Central Statistical Organisation in India may want him to wait till they come up with revised growth estimates taking into account better than expected foodgrain production numbers, but grant Mr. Aziz his day in the sun.

There is no doubt that the Pakistan economy has shown signs of revival and growth in the last 18 months, after a decade of low growth, increased poverty and external economic dependence. The 1990s was the decade that made all the difference between India and Pakistan. Between 1950 and 1990, Pakistan was ahead of India on many economic indicators. As long as agriculture and agro-based industries had a dominant share of national income, Pakistan had an advantage given its natural resource endowments.

In the 1990s, India surged ahead on two counts, first the growth of a competitive manufacturing sector and second the growth of the services economy. The emergence of new pockets of agrarian prosperity, especially in eastern India, also helped broadbase Indian economic growth. However, the underlying factor that distinguishes India's growth process from that of Pakistan is the savings and investment rate. The Indian middle class learnt the saving habit, helped along by the creation of suitable financial instruments and institutions. Consequently, India's savings and investment rate doubled in two decades hitting 25 per cent in the 1990s. Pakistan's investment rate has remained in the low teens.

Without stepping up the domestic investment rate, and Mr. Aziz has set a target rate of 18 per cent for year 2005-06 against last year's 15.6 per cent, Pakistan cannot hope to sustain upwards of 5 per cent growth per annum in the medium term. This despite a favourable external environment that has helped Pakistan recover in the past year. For close to a decade now, Pakistan has been unable to register more than 4 per cent growth in any year.

September 11, 2001 was an important milestone in Pakistan's economic history. The post-9/11 campaign against terrorism helped Pakistan economically in a number of ways. The increased scrutiny of bank accounts of Pakistanis abroad encouraged many of them to transfer their savings from foreign banks to banks at home. A return flight of capital from the non-resident Pakistani began, contributing significantly to the burgeoning foreign exchange reserves, with NRP remittances accounting for 40 per cent of its US $ 10.5 billion forex reserves, now equivalent to 11 months of imports.

This was compounded by debt rescheduling and write-offs by Pakistan's bilateral donors and access to easy external loans and credits. Favourable market access to Pakistan's textile exports also helped. Clearly, Pakistan milked the post-9/11 opportunity well. However, to be fair, Mr. Aziz and General Musharraf took bold pro-reform steps to improve government finances and build investor confidence. Pakistan's fiscal deficit is down to 4.5 per cent of GDP and a target rate of 3 per cent has been set for 2005-06. With inflation rate contained at 3.3 per cent and a 15 per cent growth in tax revenues, Mr. Aziz feels confident that Pakistan has turned the economic corner.

On that last conclusion the jury is out. The low rate of investment is a symbol of low confidence in the future of the country. The recent surge in forex reserves should not blind Pakistan's policy makers to the fact that the most productive elements of Pakistani society may not see much of a future for themselves in their homeland if terrorism and *jehadism* run amok and constantly challenge investor's confidence.

Domestic social and political instability is not a challenge that Pakistan faces alone. Almost every country in the region is faced with this challenge. Sri Lanka's proud economic record of the 1960s and 1970s was wasted by two decades of terrorism. Nepal faces this challenge today. Parts of India do too. Gujarat cannot hope to recover its economic record of the 1980s and early 1990s, if it does not eschew the politics of confrontation. Punjab has suffered economically from a decade of violence. If hopes of economic growth have revived in Bangladesh it is because the country has so far been able to tame these forces of political destabilisation. But given the activities of Pakistan's Inter-Services Intelligence (ISI) in that country, this peace may not last.

Pakistan must draw the right political lessons from the South Asian growth experience. The economics of growth cannot go hand in hand with the politics of hatred. Peace in the region is vital to the region's economic prosperity. The falsity of Pakistan's fanciful imagination of the past that it can hurt and bleed India with terrorism while simultaneously prospering to become a stronger power has been demonstrated beyond doubt in the 1990s.

It is against this background that Mr. Aziz's budget speech holds out hope for the region and for our bilateral relationship. He has brought economic performance back to the centre-stage of his government's concerns. He has promised higher growth, reduced poverty, increased investment and more employment. He cannot deliver on any of these fronts without ensuring political and social stability and regional peace. If Pakistan begins to understand that to rejoin an economic race with India, it must end the campaign of terrorism and resolve the domestic consequences of its external policies, it will augur well for the region as a whole.

South Asia can rise and shine together

WHEN Timothy Ong, the co-chairman and publisher of *Asia Inc.* a monthly business magazine from Singapore, recently drew the attention of participants at a conference on Asia to what was happening on the Karachi Stock Exchange (KSE), his audience just yawned. Karachi? Do they have a stock exchange? They do, and KSE is setting the pace for the bull run in South Asia. So, it was not surprising that Karachi's investors smiled in approval when Standard & Poor's Rating Services, the international credit rating agency, revised Pakistan's sovereign credit rating outlook from 'stable' to 'positive'. Not surprisingly, that news did not make waves in the Indian media. But then, nor has the good news from our other South Asian neighbours.

While India is 'rising' and 'shining', so is most of South Asia. While India will lead the region with an expected 7.0 per cent growth this year, Pakistan will not be too far behind with upwards of 5.0 per cent growth; nor will Bangladesh or Sri Lanka, with both countries expected to log in close to 6.0 per cent growth in 2003. A regional growth acceleration has positive externalities for all since investors at home and abroad will begin to take a more benign view of South Asia as a whole. For India, that will be good news.

In revising Pakistan's outlook, S&P have said, "The outlook revision reflects improved fiscal and macroeconomic performance, growing external liquidity and continued structural reforms under Prime Minister Jamali's government. Since coming to power about a year ago, the Jamali-led coalition government has generally remained steadfast in practising prudent economic management."

The Pakistan government has been able to reduce government deficit to a 27-year low of 4.4 per cent and persist with structural reforms. Interestingly, the S&P review states, "This progress comes despite a lack of public support, a difficult external environment, and domestic political uncertainties created by the ongoing impasse between the government and opposition over the Legal Framework Order."

With an inflation rate of 3.1 per cent and a growth rate of 5.8 per cent, the highest in a decade, and rising forex reserves, Pakistan has a healthy overall macroeconomic profile. This can only improve if its peace overtures to India strike root at home. Of course, S&P warns that any backtracking on reforms and any slowing down of fiscal stabilisation could reverse the rating outlook. Which is why Pakistan could have, for the first time in years, a stake in an improved overall political and economic environment in the region.

While Pakistan is just about reappearing on investors' radar screens, Bangladesh has had a good economic tale to tell in recent years and this too can become a better tale if it decides to get down to business with India and eschews the temptation to be troublesome.

The other emerging good tale in the region is Sri Lanka. After years of low growth and crisis, Sri Lanka registered upwards of 5.5 per cent growth this year and could see even better performance if peace sustains and its bid to link itself into India's growth process through a 'comprehensive economic cooperation agreement' bears early fruit. Unfortunate Nepal apart, all other members of the South Asian Association of Regional Cooperation will meet in Islamabad next month against this backdrop of improving economic performance.

However, there is a caveat and a shadow lurking. The growth recovery in the region is still tenuous and can be wasted if the region's political leaders do not demonstrate the required courage to buy peace within each country and across. South Asia's century is yet to begin and it cannot, without regional peace and stability.

To underscore the importance of a conducive regional political environment for economic growth is not to suggest that there is a 'peace dividend', in the traditional sense of that term. A 'peace dividend' is normally understood as the money available for development that can be diverted from defence. It will take a long time before governments in the region can really hope to monetise such a dividend, for a variety of reasons.

In India's case, the so-called 'peace dividend' is minimal for at least three reasons. First, because our defence budget is already quite modest, contrary to popular belief. At less than 3.0 per cent of GDP, there isn't much of a squeeze that can be exerted on it. While pensions and salaries will continue to be a major component of this expenditure, the desperate need for defence modernisation will mean that India will have to find resources for defence even if 'peace' with Pakistan is assured.

Second, India's security concerns transcend Pakistan and in addressing these, the country will have to spend even more on higher-cost modern technology. Third, apart from the regular defence expenditure India will have to continue to spend on internal security and on modernising the response to terrorism.

Hence, one must not exaggerate the significance of the conventionally understood 'peace dividend' in the fiscal sense. The financial savings to the exchequer from increased regional security could be minimal in the medium term. However, what is more important is that improved relations between India and Pakistan can alter investor sentiment in the region as a whole. This would benefit not just India and Pakistan, but Bangladesh, Nepal and Sri Lanka.

To what extent the governments in South Asia can make the regional security environment more conducive to economic growth will depend on a variety of factors. It will certainly depend on the maturity and self-confidence of the national leadership within each country. It will depend on the willingness of the governments to curtail the role of 'non-state' actors, including rogue elements within each country's security and political establishment. It will, above all, depend on public awareness of the economic cost in lost opportunities, the region is paying by pursuing antagonistic politics.

Those who celebrate 5.0 per cent to 7.0 per cent growth in the region should know that the region as a whole will need peace for it to log 8.0 per cent to 10.0 per cent growth. That is the 'peace dividend' waiting to be encashed.

35 COLUMN

Economic consequences of J&K elections

THE most significant policy statement of Prime Minister Atal Bihari Vajpayee with a direct bearing on the economy was his assurance this week that "there will be no war" between India and Pakistan. There has never been such a categorical assurance from the government since December 13, 2001. Mr. Vajpayee's assurance of no war, stated in an interview given to a British newspaper, did not secure the attention it deserved at home. It should calm investors, businesses and the markets who are unnerved periodically by irresponsible and myopic warmongering by hotheads at home.

What could have prompted Mr. Vajpayee to offer this assurance? Some have speculated that he was "putting his best diplomatic foot forward" to create the right atmosphere for his meetings in Europe. It is possible, though, that there is more to the Prime Minister's assurance than diplomatic nicety. The key motivating factor is the successful conclusion of the elections in Jammu and Kashmir. In the face of terrorist violence, the sullen boycott by some groups in the Kashmir valley and adverse Pakistani propaganda, the completion of the electoral process, irrespective of the final outcome marks a major step forward for India.

It is the resultant sense of satisfaction that is reflected in the Prime Minister's assurance. Hotheads in the Sangh Parivar and adventurists in government may yet want to 'teach Pakistan a lesson or two' and they may rubbish Mr. Vajpayee's statesman like assurance. They will be wrong to view this assurance as a sign of weakness or reflecting an absence of strategy.

Rather, the PM's assurance is not only based on a considered strategy in dealing with Pakistan's 'proxy war', but it is also based on a correct perception of what ought to be India's priorities, now that elections in J&K are over. A conventional war with Pakistan is not going to solve the problem of *jehadi* terrorism. Instead, it can hurt economically and diplomatically.

Does this mean that the troops massed along the border with Pakistan should be demobilised? Most certainly not. The mobilisation of troops was wrongly viewed as preparation for waging war. It was meant to exert pressure on Pakistan in a variety of ways and the strategy is working. Those who interpreted the mobilisation of forces as a signal of war came to wrong conclusions and needlessly raised an alarm.

By not explaining its strategy clearly the government may also have contributed to, on the one hand, raised expectations at home that Pakistan will now be 'taught a lesson' by military means, and on the other hand, to excessive alarm abroad of a possible nuclear conflagration, resulting in the infamous 'travel advisories'.

Now that Mr. Vajpayee has said that India does not intend to wage war, the government must clearly explain the rationale for the continued mobilisation of troops along the border, even if it is scaled down. Just as East and West Germany had, and North and South Korea continue to maintain fully mobilised troops along their borders, India may have to now continue with the policy of a higher degree of troop mobilisation and war readiness along the Line of Control, even if not the entire border, for a considerable period of time to be able to exert pressure on Pakistan.

Highly placed sources in the government claim that a clear strategy in this regard has already been developed and communicated to the armed forces. This will have to be followed by wider communication to the political class as well as to the media so that exaggerated expectations or ill-informed criticism of the mobilisation does not continue.

More to the point, the armed forces will have to devise means by which the troops are able to live normal lives, are able to be with their families for longer periods of time and do not develop battle fatigue. The experience of South Korea shows that this can be ensured without hurting either the morale of the forces or the health of the Indian economy.

The positive economic consequences of a return to normalcy in J&K and of subdued terrorist activity can be shared by both India and Pakistan, if the leadership in both countries is forward-looking and wise. The economic gains of increased stability can more than pay for the cost of increased mobilisation and battle alertness. To work this strategy successfully India must adopt a pro-active diplomatic gameplan that brings pressure on Pakistan to seek normalcy and recognise the legitimacy of the democratic process in J&K.

The elections are the starting point of normalisation in this regard and must be followed up by positive initiatives that empower the local political leadership in J&K. A wise policy in J&K can have hugely positive economic externalities for India, and for Pakistan if its leadership is also wise. Excessive belligerence on the part of the ruling alliance in New Delhi or deviousness on the part of the ruling clique in Islamabad can only be self-destructive to both countries.

Hopefully, Mr. Vajpayee's forthright statement will set at rest persistent speculation regarding the prospect of war in South Asia. This ill-informed speculation, fuelled by loose talk by short-sighted warmongers, has hurt the economy. While economists in the United States are beginning to worry about the negative economic consequences for the US and the world economy of a war against Iraq, not many economists in India are as yet articulating more forcefully a similar concern about the negative economic consequences of war.

To be sure, after the Kargil war, I did take the view that the economic and fiscal impact of the Kargil war was not too high. It was an affordable war, though not in human terms. Even now the Indian fisc and the economy can afford a war. But the economic cost of Kargil was outweighed by the political and diplomatic benefits because that war was thrust on us.

The economic costs of a conventional war initiated by India are likely to be more than the diplomatic or political benefits of 'teaching Pakistan a lesson'. It is such cool and wise calculation that must have encouraged Mr. Vajpayee to offer that reassurance on war. Moreover, the voters in J&K have taught Pakistan a lesson, thank you!

The business of other neighbours

PAKISTAN'S General Pervez Musharraf can taunt India to his heart's delight about the South Asian 'big brother' having problems with all its smaller neighbours, but if he's attentive the difference should sink in.

While Pakistan and India talk only about territory and terrorists, our other neighbours are all talking business and economics with India. Just look at the agenda of the heads of government of each of India's neighbours, including China, on their recent visits to this country. It is all focused on trade, investment and infrastructure building.

If the conversation with China is about information technology, with Bangladesh it is about natural gas. If with Afghanistan it's about technical assistance and aid, with Nepal and Sri Lanka it is about freer trade. Step out of 'South Asia' and take a look at 'Southern Asia'. The bilaterals with Iran, Myanmar and Thailand are all about trade, energy and infrastructure.

The visit to India this week of Sri Lanka's Prime Minister Ranil Wickremesinghe, therefore, followed an expected and familiar pattern. India must seize the moment and take a long-term and broader view of this nascent economic engagement with the southern Asian neighbourhood, being more generous to our less developed neighbours rather than churlish, protocol bound and insisting on reciprocity in extending preferences.

There is a website, www.indolankafta.org, on trade cooperation between India and Sri Lanka, maintained by Sri Lanka, with a hopeful homepage in bright yellow and green. There is no reason to be pessimistic about improved India-Sri Lanka trade and economic relations and this website tells us why. The opportunities for more business between the two countries are enormous and can only grow. Indeed, they must grow and in the near term, more in favour of Sri Lanka. That is a necessity that India must come to terms with.

There is far too much resistance in India to doing free trade with our smaller neighbours. The reasons are understandable and have nothing to do with India's perceived 'big brother' attitude. It's the opposite. Defensive Indian producers in one sector or another are worried about the competition. This explains the higgling and haggling that accompanied the signing of the India-Sri Lanka Free Trade Agreement and the renewal of the trade agreement with Nepal. With Bangladesh too, there is much hardnosed negotiation going on.

The problem is that India is caught in a paradox. It is the largest economy in the region but not secure enough in economic terms to be more open to its smaller neighbours. Thus, while large continental economies like the United States and China are happily signing away FTAs with their smaller neighbours, and countries at similar levels of development in Latin America and South-East Asia are able to draw up FTAs too, India is unable to muster up the confidence to pursue this track on the trade front with its smaller neighbours.

That explains why the external affairs ministry is trying hard to explain to the commerce ministry that letting our neighbours run a trade deficit against us is not such a bad idea at all. India has a huge trade surplus with Sri Lanka, and that should be reversed. Perhaps trade alone cannot bridge this gap unless India relaxes the local content requirement with respect to third country products exported from Sri Lanka to India. This is difficult. Perhaps Indian companies can help by setting up production bases in Sri Lanka for re-export home.

There could be a way of resolving the problem if there is a will and such political will was on full display this week during Prime Minister Wickremesinghe's visit. Following up the initiative taken by Sri Lanka President, Chandrika Kumaratunga, in 1998, Mr. Wickremesinghe pushed for a widening of the scope of bilateral economic cooperation and a speeding up of the process of economic integration.

The positive tone of Mr. Wickremesinghe's visit as well as the good news from Bangladesh about increased economic cooperation with India, and the successful conclusion of the India-Nepal trade talks a few weeks ago, suggest that India's relations with its 'other' neighbours are on safe track. The bilateral economic agenda has moved beyond trade to include investment, especially in the infrastructure sector, power, petroleum and natural gas, roads, railways, ports and so on.

If on the trade account India has a surplus, given the basket of goods traded, this can be balanced elsewhere with Indian investment creating jobs in neighbouring countries and India purchasing commodities like natural gas from Bangladesh. To ease the flow of trade, India should be generous enough to concede the demand that more ports are open to receive tradeables from the neighbours. Thus, the restriction of Sri Lankan exports to two Indian ports is limiting and naturally Sri Lankans complain.

The Indian mindset of seeking reciprocity, if not outright concessions, was partly shaped by the fact that our external economic relations have been largely with more developed industrial economies. We are still new to this experience of being the economically better placed and being required to extend support and help to smaller neighbours. Such generosity is not required in Pakistan's case given the proxy war that country wages against us. However, in dealing with our other neighbours, we must be generous and forward-looking.

The time has also come to widen our concept of our neighbourhood. It is no longer limited to 'South Asia' as conventionally defined by Western analysts. Iran, Afghanistan and

Myanmar are certainly our neighbours. The South Asian Association for Regional Cooperation must in fact be renamed the Southern Asian ARC and these three countries should be invited to join it.

Equal attention should be paid to deepening our business and economic relations with the Association of South-East Asian Nations. India should be a more active commercial nation in the region, living and trading in peace with nations around, with trade and investment flows cementing a new economic relationship and offering the assurance of regional security. We would then not feel so harassed by the taunts of one pesky neighbour.

IT and the e-Economy

The ballast for India-US relations

THE most enduring phrase describing the nature of the bilateral relationship between India and the United States of America during the Cold War era comes from the title of Denis Kux's book on Indo-US relations, *Estranged Democracies*.[1] More recently, though, the two democracies have been described as "natural allies".[2] Clearly, the end of the Cold War and India's 'new economic policies' of trade and investment liberalisation have opened a new chapter in the bilateral relationship.

However, despite a high degree of 'people-to-people' contact over the years, the commercial and economic engagement between the world's two largest democracies has not been sizeable enough, particularly from the US perspective, to lend weight to India's causes and interests in the United States. The comparison in recent years has been with China which today effectively subsidises the standard of living of the average American citizen through the export of low-cost consumer goods to the US. India has never been such an

---

1. Denis Kux, *Estranged Democracies: India and the United States, 1941-1991,* Sage Publications, New Delhi, 1993. Other interesting analyses of Indo-US relations in the Cold War period are offered in Satu Limaye, *U.S-Indian Relations: The Pursuit of Accomodation,* Westview Press, Boulder, 1993; Gary Bertsch, *et al.* (Edited), *Engaging India: U.S Strategic Relations with the World's Largest Democracy,* Routledge, New York, 1999; Harold Gould and Sumit Ganguly (Edited), *The Hope and the Reality: U.S Indian Relations from Roosevelt to Reagan,* Oxford & IBH Publishing, New Delhi, 1993.

2. A phrase used by Prime Minister Atal Behari Vajpayee on a visit to the United States in 1998, describing Indo-US relations.

important political or economic partner for the US, even though the US remains India's most important economic partner. The renewed attempt by both India and the United States to find a new equilibrium in their relationship in the post-Cold War period has spurred a search on both sides for a 'ballast' that will enable the faster and more stable progress of the ship of Indo-US relations.[3] At the turn of the century it now appears that we may have found in the information technology sector and in the larger 'electronic economy'—the 'e-economy'—the required ballast for the stable and energetic progress of our bilateral relationship.

This chapter draws attention to the nature of the opportunity afforded by IT and the e-economy and lists the kind of policy issues both countries have to grapple with if the Indo-US economic interaction has to accelerate, becoming wider and deeper and laying the foundation for a larger and more enduring basis for a meaningful and sustained relationship between our two great democracies. Apart from the commercial and business opportunities that the e-economy offers the two countries, we also point to the cultural and social interaction that it enables between the peoples of both democracies.

From 'estranged democracies' to 'engaging economies'

In dubbing India and the US 'estranged democracies' Denis Kux was suggesting that while the two occasionally warmed up to each other through episodic engagement, the general tenor of Indo-US relations during the entire Cold War period was marked by US disinterest and at times suspicion and Indian prickliness and at times hostility.

While Kux's focus is on personalities, and personalities do seem to have counted on both sides, the fact is that as long as the United States viewed Pakistan as a 'frontline' State and ally against communist Soviet Union, and as long as India remained deeply suspicious of

---

3. I recall Marshall Bouton (Asia Society, New York) referring to the need for an economic 'ballast' to stabilise Indo-US relations at a seminar at ICRIER. More recently, Stephen Cohen has also expressed the hope that "... economic ties, ...will eventually provide the ballast for a more stable US-Indian relationship because the economies of the two countries are complimentary", in *A New Beginning in South Asia*, Brookings Policy Brief #55, January 2000.

both Pakistani and US motives in the region, there was little chance of any real 'engagement' between the two countries, notwithstanding the genuine warmth in the people-to-people interaction and the increasing level and range of US business interest in India.

The fact that Indo-US 'political' relationship was at best 'lukewarm' during the Cold War period implied that while India and the US maintained an active economic relationship, it was nowhere near the kind of economic engagement that the US was involved in with and South-East Asia and subsequently even China. From an American perspective India was a marginal strategic and economic player.

The purpose of this essay is not to examine why this was so. We merely acknowledge this as a fact. However, we must add here that this was not a natural or inevitable state of affairs given India's desire to maintain an independent foreign policy and its commitment to a policy of 'non-alignment' during the Cold War era. Indeed, as early as in 1949, Prime Minister Jawaharlal Nehru underscored the importance of the United States to the Indian economy and welcomed US investment in India, a fact that is not widely known and acknowledged in the literature on Indo-US relations.[4] Nehru did not see a contradiction between his firm adherence to non-alignment and to India's economic sovereignty and closer economic relations with the United States. If Indo-US economic relations remained stunted in the Cold War period it was initially because the US had other priorities and only subsequently, during Indira Gandhi's tenure, because India pursued a more inward-looking model of industrial development.

The overall nature of India's 'inward-oriented' economic policies meant that foreign trade and foreign investment played a less than significant role in the national economy. India's share of world trade in fact declined from around 2.0 per cent in the early 1950s to around half a percent in the 1970s. Even so, the US remained a major source

---

4. See Sanjaya Baru, "The Economic Dimension of India's Foreign Policy", *World Affairs*, (Geneva/ Delhi), Vol 2, No 2, April-June 1998 (Reprinted as Chapter 2 in this volume).

of aid and trade for India, emerging as the single largest trade partner by the 1970s, and an important partner in India's quest for food self-sufficiency, through its support for India's 'green revolution'. Thus, more than any specific anti-US bias in Indian foreign policy, it was India's general economic policy of 'inward-orientation' and a preference for domestic enterprise over foreign multinational enterprise, which was responsible for the low level of Indo-US economic interaction in the Cold War period.

The end of the Cold War is only one of the three major factors that have contributed to a shift in Indian attitudes towards greater economic engagement with the United States.[5] The other two *equally* important factors are—first, the structural changes internal to India's political economy that constitute the basis of a new political consensus in favour of economic liberalisation and the outward-orientation of economic policy in India;[6] second, the demonstration effect of the' Asian Economic Miracle', in particular the 'wake-up' impact of China's 'new economic policies' and its impressive economic performance in the 1990s, particularly in attracting foreign investment, boosting China's exports and modernising her economy.

Together, all these factors have contributed to the beginning of a new chapter in Indo-US relations in the 1990s, some even refer to this change as a 'paradigm shift'.[7] While the jury may still be out on whether or not there has been a 'paradigm shift' on both sides, the fact is that there is now growing recognition within the foreign and economic policy community in the United States and India that

---

5. On the significance of the end of the Cold War see, Selig S. Harrison and Geoffrey Kemp, *India and America After the Cold War: Report of the Carnegie Endowment Study Group on US-Indian Relations in a Changing International Environment*, Brookings Institution, January 1993. Also see, Mohammed Ayoob, "Potential Partners: India and the United States", *Asia Pacific Issues*, East-West Center Paper No. 42, December, 1999.

6. On this see, Sanjaya Baru, "Continuity and Change in Indian Industrial Policy", in T.V. Satyamurthy (Ed.) *Industry and Agriculture in India since Independence*, Vol 2., Oxford University Press, Delhi, 1995. and Sanjaya Baru, "Economic Policy and Development of Capitalism in India: The Emergence of Regional Capitalists and Regional Political Parties", in Francine Frankel, *et al.* (Ed.), *Transforming India: Social and Political Dynamics of Democracy*, Oxford University Press, New Delhi, 2000.

7. The two governments have attempted to capture this 'paradigm shift' in a statement jointly issued by President Clinton and Prime Minister Vajpayee during the former's visit to New Delhi in March 2000. "India-US Relations: A Vision for the 2151 Century", Appendix One.

the world's two largest democracies must pursue a closer and more enduring relationship based on greater economic engagement. In the United States this view was first articulated in the Report of the Independent Task Force of the Council on Foreign Relations on "A New US Policy Toward India and Pakistan" (1997), and most recently expressed again in the *Open Letter to the President,* (March 2000) issued by the "Independent Task Force on US Policy Toward South Asia", co-sponsored by the Council on Foreign Relations and the Brookings Institution.[8]

The 1997 Report observed, "The United States should significantly expand its bilateral economic, political and military ties with India and Pakistan simultaneously. It is both possible and desirable to delink the two bilateral relationships and transcend the zero-sum dynamics that have often plagued the region (and US policy) in the past. The time is ripe, in particular, for the United States to propose a closer strategic relationship with India, which has the potential to emerge as a full-fledged major power. The relationship would be based on shared values and institutions, economic collaboration including enhanced trade and investment, and the goal of regional stability across Asia."

India's 'new economic policies' of greater outward-orientation and a more liberal foreign trade and investment regime, first introduced by the government of Prime Minister Narasimha Rao in 1991 and subsequently pursued by successive coalition governments of the United Front and the National Democratic Alliance, have enabled greater economic engagement between the two countries. As noted by Bertsch, Gahlaut and Srivastava, "There is some recognition in both India and the United States that their overall economic and political vectors are intersecting. So far, in many respects, the United States has adopted a wait-and-see approach about the success of the Indian economic programme. On the Indian side, this has resulted in a growing sense of frustration. They would prefer

---

8.   Open letter to the President, Statement issued by the Independent Task Force on US Policy Toward South Asia, Co-sponsored by the Council on Foreign Relations and the Brookings Institution, March 13, 2000.

that the United States be deeply involved in this process rather than an interested bystander. Such hands-on cooperation would also translate into greater understanding and trust, elements that could prove vital to deepening and widening their bilateral relationship."[9]

This nascent bilateral economic relationship may have developed further in the 1990s if the US had been more appreciative of India's national security concerns. The obsession of US policy makers with nuclear non-proliferation and their willingness to hold the rest of the bilateral relationship hostage to the US nuclear agenda slowed down the pace of Indo-US bilateral trade and investment flows. This is borne out by the fact that new economic partners like South Korea and Singapore rapidly increased their share of Indian trade and investment flows during the 1990s.

The unfortunate decision of the US government to impose economic sanctions on India after the Pokhran-II nuclear tests further hurt the bilateral economic relationship, not so much in material terms as much as in psychological and political terms. India was deeply disappointed by the tone of admonishment emanating from certain quarters in Washington DC and it took successive rounds of 'strategic policy' talks between Strobe Talbot of the US State Department and Indian foreign minister Jaswant Singh to restore balance to the relationship. While the sanctions did not have a major impact on the Indian economy, they did impact on trade and investment flows, which were dependent on US Exim Bank and other institutional support.[10]

While the US hurt both itself and the bilateral relationship by imposing economic sanctions on India, some other countries in fact benefited by refusing to do so. South Korea, for instance, succeeded in further improving its trade and investment relationship with India emerging as the single largest source of foreign direct investment

---

9. pp. 267, Bertsch *et al.* (1999) *op. cit.*

10. Early estimates of the impact of US sanctions on the Indian economy placed this at around US$ 20 billion. However, subsequent estimates put this at no more than US$ 2 billion over the two year period 1998-2000. Also see, Fred Bergsten, "Do Economic Sanctions Work?", ICRIER *Public Policy Lecture*, March 1999.

in India in 1998-99. By distancing itself from the G-8 and P-5 stance on India's nuclear status, France has also improved the profile of its economic relations with India.

The US has not yet officially altered its policy of opposing the Indian nuclear deterrent and is still not willing to see India recognised as a nuclear weapons power within the ambit of the NPT. However, there is increasing recognition within policy circles in the US that India and the United States must transcend such differences and build a new relationship.[11] There is greater willingness on the part of the US to recognise the relevance and credibility of the Indian nuclear deterrent. Clearly, no Indian government will roll back the deterrent, nor indeed can India not be expected to fully develop the delivery, 'control and command' system required to ensure the credibility, survivability and durability of the deterrent. However, keeping differences on such issues aside India and the US have now agreed to work together on a range of issues, economic and otherwise, at the bilateral level and at the regional, multilateral and international levels.

It is therefore not surprising that more recent policy statements on Indo-US relations have had to reiterate the importance of improved economic interaction between the two countries. The March 2000 Statement of the Independent Task Force on US Policy Towards South Asia, sponsored by the Council on Foreign Relations, had to proffer the following advice to the US President:

"You should use those inducements you have at your disposal — including waiving US opposition to international financial institution lending for non-basic human needs purposes and reducing the number of Indian firms currently limited in what they can receive from US companies — in order to underscore the US commitment to

---

11. This sense of 'realism' is most evident in the *Open Letter to the President,* of Independent Task Force on US Policy Toward South Asia, co-sponsored by the Council on Foreign Relations and the Brookings Institution. March 13,2000 (available at: www.brooke.edu). The letter states: "It is essential to resist the temptation to place ambitious, nuclear weapons-related goals at the center of US aims. Any attempt to persuade India to eliminate its nuclear arsenal will fail (and poison the atmosphere for the constructive discussion of other issues ...Nor are you well placed to pressure India to sign the CTBT given the failure of the US Senate to ratify the treaty."

expanding economic ties and improving US relations with India across the board."[12]

In setting out the key objectives of the President's tour of South Asia (India, Pakistan and Bangladesh) the *Open Letter* suggests that as far as US goals in India are concerned the most important objective ought to be "to build a post-Cold War relationship with India that expands economic and other forms of interaction and cooperation between the United States and India." Both sides are therefore, increasingly underscoring the importance of economic relations in Indo-US relations.

Admittedly, both countries have to come to grips with a variety of policy challenges before this relationship can be regarded as being stable and sustainable.[13] On India's part, we must continue to pursue the policy of economic reform and liberalisation to enable a higher degree of economic engagement between India and the world, in general, and India and the US, in particular. On the part of the US, it must not only come to terms with India's declared nuclear status and acquire a better appreciation of India's security concerns, but must also be more sensitive to Indian concerns relating to the challenge of globalisation and liberalisation within a democratic framework in a developing country.

The ongoing 'strategic dialogue' between the two governments, the recently launched 'dialogue of democracies' and the new 'architecture for institutional dialogue' on a range of economic and political issues initiated during the visit to India of US president Bill Clinton and supported by the statement of the two Heads of Government on a bilateral "Vision for the 21st Century", which talks of a 'qualitatively new relationship' between the two democracies, can help reinforce the process of coming together of the two nations.

---

12. *ibid.*

13. For a lucid and frank listing of Indian complaints and concerns with US policy in South Asia and policies relating to trade, technology transfer and national security see Jairam Ramesh, "Yankee Go Home, But Take Me with You: Yet Another Perspective on Indo-American Relations", *Economic and Political Weekly* (Mumbai) December 11-17, 1999; and *Asia Society* (New York), 2000.

However, the key to an improved Indo-US relationship in the new century lies in enhanced economic and cultural interaction. It has increased two-way trade and capital flows and the freer movement of professional skills as well as increased cultural and social interaction through the new media, which will create the stabilising ballast in the bilateral relationship. In this essay we look at the emerging role of information technology, software services, electronic commerce, the Internet and the electronic media in improved Indo-US economic relations.

Recent trends in Indo-US trade and investment

The United States is India's largest trading partner; export destination and source of foreign direct investment. The two-way trade in 1999 was in excess of US $12 billion, which implies more than a 100 per cent increase since 1992 (Table 37.1). The US is one of the few trade partners with which India enjoys a substantial trade surplus, and in fact this trade surplus finances to a large extent the trade deficit India has with the oil-exporting countries. In other words, India's dependence on imported energy from the Middle East is in part mitigated by the trade surplus it enjoys *vis-à-vis* the US. In this sense, the positive balance on trade with the US has a critical national security dimension for India since this ensures in part India's energy security.

The trade data provided here refers only to merchandise trade and does not capture 'services exports' like software and data processing exports and inward remittances from temporary emigrants like software engineers. There are no official estimates of income from such 'exports', but more on this later. Indian exports to the US are estimated to have increased by an average rate of 14.2 per cent in dollar terms since 1992. This is above the average rate of total export growth for India for this period. Imports from the USA have been fluctuating. After growing by 44 per cent in 1993, they dropped by 18.5 per cent in 1994, and rose again by 44 per cent in 1995. Their rate of growth fell to 0.6 per cent in 1996, increased to 8.9 per cent in 1997 and declined by 1.96 per cent in 1998. Understandably, therefore, the volume of Indo-US bilateral trade remains a small fraction of USA's global trade. While US exports to India account for nearly 12 per cent of India's non-oil imports and US is the destination of 18.9 per cent of India's exports, USA's trade turnover with India constitutes less than 1 per cent of its global trade. By contrast, India's share of US imports has been rising gradually and has increased from 0.84 per cent in 1997 to 0.90 per cent in 1998. India ranks 23rd among countries that export to the US.

Table 37.1

India's Trade with US, 1992-99 (in US$ Million)

	1992	1993	1994	1995	1996	1997	1998	1999
Exports to US	3,781	4,551	5,302	5,736	6,169	7,321	8,225	9,083
Imports from US	1,914	2,761	2,296	3,296	3,318	3,616	3,545	3,707
Trade Turnover	5,695	7,312	7,598	9,032	9,487	10,937	11,770	12,790
Trade Balance (Favour of India)	1,866	1,790	3,005	2,440	2,851	3,705	4,680	5,376
Trade Surplus as Percentage of Total Turnover	32.0	24.5	39.5	27.0	30.0	33.9	39.7	42.0

Source: Commerce Wing, Embassy of India, Washington DC.

There has been a considerable change in the composition of Indo-US trade. While six items account for nearly three-fourths of Indian exports to the US, namely textiles and clothing, cut and polished non-industrial diamonds, carpets, shrimps and prawns, footwear, leather goods and cashew nuts, India has also been exporting machinery, dyes, iron and steel, chemicals and a range of food items.

Conventional trade economics, however, imposes a constraint on the economist's ability to appreciate the actual level of Indo-US trade today. With the services sector playing an increasingly important role in the growth process of both the US and India and with information technology and the electronic economy emerging as the key area of bilateral commercial interaction, it has become necessary to widen the definition of trade to include trade in services. This is easier said than done. There are no readily available statistics on the two-way trade in e-economy areas like software services, data processing and e-commerce. Hence, official trade statistics only refer to merchandise trade which underestimates the actual trade relationship between the two economies.

US investments in India

There has been a sustained increase in investments by US companies in India in the 1990s (Table 37.2). While the share of 'actual' US investment (as distinguished from 'approved' investment[14]) as a proportion of 'total actual' foreign investment has increased, though in a cyclical manner, 'approved' US investment proposals have not kept pace with the overall increase in FDI approvals (Table 37.3). The share of the US has slipped from as high as 32 per cent in 1992 to a mere 11 per cent in 1999. However, on average the US remains the single largest source of foreign investment in India. South Korea has emerged as an important new investor in India, while Japan's share has gone down in the 1990s.

The sudden spurt in 1993, 1997 and 1999 can be attributed to specific large projects coming in, like Enron in 1993. Of the total foreign investment approvals in the period 1991-99, the United States had the highest share of over 22.0 per cent. Much of this investment has been in the infrastructure sectors like energy (oil refinery and power) and telecommunications, with the automobile, processed foods and

Table 37.2

US Investment in India, 1991-99 (Rs. Million)

	1991	1992	1993	1994	1995	1996	1997	1998	1999
Approval (US)	1,859	12,315	34,619	34,881	70,544	1100,559	135,698	35,620	17,260
Actuals (US)	278	1,148	4,527	3,731	6,769	9,484	25,895	14,300	15,399
Total Actuals	3,514	6,752	17,859	29,717	63,694	84,406	120,892	88,476	59,454
Actuals (US) as Share of Total Actuals	7.9	17.0	25.0	12.5	10.6	11.2	21.4	16.0	25.45

Source: *SIA Newsletter,* Ministry of Industry, GoI, 1999.

14. Since foreign investors have to secure an 'approval' to invest in India from the Foreign Investment Promotion Board (FIPB), prospective investors first seek an approval and then may wait for a period before 'actually' investing. Hence 'approvals' can be different from 'actuals'.

Table 37.3

Country Share of Foreign Investment Approvals in India (Percentage)

Country	1992	1995	1999 (up to Sept.)	Total
US	31.6	21.9	11.2	22.3
Mauritius*	0	5.6	12.4	10.1
UK	3.1	5.4	10.6	7.4
S. Korea	1.0	1.0	13.5	4.4
Japan	15.7	4.7	5.8	4.4
Germany	2.2	4.1	4.1	3.7
NRI**	11.3	2.2	1.5	3.9
Euro-Issue***	0	3.7	11.9	10.7

Source: SIA Newsletter, Ministry of Industry, GoI, 1999.

Note: *: Mauritius has emerged as an important source of FDI because of a tax-avoidance treaty with India. Many multinational and some Indian companies invest in India through Mauritius-based subsidiaries.

       **: NRI stands for Non-resident Indian.

       ***: Major Indian companies have been accessing lower cost foreign funds through Euro-issues.

services sector also attracting US investment. The new insurance policy, which permits minority foreign participation, is expected to attract US companies into the Indian financial sector.

Most of the Fortune 500 companies have operations in India and all the major IT companies have also started operations here. While US companies have been slow in arriving in India, with Japanese, South Korean and European companies being more aggressive, there is no doubt that India has now secured an important place for itself in the medium-term corporate plans of most major US multinationals.

While there is no doubt that investment in the infrastructure and financial sectors may account for the dominant share of US investment in India in the near future, the services sector, especially IT, media and entertainment sectors, is expected to secure an increasing share of inward investment. Such investment will not just be aimed at the Indian market but also at the world market. In other words, the e-economy may emerge as the most important sector for export-oriented US investment in India; automobile, processed foods and services sector also attracting US investment. The new insurance policy, which permits minority foreign participation, is expected to attract US companies into the Indian financial sector.

Trends in the e-economy

For decades there has been a certain stability in the composition of the two-way trade between India and the US. India exported mainly textiles and garments, leather goods, gems and jewellery and some food products, and imported from the US foodgrains, machinery and other capital goods. While oil-exports shaped the strategic relationship between the US and West Asia, the export of low cost and good quality consumer durables, household electronics and new technology products shaped US economic relationship with most of East and South-East Asian countries. China secured a strategic foothold in the US market by first displacing some of the South-East countries and subsequently becoming the major source of low cost consumer durables, toys and household goods. India has never been able to identify a strategic trade sector and the one area in which it had a comparative advantage, namely textiles and garments; it wasted away through the pursuit of shortsighted domestic industrial policy.

All this has begun to change for India in the electronic age. India's historical investment in mathematics and the sciences, its more recent policy of providing public investment in science and technology teaching, the spread of good quality engineering colleges, particularly in peninsular India, and the relatively uninhibited development of new enterprise in the 'unregulated' 'new economy' have combined to impart to the Indian information technology sector a competitive advantage in the global e-economy.[15] Indian enterprise readily exploited this advantage in the fastest growing e-market in the world, namely, the United States.

Surprisingly, however, there is no official database on the Indian e-economy. No agency of government or industry organisation collects comprehensive information on the number of firms, the value of services and output, total employment and so on. The only available source of comprehensive nationwide information on the e-economy

---

15. On the factors that contributed to the software industry emerging as an 'island of competitiveness' in India see M. Patibandla, D. Kapur and B. Petersen, "Import Substitution with Free Trade: Case of India's Software Industry", *Economic and Political Weekly,* April 8, 2000, pp. 1263-1270.

is the National Association of Software and Service Companies (NASSCOM). Nasscom's *The IT Software and Services Industry in India: Strategic Review 2000,* is the only important source of information. This publication incorporates information from the Nasscom-McKinsey Study Report on the Indian software industry (1999).[16]

The Nasscom report claims that, "With a compounded annual growth of more than 50 per cent between 1990 and 1999, the Indian IT software and services sector has expanded almost twice as fast as the US software sector did during the same period, though from a smaller base" (Table 37.4).

Table 37.4

Information Technology Industry in India (US$ Million)

	1994-95	1995-96	1996-97	1997-98	1998-99
Software-Domestic-Exports	350	490	670	950	1,250
	85	734	1,083	1,750	2,650
Hardware-Domestic-Exports	590	1,037	1,050	1,205	1,026
	177	35	286	201	4
Peripherals-Domestic-Exports	148	196	181	229	329
	6	6	14	19	18
Training	107	143	183	263	302
Maintenance	142	172	182	221	236
Networking & Others	36	710	156	193	237
Total	2,041	2,886	3,805	5,031	6,052

Note: Domestic Market = Domestic Production + Imports

Source: Nasscom, New Delhi (cited in Patibandla *et al.,* 2000).

Nasscom estimates that in 1999-00 software exports may account for more than 10 per cent of India's exports, with this share rising to 20 per cent in 2002-03. The Government of India's annual *Economic Survey* states that in 1998-99 there was a 54 per cent increase in software exports, but does not mention on what basis this figure has been arrived at. Apart from this we have no other official estimate

---

16. Dewang Mehta (Edited), *The IT Software and Services Industry in India: Strategic Review 2000,* National Association of Software and Service Companies, New Delhi, 2000.

of income, output and trade in the IT sector. The Electronics and Computer Software Export Promotion Council recently reported that in 1999-00 export of software services and electronics grew at 35 per cent in rupee terms and placed at Rs 24,025 crore ($ 6 billion). The sector thus contributed 15 per cent of the country's total export earnings in 1999-00 compared to 12 per cent in 1998-99, with Rs 17,775 crore ($ 4.44 billion) worth of exports. India's share of the cross-country customised software development market has reportedly increased from 12 per cent in 1991 to 19 per cent in 1999.[17] The market capitalisation of listed software companies in India was US$ 42 billion as on 30th December, 1999. Up from US$ 4 billion on 1st January, 1999. IT-enabled services have been estimated to have generated 40,000 jobs and earned revenues of Rs 2,030 crore in 1999.

Location of software companies

The Indian e-economy has an identifiable geographical character. It encompasses peninsular India and the hinterland of the national capital, Delhi. Of the top 600 companies as many as 409 companies have headquarters located in the six peninsular cities of Mumbai, Bangalore, Hyderabad, Chennai, Pune and Thiruvananthapuram, covering the five Indian states of Maharashtra, Karnataka, Andhra Pradesh, Tamil Nadu and Kerala. The Delhi region, however, (including Gurgaon and NOIDA) accounts for as many as 111 companies.

Type of software services

Till the mid-1990s the export of 'professional services' (body-shopping) dominated software services business in India. However, in the second half of the Nineties there has been a diversification in the structure of services offered both for the domestic and export markets. While professional services still account for the largest share of software service exports, in the domestic market products and packages account for a higher share of the business (Table 37.5).

---

17. *The Times of India*, June 1, 2000.

Table 37.5

Structure of Software Activity in India, 1998-99

Software Activity	Domestic Market		Domestic Market	
	Rs. Million	Percentage	Rs. Million	Percentage
Projects	14,100	28.5	39,950	36.50
Professional Services	2,500	5.0	48,300	
Products & Packages	23,900	48.5	8,650	7.90
Training	2,300	4.5	1.72	
Support & Maintenance	2,000	4.0	4,650	4.25
IT-enabled Services	4,700	9.5		5.48
Total	49,500	100	1,09,400	100

Source: Nasscom Strategic Review, 2000.

The revenues from 'training' shown in the table include revenues related to sale of products, projects execution and corporate training. The domestic market's revenue does not include any figures pertaining to in-house development by end-users. Even though the focus of the Indian e-economy has been on the export market, the domestic market has also grown impressively. According to Nasscom, domestic software companies launched over 122 new software products and overseas companies in the Indian market launched over 158 new software products.

Most Indian software companies have been engaged in developing application software for the banking, retail and distribution, manufacturing and government sectors. According to Nasscom there has been a diversification more recently into transport, hotels, insurance, communications and defence. The global export market, with the domestic market still relatively underdeveloped, still largely dictates the structure of output of the software companies. However, as IT and the knowledge-systems begin to be adapted by the 'old economy', a domestic market for the 'new economy' will also begin to grow.

Software export market

The significance of the US for the Indian e-economy becomes clear when we look at the direction of India's software exports. In

1998-1999, the US market accounted for nearly 58 per cent of total Indian software exports. The European market absorbed 23 per cent of total software exports, while East and South-East Asia (mainly Japan and Singapore) accounted for a little over 8.0 per cent of the export market (Table 37.6). In short, the United States is the single largest market for Indian software and services exports and will remain so in to the near future.

Table 37.6

Direction of Indian Software Exports, 1998-99

Region	Export Revenue	Percentage Share
Australia & N. Zealand	2,166	1.98
Japan	4,271	3.90
Singapore	2,047	1.87
East & S.E. Asia	8,921	8.15
West Asia	1,642	1.50
Germany	3,825	3.50
UK	12,240	1.19
Europe	25,096	22.94
US	63,430	57.98
Rest of the World	5,287	4.84
Total	109,400	100.00

Note: Individual rows do not add up to 100 per cent since some countries have not been included here.
Source: Nasscom Strategic Review 2000.

In terms of the type of services exported, Table 37.5 shows that in 1998-99 professional services and projects continued to dominate the export business, though more recently the share of IT-enabled services is reportedly increasing. Of the total export business as much as 58 per cent is estimated to be onsite services while 34 per cent is offshore services and about 8.0 per cent of exports is in the form of products and packages. It is widely expected that the share of offshore services based on real-time and online programming and software development will increase, particularly with respect to developed country markets. The software industry expects to reach an export level of US$ 6.3 billion in 2000-01 and US$ 10 billion by 2001-02 and is aiming at a target of US\$ 50 billion of annual IT software and services exports by 2008.

If the goal of an annual export trade of US\$ 50 billion is attained, software exports will emerge not only as India's single major export item, but they will also become a major strategic asset for India, adequate to finance the import of food, high technology and, perhaps, even oil. The critical importance of attaining this level of exports and of maintaining its share of the highly competitive US market cannot be over-emphasised. Even if other market opportunities present themselves to the Indian software exporters the US will remain a strategically important market.[18] Even if the share of the US market were to drop to a half of total export of software services from India, we are talking of exports up to US\$ 25 billion, which is twice the value of total Indian exports to the US this year.

However, if software and services exports have to acquire such a high profile, two things are needed. First, the creation and modernisation of the required infrastructure in India; and, second, continuous product development and quality improvement to meet the needs of a changing and highly competitive market. India and the United States can work together through 'win-win' collaborative projects to enable both these. First, the US companies can invest in India's telecom and related infrastructure to improve the speed and quality of services being provided. Second, US companies can invest in India in IT research and new product development. Given the fact that the US market is the most important destination for Indian software and services exports, it is the US that will benefit from such development.

The US e-market and India

The United States is a global leader in the e-economy. It dominates the IT market, especially in hardware and packaged software. The

---

18. Germany, France, UK, Singapore, South Korea and Japan have been actively seeking Indian software service exports, liberalising their immigration policy to enable the movement of natural persons. In accessing these markets Indian software engineers are constrained by their lack of knowledge of European and Asian languages, other than English. Acquisition of new language skills can widen the export market for the Indian e-economy.

overseas market accounts for more than half the sales of most US vendors of mainframes, midrange computers, workstations and PCs. Emphasis on investment in R&D and on development of the domestic market for the new technologies helped ensure US leadership in these areas.

However, the US faces a shortage of skilled workforce and will continue to do so. This is precisely where the India-US synergy works best because India can help bridge the manpower gap in IT services and software. As the Nasscom *Strategic Review* observes, "A win-win situation has been created by the cooperation between Indian and US companies in the IT sector. Indian companies offer competitive advantage to the US for outsourcing software requirements by providing quality and price performance in software solutions. By aligning with Indian software houses, US companies are also able to gain competitive advantage for exports to Europe and Japan through timely and efficient deliveries."[19]

It is not surprising, therefore, that the US remains India's largest export destination and the most important source of hardware and new technology for India. Increasingly, US and Indian companies will begin to work together to penetrate third markets. This is already happening with respect to European markets. Indian software professionals are teaming up with US companies to offer their services co-jointly to European customers. The growing demand for Indian software professionals in Europe and developing Asia will widen such business opportunities.

If the Indian e-economy grows at the rate of 50 per cent over the next half a decade, as it has over the last one, and if no new entry barriers are erected by developed countries, India can see earnings of nearly US$ 50 billion per year from software and services exports. The US trade alone is likely to be around US$ 25 billion. This will create an unprecedented commercial relationship between India and the US in the next five years.

---

19. *Nasscom Strategic Review, 2000.*

The e-economy's SWOT analysis

The *Nasscom Strategic Review* offers a comprehensive SWOT analysis for the Indian e-economy, which should help identify the policy issues, which require to be addressed for the Indian e-economy to remain competitive. The main strengths are—high quality and competitive pricing of Indian software and services; availability of a large pool of knowledge workers with requisite computing and language skills; easy access to latest hardware technology given India's liberal import regime in this area; flexibility, adaptability and reliability of Indian professionals, ability to undertake offshore software development through datacom links, availability of local enterprise and skills, the Indian diaspora, especially the active and productive two-way links between Indians and Indian Americans in the US.

The main weaknesses identified are inadequate infrastructural support in India (ranging from telecom and power to urban facilities, schooling and other lifestyle services), low level of PC use and Internet penetration, low level of domestic technology development, inadequate availability of venture capital funds, and limited domestic market for knowledge-based technology and products. The reports of National IT Task Force as well as the *Nasscom Strategic Review* have clearly identified the policy homework for the Indian government. The new IT policies enunciated through the new Indian IT Bill (May 2000) should help create the legal framework within which these issues can be addressed better. The bottom line, however, is new investment in high-speed data networks, improved telecom and power infrastructure and a sustained improvement of the human capital infrastructure -in the schools and technical institutions.

While the Nasscom study expresses familiar optimism about the enormous opportunities that exist for the further development of the Indian e-economy, based both on the domestic market as well as the international market, it also identifies specific threats. These are, apart from the inadequate and low quality infrastructure already referred to, mindless governmental interference, supply constraints imposed by slow growth of skilled manpower at home, and demand constraints imposed by neo-protectionism abroad and, finally, competition from other countries in the developing world, particularly in Asia.

There is now widespread recognition that having celebrated India's early emergence as a player in the global e-economy, India may lag behind other rivals, particularly China, South-East Asia, Israel and Eastern Europe if it does not develop adequate infrastructure at home, particularly the communications, power and research infrastructure, and does not produce good quality skilled professionals in adequate numbers to meet the growing demand at home and abroad. Nasscom has recently alerted the government to the danger of India falling by the wayside in the global e-race.

e-Business: US corporations and Indian entrepreneurs

The essential importance of the e-economy in Indo-US bilateral relations is that this is one sector in which the two countries are able to relate as equals with a spirit of 'give-and-take' establishing a 'win-win' relationship. The old paradigm of one-way dependence and a relationship of unequals is giving way to a new paradigm in which Indians see themselves as making a contribution of their own to the bilateral relationship and not merely being recipients of aid and largesse. Not only have US companies benefited from trade and investment in the IT sector, but the US economy has also benefited by securing access to India's low cost but good quality software programming skills and from the incomes and jobs created by Indian entrepreneurs in the US. This offers a balance to India's gains from access to new technology, new markets and new jobs.

India gains by securing access to the US market and by receiving US investment and technology in the Indian e-economy. The US gains by securing access to low cost Indian services and pro-active Indian enterprise, which in turn creates new products, jobs and incomes in the US e-economy. Clearly, this is a win-win relationship.

US investment in Indian e-economy

While Indian companies like Infosys, Wipro, Satyam and Tata dominate the Indian software industry, many foreign companies, mainly US multinationals, have also registered their presence among the top 50 companies operating out of India. As many as 50 US companies, including IBM, Microsoft, Baan, Hewlett Packard,

Honeywell, Hughes, Lucent, Digital, Sun Microsystems, Texas Instruments, Quark, Metamor and Novell are all involved in new product development through companies based in India and another 25 companies are engaged in providing software services and support to parent companies in the US.

In 1998-99, more than 203 Fortune 1000 companies outsourced their software requirements to India, up from a mere 23 in 1990. What *Annexure One* does not list is the names of US companies that are using software developed in India. Airlines like United Airlines (apart from Swissair, Singapore Airlines and British Airways) use Indian software and so do American Express, Wal-Mart, Citibank, Morgan Stanley, General Motors, Sony, Boeing, Reebok and so on. The competitive advantage that Indian software sourcing is giving US companies has created a win-win synergy between large US corporations and the Indian IT industry. US companies have also become more competitive in third markets, like Europe and East Asia, by sourcing their software requirements from India. It is this forward-looking perspective of US corporations that has contributed to the US being the largest market for Indian software exports. *The Nasscom Strategic Review* expects that the US would "continue to dominate India's exports of IT software and services."[20]

The listing of Indian IT companies in Nasdaq opens up new opportunities for US capital in India. Also, the opening up of the venture capital business in India to foreign investors should attract considerable investment from the US, where venture capital business has developed the most and Indian investors have emerged as successful entrepreneurs in this business. Organisations like The Indus Entrepreneurs (TIE), headquartered in California's Silicon Valley have been playing a catalytic role in promoting Indo-US links in this area.

New opportunities in the e-economy

The focus of Indo-US e-trade has so far been on IT software and services. These will remain the mainstay of the business in the near

---

20. *ibid*, pp.63.

future as more and more US companies locate their software development and data processing facilities in India and new opportunities for Indian professionals are created in the US economy.

Going beyond existing areas, the Nasscom-McKinsey study has identified new sectors in which trade and investment opportunities are likely to emerge. These are:

- IT services: web enabling legacy systems, e-commerce/extended enterprise applications, standards based application integration, knowledge management, and convergence applications.

- Software products: emerging 'slivers', productisation, and embedded software.

- IT enabled services: HR services, remote customer interaction, data search, integration and analysis, and engineering and design services.

- E-businesses: domestic business-to-business, and NRI-oriented business-to-consumer.

- Domestic market: large corporate users, electronic government and increased consumer spending.

Indian software companies expect to see a boom in IT-enabled services, particularly in the US market. These services include call centres, medical transcription, back office operations, revenue accounting, insurance claims processing, legal databases, payroll records, logistics management, content development/animation, entertainment software, graphics and design, computer animation, and so on.

What does all this mean for the Indo-US relationship? Apart from the purely economic aspect of incomes and employment being generated by the e-economy, we must also draw attention to the increased social and cultural interaction this has enabled. The three most important areas in which such 'people-to-people' interaction between the two nations has been enhanced by the new economy are—entrepreneurship, infotainment and the Internet, and IT-enabled services. In the next two sections we return to a discussion of the first two areas. Here we comment briefly on the cultural role of IT-enabled services.

This phenomenon is best captured by the following report from the *Far Eastern Economic Review*:[21]

"Janet Williams is 23 years old. She works at GE Capital, a division of the giant American conglomerate General Electric. A typical day for Janet begins at 8 a.m. New York time, as she begins phoning GE credit-card holders in places like Boston and Washington to remind them to pay their bills: 'Hi. My name is Janet and I'm calling from GE Capital', she says in her friendliest voice. People answering her calls have no way of knowing that Janet is sitting in Gurgaon, a town on the outskirts of Delhi. Or that her real name is Pooja Atri and that she picked up her American accent partly by watching 'Baywatch'.

"GE Capital's facility in Gurgaon, Haryana, is teeming with pseudonymous 20-something Janets, Als and Sandys. Some take incoming toll-free calls, bounced by satellite to India. Most have never set foot in the United States. But they spend a large chunk of every day (or night) chasing credit-card debtors, assessing medical claims, approving car loans, answering customer queries, in short, acting as cogs in a giant machine that hums along smoothly half a world away. Many have college degrees and earn \$ 3,000-\$ 5,000 a year. Their counterparts in the US are usually less educated but command wages of \$ 18,000-\$ 20,000 a year."

Thousands of young, educated and articulate Indian men and women are dealing on a day-to-day basis with US citizens through satellite telephony, the Internet and satellite television. The impact of such IT-enabled social and cultural interaction on political attitudes is already palpable. The famed 'anti-Americanism' of middle class India in the Cold War period is history and, as was evident during the travels of President Bill Clinton through India, there is a new familiarity, which is breeding friendship rather than contempt.

---

21. *Far Eastern Economic Review,* 23: September 2, 1999.

IT-enabled services have created a stake in improved Indo-US relations for a new generation of IT-enabled youth whose livelihood is today dependent on this business. While this is true for anyone employed in an export industry, the IT-enabled services have enabled cross-country and cross-cultural 'people-to-people' interaction between the service provider and the customer which is unprecedented in the history of Indo-US relations, or indeed in the bilateral relationship between any two nations so separated by history and geography.

Indian enterprise in the US

The flowering of Indian enterprise in the US e-economy has enabled the development of new businesses generating new jobs and incomes for US citizens at home and trade and employment opportunities for Indians both at home and abroad.

The successful listing of Bangalore-based Infosys and Wipro on Nasdaq, the popularity of Sabeer Bhatia's 'Hotmail', the emergence of Indian American billionaires in the US e-economy and the phenomenal growth of Indian software exports has suddenly raised the profile of the Indian e-economy globally. Going beyond the headlines, the emergence of a new first-generation Indian American entrepreneurial community in the e-economy has added a new dimension to the people-to-people interaction between India and the US. While the political influence of the over one million strong Indian American community has been growing and is reflected in the increased influence of the Indian American lobby in the US Congress, the emergence of the e-entrepreneur in areas like Silicon Valley in California, has helped impart to the Indian American community a new and high profile for the first time. Popular jokes like "Silicon Valley smells of curry" and "you can get a job more easily in Silicon Valley if you were named Murthy rather than Murphy" have come to symbolise this newly acquired favourable profile of the Indian American *e-community.*

The most authoritative study so far undertaken of this phenomenon of Indian American enterprise in the e-economy is the widely quoted study of AnnaLee Saxenian, *Silicon Valley's New*

Immigrant Entrepreneurs (1999).[22] Saxenian's study, which is perhaps already dated since the boom in Indian enterprise in the region continues unabated, begins with the bald assertion, "when local technologists claim that "Silicon Valley is built on ICs", they refer not to the integrated circuit but to Indians and Chinese engineers." Saxenian records the high incidence of Indian American owned enterprises in Silicon Valley's e-economy and adds, "Silicon Valley's Indian-born engineers have played a ...(role) linking technology businesses in Silicon Valley with India's highly skilled software programming and design talent. These long-distance social networks enhance economic opportunities for California and for emerging regions in Asia."

Saxenian quotes a Dun & Bradstreet database on technology firms started since 1980 that shows that close to one quarter (24 per cent) of Silicon Valley's technology firms in 1998 had Chinese or Indian executives. "Of the 11,443 high-technology firms started during this period, 2001 (17 per cent) were run by Chinese and 774 (7 per cent) by Indians. In 1998, these companies collectively accounted for over $16.8 billion in sales and 58,282 jobs."[23]

Saxenian does not find any evidence to suggest that the arrival of Indian Americans in Silicon Valley has displaced any local persons from their jobs. Rather, she suggests, their entrepreneurial activity has created new incomes and employment opportunities for the region. Moreover, she says, "Skilled immigrants contribute to the dynamism of the Silicon Valley economy, both directly, as engineers and entrepreneurs, and indirectly, as traders and middlemen linking California to technologically advanced regions of Asia."[24] Elsewhere she adds, "Immigrant engineers provide the critical contacts, information, and cultural know-how that links dynamic—but distant—regions in the global economy."

---

22. AnnaLee Saxenian, *Silicon Valley's New Immigrant Entrepreneurs*, Public Policy Institute of California, San Francisco, 1999.

23. *ibid*, p.25.

24. *ibid* pp.ic-x, p.27 and p.56.

While Saxenian's study is based on the results of the 1990 Census and her own survey of the region, the US 2000 Census will provide a much better picture of the presence of Indian American enterprise in the region since there has been a significant increase in their presence in the e-economy in the second half of the 1990s. Responding to local concerns about competition in the job market from immigrants, Saxenian says, "The national debate over the increase of HI-B visas for high-skilled immigrants focused primarily on the extent to which immigrants displace native workers. Yet we have seen here that these immigrants also create new jobs and economic linkages in their role as entrepreneurs."

Saxenian's observation that, "In contrast to the close collaboration between Taiwan's policy makers and US-based engineers, there has been almost no communication at all between the Silicon Valley engineering community and India's policy makers—even those concerned directly with technology policy," is no longer valid. The government of India as well as the State governments of some key states like Andhra Pradesh, have actively sought advice and assistance from Silicon Valley entrepreneurs to improve the interaction between Indian and US companies and professionals in the e-economy. US-based e-entrepreneurs and venture capitalists now organised into groups like The Indus Entrepreneurs (TIE) are actively engaged in policy making in India as members of key advisory groups on IT policy. The 'Knowledge Trade Initiative' launched during President Clinton's visit to India, and the new Information Technology Bill passed by the Indian Parliament in May 2000 offer a new framework for greater interaction between Indian and US-based Indian American and other IT companies.

Going beyond national policy, Indian Americans have emerged as active lobbyists at the provincial or State level in India pressuring state governments to pursue forward looking policies aimed at stimulating the growth of the e-economy. The influence of the Indian American Telugu community on policy making in Andhra Pradesh as well as on the investment decisions of major US corporations has been visible in recent months. The success of some Software Technology Parks in India, particularly the ones in Hyderabad and Bangalore, in encouraging new local enterprise in the e-economy have also helped strengthen the two-way entrepreneurial link between the two countries.

e-Business in media and infotainment and the digital diaspora

In documenting the trade, investment and entrepreneurial links between the Indian and US *e-economies* we have so far focused only on the 'commercial and economic' aspects of role of the e-economy as a 'ballast' for Indo-US relations. There is an equally important social and cultural aspect to the e-economy link, which is gaining in importance. This is the range of people-to-people interaction that is enabled by the continuous contact through the Internet, the infotainment business and the media. The intensity of this interaction, first made possible by the fact that we are both liberal democracies with assured human rights and access to information, is enhanced by the nature of the new media technology and its easy and widespread access and reach.

Hollywood cinema, the worldwide web, satellite television and such like have enabled much greater unrestricted people-to-people contact, both business and cultural, between the two countries. The level of such interaction between India and the US, so far largely mediated through the diasporic network of Indian Americans, is unparalleled by any other bilateral interaction. The new information technology combined with its low cost and easy access has built new bridges between the two countries, which have already altered popular perceptions of each other, especially of India in the US.

This is an important political development to the extent that it has blunted the edge of residual anti-Americanism in Indian political life. The popular reception accorded to President Clinton, particularly by Members of the Parliament and in such cities as Hyderabad, testifies to the impact of this new cultural and social interface between our two nations. An increasing number of Indians have become consumers of US media and infotainment output, while US consumers are increasingly buying India-made software programmes, multimedia products and infotainment products.

The spread of Internet and growth in PC sales has contributed to this phenomenon. Annual sales of desktop personal computers have crossed the one million mark, with annual turnover topping US$ 1 billion.[25] "India's PC industry tops $ 1 billion", according to a recent report, 1999 witnessed a 49.26 per cent growth in desktop PC sales, the number of units sold increasing from 680,000 in 1998 to 1,015,000 in 1999. The sales turnover rose 38.8 per cent to Rs 45.4 billion. Half these sales were in non-metro cities and mostly to individuals rather than government or corporations. In 1999, first-time PC users accounted for as much as 40 per cent of all sales. With Internet penetration still as low as 0.5 per thousand population and e-commerce spending estimated to be a mere $ 4 per subscriber, the future potential for growth in this segment of the e-economy is enormous. Market surveys project Internet subscribers in India to increase to a total of 1.3 million by end 2000.

The increased demand and the search for improved speed and quality data transfer will increase the market pressure for new infrastructure. This will drive policy forcing the government to allow entry of new investment.

The new media has also enabled the creation of a new 'dot-com community' both within India and globally, within the Indian diaspora, creating a 'dotcom diaspora' which has become active and creative. The Indian middle class's ability to use the English language and the availability of computing skills has fuelled this process. The social interaction that the new communication technology has enabled worldwide has increased the two-way flow of information between India and the United States, now home to more than a million Indian Americans.

The proliferation of cyber-cafes, dotcom businesses and the free spread of satellite television in India have created the required infrastructure for enhanced Indo-US social and cultural interaction. The fact that India is a democracy with a large English-speaking middle class has helped in this. The success of the Indian computer

---

25. *India Abroad News Service,* "India's PC industry tops $1 billion", May 9, 2000 (www.siliconindia.com).

scientists and the *e*-entrepreneurs in the US has helped reinforce the significance of the US in this new e-economy. If India persists with its liberal media policies this bond between the two countries will clearly transform 'estranged democracies' into 'engaging democracies'.

Not surprisingly, therefore, issues relating to the 'infotainment business', such as policy on internet access, media, broadcasting and entertainment industries and so on have become key issues in the Indo-US policy dialogue on the e-economy. India is in the process of creating the required policy framework to enable globalisation of the Indian media, entertainment and broadcasting industries, including such niche areas as computer animation where the Indian and American film industry have been able to cooperate and launch joint ventures. At a meeting in November 1999, the Joint Indo-US Business Council recorded the following in a statement titled, *Unleashing the Potential: A New Agenda in Indo-US Economic Cooperation.*

The Indian broadcasting and entertainment sector nurtures a vast wealth of creative resources. In the coming years, India has the potential to become a major entertainment content and service provider to world markets. At the world level, this knowledge-based industry is currently led by a few major institutional players, most of whom are based in the US. The US is a major potential market for Indian entertainment products. As two of the world's largest players in information-based industry, the US and India can work together to assure a liberal global trading regime for entertainment services and products—something that neither country can achieve alone. More than any other country, the US can supply the investment, expertise, technology to facilitate two-way trade in entertainment services and content necessary to bring India's entertainment industry to global scale, reach and standards.

The broadcast industry has a vital role to play in building a market for entertainment industry products. At present, television and radio provide the most broadly accessible medium for promoting audience interest in new and established artistic creations. Even a brief perusal of programming in India demonstrates how foreign participation in the Indian market has stimulated a rapid increase in the quantity and quality of news, sports and entertainment programming for the Indian consumer and foster the rapid growth of an indigenous private industry. The US is India's natural partner in the broadcasting and entertainment industries.

The USIBC has put forward a policy agenda for enabling increased US investment in India. This must be matched by an Indian agenda for market access in the US. Apart from media and infotainment business, the new information technology can also help educational programmes in India, building databases and virtual libraries and increasing access to information. Admittedly, India has to address issues of intellectual property protection, just as the US must address Indian complaints about market access and access to new technology, as well as concerns relating to mergers and acquisitions and oligopolistic trade practices.

The scope for Indo-US interaction in this business far exceeds the business opportunities available for a few US corporations in India. The e-economy opens up new opportunities for joint enterprise between Indians and Americans in the media and infotainment sectors. More importantly, it enables the Indian American community in the US to be more involved in joint business enterprises in the media and infotainment sectors. All this has been made possible by the Internet and satellite television, which has created a global 'digital diaspora'.

The digital diaspora

The Internet and the 'dotcom' revolution have created an Indo-US 'digital diaspora' that is further enhancing the cultural and social interaction between the two democracies. In a fascinating essay on the emergence of a 'digital diaspora' and the manner in which the Internet has enabled greater interaction between Indians in North America and India, Patel says:

"The Internet is very much at the heart of globalisation; indeed it is its central nervous system. Globalisation is really a complex set of processes occurring in the social, cultural, political, economic and; most importantly psychological areas.

"Many South Asians in the diasporas, especially in North America, are very much part of this global revolution; indeed, they are, by the very nature of their having been uprooted and living outside their ancestral homelands, at its forefront."[26]

Patel quotes a Canadian analyst of the Internet to say, "The ability to exchange messages with individuals on the other side of the planet and to have access to community information almost instantaneously changes the dynamics of diaspora, allowing for qualitatively and quantitatively enhanced linkages."[27]

The relevance of this observation to the role the Internet has played in bringing the Indian diaspora together, particularly Indian Americans in the US and their families in the home country is easy to appreciate. The role that the online media has played to mould perceptions in the US and India during the Kargil War of 1999 is an example of how the digital diaspora can help improve Indo-US relations.

Clearly, there is more than mere business interest at stake for both India and the US when they endeavour to create the framework for increased trade and exchange of information and entertainment through the global e-economy. The Internet and the electronic media are bringing the world's largest democracies together in a way that neither had experienced or anticipated before. The fact that both countries are open and liberal democracies with a free media has enabled this interaction. Thus far the interaction has been limited, sporadic and unregulated. A regulatory framework with liberal rules of the game will enable mutually beneficial and organised intercourse between the two nations.

The policy challenge

The dynamism of the e-economy, globally as well as in India, has meant that policy makers and regulators have not been able to

26. Dhiru Patel, "Modem Technology, Identity and Culture: The South Asian Diasporas", Paper presented at the *International Conference on Culture and Economy in the Indian Diaspora,* India International Centre, New Delhi, April, 2000 (*mimeo*).

27. K. Karim, *From Ethnic Media to Global Media: Transnational Communication Networks Among Diasporic Communities,* Ottawa, Department of Canadian Heritage (quoted in Patel, 2000).

keep pace with technical change and market expansion. Any comment either on the state of technology or on the structure of the industry may soon become dated. Indeed, so dynamic has this sector been that any comment on the policy framework also runs the risk of becoming obsolete given the pace at which policy has been changing.

In India the e-economy grew virtually free of any public policy restraint or support till recently with the N-sector being left largely to its own devices without there being an active policy of support or a framework of regulation. Thus, the development of the Indian e-economy is a testimony to Indian private enterprise. Governmental support was however present in two forms, public investment in high quality technical training institutions like the Indian Institutes of Technology; and, public investment in electronics industry and in related user industries like space, defence, aeronautics, nuclear and missile development. Effective public regulation, however, followed rather than guided the development of the e-economy. This is true both for computer software and services as also for the infotainment industry.

Once the government recognised the importance of the IT sector and India's comparative advantage in this area, as series of policy initiatives were taken to make the government a more effective partner and promoter of private enterprise. Official policy has been framed within the very liberal perspective offered by the National Task Force on Information Technology and various other committees.

The US-India Business Council drafted a 50-point policy agenda covering the entire gamut of Indo-US economic relations at its meeting in November 1999. The Indian government has addressed much of this agenda and some issues have been addressed by the US, particularly relating to visas. But others remain. The key policy issues in the specific area of the e-economy relate to the following areas:

i.   Infrastructure—telecom, power, bandwidth, satellite links.

ii. Training and skill development.

iii. Venture capital.

iv. Intellectual Property Protection.

v. E-commerce regulation.

vi. Movement of natural persons (HI-B visas).

vii. Access to new technology (role of sanctions).

viii. Spread of IT to traditional sectors—industry, services, agriculture, government, education.

ix. Foreign investment policy.

In each of these areas the Indian government has been taking several initiatives and policy has been dynamic, yet the unfinished agenda is huge. The Information Technology Bill, passed by the Parliament in May 2000 and give Presidential assent in June 2000, facilitates the regulation of e-commerce and related issues like e-crime. The enactment of the IT Bill was an important step in creating the legal framework for increased e-commerce and for increased flows of foreign investment into the Indian e-economy. The liberalisation of rules pertaining to foreign investment in the IT sector as well as in venture capital and e-commerce is another important step forward. In 1999-00 it was estimated that there were 25 venture capital companies in India managing a total of about $ 1.3 billion of start-up capital. The new policy opening the business to foreign investors will increase funding considerably. The next step would be a new policy framework towards investment in media, entertainment and broadcasting.

If the funds constraint is thus being eased, a major infrastructural constraint remains in the limited bandwidth available in India. According to NASSCOM only about 325 MBPS (megabytes per second) is available out of India today, while the demand from India's flourishing software, business application and dotcom industries has accelerated to 5 GB (gigabytes), a staggering 15-fold shortfall. Demand is forecast to increase 1000-fold in the next five years. If the bandwidth crunch is not resolved, in the next eight years, India could loose more than $ 22 billion in revenues and 6,50,000 jobs, according to NASSCOM estimates. McKinsey & Co. recently forecast that India's IT industry will generate $ 87 billion in annual revenues, $ 225 billion in market value, and 2.2 million jobs by year 2008. The urgency of creating the required bandwidth and related infrastructure cannot be over-emphasised.

Equally important is the investment in training, skill development and education. Rivals like China, Israel and others can easily overtake India as a 'software superpower' if it does not widen the base of high quality manpower. The existing good quality institutions are not adequate for the demand being generated. A mere quantitative increase in supply of manpower from poor quality institutions can only hurt India's brand image in the global marketplace built so painstakingly and assiduously over the years by the excellence of teaching and training at the IITs.

For its part, the United States must also pursue a more forward-looking and liberal policy with respect to trade in services in the e-economy. While the US has taken some steps in increasing the number of H1-B visas, its policy with respect to the 'movement of natural persons' and trade in software services is far more restrictive when compared to its policy with respect to trade in goods and movement of capital.

Restrictions to the movement of natural persons can be broadly grouped into four categories, relating to immigration related regulations concerning entry and stay of service providers:

(i)   regulations concerning recognition of qualifications, work experience, and training;

(ii)   differential treatment of domestic and foreign service personnel; and

(iii)   regulations covering other modes of supply, particularly on commercial presence, which indirectly limit the scope for movement of natural persons.

Indian software professionals have faced entry barriers in developed country markets, including in the US, and these barriers restrict the scope for trade in the e-economy where technology often comes embodied in human skills. Furthermore, in the specific case of the United States, the H1-B visas issued to temporary immigrants cover all categories of professionals and do not distinguish software professionals. It may be useful to create a new visa category that can enable the quick disposal of visa applications made by software professionals.

The US must also address domestic policy issues like imposition of social security taxes and double taxation of temporary immigrants. Indian software professionals working in the US on temporary projects have been made to pay tax on their income in the US, even though they pay taxes back home. They have also been made to contribute to social security without securing the benefits. Social security contributions have become 'trade taxes' on Indian software professionals deputed abroad and have tended to erode their cost advantage relative to US software professionals.

Both India and the US are trying to arrive at a consensual position on issues relating to e-commerce and trade in services in the WTO. This process must continue and the US must take a long-term, forward-looking perspective rather than be driven by domestic lobbies and short-term objectives. Such a perspective can widen the basis for trade in the e-economy.

India has found a new source of economic growth and, more importantly, a means of enhancing its share of world trade in the e-economy and in software exports. Given the central importance of the US market to this trade it is clear that Indo-US economic partnership is set to experience a qualitative improvement in the immediate future if this trade is fostered. However, to be able to exploit the emerging opportunities India must persist with a forward-looking trade and investment policy in the e-economy and invest in the required infrastructure. For its part, the US must remove barriers to trade and the movement of professionals. This in turn will create further avenues for Indo-US economic cooperation. The burgeoning size of the e-economy and of trade and investment flows in this sector will, for the first time, create a huge commercial and entrepreneurial stake in improved Indo-US relations on both sides. This will be the most important component of the economic ballast to Indo-US relations in the years to come.

38 ESSAY

India, China and the Asian neighbourhood

Issues in external trade and foreign policy

TRADE has for long been an important aspect of the relations between countries. In the post-Cold War period it has become even more so with geoeconomics and globalisation casting a shadow on geopolitics and the role of political ideology in international relations. One country which has understood the significance of trade in external relations is China. Trade policy, albeit a blunt instrument of foreign policy, has acquired a higher profile in fostering bilateral relations between nations. India has been slow to appreciate this aspect of foreign trade, but an effort has been made in the last decade to increase India's share of world trade as well as pursue regional and bilateral preferential trading agreements with a view to economically engaging not just the major industrial economies but also the newly industrialising Asian economies and India's own neighbours.

However, economists continue to neglect this foreign policy dimension to trade. While those suspicious of outward-orientation and trade liberalisation, view any increased external engagement as inherently risk-prone since it exposes the economy to the vagaries of global market forces, others tend to underplay the political economy of trade liberalisation, viewing the gains from 'trade openness' purely in economic terms with an exclusive focus on multilateral trade regimes. Neither have paid much attention to the political economy of regional or bilateral trade relations, in the context of India's greater outward-orientation. However, the fact remains that even large trading nations like the United States, Japan, and even the European Union continue to place a great deal of emphasis on bilateral trade relations even as they actively participate in multilateral forums like the WTO. Even China, which has been more focussed on bilateral and regional trade arrangements because it was out of the WTO, continues to pay attention to these relations even as it seeks WTO membership.

Hence, it is not altogether out of place for India, newly re-emerging as a trading nation, to try and seek increased market access through regional and bilateral trade agreements even as it remains actively engaged with multilateralism through the WTO. The purpose of this chapter is to examine recent trends in China's and India's external trade with their southern Asian neighbourhood, pointing to China's growing profile as a major trading nation in the region.

China's relentless pursuit of world markets and its drive to seek membership of the WTO has created new challenges for India in the sphere of trade and foreign policy. China has not only made commitments to liberalise trade going well beyond India's commitments in the WTO, but it has also been able to increase its trade engagement with major Asian countries in India's neighbourhood. To the extent that trade is an important aspect of international relations, India must also pay greater attention to its Asian neighbours and continue to increase its share of world trade by becoming a more competitive and open economy.

India's increasing outward-orientation in the 1990s, the liberalisation of its external trade and foreign investment policies, has undoubtedly increased the importance of foreign trade in India's growth process. India will have to sustain a higher rate of growth of exports both in order to service the expected increase in imports and the foreign exchange outflow on account of increasing profit repatriation by foreign investors. Given this increasing importance of foreign trade, recent trends in India's export performance draw our attention to the important relationship between economic growth, trade policy and national security.

Regional trends in India's recent export performance

After a rapid acceleration of export growth in the mid-1990s, responding to both exchange rate and macroeconomic policy changes, India's export growth slowed down in 1996-99. In 1998-1999, in particular Indian exports were hurt by the Asian economic crisis, with exports to the ASEAN economies and Japan falling sharply that year. Apart from the economic crisis in some Asian countries and in Russia, it is possible that economic sanctions and political measures adopted by some countries in the wake of India's nuclear tests in May 1998, particularly by China, Japan, Australia and some EU countries, may have also caused the decline in export growth in the second half of 1998.

The recovery in export growth in the second half of 1999 has also been largely on account of the remarkable turnaround in the trade with ASEAN economies and with China, Hong Kong, Russia, USA and UK. While underlying economic factors have undoubtedly played a role, it is possible that the easing of political factors, with the nuclear issue partly receding into the background with India mending fences with China, EU and USA, may have also helped.

Some recent trends in China's export performance

China's remarkable export performance and its emergence as a major trading nation in the 1990s has been widely commented upon by economists. China's drive for economic modernisation and accelerated national income growth has helped China emerge as a major trading nation during the 1990s. China has widened the distance between itself and India in world trade and, in the process, not only increased its share of world trade but also its share of trade of several countries in India's neighbourhood. This paper examines recent trends in China's bilateral trade with a range of countries in India's neighbourhood and discusses the foreign policy dimension of China's growing market penetration in Asia.

At the time China launched its economic modernisation and liberalisation programme in 1978, its total external trade amounted to US$ 20.6 billion, which accounted for 8.8 per cent of its GDP. By 1998, China reported external trade amounting to US$ 324

Table 38.1

Indian Export Performance-Trends in Country Share

Region	Growth Rate (April–November)			Country Share	
	1997	1998	1999	1998	1999
World	3.5	-2.8	11.7	100	100
Asia (excl M. East)	-1.7	-20.6	18.2	23.1	24.5
China	0.7	-26.6	24.3	1.2	1.4
Hong Kong	6.1	-9.6	27.8	5.3	6.1
Indonesia	5.0	-73.6	91.2	0.41	0.70
Malaysia	1.5	-44.5	43.9	0.91	1.17
Philippines	48.3	-60.1	20.6	0.33	0.36
Singapore	-38.1	36.5	1.47	1.80	-14.7
Thailand	-14.7	-11.1	32.4	0.93	1.10
Vietnam	1.1	5.5	8.3	0.38	0.37
ASEAN-6	-	-	38.5	4.43	4.43
Middle East	4.1	20.6	5.9	11.5	10.9
Russia	13.8	-20.5	37.9	2.10	2.6
UK	3.6	-13.3	15.7	5.7	5.9
Japan	-5.1	-16.1	2.4	4.92	4.51
Australia	15.3	-10.5	4.9	1.2	1.2
Africa	15.7	12.8	-9.2	6.5	5.3
USA	1.6	8.2	16.5	22.0	22.9
Europe	4.2	-3.8	9.8	30.8	30.3

Source: *Direction of Trade Statistics* (various years), World Trade Organization.

billion, estimated at 34.0 per cent of its GDP.[1] The average annual growth of total trade (imports and exports) during the period 1978 to 1998 was upwards of 15.0 per cent per annum, more than the average growth rate of GDP.

Even prior to that, Tendulkar has calculated, the exponential rate of growth of export volumes for China during the period 1973-1983 to be as high as 9.6 per cent compared to India's 5.1 per cent.[2] According to Tendulkar, while India's export growth improved in

---

1. Date accessed from www.chinaonline.com.

2. Suresh Tendulkar, "Exports in India's Growth Process", *ICRIER Working Paper,* 1999.

the 1990s, to an exponential rate of growth of 8.83 per cent in 1984-1995, China's remained higher at 9.53 per cent. For the period 1987-96, China's total exports grew at 15.51 per cent per annum while India's grew at 10.89 per cent per annum. More specifically, China's manufactured exports grew at 19.37 per cent during this period compared to 11.89 per cent for India. This enabled China to increase its share of total world exports from 1.9 per cent in 1987-90 to over 3.0 per cent in 1993-96, compared with an increase from 0.6 per cent to 0.7 per cent for India for the relevant years. it may be useful to recall that in 1950 India's share of world trade was around 2.0 per cent while China had a share of only 1.4 per cent, which then declined to 0.8 per cent in the early 1970s before gradually recovering in the 1980s.[3]

This phenomenal increase in its foreign trade enabled China to emerge as a major trade partner of the OECD economies as well as of its neighbouring Asian economies. According to Surjit Bhalla's estimate, while world exports to industrialised countries grew at 4.9 per cent per annum during the 1990s, China's exports to these countries grew at 17.0 per cent.[4] Thus, China's share of exports to industrialised countries increased from 1.7 per cent in 1990 to 3.7 per cent by 1997. Tendulkar's study offers a comprehensive picture of the structure of China's exports in the period 1987-96 and comes to the broad conclusion that, "China's industrial exports were found to be more diversified than those of India at the 3-digit SITC level. This was traced to the very high growth rate of value of aggregate exports at 18.7 per cent per annum during 1986-97."

---

3. China switched its foreign trade policy as part of its economic modernisation strategy and opted for increased external trade with the developed market economies from the 1970s. See Teng Weizao, "Socialist Modernisation and the Pattern of Foreign Trade ", in Xu Dixin, *et al.*, *China's Search for Economic Growth*, New World Press Beijing, 1982. To quote, "We must use foreign capital and foreign tade in a planned way so as to speed up the modernisation of the economy. We must not build an inward-looking economy based on a 'closed door' or 'semi-closed-door' policy."

4. Surjit Bhalla, "Chinese Mercantilism: Currency Wars and How the East Was Lost", *ICRIER Working Paper*, 1999.

In sum, a strong performance in external trade has been an important aspect of China's growth acceleration during the 1990s. Equally importantly, China's emergence as a major trading economy has so far been welcomed by the rest of the world and, despite China not being a member of the World Trade Organization (WTO) till now, it has not encountered any resistance to its exports in any country.

Bhalla's paper also makes a political economy point that China was 'favoured' by the United States, IMF and World Bank during the 1990s and allowed to emerge as a major exporter to the West using 'beggar-thy-neighbour' trade and exchange rate policies. Not surprisingly, therefore, a recent Chinese assessment of its foreign trade observed:

"We should, on the foundation of continuing to increase market share in traditional markets, and the precondition of faster expansion in the African market, continue to greatly expand new markets including Africa, Latin America, Oceania, and Europe, with special emphasis on the Commonwealth of Independent States and Eastern Europe, and also continue the market diversification strategy."[5]

Understandably, both for India and China the biggest trade partners are the US and EU. Together, these two markets account for 37.6 per cent of India's exports and 27.4 per cent of China's direct exports and over 30 per cent of China's total exports to these market (that is, including the re-exports through Hong Kong). While Hong Kong is China's top export destination, much of this trade is due to Hong Kong's entrepot status and is meant for re-export to rest of the world. In fact 're-exports' constitute a good 85 per cent of Hong Kong's total exports, with 'domestic' exports constituting just 15 per cent, and in 1977 China accounted for 37 per cent of total re-exports from Hong Kong. For China the Pacific rim is the more important export market. China's top export

---

5. Chen Jiaqin, "Analysis of China's Foreign Trade Trends", in Liu Guguang, *et al.* (Edited) *Economics Blue Book*, Centre of Asian Studies, University of Hong Kong, 1998.

destinations include USA, Japan and South Korea, apart from Hong Kong. For India, the trans-Atlantic market is more important (Table 38.2).

Table 38.2

Top 10 Export Markets for China and India,
1995-97 (Percentage Share)

	India		China	
1	US	18.0	Hong Kong	23.0
2	Japan	7.5	US	18.0
3	UK	6.3	Japan	19.0
4	Germany	6.5	S. Korea	5.0
5	Hong Kong	5.7	Germany	3.7
6	UAE	4.8	Netherlands	2.4
7	Belgium	3.7	Singapore	2.4
8	Bangladesh	2.7	UK	2.0
9	Russia	3.1	Taiwan	1.9
10	Italy	3.1	France	1.3
	Share of Top Two (i.e. US + Japan)	25.5	Top Two Excl. Hong Kong (i.e. US + Japan)	37.0
	Share of US + EU - 4	37.6	Share of US + EU - 4	27.4

Note: Almost all Chinese exports to Hong Kong are re-exported to rest of the world. The US is the single largest destination of Hong Kong's re-exports, accounting for a fifth of total Hong Kong re-exports. Hence, actual importance of US market is larger than is suggested by the figure given in the above table. China's top 9 direct export destinations are also among the top 10 markets for Hong Kong re-exports, which are mostly goods Chinese mainland origin.

Source: *Direction of Trade Statistics* (various years), WTO.

India and China—Bilateral trade with Southern Asia

Table 38.2 and 38.3, viewed together with the accompanying charts, sum up the trends in China's and India's total trade and, in particular export trade, in recent years. The most important conclusion we can arrive at from this data is that China is fast emerging an important trade partner of a range of countries around India, particularly the ASEAN economies. More importantly, from out of a total of 13 countries in 'southern Asia', ranging from Central Asia and Iran to South and South-East Asia, it is only with three countries that India has a higher share of their respective total external trade than China. These three are Nepal, Sri Lanka and Bangladesh. China has overtaken India in Myanmar as well as in

TABLE 38.3

Share of India and China in Total Trade of Some Asian Countries, 1991-97 (Percentage)

Year/Region	Myanmar	Indonesia	Malaysia	Singapore	Thailand	Vietnam	Bangladesh	Sri Lanka	Pakistan	Kazakhastan	Uzbekistan	Iran	Afghanistan
1991													
India	3.19	0.51	0.84	1.13	1.49	0.62	4.25	4.62	0.61	N.A.	N.A.	1.15	4.3
China	25.78	3.67	2.03	2.46	2.25	0.79	3.29	2.10	2.81			0.63	5.5
1992													
India	5.78	0.47	0.97	1.08	0.55	0.47	4.38	5.35	1.13	N.A.	N.A.	1.43	3.5
China	23.3	3.51	2.17	2.48	2.19	2.15	3.52	2.10	2.85		11.68	0.99	4.9
1993													
India	5.85	0.67	0.66	1.02	0.72	0.39	6.23	5.29	0.74	0.59	0.13	1.26	4.3
China	24.3	3.35	2.48	2.70	1.60	3.1	3.3	2.23	2.97	16.98	3.93	1.98	9.5
1994													
India	5.60	0.87	0.79	1.02	0.72	0.43	6.79	5.56	0.73	0.59	0.23	1.98	3.8
China	22.4	3.85	2.78	2.47	2.32	4.45	4.29	2.05	2.92	3.17	3.11	1.18	8.7
1995													
India	4.95	1.01	0.91	1.15	0.71	0.69	10.70	5.84	0.62	0.17	0.28	2.39	3.1
China	23.8	3.97	2.37	2.80	2.87	6.25	6.43	1.91	3.21	3.60	2.02	1.46	3.4
1996													
India	4.99	1.50	1.24	1.20	0.68	0.67	10.19	6.71	1.18	0.18	0.17	2.68	7.2
China	18.8	3.93	2.39	3.05	2.96	5.43	6.47	1.75	3.24	4.85	2.35	0.84	4.8
1997													
India	5.67	1.39	1.21	1.29	0.74	0.59	7.6	5.86	0.88	0.49	1.97	2.20	4.7
China	20.6	4.23	2.61	3.77	3.32	6.60	6.19	1.73	3.62	4.59	2.52	2.61	4.6

Note: India/China total Trade (X+M) with Country X
Total Trade (X+M) of Country X

Source: *Direction of Trade Statistics* (various years), WTO.

Vietnam, a country that China invaded barely two decades ago and has long been regarded by India as a 'friendly' country.

China has been able to accelerate its trade with these countries mostly from the mid-1990s. While China's trade with ASEAN economies is characterised by fluctuations, in the case of Myanmar and Vietnam we are able to see a sudden but sustained growth in trade in the 1990s. It may be pertinent to note that in Myanmar's case, China's export growth may be linked to new and increasing Chinese investment in the infrastructure sector including ports, railways and road construction as well as the growth in defence-related trade, particularly armaments exports. Not surprisingly, therefore, China accounts for only 5 per cent of Myanmar's export trade, but for 12 per cent of the latter's imports. Interestingly, India has a higher share of Myanmarese exports, at 13 per cent, being Myanmar's second largest market after Singapore (16 per cent), but does not even figure among the top 15 exporters to Myanmar.

In the case of Pakistan, defence exports may play an increasingly important role in defining Chinese exports to that country. It is useful to underline the fact here that China's three largest markets for its defence exports are Pakistan, Myanmar and Bangladesh, in that order. China and Hong Kong together account for 10 per cent of Pakistan exports but for only 5 per cent of its imports. While the US and EU remain Pakistan's major trade partners, India does not figure in the list of top 20 trading partners.

It is interesting to note that even with the three countries with which India enjoys a larger trade relationship than China, namely Sri Lanka, Nepal and Bangladesh, India in fact enjoys a massive trade surplus, which remains a sore point in their bilateral relations with India. Of course, China similarly enjoys a trade surplus with Pakistan, but with many ASEAN economies it has a trade deficit.

While India accounts for 16 per cent of imports into Bangladesh, its share of Bangla exports is a mere 1.0 per cent. The US and EU are the major destination for Bangla exports, accounting for 82 per cent of all Bangla exports, but their share in Bangla imports is a lowly 18 per cent. China and Hong Kong together account for 16 per cent of imports into Bangladesh, though exports to these markets account for only 3.0 per cent of Bangla exports. The structure of Nepal's and Sri Lanka's trade is similarly distorted. USA and EU are the major markets for both countries (70 per cent for Nepal and 66 per cent for Sri Lanka), but their share in imports is still very low. In the case of Sri Lanka, India is not an important export destination, but it accounts for 9.0 per cent of all imports. Japan, Korea, ASEAN and Hong Kong-China are other sources of imports. In the case of Nepal, India has an overwhelming presence, accounting for 27 per cent of its exports and 34 per cent of its imports. But Hong Kong is emerging as an important source of imports into Nepal (26 per cent share of total imports), which suggests that cheap Chinese goods may be coming into India through Nepal *via* Hong Kong.

The policy prescription for India is obvious. Not only must it raise its overall trade engagement with her neighbours, but it must pursue policies which can alter the trade imbalance in favour of its smaller neighbours, particularly Nepal, Sri Lanka and Bangladesh. Admittedly, this is easier said than done but India can, for instance, undertake unilateral trade liberalising measures. Equally importantly, Nepal and Bangladesh can, in particular, improve their trade balance by exporting power (hydel from Nepal and natural gas from Bangladesh) to India.

Another trade related concern India has with respect to China is the threat from dumping, already referred to above. In Sri Lanka, we have the recent episode of an Indian company manufacturing automobile tyres in Sri Lanka coming under severe competitive pressure from cheap Chinese imports. The Indian company was till recently exporting tyres to Sri Lanka and only recently decided to set up production facilities on the island. Even as the company's locally manufactured output hit the markets, China 'dumped' tyres in the Sri Lankan market deeply hurt this Indian company.

China has used its opaque exchange rate structure and export subsidy policy to subsidise its exports worldwide and, in particular, in developing economy markets. In its pursuit of market shares and its endeavour to compete out its Asian rivals China has adopted aggressive tactics. Its proposed membership of the WTO will hopefully bring it within the ambit of multilateral discipline and encourage greater transparency in its domestic economic policies. It is not surprising, for these reasons, that China has not only driven a hard bargain in seeking WTO membership, but it would like to come in as a 'developing country', securing the few advantages that status still confers on WTO members.

Two important points stand out from this descriptive account. First, that China is emerging an important trading nation in this region, particularly as an arms supplier and as a source of cheap consumer goods. Second, that India must address the problem of its trade surplus with all its neighbours if it wants to assuage their feelings and compete with China as a market for their exports.

Trade policy and foreign policy

External trade has for centuries been one of the most important forms of contact between nations. Not surprisingly, trade policy has come to be recognised as an important element of foreign policy and, as aptly summed up by Richard N. Cooper in his influential essay entitled *Trade Policy is Foreign Policy*, "historically trade issues frequently intruded into, and occasionally even dominated, high foreign policy among countries."[6] Cooper believed that in the post-Second World War period the Cold War had pushed political issues to the fore in the foreign policy of the trans-Atlantic powers and reduced the profile of trade issues. Writing in 1972, Cooper was urging US policy makers to take trade policy issues seriously and not be obsessed by Cold War concerns regarding strategic and political issues. With the end of the Cold War, however, trade policy issues have come to dominate 'high foreign policy' in the 1990s. The completion of the Uruguay round negotiations, the unilateral application of US-EU bilateral trade laws by the Bush and Clinton administrations and the US-China and US-EU bilateral trade disputes have come to occupy as much of the foreign policy and strategic policy mindspace in major capitals of the world as

---

6. R.N. Cooper, "Trade Policy is Foreign Policy", *Foreign Policy* Winter, 1972.

negotiations on nuclear disarmament, NATO expansion and political disputes in the Middle East, Eastern Europe and South-East Asia.

What is important to recognise, however, is not so much that in the post-Cold War period trade policy has again come to overtake political and strategic issues, which it has not, but that trade policy is becoming increasingly enmeshed with foreign policy and security issues. Cooper quotes in his essay the deposition made by the economist and strategic policy analyst, Thomas C. Schelling to the US Congress Commission on "National Security Considerations Affecting Trade Policy" (Washington DC, 1971). Schelling told the Commission:

"Trade policy can be civilised or disorderly, US trade policies can antagonise governments, generate resentment in populations, hurt economies, influence the tenure of governments, even provoke hostilities.... Aside from war and preparations for war, and occasionally aside from migration, trade is the most important relationship that most countries have with each other. Broadly defined to include investment, shipping, tourism, and the management of enterprises, trade is what most of international relations are about. For that reason trade policy is national security policy."

If this view of trade policy is accepted then, apart from negotiating 'multilateral' agreements on trade liberalisation and market access, large countries like China, India, the US and so on must pay added attention to their bilateral trade relations with key partner countries. It is not surprising that both the US and the EU participated as actively in the negotiation of the Uruguay Round agreement as they did in creating NAFTA and the EU 'single market'. Indeed, the post-Cold War period negotiations for the 'eastward' expansion of NATO have gone parallel to negotiations on EU enlargement to include Hungary, Czechoslovakia and Poland. Similarly, even as China has pursued membership of WTO over the last five years, it has assiduously built up its bilateral trade relations with the US, EU, Japan and its key neighbours.

India has understandably supported China's admission into the WTO. However, we must bear in mind the fact that while China's entry into WTO may help strengthen the hands of the so-called 'developing countries' and bring China under WTO discipline and dispute settlement system, it will also exert additional pressure on India to increase the pace of trade liberalisation. China is not only already ahead of India, in terms of trade openness, but its commitments are also ahead of India's. In canvassing for WTO membership, China has made some bold offers on tariff bindings, agriculture, TRIMs and TRIPs to the US.[7]

For example, China has offered to reduce its average tariff rate to about 9.44 per cent, with all tariff lines bound and only a few exceptions, by year 2005. This compares with India's current plans to bring the average tariff rate to a little below 30 per cent by 2005. China has offered to 'fully comply upon accession' to the TRIMs agreement, with no transition measures. In agriculture, China has offered an average tariff of 17 per cent by end 2004, with all tariff lines bound. It has also agreed to eliminate all export subsidies. In other areas too, China's 'offers' go beyond India's existing commitments. China may have promised more than it can or intends to deliver. It is also better placed than India to make bolder offers, given its higher foreign trade to GDP ratio, its much higher foreign exchange reserves and a generally stronger external economic profile. Nevertheless, the fact is that China's aggressive pursuit of a forward-looking liberal trade policy can further pressure India into increasing its own pace of trade liberalisation. Is India capable of bearing such pressure? There is no gainsaying the fact that trade policy, multilateral, regional and bilateral, is an important element of national security policy, albeit a blunt instrument of foreign policy.

In the Cold War era China often accused the US of attempting its 'encirclement' by its alliances with Japan, Korea, ASEAN, Pakistan and even India. While the US has moved away from its 'encirclement' strategy to seek greater 'engagement' with China,

---

7.   Daniel H. Rosen, "China and the World Trade Organization: An Economic Balance Sheet", Institute for International Economics, Washington DC, 1999, www.chinaonline.com.

particularly in the economic sphere, China may in fact be adopting this 'encirclement' paradigm against India. Thus, not only has China built key strategic alliances with Pakistan and Myanmar, but it has also made trade a focus of its increasing economic 'engagement' with India's neighbours. This strategic 'encirclement' of India has extended beyond Indian borders to include countries like Vietnam, a foe of China in the past and a friend of India for a long time. Today, China's trade with Vietnam is several fold larger than India's trade with that country.

India has strategic interests in the Indian Ocean region and should improve its strategic equation with Iran, Central Asian republics, the Gulf States and the ASEAN economies, particularly Singapore, Thailand and Indonesia. To pursue its legitimate foreign policy goals, India must deepen and widen its trade and investment relations with each of these countries. If India fails in this regard, its economic encirclement by a rapidly growing trading power, China, can lay the basis for its political and strategic encirclement.

Apart from pursuing bilateral initiatives like the India-Sri Lanka Free Trade Agreement, India must also actively ensure that trade and economic cooperation become the focus of regional associations in this part of the World. Regrettably SAARC has not been an effective forum for increasing trade and economic cooperation in South Asia. Not only have SAARC initiatives like SAPTA and SAFTA moved slowly, but new initiatives like the recommendations of the SAARC Eminent Persons' Group on forming a South Asian Economic Union and such like have been aborted. Notwithstanding the slow progress of SAARC, India must retain its interest in regional cooperation and also invest greater resources and diplomatic energy in new regional economic groups such as BIMSTEC (Bangladesh, India, Myanmar, Sri Lanka and Thailand Economic Cooperation) and IOR-ARC (Indian Ocean Rim Association for Regional Cooperation). BIMSTEC can not only help improve trade relations with Bangladesh, Sri Lanka and Myanmar, but it will also act as a bridge to ASEAN, a part of Asia where China looms large and India's engagement is eagerly being sought, especially by Thailand, Indonesia, Vietnam and Singapore.

Finally, a part of Asia where China is fast emerging an important economic partner is Central Asia. China has been liberal in investing in Kazakhstan and this investment, particularly in the infrastructure sector, has driven their trade relationship. China's share of Kazakh, Uzbek and Afghan external trade is higher than India's. While China's share of Iran's trade is still small, India should pay greater attention to its strategic and economic relations with Iran particularly in the aftermath of Pakistan's declared nuclear stance. China's interest in Central Asia is strategic. It hopes to be the link between Central Asian oil and natural gas and the energy deficit markets of East and South-East Asia. Central Asian energy requires the East and South-East Asian markets and China is offering the route for the land-based pipelines. If China succeeds in this venture, not only will it build permanent and strategic links with Korea, Japan and the ASEAN economies, but India will be further marginalised in the region. India, Iran and the United States must, therefore, come closer and explore the possibility of greater plurilateral economic cooperation in the region.

Several policy conclusions follow from this study with respect to domestic and external economic policy, investment in trade-related infrastructure, regional and bilateral economic relations and the creation of new alliances of friendship with strategic partners both within the region and outside, all aimed at ensuring a strategic equilibrium in Asia, between India and China. A strategic disequilibrium in Asia, favouring China, can have adverse consequences for the global economic and political order, not to speak of India's own national security interests.

Trade policy is intimately linked with foreign policy and national security. India's desire and need to increase its share of world trade suggests that it must learn to walk on two legs—on the one hand being actively engaged in the multilateral trade process and undertaking domestic economic reforms, aimed at improving the competitiveness of Indian exports, and on the other hand, pursuing regional and bilateral initiatives. These need not be confined to our immediate 'South Asian' neighbours, but must extend to our wider 'Southern Asian' neighbourhood, as well as to our key trade partners like the United States and the European Union. This strategy suggests itself even more in the context of China's increasing integration into the world economy, its growing political clout and its rising competitive ability *vis-à-vis* India in the region around us.

to our key trade partners like the United States and the European Union. This strategy suggests itself even more in the context of China's increasing integration into the world economy, its growing political clout and its rising competitive ability vis-à-vis India in the region around us.

39
COLUMN

Mr. Rao goes to Washington

INDIA and the United States of America have never been enemies, the US deputy secretary of State, Mr. Strobe Talbott, reminded the Prime Minister, Mr. P.V. Narasimha Rao, adding, however, that the two have never been particularly good friends either. While the contents of the 45-minute one-to-one meeting between Mr. Rao and Mr. Talbott are not yet public knowledge, in his candid conversations with Indian officials and diplomats Mr. Talbott made it very clear that the United States would like Indo-US relations to emerge out of the mire of suspicion and neglect, and 'turn a new leaf'.

It is not without significance that the US has accepted India's position that the relationship must be defined independently of Pakistan. India views itself as a regional power in Asia and would like to relate to the US on the basis of its national and international concerns, and not merely on the basis of its bilateral ties with Pakistan.

While all this augurs well for Mr. Rao's visit to Washington, Mr. Rao has not been carried away by the overt enthusiasm of Mr. Talbott who offered assurance that the Washington visit will be 'more successful', than Mr. Rao's visits to any of the European capitals. Indian diplomats were happy to hear these words, but bade goodbye to Mr. Talbott, fully aware of the still tenuous nature of the Indo-American relationship. There is probably no illusion in the Prime Minster's mind, therefore, that his visit to the United

States might not really be a major turning point in what has been an essentially low-key, though often frustrating and irritating, and sometimes rewarding, relationship.

However, merely because no dramatic results are expected and because there is growing anger in India about the insensitivity of the Clinton administration towards Indian sensibilities, the Prime Minister is obviously not going to turn down an opportunity to explain current thinking in India on economic, defence and other issues to a new generation US president. The official view is that a visit to the US is long overdue considering the fundamental changes that have taken place in the world and in India since the last visit of an Indian Prime Minister in 1985.

Those who are concerned about the 'secret' meeting in London, between US and Indian diplomats, will do well to recall that Mr. Rao's route to Washington has been a circuitous one. On his way to the American capital at the end of his third year in office, Mr. Rao has halted at several interesting and important stations. In India's neighbourhood, he has made highly successful visits to Iran, China and some of the Central Asian republics. India's relations with some of the former Soviet republics is still very satisfactory, even if Moscow remains preoccupied with itself and the West and, despite Mr. Yeltsin's successful visit to India, has not been able to rebuild on the foundation of the past.

In the East, he has visited Tokyo and Seoul and also established a friendly and rewarding relationship with some of the key ASEAN countries, including Malaysia, Thailand and Singapore. In the West, he has travelled to Paris, Bonn and London. The only important capital that Mr. Rao has not visited is Moscow. And thereby hangs a tale.

It is now commonplace to suggest that in the post-Cold War world, India must arrive at a *modus vivendi* with the US. However, the significance of Mr. Rao's itinerary has not been lost on the US. Rather than go straight to Washington and leave his calling card with a president who has still not found the time or the inclination to appoint an ambassador to his country, Mr. Rao chose to first call on a dozen different friends to show that we can still live with honour in the unipolar world. In security terms, the visits to Iran and China were both important and useful. In economic terms, the visits to Japan and the EC capitals were equally useful. A sub-continental economy like India, with a vast market at home and in search of new technology and markets abroad can live comfortably with the friends that Mr. Rao has already called on. However, its Prime Minister can ill afford to be churlish and petty-minded and decline an invitation to visit the US merely because a bumbling Mr. Bill Clinton has been unable to evolve a mature, long-term policy for South Asia based on America's social, political and economic interests rather than her arms industries' short-term business interests.

If the entire debate on Indo-US relations and the advisability of Mr. Rao's visit to the US at this juncture has become bogged down in the controversy relating to nuclear non-proliferation, no one but Washington is to blame. Rather than keep the focus of the Indo-US relationship on economic issues, given that the US is the most important trade partner for India and now the largest source of foreign direct investment, the Clinton administration has ill-advisedly chosen to retain nuclear non-proliferation on top of its agenda. Even at this stage, if Mr. Clinton would really like to see Indo-US relations take a turn for the better, he should end his obsession with the NPT and build bridges through an improved trade and investment relationship.

Indeed, the fact is that while the Indian and US policymaking elites have found each other frustrating and irritating, the bond between the intellectual-business-social—political elites of the two countries is today stronger than at any other time in the past. More importantly, India's establishment and anti-establishment elites are more closely linked to the US than any other country. Even Britain is no longer in this cultural position, for most Indians who live in Britain have either delinked themselves from India or belong to the politically and economically less influential trading and middle classes.

On the other hand, the professional Indian middle class, the new entrepreneurial groups in the sub-continent's more developed regions of western and southern India, as well as the big business class in India have a closer rapport with the US than any other country. Mr. Rao is aware of this crucial sociological fact which defence strategists and diplomats often forget. He recognises that the US is the 'Mecca' of India's 'new business and professional classes' and to retain the support of the latter, he must befriend the former. He is aware of the fact that government-to-government relations between the two great democracies lag far behind the people-to-people relations.

Given this ground reality, it is only natural that an Indian Prime Minister should want to engage the US government in a discussion on a wide range of issues confronting the two countries, and the global community, at the turn of the century. While Mr. Clinton has so far shown little appreciation of the 'ground reality' of a strong Indo-US economic and cultural relationship and has wasted an year of his increasingly damaged presidency, he might finally be discovering the value of doing business with India. Hence, the invitation to Mr. Rao.

This optimistic view of Mr. Rao's visit is at variance with the environment of dismay and hostility that has begun to build up, partly due to US manoeuvres on the road to Marrakesh, the proposed F-16 sales to Pakistan and the ham-handed manner in which the Indian government, including the Prime Minster's office, have handled the discussions in London. Inept bureaucracies on both sides are damaging a valuable relationship, and it is necessary that both Mr. Rao and Mr. Clinton do some house-cleaning before they meet.

regions of western and southern India, as well as the big business
class in India have a closer rapport with the US than any other
country. Mr Rao is aware of this crucial sociological fact which
defence strategists and diplomats often forget. He recognises that
the US is the 'Mecca' of India's new business and professional classes,
and to retain the support of the latter, he must befriend the former.
He is aware of the fact that government-to-government relations
Minister should want to engage the US government in a discussion
on a wide range of issues confronting the two countries, and the
global community at the turn of the century. While Mr. Clinton
has so far shown little appreciation of the 'ground reality' of a

40 COLUMN

Beyond nuclear policy

A wider perspective on signing CTBT

THE economy, it is said, is far too important a matter to be left
entirely to economists. National security, it must be said, is also
far too important to be left entirely to nuclear strategists. The
decision of whether India should agree to sign the Comprehensive
Test Ban Treaty (CTBT) or not cannot be taken within the narrow
perspective of nuclear policy alone, though this will be the primary
consideration, but within a wider national security perspective.

Our nuclear policy has not been shaped by military
considerations alone. It is central to our economic and energy
security and is embedded in a comprehensive national security policy.

It is this wider perspective that informed India's decision to
maintain a posture of 'ambivalence' and undeclared capability till
1998. While India initially endorsed and co-sponsored the CTBT,
linking it with universal nuclear disarmament, the manner in which
the treaty came to be drawn up and, more importantly, the indefinite
extension of the Nuclear Non-proliferation Treaty (NPT), which
legitimised the nuclear status of the five UN Security Council
members, with the support of the so-called 'non-aligned movement',
queered the pitch for India's refusal to sign CTBT in 1996. These
columns of The Times of India played an important role at the time
in moulding public opinion against the CTBT. This decision was
articulated as an opposition to 'nuclear apartheid' as well as based
on security considerations given the ongoing nuclearisation of our
neighbourhood.

The Shakti tests of May 1998 have qualitatively altered the scenario. The main reason for not signing in 1996 no longer holds. Questions relating to the technical adequacy of those tests, raised by ill-informed or motivated critics, are red herrings. Such critics must then demand more tests now, not an unending freedom to test. The considered view of the nuclear establishment is that the Shakti tests are adequate for the credibility of India's minimum nuclear deterrent.

The military challenge ahead is in the field of missile technology, developing the delivery, command and control system. This agenda must be pursued and is not constrained by adherence to the CTBT.

India would not have found itself in the current predicament if it had conducted its tests in 1996 and then signed the CTBT, a strategy adopted by France and China. The important question is why did India not test in 1995 or 1996? Was the reason purely political, did the Congress and the United Front governments oppose testing in principle while the Bharatiya Janata Party was for it? Or, did wider economic and diplomatic considerations hold the Narasimha Rao, Gowda and Gujral governments back, while the Vajpayee government no longer felt constrained by them? Consider the facts.

First, none of India's major political parties overtly favoured testing till 1997. The election manifestoes of each of these parties for the 1996 general elections stand testimony to this fact. Everyone spoke of 'retaining the nuclear option' and fighting for universal nuclear disarmament. It is only in 1998 that the BJP manifesto referred to "exercising the nuclear option" and "inducting nuclear weapons". Clearly, the indefinite extension of NPT and the terms of the CTBT as adopted altered perceptions in India. Two options were left for India. To test, go overtly nuclear and sign, or to give up nuclear capability forever. Both options had their advocates in India, but within government there was a consistent view from the late 1980s that India must respond to the nuclearisation of its wider neighbourhood. Prime Minister Vajpayee finally took the decision to go overt in April 1998.

What held his predecessors' governments back and what enabled Mr. Vajpayee to go forward? The single most important factor was the wider economic and diplomatic environment. The Indian government felt far too constrained by external pressure in 1995 and 1996. As much has been conceded by Prime Ministers Rao and Gujral who wanted to follow the Chinese example of testing and signing but were advised that the economy may not be able to withstand the pressure of sanctions. Whether this was factually an accurate assessment of the state of the economy at the time or not is moot. The fact is that they were prepared to believe the argument that India will not be able to withstand the impact of sanctions.

Prime Minister Vajpayee took the view that the economy could withstand sanctions and he proved correct. India tested, the sanctions came, but proved to be less hurtful than widely imagined. India has been subject to bilateral sanctions, mainly by the US and Japan, and multilateral sanctions imposed through restraints on World Bank lending imposed by the G-7 countries. These sanctions are still in place, so are the many pre-Pokhran-II sanctions. Sanctions offer an opportunity for indigenous development, they also impose costs. There are times when the burden of such sanctions have to be borne by a nation, there are times when it can be asked why this is still necessary.

Fortunately, the Indian economy has performed adequately well in the last year to enable the country to withstand the full impact of sanctions. However, the time has come to ask whether any larger strategic and security purpose is served by continuing to hold out on CTBT. If the country genuinely believes that it is not in our security interest to sign the CTBT, a view correctly taken in 1996, then we must continue to refuse signing the treaty whatever the economic and diplomatic cost. However, if no serious security interests are involved, why should we remain stuck on dogma, dubious principle and a negative attitude to the rest of the world? Moreover, we must weigh the costs of our defiance against the benefits of cooperation within a wider perspective of national security which takes into account our economic and technological priorities and concerns. A robust nuclear energy programme is as much an investment in national security as building a nuclear deterrent.

The national debate on India's adherence to CTBT must not be confined just to the technical aspects of our nuclear weapons capability, important as they are, but must be within the framework of a vision of our economic and social priorities, our relations with a range of friendly countries including our wider Asian neighbourhood, Europe and the United States and our commitment to genuine universal nuclear disarmament.

Who's afraid of Entities List?

THE United States government has now targeted what it believes to be India's 'military-industry' complex, the public and private sector companies engaged in defence-related production and services, with its 'Entities List'. This is all part of the 'Big Power' scare tactics and India will have to learn to live with such pressure tactics if it is serious about playing the nuclear game. The US government's action will hurt and a back-of-the-envelope calculation from a senior foreign ministry official yields a figure of about 300 to 400 million US dollars. That's the kind of pain an aspiring nuclear power must learn to bear. There's no free lunch in the security business.

There's even a positive way of looking at the US action, as some senior scientists at the defence research laboratories do. "Sanctions have helped us," says a scientist at Hyderabad's Defence Research and Development Organisation (DRDO). "Many of the projects which were on hold till recently because the government preferred to place import orders rather than allow domestic production, are now getting cleared because imports have been hurt by US sanctions." In Bangalore, a scientist at an aerospace research facility says his company was an importer of certain rocket parts from a US firm and had been pushing the US supplier to set up a joint venture production facility in India. "They refused to do this and we continued to depend on imports. When the sanctions came the US company agreed to jump them by going in for a joint venture. We are close to sealing that deal and I hope sanctions continue for some time because that will help indigenisation," says this upbeat scientist. Indian government officials are not off the mark when they suggest that lobbying by interested US corporations has helped soften the impact of the first round of nuclear sanctions.

Undoubtedly US sanctions will hurt and one must try and shake them off, but it is equally important for policy makers and businessmen to see how they can make the best use of a situation created by these sanctions. There has been much justifiable consternation within the domestic business community about the Entities List and the inclusion of major Indian corporates. Jamshed Godrej of Godrej & Boyce, an affected party, has rightly said that, "India has a space programme and it is legitimate for Indian companies to participate in it." One can only express regret that the US administration is still pursuing Cold War tactics of hurting the industrial and technological potential of countries like India when it should in fact be actively involved in augmenting this potential in the large interests of global peace, prosperity and the democratic way of life.

No one can better appreciate the benign link between defence-spending and people-friendly technological development better than the United States. For years, the US military budget has sustained civilian research in such a wide range of areas as food processing, medical care, information technology and entertainment. The Internet is a spin-off from defence spending.

In his celebrated book, *The Work of Nations*, former US labour secretary, Robert Reich, draws our attention to the beneficial civilian uses of defence-related spending and how this was repeatedly used by the US administration to justify pouring billions of dollars of taxpayers' money into defence projects. Says Reich: "...billions of dollars dedicated to researching, designing and constructing intricate and complex weapons systems...also generate technologies with commercial possibilities. Defence contractors invented small transistors, which eventually would find their way into everything from television to wristwatches. Also from the military-industrial complex...would emerge hard plastics, optical fibres, lasers, computers, jet engines and aircraft frames, precision gauges, sensing devices, and an array of electronic gadgets, many of which have also created commercial advantage for America's core corporations."

When a group of engineers working on advanced computer systems in California decided a decade ago that they did not want to be involved with the Star Wars project and would refuse all funding that had any links with it, they suddenly discovered they were out of any funding. Star War budgets had come to so completely dominate research in computer sciences that there was no way of not touching that money! The R&D spin-off of defence spending in the US has been adequately documented.

It is only natural that a country like India will also try and make use of such externalities and, if anything, there is greater need for a closer link between the Indian corporate sector and defence R&D.

Businessmen who have dealt with defence R&D organisations are convinced that if the government should allow greater cooperation between the public and private sector, leaving R&D and product development to the public sector and manufacturing and marketing the product to the private sector, then there is a vast potential waiting to be tapped in such areas as medicine and medical care, food processing, automobiles, metals and engineering, aviation, telecommunication and so on. India is still at the nascent stage in the development of a productive link between defence spending and industrial and technological development. A domestic 'military-industrial' complex, with potential benign spin-off for development, is in the making and should be encouraged. The US action last week will undoubtedly scare away some of the private sector companies. That is what the action is intended to do. But the path to progress lies in developing this synergy and creating a mixed economy in defence-related production.

Dotcom diaspora

World wide web of overseas Indians

IF Silicon Valley smells of curry, the Hotmail directory reads like an Indian epic. Just look at the names of all those account holders and the dotcomers. No single community has perhaps networked as much through the web as has the Indian diaspora. If British colonialism helped spread Indians worldwide, the English language is today helping reconnect communities through the Net. For thousands of urban middle class Indians, the Internet is a family get-together.

Anthropologist Johanna Lessinger from the University of New Hampshire, USA, reports from her study of 'Indian immigrants in the United States' that for many middle class Indian Americans in the US, "the house-hold bills found most burdensome were long-distance phone bills". No wonder it took an Indian like Sabeer Bhatia to think of 'Hotmail'. The Internet and e-mail are at the heart of the globalisation of the Indian middle class.

Sociologist Dhiru Patel, a diasporic Indian from the department of Canadian Heritage, told an international conference on 'Culture and Economy in the Indian Diaspora' in New Delhi earlier this month that, "online media has become the 'collective brain' of the Indian diaspora". Patel quoted a fellow researcher, K. Karim, as saying that, "The ability to exchange messages with individuals on the other side of the planet and to have access to community information almost instantaneously changes the dynamics of diaspora, allowing for qualitatively and quantitatively enhanced linkages."

'Diaspora', according to Oxford historical Steven Vertovec, is the term often used today to describe practically any population which is considered 'deterritorialised' or 'transnational', that is, "whose cultural origins are said to have arisen in a land other than which they currently reside, and whose social, economic and political networks cross the borders of nation—states or, indeed, span the globe". By this definition, people of Indian origin worldwide may well be the world's most dispersed diaspora.

The Indian diaspora, most recently estimated to be upwards of 12 million, is by no means homogeneous. To begin with, overseas Indians come in two distinct categories—first, 'people of Indian origin' (PIOs), resident nationals of many countries across the world, from Fiji to East Africa, from Coventry to the Caribbean. They are normally two or more generations away from India. Second, 'non-resident Indians' (NRIs), first-generation expatriates still firmly linked with their families back home, many still Indian passport holders. Both groups are as diverse as their home country, in terms of language, class, caste, ethnicity and religion. However, what is increasingly common to the more dynamic sections of the diaspora is their link to the web, driven as much by their business need as the desire to network with the diaspora.

A good part of the e-networking till now may have been confined largely to the NRI community, but as net communities spread, multiply and diversify the Internet is emerging as the most important link for India's English-language speaking global diaspora. India's open democratic system which has enabled the easy proliferation of the Internet and net-cafes and clubs, has opened up the web to anyone who can afford to pay a rupee per minute of usage, with rates going down.

While the Jewish diaspora is also highly wired in to the web (recall the web community electing former Israeli Prime Minister Yitzhak Rabin as the 'man of the century' outscoring Mahatma Gandhi), the Indian diaspora appears to have stolen a march over overseas Chinese whose web-networking has been limited by China's intrusive and restrictive laws relating to Internet access. The fact that the English language is the *lingua-electronica* has also given a decisive advantage to Indians, at home and overseas. Not surprisingly, the Chinese and other East Asians have launched crash courses in learning English. Indeed, if we continue to neglect the teaching of English in India, the East Asians may well overtake us and we may have lost a historical advantage.

Indians and people of Indian origin not only communicate with their family through the Net, they now perform online *pujas*, exchange greetings, buy and sell property, access news, information and entertainment and, influence thinking across the world and abuse each other. Nowhere is the intense caste-animosity that lies behind politics in Tamil Nadu more manifest than on the web. Just check out the website for 'socio-cultural Tamil'.

Till early this century, it took between two to six months for overseas Indians to meet up with their family back home, travelling as they did by sea. While air transport in the post-war period reduced time, it increased cost of travel. Telephones became the most cost-effective but ineffective means of keeping in touch. Surprisingly, the Indian print media did not reach out to this community till recently and the first major diasporic publication came from the US rather than India. The Net has changed all that.

The creation of a global Indian 'dot-community', dubbed by a journalist friend as "dot-*kaum*", has had the dual impact of allowing Indians to access the world and the Indian diaspora to reaccess India, both instantaneously. This easy accessibility creates a community and that community creates new possibilities—economic, cultural, diplomatic. Consequently, despite its low share of world trade, India may acquire a high share of global, social and cultural interaction.

This is already apparent in the growing reach of the Indian infotainment industry. The diaspora is both a consumer and generator of media raw material and the final product. Words, ideas, music, information, images, experiences, concerns, causes go back and forth between Indians at home and overseas reinforcing old attachments and loyalties, creating new ones and allowing dual identities to live together. Few nations in the world are likely to experience this phenomenon as intensely as the Indian digital diaspora and the dot-community will.

However, to be able to really derive the benefit of the new economy we must invest considerably more in the required infrastructure, the communication hardware, and in qualified people who can generate the information software. Projects like Sankhya Vahini help create that infrastructure. Regrettably, this innovative project which combines commercial utilisation of cyberspace with an expansion of the knowledge network, has generated avoidable controversy which must be put to rest. Equally, Indian dotcom companies must also invest in high quality infotainment software so that we don't remain mere consumers of other people's output but are also able to generate world class output of our own.

Terms of engagement

WASHINGTON DC: A window of opportunity has opened for initiating a new phase in the relations between India and the United States and, despite the postponement of US President Bill Clinton's visit due to the Lok Sabha elections, there is enough evidence of a sincere commitment in the second Clinton administration to improved Indo-US relations.

That the United States is presently serious about a major turnaround in Indo-US relations came through very clearly in a range of statements made by senior officials of the US state and defence departments, as well as several 'India-watchers' at a two-day 'strategic dialogue' between Indian and US strategic, foreign and economic policy analysts at the Institute for National Strategic Studies at the National Defense University, Washington DC, recently.

Since the participants at the seminar spoke on a 'non-attributable' basis it will not be possible for us to quote individuals here. However, the message that came through loud and clear was articulated by one US official in the following words, "We want to change the tone and tenor of our relationship with India and not define our relationship by our differences. We benefit from hearing what India has to say. We ignore India at our risk." This official went on to quote Mr. Thomas Pickering, the former US ambassador to India and Russia and currently under secretary in the state department, as stating that it was now the intension of the Clinton administration to "under promise and over deliver" in dealing with India so that no exaggerated expectations are generated and there is no destructive disappointment if things go wrong.

US officials now draw a parallel between the United States' prickly relations with its allies, in particular the European Union and Japan, and the sparring relationship with India, arguing that latter relationship is potentially so broad based that there will be areas of mutual agreement and areas of disagreement. Said a US official, "Indo-US relations should be like the US-EU relations, marked by 'successful problem-solving'. They are complex but characterised by close cooperation and trust." Another state department official held the view that, "There is no single item on the Indo-US agenda. No obsession with one single issue. There is now a willingness on the part of the US to work beyond prickly issues." While the prickly issues were not always explicitly spelt out, participants at the conference were clear that these referred to US concerns about India's nuclear programme. However, one US official borrowed the paradigm of chaos theory to suggest that there is "...no centre of gravity in Indo-US relations. It is a weakly chaotic and dynamic system."

If these quotable quotes are not convincing enough, here is a another quote from a senior state department official who reported the US assessment of the meeting between Prime Minister Inder Kumar Gujral and US Secretary of State Madeline Albright, when the latter visited New Delhi in late November. The broad-ranging discussion between the two, said the US official, "...was a conversation between global powers. It covered global issues like the reform of the United Nations, Iraq, problems in West Asia and so on. The US-India relationship is now an independent free-standing structure. It is independent of the Cold War, of China, of Pakistan.... It is based on an independent structure."

In a nutshell, the second Clinton Administration has come to a clear understanding that it must rebuild its relationship with India on the foundation of enduring cultural and social links and emerging and deepening trade and investment links, without allowing earlier concerns and suspicions on political and security related issues to stifle a potentially mutually rewarding relationship.

In an essay on the US and South Asia that has already had wide circulation in Washington DC published in the influential journal *Current History* (December 1997), Selig Harrison, a doyen among the dwindling tribe of India specialists (author of *India: The Most Dangerous Decades*, 1960) calls for a "positive and constructive" relationship between India and the US. Harrison says, "To remove the 'bristling feeling' from their relations, both the United States and India will have to show greater sensitivity and forbearance. The United States will have to learn that it cannot cling forever to its self-appointed role as the 'only superpower'...and India will have to recognise that political and economic accommodation with the United States is a necessary pre-condition for its own achievement of superpower status." Harrison has outlined a possible Indo-US 'bargain' on the nuclear issue which can remove the 'bumps' and US laws that prohibit hi-tech exports to India and prevent Indo-US cooperation in the nuclear field.

It would be incorrect to suggest that the Washington conference was gung-ho about Indo-US relations. Participants on both sides were acutely aware of the history of missed and wasted opportunities, of mutual suspicion, of contradictory pulls and pressures in both countries and, above all, of India's insignificant share in the American mind-space, both within government and among the public, especially the media. If there is a constituency for India in the US it is within the business community, as one US official put it, "...every major US corporation now having a base in India." But even here, China has an overwhelming presence and India has a long way to go before it can equal China's appeal to US investors.

What is interesting, however, is the positive perception of the US strategic policy community about India's economic future. As one analyst at the National Defense University puts it, "On present trends, India is likely to become the clearly pre-eminent regional power (in South Asia). Indeed, as the difference (between India and Pakistan) in economic growth rates becomes clearer, the trends in

India's favour will affect perceptions. India will be seen as the power of the future, and that will in turn multiply its power in the present."

Influential sections within the United States government and within the business and strategic policy community are convinced that the US must strengthen and deepen its relationship with India. There is an air of pragmatism in Washington DC, shorn of Cold War shibboleths and the US seems to be interested in 'engaging' India in a new relationship. The question is, are we ready, willing and adequately prepared to be so engaged? The world is waiting for an answer, but may not wait for long.

Long and short of India-US relations

WASHINGTON DC: After climbing the slopes of successful summitry and basking in the sunshine of a new engagement, the bilateral relationship between India and the United States of America seems to have hit a plateau. Naive optimism about being 'natural allies' has given way to sober realism bordering on frustration that the more things change the more they remain the same.

Nothing has contributed more to this new realism than the fallout of the 9/11 terrorist attacks and the US reassessment of its relations with Pakistan. Even though the US remains sceptical about General Pervez Musharraf's commitment to the war against *jehadi* terrorism, the 'P-word' will continue to haunt Indo-US relations in the medium term. In the 'long run' India and the US will be partners on many fronts, but in the 'short run' the partnership with Pakistan is important for the US.

That, in a nutshell, is the message from within Washington DC's 'beltway', the epicentre of foreign policymaking in the US. Several US interlocutors participating in a India-US bilateral dialogue, jointly sponsored by the Confederation of Indian Industry and the Aspen Strategy Group, a Washington DC-based policy arm of the Aspen Institute, Colorado (USA), were categorical in their view — the US and India have much in common as multi-cultural democracies, as strategic partners in the Indian Ocean region from Aden to Singapore, and there is depth to the people-to-people relationship reinforced by India's presence in the knowledge economy, but if India could improve its relations with Pakistan it can help bilaterally too.

From a US perspective nothing would be better than to have both India and Pakistan on its side, with both resolving their differences amicably. However, fully aware of its strategic importance to the US, Pakistan is currently in no hurry to improve its relations with India. Hence, what is theoretically not a zero-sum game has in practice ended up being so and as long as this is the case, the strategic engagement between India and US may get hedged in.

The CII-Aspen dialogue is a unique ensemble. In the world of 'track two dialogues', the semi-official interaction between nations through former policy makers, policy analysts and others capable of shaping opinion both within government and in civil society, the CII-ASG dialogue is a rare example of an industry association providing a diplomatic platform. Track two interactions are normally facilitated by academic institutions and think tanks. It is perhaps a measure of the straitjacket into which many academic institutions in both countries have fallen that previous bilateral track two interactions proved to be stillborn while this one has gotten off to a good start.

The Indian team is led by industrialist Ratan Tata and India's former ambassador to the US, Naresh Chandra, while the US team is led by strategist Henry Kissinger and ASG's co-chair Joseph Nye. Both teams include businessmen, retired officials and diplomats, strategic policy analysts, politicians and editors. The rules of engagement are that all comments are off-the-record and no one can be quoted but participants are permitted to write on the issues discussed.

The group's meetings in January 2002 (Udaipur) and August (Aspen) were marked by remarkable warmth and frankness, with participants on both sides speaking candidly, not sermonising, and showing empathy for the other side's viewpoint. However, the hope expressed by some at Udaipur—that Pakistan would not become a fetter in India-US relations—was stated with less assurance in Aspen. How the two countries manage their relations with Pakistan will willy-nilly shape the bilateral relationship in the short term.

If, despite this, the strategic engagement is proceeding apace it is partly on account of the importance of the Indian American community to the bilateral relationship and partly a consequence of growing US concern about China's rising military and economic profile. Undoubtedly, the China factor counts for more with the Bush administration. New military-to-military relations between India and US have also helped and the Pentagon today appears better disposed towards India than the State Department, notwithstanding reports of F-16 nuclear-capable fighter jet sales to Pakistan, which India has taken a dim view of.

India has more friends in the Pentagon than the State Department and undoubtedly more in the US Congress. *The New York Times* columnist Tom Friedman put it very well when he said that while General Powell may like General Musharraf, General Electric prefers India! But Indian diplomacy in US is presently not as deft and sure-footed as it has been in recent years.

Relations are still lukewarm in trade policy. The skirmish between US trade representative Robert Zoellick and commerce minister Murasoli Maran and their face-off at the World Trade Organization's Doha ministerial meeting has left unhealed wounds on both sides. US trade officials still view Mr. Maran's stance as isolationist and are unwilling to see India's tactics at Doha, aimed at postponing the day of reckoning on the Singapore issues, as having wider developing country support. India still chaffs at US's bulldozing tactics and at attempts to use bilateralism and regionalism as a weapon against deadlocked multilateralism. However, there is interest in a bilateral engagement on trade policy and this is likely to happen on 'track two'.

Clearly, Pakistan and trade policy are the two areas on which India and the US must spend more time to iron out differences. Another, albeit related area, is nuclear strategy. While the Bush administration has eased off on non-proliferation, the issue could resurface anytime. More importantly, India remains perplexed by US silence on Pakistan's nuclear blackmail this summer and is unhappy that controls on dual use and high-tech exports continue.

While Indo-US economic relations are not exactly 'as flat as a *chapati*', as US ambassador Robert Blackwill complained, they can be placed on firmer ground for the long-term if the Indian economy performs better, delivering up to 7 per cent growth, and is more open to foreign investment and trade. It is on the foundations of a more vibrant economy that a firmer basis of long-term engagement with the US can really be built.

The big deal about no big deal

WASHINGTON DC: Within a week of an official announcement by the United States government that the current six month duration for visitor's visas will be reduced to 30 days, over 25,000 Indian Americans have already signed a petition widely canvassed through the Internet protesting the move. If you have an e-mail address and have a relative in the US chances are you have already read the petition. It's making waves in Indian American cyberspace and thousands of young non-resident Indians in the US who look forward every year to visits from elderly parents are sad and angry.

"This is one more fallout of '9-11'," says an official at the Indian Embassy in Washington DC, "and there is more to come." The Indian Embassy has been informed that during the course of this year as many as 25,000 Indian passport holders may be asked to return home by US immigration authorities on grounds of overstaying their visa or to alter their visa status or simply because they no longer have the job that brought them here in the first place as H1-B visa holders.

Indian Americans are still hopeful that they can get the Bush administration to take a re-look at the 30-day order but Indian diplomats are less sanguine. The dim outlook of some Indian diplomats here is partly a reflection of the fact that Indo-US relations have hit a plateau and if the cooperation on the security front is set aside, there isn't much else happening.

On the political and security side much has happened and there is now a certain stability and depth to that relationship. This is best reflected in the fact that both countries have shied away from making a big deal about increased maritime security cooperation with Indian naval vessels invited to escort US ships between the Persian Gulf and the Malacca Straits. This decision on the part of the Bush administration has sent an important signal across the world that India will play the key role in the security of the sea lanes in the Arabian Sea and the Bay of Bengal spanning the region from Aden to Singapore—British India's 'sphere of management'.

There is similar good news about increased defence cooperation even if the US government has not lifted all hi-tech sanctions. In the fight against terrorism there is quite cooperation going on. But that's about it. This high level of engagement on the security side is not being matched by a similar engagement on the economic policy front. "There isn't enough happening on the economic front and that's not good. India must do more on the trade front," says James Clad, an old India enthusiast who has just joined the Bush administration.

The reference on trade is perhaps to two separate things that worry Americans. First, the low rate of growth of US exports to India in recent months, and second, the 'Cold War' following the open spat between Indian commerce minister Murasoli Maran and the US trade representative Robert Zoellick at Doha. Many do-gooders have been trying to get Mr. Maran and Mr. Zoellick to just talk to each other, forget getting them to agree with each other, and that's not happening.

Notwithstanding the domestic problems faced by that 'five-letter word' Enron, it remains a bone of contention with India. "There will be no US investment in the Indian power sector for the next five years," says an Indian official at a multilateral agency. If US investment in Indian infrastructure is drying up and if there is little interest in manufacturing at a time when domestic investment in India is still to pick up, the only area of any likely action is services.

"The services sector can do for Indo-US economic relations what manufacturing did for US-China trade," says Devesh Kapur of Harvard University. Indeed, that is the only sector in which there is action, despite the tech slowdown. However, here too the greater action will be in data processing and out-sourcing of software development, with the work being created in India. The huge inflow of temporary workers into the US is going to dry up with the US clamping down on immigration. This means India will have to improve its domestic infrastructure, especially telecom and power and generate adequate manpower, competing with Israel, Philippines and other East and South-East Asian countries.

All this is in the future. Right now the level of activity in the services sector, including the IT sector, is not providing enough of an economic ballast to a still nascent strategic relationship. The cooperation on the security front can not by itself sustain the bilateral relationship or take it to the level of the current engagement between China and the US. More to the point, if a democratic party administration comes to power some of the old nuclear non-proliferation obsessions can easily come to the fore re-introducing rancour into the strategic discourse.

If and when that happens there must be enough of an economic ballast to counter any such resurgence of political dissonance. Indeed, while the nuclear issue is not on the Bush government's agenda, there is already rising anxiety about increasing communal tension within India and the slow pace of progress on a resolution of the Kashmir issue. While the pro-Israel Jewish lobby can help upto a point in deflecting criticism on the communal situation in India, even this lobby would like to see more business opportunities in India and there has to be a commercial 'quid' to the political 'quo'.

That brings business and economics back into focus in the bilateral relationship. American interlocutors do not have the patience to listen to explanations about how the reason for such a low level of economic engagement has nothing to do with any anti-US bias but is the product of India's economic slowdown. At a time when China is still clocking upwards of 7 per cent growth and East and South-East Asia are getting back on track, few have the patience to wait for India to get its act together. If we remain obsessed with our domestic political and communal politics, and continue to neglect the economy, the world and the US will move on leaving us to deal with our own devices and desires. So who cares!

India and US

Out of the South Asia box

WITH Ms. Madeleine Albright coming to New Delhi weeks after Bill Clinton, a question naturally comes to the fore. Why do US leaders always come so enthusiastically to India after demitting office? Is this country just a tourist destination for retired American leaders or what? One of the continuing frustrations of Indians dealing with the United States is the latter's short attention span and superficial interest in this country. The relationship has been long on sentiment, short on substance.

Silicon Valley, business outsourcing, the contribution of Indian Americans to the emergence of the US as a knowledge economy superpower and India's economic resurgence and external liberalisation have, of course, combined to help change that. The end of the Cold War and the emergence of the *jehadi* threat has widened the scope for cooperation between the world's largest democracies.

However, the positive factors that have contributed to an improved bilateral relationship between India and the US, leading to Prime Minister Atal Bihari Vajpayee dubbing the two countries "natural allies", are diluted to an extent by the US continuing to view India through the South Asia prism. The very concept of 'South Asia' is an Americanism dating back to the period when the US State Department had little interest in India apart from the fact that it was Pakistan's neighbour and the latter was a military ally in the region.

To be sure, the India-US engagement does span a wide range of interests and concerns going beyond Pakistan and nuclear proliferation. For precisely this reason, and given the long distance the India-US relationship has traversed since the 1960s and the wide-ranging nature of our bilateral relationship now, it is a pity that the New York based Council on Foreign Relations (CFR) and The Asia Society (TAS) chose to put together a report on India-US relations within the restrictive framework of South Asia, focussing excessively on the Kashmir issue and the India-Pakistan nuclear threat. The frame chosen for the report unwittingly shapes the picture drawn within.

In itself, the CFR-TAS report on *New Priorities in South Asia: US Policy Towards India, Pakistan and Afghanistan* (2003), jointly written by diplomats Frank Wisner, Nicholas Platt, Denis Kux and scholars Marshall Bouton and Mahnaz Ispahani is balanced and realistic. Both Indians and Pakistanis will quarrel with something or the other in this report, as indeed many already have, and some Americans may also be dissatisfied with some of the recommendations. That, however, is not the report's real weakness from an Indian perspective. For an Indian, the so-called 'South Asian' setting in which the bilateral relationship is viewed would appear as being rooted too much in the past and not adequately forward-looking.

The key recommendations of the report, barring the ideas on Kashmir, will be generally and genuinely welcomed in India. The need to work to expand political, security, military and intelligence cooperation between US and India; to intensify both official and unofficial dialogue on economic and trade issues; the idea of a bilateral free trade agreement for trade in services; the need for the US to ease restrictions on high technology cooperation with India in civilian sectors; for US to treat India as a 'friendly' country in granting export licences in defence and high-tech sectors; the need for India to be more open to foreign investment and trade and pursue market-friendly economic reforms to boost economic growth and facilitate easier academic exchange and people-to-people contact with minimal governmental interference.

Who in India can object to any of these suggestions, barring those who are congenitally anti-American or are unwilling to accept the reality that the US is a 'South Asian' power, with its forces based in Pakistan and Afghanistan and with long-term interests in the region's energy resources and nuclear capability.

While the CFR-TAS report's specific recommendations are in fact not made within a South Asian framework and are relevant to a wider engagement between India and the US, the thrust of the report and the timing of its publication, on the eve of Prime Minister Vajpayee's visit to Pakistan gives the impression that a more myopic South Asian agenda has shaped the report. The report's authors must move quickly to dispel that impression if the report is to have a wider appeal in India.

India and the United States are indeed destined to be 'natural allies'. But this was a forward-looking statement of Mr. Vajpayee, not an assessment of the reality today. As the Indian decision on Iraq, reflecting domestic public opinion rather than emerging strategic thinking within the policymaking establishment, showed there is a political distance to be covered before India and the US can really think of each other as 'natural allies' in Asia.

There is an economic distance as well. The CFR-TAS report underscores both tasks at hand. While the report's views on the Kashmir issue have already, and understandably, evoked a sharp response from Indian commentators, its' assessment of the situation in Pakistan and the policy options for the US and Pakistan government have drawn sharper responses from within Pakistan. That Pakistani commentators are unhappy with the CFR-TAS report is no consolation for those Indians who see a huge untapped potential in India-US relations being held hostage to US's myopic policy in the region.

The time has come for both the US and India to view each other from a non-South Asian perspective. The proposed visit to New

Delhi of a senior State Department official, Matt Daley, dealing with East and South-East Asia perhaps signals an interest in understanding India's resurgent relationship with wider Asia. US think tanks too must begin to view India within this wider Asian, indeed global, spectrum.

The CFR-TAS report correctly calls for greater interaction between Indian and US scholars and researchers. While there are today more 'India' chairs in the US, as opposed to 'South Asia' centres, the study of India should be conducted within a wider Asian setting. Hopefully, the next CFR-TAS report will examine US-India relations within this broader perspective and not worry overly about a bilateral dispute on Kashmir that India and Pakistan should ideally be able to resolve together.

47 COLUMN

Putin Russia in perspective

TWO and a half years after his previous visit, Russian President Vladimir Putin will be back in India next week, testifying to the durability of a trusted friendship. With few other major powers in the world, does India feel more comfortable than with Russia. Yet, with few other major powers is India's economic relationship so badly off as it is with Russia. Can India and Russia sustain their longstanding and trusted friendship without a strong economic foundation? Difficult.

While concerns about national security and the dynamics of geopolitics continue to shape relations between nations, business and economics have moved centre-stage in international relations. India and Russia have similar security concerns—they worry about terrorism, about national integrity, about the global imbalance in the distribution of power in a unipolar world. They have an enduring pact in defence cooperation and India continues to depend on Russia for critical defence equipment.

However, neither shared security concerns nor periodic defence purchases can hope to restore the warmth between the two that was once palpable unless both countries are able to rejuvenate a fading economic relationship. More to the point, bilateral relations in today's world are increasingly defined by people-to-people interaction, both business and social, and less so by the needs of the State and the whims of politicians in office.

In 1990, the region now dubbed the Confederation of Independent States (CIS) accounted for over 16 per cent of India's exports. By 1993, this share collapsed to 3.3 per cent, a catastrophic decline in bilateral trade from which neither has yet recovered. Russia today accounts for a mere 2.58 per cent of Indian exports. The United States (US) was behind CIS with a share of 14.73 per cent. Greater China (mainland plus Hong Kong) accounted for just 3.39 per cent of Indian exports that year. By 2000, while Russia's share in Indian exports was down to a mere 2.5 per cent, that of the US increased to 22.8 per cent and of Greater China to 8.25 per cent.

Apart from political uncertainty and the disruption in the functioning of the Russian economy after 1991, the collapse of the special rupee payment arrangement with India also contributed to the sudden attrition in the extent of Russia's business interaction with India. The increase in India's share of world trade from around 0.5 per cent in 1990 to 0.8 per cent by the end of the decade was almost entirely due to an increase in India's exports to the US, on the one hand, and to industrialising Asia (ASEAN and China in particular), on the other.

So marginal has Russia become to India's export strategy that the Union commerce ministry's Medium Term Export Strategy, 2002-2007, does not even discuss India's exports to Russia as a separate subject, as it does the trade with the US, European Union and Japan. The export projections for 2002-2007 forecast a 14 per cent growth in Indian exports to the US, 17 per cent growth in trade with Africa, 8 per cent growth in trade with western Europe and 6 per cent in the case of eastern Europe and Russia.

Interestingly, the export forecast for Russia is not based on decadal record in 1990s, as in other forecasts, but on more recent trends because the Russian economy has bottomed out and is on a recovery path. President Putin has been able to turn Russia around and last year it recorded an impressive 5 per cent rate of growth. If India-Russia bilateral economic relationship has to be strengthened, the past cannot be a guide to the future. The time is ripe for some fresh thinking.

There are many ideas in the air. Russia has agreed to reinvest part of the rupee debt owed by India to the Soviet State in India and is therefore looking for opportunities in the privatisation programme. Resolving this issue can liquify the relationship a bit. The Russian aluminum company, RusAl, hopes to be able to pick up some stake in NALCO. There are other public enterprises that Russian companies may be interested in and we should enable that investment to come in, both because of past Russian commitment to Indian industrialisation and, more importantly, because in many cases Russian companies can bring both new technology and access to new markets with new investment.

Going beyond trade, there are many business opportunities opening up in Russia. Gutsy and risk-taking Indian entrepreneurs have made it big in the Russian market in recent years in businesses ranging from pharmaceuticals to tyres and from restaurants to steel mills. However, Indian business is up against two hurdles in the resurgent Russian market. First, competition from cheaper Chinese goods, and, second, the weakness of Indian brands.

The competition from China can in fact be overcome if Indian companies pay greater attention to product quality because, unlike in the western market where Chinese goods are mostly imported by western multinationals that have set up production bases in China, the Russian market gets goods made by Chinese firms all of which are not necessarily of good quality. The 'Made in China' brand is, therefore, not yet as strong in the Russian market as it is in the US market. This offers an entry point to better quality Indian goods.

Some Indian companies have started exploiting this opportunity. Mahindra and Mahindra will be selling Scorpio in the Russian market. Many other Indian companies have set foot in Russia but have not been aggressive enough. The window of opportunity now available may get closed when cheaper Chinese goods come better made.

Energy, science and technology and education and culture are also areas where more cooperation is possible if both sides are more imaginative. Despite its economic decline, Russia still has a huge pool of well qualified engineers and scientists, many of whom are being employed in the US and in China. For an entire decade we have failed to make use of this resource.

While the US, EU and Japan will remain India's more important economic partners for a long time, there is much potential in India-Russia business and economic relations waiting to be tapped. However, political summits and defence deals no longer bring nations as close as business, tourism and cultural interaction can. India's people-to-people contact with Russia lags woefully behind its potential and language and the mountains are not the only barriers.

G-8 Summit

Not just because it's there

WHEN George Leigh Mallory, who made the first recorded, albeit aborted, attempt at climbing Mount Everest, was asked why he tried he replied famously, "because it's there". Prime Minister Atal Behari Vajpayee could well say the same thing if asked why he's headed to France next week to make his way up the G-8 Summit.

G-8 was fast becoming an anachronism, an outdated club of self-important nations in a rapidly globalising world. Imagine a group that has often been described in the media as the "boardroom of the world" including Italy and Canada and excluding China and India! Little wonder that a seasoned American diplomat like Richard Holbrooke, who may well have become the United States (US) secretary of state if Al Gore had become US President, took the view that it was time to wind up G-8.

That the G-8 have been defensive about their stilted composition is clear even from their website (www.g8.fr). Offering replies to a few FAQs about G-8, the website poses the question, "Why eight and not more or less?" but puzzlingly shies away from answering it! The one defence the website offers for G-8 may sound a bit odd in the post-Gulf War II world. It says G-8 plays a "real and important role, because it has a huge cooperative and driving capacity and because a good understanding among G-8 members is vital to the smooth running of the major international organisations." Go tell that to the beleaguered United Nations Secretary-General Kofi Annan!

Partly in recognition of its growing irrelevance in an increasingly globalised world marked by new centres of economic power and partly because of France's desire to cock a snook at American unilateralism and underscore the reality of the emerging multipolar world, Paris decided to invite a clutch of 'emerging economies' including Brazil, China, India and South Africa to the Evian Summit next week. For G-8 to truly ensure the 'smooth running' of international organisations and the global economy it must become at least the G-10, with China and India on board on a permanent basis.

That said, we must be honest enough to recognise that India is a step behind China on most economic criteria that will be used to judge G-8 membership qualifications and, therefore, runs the risk of finding G-8 becoming G-9 before it is willing to become G-10! Perhaps neither the trans-Atlantic powers nor Japan would like that and therefore will prefer China and India walking in together rather than sequentially.

Even so, Mr. Vajpayee and our political leadership must remain alive to the fact that there is homework yet to be done on the economic side to sit at a global high table like G-8 because membership there is defined more by global economic capabilities than population size or political, diplomatic and strategic power.

Given what defines G-8, Prime Minister Vajpayee must go prepared to talk business, trade and economics. Not just terrorism and environment. True, the G-8 have widened their concerns in recent years to worry about weapons of mass destruction (WMD), poverty, environment and human rights. There has always been an emphasis on democracy in G-8's self-image. Russia was invited only after it became a democracy, though China has not been asked to pass that test yet! India must not allow any dilution of that part of G-8's agenda. The group must remain wedded to its core principles of free enterprise and democracy.

However, Mr. Vajpayee must resist the temptation of scoring points on such aspects of G-8 agenda where India shines more brightly than China. Rather, he must accept the fact that G-8 is a summit of the world's more powerful and open economies, it was conceived as such in the midst of a global economic crisis in the 1970s and it remained pre-occupied with global finance, energy flows, debt crises and free trade.

Given this background, Mr. Vajpayee must project India's commitment to building a more robust and open economy, to greater interaction with other industrial and developing nations and to internal economic reform and modernisation. It is India's economic performance and promise that G-8 will want to hear about. India's commitment to multilateral trade agreements, to global rules of the game in the market for goods, services, finance and capital.

While Mr. Vajpayee has been a 'foreign policy Prime Minister' his interests even on the diplomatic side have remained largely confined to geopolitical and diplomatic challenges rather than the economic ones. At the Evian Summit Mr. Vajpayee may run the risk of losing his audience's attention if he only speaks about terrorism and WMD.

He must focus greater attention on India's economic record and his economic agenda and how India remains a credible voice of the developing world in multilateral economic fora. The G-8's Okinawa Summit called for a Global Information Society, a cause India must embrace and show its record of achievement on this front.

India's current robust external economic profile and our record in the services sector should enable Mr. Vajpayee to self-confidently take on the obligations and opportunities of globalisation. Demanding adherence to principles of multilateralism even by the developed economies, while committing India to these, rather than adopt defensive postures, whining and complaining about the big bad world, as many in the Sangh Parivar would like to do.

G-8's Evian Summit will be the first major international debut of China's Hu Jintao who goes there after being marred by SARS. China remains the toast of such conclaves and Mr. Hu may well overshadow Mr. Vajpayee if he talks business while Mr. Vajpayee worries about terrorism. It is, therefore, imperative that Mr. Vajpayee talks business and means business. His policy sherpas must prepare him accordingly for this summit. Then alone would going to the Evian Summit make sense. If not, it would amount to a lot of huffing and puffing for no good reason.

Business in command

China's cultural counter-revolution

SHANGHAI: The only thing red about China, it appears, is the generous spread of lipstick that the post-Mao generation of young women wear with nonchalance. On Beijing's Tiananmen Square, in the industrial boom towns of south-eastern China, on the glitzy Shanghai bund, Chinese youth are 'modernising' with a vengeance.

"The Mao jacket has too many buttons," says Mr. Xue Liang Cai, editor-in-chief of the *Suzhou Daily*, offering an explanation for the sartorial transformation in China, "now people like to wear loose fitting clothes". If Mr. Xue is using this as a metaphor for the more enduring social and cultural transformation underway, he does not betray the intention, preferring to remain poker-faced. Despite the sartorial assertiveness of individualism, the Chinese who meet foreigners remain secretive, always parroting the party line and only rarely speaking their mind. Younger, urban Chinese are, however, willing to be more open with their views.

"There is a new class in China today," says an American businessman at a trendy jazz bar in Shanghai's Peace Hotel, "the young, upwardly-mobile professionals who man the new business operations that Deng's modernisation has unleashed, they are China's yuppies". You can call them "Chuppies".

In the industrial boom town of Wuxi we meet a 'chuppy', Mr. Zhao Ming, smart, quick-witted, impeccably dressed, a member of the Communist Party, he waxes eloquent about China's 'economic miracle'. Guiding us around Wuxi's prosperous suburbs, with their hi-tech industries and new 'villas' for 'businessmen', he expounds the three qualifications of a successful manager—'knowledge of Japanese or English language, computer skills, ability to drive a car'. Says Mr. Shao, "There is nothing like capitalism and socialism these days. Everyone is practical, they are interested in business and in improving their standard of living. We are now pragmatic."

Business is in command in Deng's China. If Mao Zedong's 'cultural revolution' was captured by the slogan 'politics in command', Deng Xiaoping's 'modernisastion and opening up' policy has made a virtue of pragmatism. This is symbolised even in the change of the name of the official newspaper of the Chinese Communist Party from its original *Red Flag* to its present *Qiushi*, which means 'Seek Truth From Facts'. At the height of the Cultural Revolution in the late 1960s, a popular slogan claimed that, "a socialist train which ran late was better than a capitalist train which ran to time". Deng's 'cultural counter-revolution' has rubbished the idea.

Indeed, as early as July 1962, before Mao launched the Cultural Revolution, Deng had told a meeting of the Young Communist League: "There is a Sichuanese saying, 'whether white or black, a cat is a good cat so long as it catches the rat'...when it comes to ways of optimising the relations of production. I rather think that we should take this attitude—to adopt whatever pattern will restore and develop agricultural output in each locality quickly and easily. If the masses want a particular pattern, then we should adopt that pattern, if necessary making legal what is now illegal." That vision has guided Deng in the nearly two decades that he has remained communist China's second 'great helmsman'. In today's China ideology is at a discount at all levels. The nation is in a hurry to become a superpower and will sup with the devil to realise that objective.

With pragmatism has come a yearning for consumerism and with it the 'get-rich-quick' syndrome. The search for material prosperity, confess many Chinese, has contributed to increasing corruption in public life. The drive against corruption is, therefore, one of the most important political battles being fought today and the teaching of Confucianism is gaining ground since this is viewed as a moral antidote. Some observers view this as an attempt by the old guard to discredit Deng's 'opening up' policy. "The campaign against corruption is really a political battle between the Dengists and the more conservative communists," says an observer in Shanghai.

The post-Mao teenager, however, is blissfully unconcerned about politics. Requests for a visit to Mao Tse-tung's mausoleum in Beijing, not included in our itinerary, were dismissed by our youthful, "my-career-is-more-important-than-politics," mouthing interpreter with the question, "what is there to see?" Mao is distant history, and his views on socialism and cultural revolution seem an uncomfortable reminder of an excessively 'ideological' past, and, perhaps, a hurdle in the race for modernisation.

China is of course modernising. Notwithstanding all the current concerns about the 'overheating' of the economy, the sliding down of the double-digit growth rate of the early 1990s into single digits (in 1995 GDP growth is expected to be 7.4 per cent) and the steady escalation of inflation, (officially predicted to be 18 per cent in 1995 and unofficially estimated at 25 per cent). China is well set on the course to emerge as a 21st century superpower—perhaps Asia's most powerful economy. The evidence is overwhelming.

In the industrially prosperous south and east, new urban centres are emerging overnight. The most dramatic example of this transformation is, of course, to be found across Shanghai's Huangpu river in the Pudong New Area. When Pudong was developed as a new business district in 1990, a mere 37 companies had established base there. Today 2,900 companies are working on 4,000 projects. Admittedly, much of this investment still comes from Chinese investors from Taiwan, Hong Kong and Singapore. Japan and Korea are big players. North America and Europe have a reduced presence today but that should not prevent the march of the industrial juggernaut. Deng has declared that Shanghai will be a global metropolis by the end of this decade on par with New York, Paris, London and Tokyo. The infrastructure is already in place. Scores of skyscrapers, workshops, hotels, recreation facilities, parks, four lane highways and so on are on the ground. "A foreign businessman will merely have to come with a cheque and buy up all the facilities he wants. The labour is available, the facilities are there and there are no glitches", confirms an Indian diplomat.

Problems exist—both economic and social—and the Chinese do not shy away from discussing them. Inter-regional and inter-personal inequalities are on the increase. The legitimisation of private property is underway and white-collar crime is a menace. These are the wages of superfast development.

As a superpower-in-making, China is interested more in "its" east-with western Europe on a distant horizon. China's west—especially Russia and India—is important only to the extent that the Chinese would like peace on their borders and good relations with their neighbours to enable them to divert all their attention and resources to rapid industrialisation. The technology, the hard-currency markets and the lifestyle will all be imported from its eastern borders and from across the Pacific. The Third World hardly matters in this scheme of things.

"There is an all-round improvement in Sino-Indian relations to the satisfaction of both sides," says an official of the Chinese foreign ministry, "and there is a broad prospect for further development. Let bygones be bygones." The scope for improved Indo-Chinese relations exists, the economic opportunities are there both in trade and investment, but neither side has paid much attention to it. Save an exceptional Indian company like Ranbaxy, few Indian businessmen have ventured to China. The level of awareness about each other is still abysmally low in both countries, perhaps more in 'eastward-oriented' China than in a 'westward-oriented' India, and gulf is likely to widen unless both Asian giants acquire a greater stake in each other's drive to prosperity.

50

Manhattan of the East

Wandering and wondering in China

REPORTING on my previous visit to China in 1995, I began my first despatch with the observation that the only thing red about the Peoples' Republic was the dash of lipstick every woman on the street sported. China's urban woman has certainly moved on since. The 'glam' look is out, the trendy look is in. It is all jeans, T-shirts and the cool, casual look. Shanghai's streets are crowded with young women shopping, chatting, kissing their boyfriends at street corners or just lazily chewing gum! Is this Manhattan or what?

A senior official of the Pudong New Area, the new city across the Bund from old Shanghai, who drove us around the high rise buildings still under construction in 1995, proudly told us, "when this is ready, it will be the Manhattan of the East". In 2001 it is, minus the terrorists!

Shanghai is not just about tall buildings, six-lane triple-deckered highways and shopping malls. It is also about a new lifestyle of a new generation of Chinese, very Manhattanish. In 1995 we visited the newly opened outlet of McDonalds to find it virtually empty with a few foreigners for customers. Today the McDonalds outlet is bustling with China's young. Thomas Friedman, the foreign affairs columnist of *The New York Times*, hypothesised in his best selling book on globalisation, *The Lexus and The Olive Tree*, that you get a proliferation of McDonalds wherever you have a spending middle class. He went on to suggest that the existence of such an upwardly mobile middle class is a guarantor of peace and stability because the middle class abhors violence and war.

China's new middle class youth will most certainly not be too enthusiastic about waging war because they are busy making love! At the twilight hour and late into the night, all along Shanghai's Bund, one finds young couples in embrace. It is a common sight in the West and in developed Asia, but for an Indian this is news. Does a young couple in any Indian city and in the most upmarket locality of any metro feel comfortable and safe doing this? They'd worry about harassment by 'eve-teasers' and lecherous bystanders and the moral police. In Shanghai no one bothers.

Sexual permissiveness is an escape valve meant to divert social energy away from a clamour for democracy and freedom of expression, a Sinologist tells us. "The Chinese Communist Party encourages sexual permissiveness, even pornography, as a way of keeping people happy so that no one can challenge its political dominance," he theorises. So I am prepared to see visible signs of this permissiveness. Yet, I am not ready to confront what I do outside Shanghai's famous Peace Hotel.

The Peace Hotel, now re-conditioned, was the only hotel with a jazz bar in the old Maoist days. A familiar watering hole for the expatriate and a popular hotel for many a visiting dignitary. Located on the Bund, it is architecturally a reminder of Shanghai's European past. Step out of its front door onto the Bund side, you face a giant statue of Chairman Mao; but if you step out into the road alongside the hotel, it opens into a huge pedestrians-only shopping mall. Bang in front of your face, as you stand at the threshold of the Peace Hotel, is a brightly lit shop with a neon sign that announces, 'Sex Shop'. Aha, permissiveness in your face.

I cross the street and step in. In London such a shop would be tucked away in the narrow lanes of Soho, in Paris one would have to go to Montmartre. Here in Shanghai we are in the heart of the city and a step away from a Mao statue. The shop is brightly lit, with three young saleswomen manning it. Three smiles greet you. There is nothing shady about this shop. Just like any other, it sells its wares, sexual gadgetry, the works—and all 'Made in

China'! Shoppers browse around, as if they were in a grocery store. India, the land of *Kamasutra* and Khajuraho, is decades away from this casual attitude and open interest.

The shopping malls are full. You jostle your way around and they all invite you in to their shops. "Come, good bargain," says the saleswoman outside a silk shop. And, what a bargain. I buy a silk tie priced at 200 yuan (US$ 25) for 50 yuan and feel thrilled. A Vietnamese delegate to the conference I am attending laughs his head off. He bargained the price down to 10 yuan! All you need are cheap flights into China and India's *bazaars* would be empty.

Shanghai epitomises the new China. Of course, the six-lane highways have enough space for bicycles and there are millions on their cycles even now. But there are more cars than in 1995 and every fourth vehicle on the street is carrying construction material— cement, steel, plastic tubes, whatever. In 1995 there was construction all around wherever you went, in 2001 they are still building. It is activity of this sort that sustains their continued 7.0 per cent to 8.0 per cent growth.

Economic growth and prosperity bring with them increased inequality. In 1995, we never saw any beggars. Today, in Shanghai's glitzy shopping mall a mother carrying a child walks up to me, points a finger at the child's mouth and asks for alms. We are standing outside a McDonalds outlet and Mao's statue is not far away.

To draw attention to this downside would be churlish, for the overwhelming impression Shanghai and Pu Dong make is of a nation on the move. There are more Indians travelling to China today than in 1995 so while in 1995 we were watched with curiosity, now more people converse. A young man sidles up to me on a street, "Indo? Indu? India?" I say, "Yes, yes, yes," as we walk briskly. The next question stops me in my tracks. He asks, "IT?"

Why does he think India is IT? "Many Indian in Pu Dong in IT," he tells me. He works for Oracle in Pu Dong, he has read about India's progress in software. "Indu good in software," he affirms.

"Thank you. Chinese good in everything," I tell him. We become friends and he walks with me for an hour. "You like Karaoke, nice girls, go to French concession, velly nice clubs." French concession is the part of Shanghai ceded to the French before liberation. We are now in the English concession, he tells me. "Here only shops, there night clubs." How predictable.

The self-confident modernisation and, indeed, westernisation of China is palpable. At the Conference on Cooperative Security and Globalisation which I am here to participate in, the conference convenor tells us the dress code for all meetings and meals is formal. It was mentioned in the invitation letter but some have turned up without ties. "You mean we gotta wear a tie?" asks the open collared Canadian delegate. "Yes, you may do that in the coffee break," comes the deadpan reply. Would an Indian conference chairperson say that to a western delegate, I wonder. China leaves you wondering about so many things, and with an urge to wander more.

Pacific blues

The US-China face-off

HONOLULU: When big wheels move even small cogs get the message. So Dr. Yonggen Xiong may not have been surprised with the eviction notice he received in his Honolulu hotel room, days after the United States and China openly argued with each other, asking him to go home to Beijing. Dr. Xiong was no Chinese spy, nor was he a scientist stealing US nuclear secrets. He was neither a soldier nor a diplomat. He was a mere scholar visiting the US to participate in a conference. To his misfortune, relations between China and the US had suddenly hit rock bottom after China caught a US spy plane and demanded an apology for the loss of a soldier's life.

Dr. Xiong had already arrived in Honolulu to participate in a conference on "Security Implications of Economic and Cultural Trends in the Asia-Pacific", at the Asia-Pacific Center for Strategic Studies (APCSS), a think tank of the US Pacific Command. A day before he was scheduled to speak at the conference he was asked to pack his bags. It was an unceremonious farewell and an interesting way to begin a conference in which participants from the United States Pacific Command and the US strategic policy community were interacting with strategic analysts and journalists from Japan, Australia, Taiwan, Korea, Indonesia, Philippines, Singapore, Fiji, Pakistan and India.

Clearly, the US did not want anyone around the conference table to miss the all too visible signs of its displeasure with China. Dr. Xiong's forced return home was transmitted to all, loud and clear. As if to make a point of the new display of anger with China, the dean of APCSS, Dr. Ron Monteperto, a former senior US State and Defence Department official exuded extra warmth towards this writer, representing India at the conference. Another small cog in the big wheel was feeling the ripple effects in distant Honolulu of the diplomatic waves made by the Oval Office meeting between US President George Bush and the visiting Indian external affairs minister Jaswant Singh.

US-China relations have for some time been marked by a 'blow hot, blow cold' courtship of sorts. As long as the Soviet Union was enemy number one, the US-China tango was entirely understandable. Under normal circumstances the end of the Cold War should have resulted in a cooling off of the relationship. Especially after the Tiananmen Square incidents one would have expected a real stepping up of pro-democracy sentiment, considering the number of changed equations between the US and its many erstwhile non-democratic allies of the Cold War era.

How come the China relationship not only survived the end of the Cold War but seemed to thrive even after the post-Tiananmen Square interlude? The US even elevated China's global stature by pushing through an inequitous nuclear non-proliferation treaty that sought to divide the world between nuclear haves and have-nots, in the process making India more firm in its resolve to go nuclear. Add to this the fact that the Clinton administration went out of its way to pamper China's ego by not only squealing on Prime Minister Vajpayee's letter to the US president on the Indian nuclear tests, which had directly alluded to the China factor in India's nuclear strategy, but also acknowledging China's role in 'South Asian' security. The end of the Cold War had not helped reduce China's importance to the US. Why?

Simple. Unlike a marginal player of the Cold War era like Pakistan, which had made a nuisance of itself by allowing anti-US Islamic fundamentalist groups to thrive on its soil, China balanced its declining political and strategic relevance to the US by increasing its economic relevance. China is the second largest trade partner of the US with a huge trade surplus. More to the point, China has locked the US into a relationship of mutual dependence whereby the US middle class household would be hurt if the US-China trade relationship is interrupted.

China has used trade as a strategic policy weapon, building a relationship of mutual benefit, not just with the US but with an increasing number of countries worldwide. China is increasingly sought as an economic partner both by European and East and South-East Asian countries. Even countries which worry about China's rising economic and military profile, do not want to hurt their economic relationship with it. By assiduously offering the potential of its huge internal market and delivering on the promise of exporting reasonable quality goods at low prices, China has forced an increasing number of countries to ignore its rising political power.

Nothing brought out the irony of this visible dualism better than the convoluted manner in which the Clinton administration defended supporting China's membership of the World Trade Organization and extension of 'permanent normal trade relations' (PNTR) to China, while at the same time it continues to isolate Cuba, waging a relentless trade war against it.

Closer home, in its own neighbourhood, countries like Japan, South Korea, Australia, Singapore are unable to decide whether China's growing power and influence is a factor for regional stability, prosperity and peace or will turn the much sought after 'Asia-Pacific Century' into a China-US century. Nowhere is this more manifest than in the attitude of these countries to India's membership of 'Asian' organisations like APEC, ASEAN+3 and so on.

The US seems clear about the kind of world we are moving into. It will be one in which the US remains the undisputed 'numero uno' but sharing power on its terms with regional powers like the EU, China, Japan, India and Russia. It will engage one or more of these nations in ensuring stability in different parts of the world. In West Asia and Africa it will share influence with the EU, in

Central Asia with Russia, in Southern Asia and South-East Asia with China, India and Japan. In the Americas it will remain the regional hegemon. China seemed quite happy with this, as long as it was allowed a share of influence in Asia. The India-US *modus vivendi* after Pokharan-II has upset China. US assertiveness on nuclear missile defence has encouraged China to reach out to new friends in Latin America and South-East Asia.

The inability of the US to shape a new bilateral policy on China without hurting its own economic interests and Japan's declining influence in Asia, its economic lethargy and military meekness, has been frustrating the US. Perhaps over-estimating its power, China over-reached itself. First, in backing Pakistan's nuclear programme, second, by deliberately increasing its economic influence in Asia and, finally, in talking tough to the US on the spy plane episode.

The Clinton administration was wimpish in its response. President Bush has decided to show who's the boss. The big wheels of diplomacy begin to move in Washington DC. Small cogs experience the impact way out in Hawaii!

52 | COLUMN

The Chinese art of economic diplomacy

HAS any economist ever calculated the 'foreign policy multiplier' of funds well spent in winning friends and influencing people? If such non-tangibles can ever be quantified, the 'foreign policy multiplier' of the US$ 1 billion that China spent shorting up the Thai baht can be expected to be a sizeable figure.

The timing was perfect for China. This significant act of economic diplomacy comes barely a month before China hosts the biggest annual meeting of the world's finance ministers and central bankers, which also attracts the largest gathering of global bankers and financiers, namely the annual meetings of the International Monetary Fund, the World Bank and its affiliates, to be held in Hong Kong. We can look forward to China's finance minister making a big deal of the support offered to the Thai baht at the Fund-Bank meeting. Its Prime Minister has understandably been making a point of it on his visit to Singapore this week.

Addressing a meeting of Singapore businessmen earlier this week, Chinese Prime Minister, Mr. Li Peng, reiterated his government's commitment to greater economic and business cooperation with South-East Asia, and has reassured the region that China's supportive hand could be depended upon in the turbulent world of money and finance. "We should seriously draw lessons from previous financial crises in the world, keep a high degree of vigilance, strengthen financial regulation, improve the financial system so as to forestall and reduce financial risks to the minimum and ensure a sound growth of the economy," said Mr. Li, speaking at a meeting hosted by the Singapore Trade Development Board.

Mr. Li added for good measure, "We are soberly aware that compared with the developed countries, the economic strength of countries and regions like ours is still relatively weak and the financial system not adequate, thus bearing financial risks which make it susceptible to the impact of the turbulence of the international financial market."

Surprisingly and regrettably, with the singular exception of *The Hindu*, no Indian newspaper, including financial newspapers, reported Mr. Li's important speech. It is a matter of shame that reportage of news from the rest of Asia, especially China, still comes to us mostly through western news agencies which have their own priorities. Not a single Indian newspaper has a correspondent stationed in China, our most important neighbour, an emerging superpower and a country whose experiments with economic policy deserve better understanding here. Even the dispatches from the lone Indian journalist in Beijing, a correspondent of *Press Trust of India,* are not regularly used by newspapers which devote more space to the sexual escapades of Princess Diana and such like news. At least one newspaper recently considered posting a fulltime correspondent in Beijing, clearly the most challenging job for any Indian journalist today, especially an economic and business journalist, but gave up the idea because it felt it could not afford the cost.

For all the talk of India's 'Look East' policy and our interest in ensuring a mutually beneficial link with 'Resurgent Asia', the media neglect of events in the region, its reluctance to invest in foreign correspondents here and its wretched dependence on western sources for news and analysis of events is unpardonable. India's patriotic, *swadeshi* businessmen, who continue to lobby the government for protection from foreign competition, should at least spend some money to ensure better media coverage of developments in China, East and South-East Asia if for no other reason than to learn a lesson or two in how to protect their interests against foreign competition.

In his Singapore address this week, Mr. Li reportedly said that some 'restrictive' measures on foreign investors and their production management in China would continue. For instance, the restriction on registration of joint ventures for say 15 or 20 years, as specified in the initial contract would hold good. After that period, these companies would be owned by the Chinese partners.

Similarly, the restriction on access to the domestic market would continue and the joint venture companies could sell only the specified 10 to 20 per cent of their production in the domestic market. The rest should be for export. Says *The Hindu* report, "Mr. Li told investors, categorically, not to look at the big markets for products like telephones or colour television for example and said no foreign company would ever be able to compete with the local firms producing them."

Mr. Li's forthrightness would warm the heart of many Indian businessmen. However, if they expect Indian prime ministers and finance ministers to talk that kind of language and not genuflect before foreign investors, they must also be prepared for the tough life the Chinese have lived in their quest for superpower status.

At a more practical level, if the Chinese mean what they say, (often they don't) then the Indian government must wake up and examine to what extent we can arrive at common positions on an issue like the Multilateral Agreement on Investment (MAI) proposed by the OECD. Mr. Li's Singapore speech goes contrary to the provisions of the proposed MAI and does not even meet the requirements of the World Trade Organization. After all, if China is serious about joining WTO, it will have to comply with the agreement on TRIMs (trade related aspects of investment measures), which explicitly prohibits linking foreign direct investment to export obligations. Will China fall in line and Mr. Li eat his word? Whatever their game plan, we must get to read more about it in the columns of our newspapers.

The 'New Great Game'

APEC, ASEAN+3 and now JACIK, an alphabet soup in a changing Asia

WHEN this column appears, I will be in distant New Zealand! Not walking the beaches that Hrithik Roshan and Ameesha Patel trampled on in that Bollywood movie that has enthused so many Indian tourists to travel down under and beyond, but to speak at a conference curiously titled "Seriously Asia". New Zealand, my hosts tell me, wants seriously to be regarded an Asian nation!

It is an understandable desire. New Zealand's major trade partners include China, Japan and Korea and, like Australia, it wants to shed some of its 'anglocentric' image and acquire a more Asian persona, also because so many Asians now live in these 'English' islands. But New Zealand's desire to be counted as Asian is part of a wider process of engagement in the region in which new equations are being established among old nations. The phenomenon driving this process is both the economic resurgence of the Asia-Pacific region and, more recently, China's emergence as a major economic and military power.

In the immediate aftermath of the end of the Cold War the world's Big Powers were first pre-occupied with reordering Europe and Central Asia. The so-called 'Great Game' of Central Asia was restarted in right earnest and to a large extent the United States made huge gains, both in 'New Europe' and in Central Asia. Even as this process was continuing, Al-Qaeda opened a new front for

Big Power rivalry in the Middle East and the War in Iraq is very much a part of the Great Game for influence in the region.

During this entire period, Asia was first busy with economic growth and then with economic crisis. The *modus vivendi* between the US and China, given the huge economic stakes both have in each other, meant that the unlocking of equations by the end of the Cold War and the geo-economics of trade and investment had been slow in moving the geopolitical tectonic plates in Asia to our east.

The Asian financial crisis of 1997-98 provided the context for a change of equations in Asia. China's emergence as a major economic power, a force for stability and stabilisation, Japan's inability to react and act imaginatively and US backing for a dubious role played by the ideologues of the International Monetary Fund completely altered the chessboard in Asia. The arrival of George Bush in the White House and his willingness to call a spade a spade in East Asia also stirred the pot. *Jehadi* terrorism and the spread of Al-Qaeda in South-East Asia increased anxieties across the region in disparate ways, altering Cold War equations. Finally, North Korea's nuclear bravado provided the final trigger. Asia to our east is busy re-examining relationships.

The most active player in this 'New Great Game' is, understandably, China. The region's fastest growing economy has economic links and a shared border with almost all the countries in the region between Central Asia and East Asia. The Old Great Game was the late 19th and early 20th century race for influence and territory between Russia/USSR and Britain in Central Asia. The New Great Game has many more players and no passive playing field to be trodden upon, unlike the Central Asia of the past. Indeed, ASEAN has actively encouraged the 'Major Powers', including the US, China, Japan, Russia and, latterly, India, to play a game of balance of power in which it retains a certain autonomy.

The arena of the new game spans the entire region from the Pacific to the Persian Gulf. The game revolves around energy flows, capital flows, control of sea lanes and access to markets. From an Indian perspective it manifests itself in a variety of ways. China's support for Pakistan's nuclear programme and its investment in the maritime infrastructure of Pakistan and Myanmar are obvious elements that have been widely commented upon. Less visible till recently was China's role in the nuclear development of North Korea and the use of North Korea as a weapon against Japan and the US. The military aspect of the game is, in some ways, more manifest. However, what is less visible is the economic game that is on.

China used the goodwill it won after the Asian financial crisis by encouraging the creation of various economic forums like ASEAN+3 (China, Japan and Korea) and the Boao Forum, and floated the idea of an Asian Monetary Fund. The memory of Chinese mercantilism is being gradually erased by the surge in China's import demand. Everyone in the region is exporting to China these days.

While India responded fairly early to the incipient signs of a New Great Game with its 'Look East Policy', enunciated as early as in 1992, we failed to give the policy much economic content with our hesitant external liberalisation. It is only in the past two years that India has engaged the region to its east more vigorously but it has some distance to travel in catching up with China and Japan. There has been a paradigm shift with ASEAN and the relationship is grounded both in economics and security, with maritime security emerging as an important area of regional cooperation.

We hope to widen ASEAN+3 into an Asian Economic Community, and as a first step into JACIK, a forum of Japan, ASEAN, China, India and Korea. Not to be left out of this game, the US has reactivated the sleepy Asia-Pacific Economic Cooperation (APEC) and used the new campaign against terrorism to widen APEC's agenda from trade to terrorism. Surely no one can deny that US is an 'Asian' power, given its military pacts with so many Asian countries.

One thing is, however, clear. While there is no doubt that China has emerged as a major economic and military power in the region, almost everybody else wants India to be actively engaged as well. For the first time after Jawaharlal Nehru tried to encourage India's Asian identity, we are once again being welcomed in Asia to our east. But to sustain this process we need to increase our economic interaction with all Asian economies. This means lower tariffs, more trade and investment flows and increased interaction with the region. Economics is the cornerstone of the New Great Game!

Business beyond borders

India-China relations show the way for India-Pakistan relations

GO to google.com and type 'China, India, relations' and you get a list of items devoted to business, culture and tourism, with just an odd one on nuclear issues or on the border dispute. Replace China with Pakistan and you get nothing but articles on conflict and terrorism. This should not surprise anyone who has followed the visit to India of China's Prime Minister Zhu Rongji and compares it with General Pervez Musharraf's visit to India.

India and China are no longer publicly arguing about borders and territory, nor about one interfering in the internal affairs of the other. That is all either *passe* or left for quieter and closed door discussions. In public we talk about doing more business and trade. Mr. Zhu travelled to Bangalore, Mr. Musharraf wanted to go to old Delhi's Jama Masjid! Therein lies the difference.

It is not as if India and China do not have unresolved political issues that divide them. China continues to lay claim to parts of India's north-east, even though it has indicated its willingness to finally grant official recognition to Sikkim's accession to India. Going beyond territorial claims, there are other political issues, including India's asylum to Dalai Lama, which bedevil Sino-Indian relations. Indeed, more seriously there are issues pertaining to China's military cooperation with Pakistan and Myanmar which worry India. The list of issues which can keep Sino-Indian relations tepid and testy is long.

Yet, India and China have been able to do more business with each other in the past decade than in the entire 20th century! Sino-Indian bilateral trade has crossed $ 3 billion and it would be double that if India's trade with Hong Kong is included. Indian companies are investing in China and *vice versa*. India's prowess in information technology has become popular knowledge in China. Walking in a shopping district in Shanghai a few weeks ago I was greeted by a stranger who first asked "Indu? Indo?" and then followed up that question with "IT?"

The bonhomie that marked Mr Li Peng's visit to Bangalore last year and Mr. Zhu's meeting with Indian business leaders in Mumbai this week shows how much increased economic interaction between the two countries has helped alter attitudes. If the Indian government now finally agrees to alter India's official map to show Aksai Chin and other parts on the other side of the so-called 'line of actual control' occupied by China as belonging to China, and finalises a border agreement making *de jure* what is *de facto*, few in India will protest.

Is there a lesson in all this for Pakistan and for India's relations with Pakistan? Of course there is and that is what governments in India have been saying for over a decade now. Business and economic cooperation can help ease political tensions and reduce the relevance of border disputes. If Pakistan wants to keep the Kashmir pot boiling it is free to do so, but just as China has come to regard India's support for Dalai Lama in the correct perspective, India may well begin to regard Pakistan's political stance in a more agreeable perspective. But there must be a quid for every quo!

India and China agreed to extend to each other the 'Most Favoured Nation' treatment in 1984, a few years before Prime Minister Rajiv Gandhi made his historic visit to Beijing. The 1990s have witnessed a blossoming of the business relationship. If the pace of trade expansion witnessed in the last five years is sustained over the next five years, China will emerge as a major business partner for India, perhaps even overtaking Japan. Geoeconomics may then well turn geopolitics on its head.

The decade following the end of the Cold War has witnessed fundamental changes in India's relations with both the United States and China. It is true that the 1990s has also seen India's relations with the rest of Asia changing, especially relations with South-East and East Asia. Equally, there has been a sustained improvement in the already good relations with Central Asia and the Gulf region. From the straits of Hormuz to the straits of Malacca, India has experienced an improvement in her relations with her wider Asian neighbourhood. This has, in part, been shaped by India's own economic growth and her greater openness to external trade and investment flows and in part by the improved relations with both the US and China.

The only relationship which is an exception that proves the rule is the relationship with Pakistan. Pakistan remains obsessed with short-term political goals and its external relationship with India remains a prisoner to its domestic politics and the politics of its national identity. During the tenure of Prime Minister Nawaz Sharif there was some evidence of a change in this world view. Mr. Sharif was willing to talk business and the meetings he had with Prime Minister I.K. Gujral in Dhaka and Colombo appeared to be the beginning of a new phase in which business and economics would come to the fore. A hopeful Pakistani economist, the late Dr. Mahbub ul Haq, wrote a series of articles in the Pakistani media educating his countrymen about what MFN meant and how this was no special concession to India but a mere multilateral obligation which could foster greater economic interaction.

General Pervez Musharraf is yet to reach the milestone that his civilian predecessors had crossed half a decade ago. As a result, when he marched to the podium at the SAARC Summit in Kathmandu last fortnight, he relegated the core issue of the Summit, namely regional economic cooperation and a time-table for increased intra-SAARC trade, to the background and tried to convert a regional forum into a bilateral summit on a patently political issue.

China's leaders have not forgotten their political differences with India, nor have territorial claims been fully given up. They have chosen, however, to push such differences under the red carpet that they have rolled out to increased business and trade. China has improved its political relations with the US and most of its neighbours, including Vietnam, through economic engagement and diplomatic mercantilism, not just crossing borders but setting them aside to do business. Surely, that's an easy lesson for General Musharraf to learn, considering he goes so frequently to Beijing!

An eagle's eye on the dragon

WHEN *The Financial Express* frontpaged a story (July 18, 2002) on the Report to the United States Congress of the US-China Security Review Commission on *The National Security Implications of the Economic Relationship Between the United States and China*, the rest of the media ignored it. Ignoring this report can only hurt us, reading it thoroughly would be rewarding. Go to www.uscc.gov for the full report.

This is not the high brow version of Humphrey Hawksley's *Dragonfire*, even though China has reacted sharply to what it views as a report written with a 'Cold War' mindset. Hawksley wrote about a nuclear conflict in Asia, the USCC has written about an even bigger potential conflict with China, an economic confrontation.

"Our relationship with China," says USCC, "is one of the most important bilateral relationships for our nation. If it is not handled properly, it can cause significant economic and security problems for our country. China is emerging as a global economic and military power, and the United States has played, and continues to play a major role in China's development."

The report comes to a rather tentative conclusion, "The Commission cannot forecast with certainty the future course of US-China relations. Nor can we predict with any confidence how China and Chinese society will develop in the next 10 to 20 years. We do know that China now ranks among our most important and most troubling bilateral relationships and believe that China's importance to the United States will increase in the years ahead. As its economy and military grow and its influence expands, China's actions will carry increased importance for the American people and for our national interests."

USCC emphasises the need for the US government to "fully understand the increasingly complex economic, political and military challenges posed by China's drive toward modernity" and to gain such an understanding it recommends allocation of more resources and the elevation of China in US foreign and national security perspective. While hoping for a 'positive' outcome, the report forewarns that the US must "be prepared for all possible contingencies".

The facts. The US trade deficit with China has grown from $ 11.5 billion in 1990 (half of total US trade with India today!) to $ 85 billion in 2000, and the US is one of the biggest investors in China. Yet, China's nuclear missiles stand directed at the US and the two countries have come close to conflict over Taiwan. The US spearheaded China's membership of the World Trade Organization and yet the USCC warns that the US "renew the Super 301 provision of US trade law and request the administration to identify and report on other tools that would be most effective in opening China's market to US exports if China fails to comply with its WTO commitments."

The detailed recommendations of the USCC report cover a wide range of areas including improving US academic expertise on China, improved translation of Chinese publications and official records and databases, improved intelligence gathering and processing, and increased pressure on China to comply with all international agreements and conventions to which it is a signatory.

A specific recommendation made is that the US Department of Defense and the Federal Bureau of Investigation jointly assess China's targeting of sensitive US weapons-related technologies, the means employed to gain access to these technologies, and the steps that have been and should be taken to deny access and acquisition. This assessment should include an annual report on Chinese companies and Chinese PLA-affiliated (People's Liberation Army) companies operating in the United States. The report also underscores China's record in nuclear proliferation, though Pakistan is not mentioned by name, and calls for sanctions to punish against such proliferation.

The overall sense of this report is to give a wake-up call to a nation that had virtually fallen in love with Chinatown, fortune cookies and Peking duck. More importantly, it seeks public investment in understanding what is happening in China. The remarkable aspect of this congressional report is its forthrightness in setting out what is US national interest and how China may challenge that. It is a measure of the self-confidence of a superpower like the US that such a candid report has been placed in the public domain and a public and informed debate has been sought. Some may rubbish the report, others may take an even dimmer view of China. But an informed debate can take place.

Have we in India undertaken such an exercise? At the Parliamentary level? Certainly not. Catch our MPs dedicating time to such a serious study of anything. However, the first and second National Security Advisory Boards (1998-2001) did put out two National Security Reviews which to this day remain classified documents even though they were written by non-governmental persons and none need regard the views expressed therein as the views of the government. Even the NSAB report was only a first step and a broadbrush picture which should be improved upon by more in-depth studies.

Atleast one important recommendation of the NSAB was that the government should invest more funds in the study of our neighbourhood. One can count on one's fingertips the number of China experts in India. Ditto for Pakistan. If the expertise on China and Pakistan is so abysmal, nothing more need be said about our understanding of Central Asia, West Asia, East Asia and South-East Asia.

Consider a question that the USCC has tried to grapple with, namely, trade with China. The USCC takes the view that increased trade with China can help facilitate China's transition to a free market economy, the development of rule of law and to more democracy. A prosperous China, it believes, will be a more peaceful country if fully integrated into the Pacific and world economies.

How should India view trading with China, now that 'Greater China' (mainland and Hong Kong) has emerged as our second largest trade partner? Should China's foray into India's IT sector be encouraged or feared? How much expertise is available in India to provide an intelligent answer to that question? Pretty little. As a result different arms of the government are pursuing different, sometimes conflicting, policies.

(Thanks is due to Jairam Ramesh and Rohit Bansal for drawing my attention to this report.)

Is India a paper tiger?

IS it a measure of his efficiency in clearing files or of his ministerial underemployment that Union disinvestment minister Arun Shourie has more books than files on his table? And why not? Consider the reading material he is wading through. Shourie may well have built up the best collection of books on China. Working on his General Cariappa Memorial Lecture, to be delivered later this year, Shourie is poring over every research paper and book he can find on analysing China, its economic performance and strategic potential. He has his priorities right. Unless India understands the nature of the challenge China poses and is likely to pose, it is impossible to get a grip on the challenge of development and governance at hand.

At a time when many of his ministerial colleagues are busy dispensing petrol pumps and other favours, grabbing land, abusing minorities or promoting obscurantism, Shourie is devouring page after page of analysis on Chinese power. Among the many books and reports, the more fascinating study is the voluminous tome entitled *China Debates The Future Security Environment* by Michael Pillsbury (National Defense University Press, Washington DC, 2000, available on the NDU website).

Citing 600 select quotations from 200 Chinese scholars published between 1994 and 1999, *China Debates* is the most comprehensive presentation available in English of how China's most eminent strategic analysts, economists and social scientists view the world they confront and their place in it. That China sees itself as a civilisational power of long standing, The Middle Kingdom, is well known. What is interesting about this collection is the confidence with which China sees itself as a nation destined to global pre-eminence and the wary contempt it has for India.

While there is recognition of the fact that the US is today the world's only superpower, it is viewed by many Chinese scholars as a 'declining power'. The world is moving towards a multipolar structure in which the US, Europe, Japan, Russia and China will be the five great poles of power. India does not figure in the Chinese calculus as a great power to reckon with. India is viewed as a 'military power' in South Asia, with a presence in the Indian Ocean region exceeding China's. If there is any area where India is seen as being ahead of China, it is in its naval and air power. But this, in the Chinese view, counts for little since India's 'Comprehensive National Power (CNP)' is way behind China's.

The analysts of power define CNP as a sum of military, economic, scientific, technological and political power. A China Academy of Military Sciences study quantifies CNP as a sum of eight variables. A total CNP score of 1.0 is a summation of a country's natural resources (0.08), domestic economic capability (0.28), external economic capability (0.13), scientific and technological capability (0.15), social development level (literacy, health and other human development indicators, 0.10), military capability (0.10), governmental capability as manifested in ability to regulate and control economic activity (0.08) and foreign affairs capability (diplomatic influence and reach, 0.08).

The US has the highest CNP score and will continue to do so into the foreseeable future, but China sees its current rank at 5, behind US, Japan, Germany and Russia and improving to 2 by the first quarter of the century. India is placed at rank 13 from which it is not expected to move very much higher. Even as they acknowledge India's superior military power in the Indian Ocean region and worry about Indian intentions in Tibet, Chinese scholars see India as a second rate economic power. Given that economic, political, social and governance capabilities are given more weightage than purely military capability, China believes that India's nuclear power status will not really alter the balance of power in the region.

To quote Pillsbury, "China's analysts write that India, as a smaller scale version of Japan, also has a militaristic, religion-based strategic culture, seeks to dominate its neighbours, has had covert nuclear ambitions for two decades prior to its nuclear tests in 1998, attempts to foment conflict between China and other nations, and has some areas of military superiority over China, such as its current navy. However, India's economic reforms are judged insufficient to catch up with China and enter the multipolar world as the sixth pole. India's CNP scores for 2010 place it no higher than number nine (according to one study) or thirteen (according to another), only about half of China's CNP score in 2010."

The scepticism of China's analysts with respect to India's CNP is not only based on doubts about economic reform but also the belief that India's fractious polity will limit her economic and military potential. Interestingly, China's Marxist-oriented scholars give low scores for India's ability to reform the public sector, close down sick public sector enterprises and raise the resources required for development. Of course, this was written before Shourie took charge of privatisation!

Ironically, while many analysts express concern about rising religious nationalism in both Japan and India, and believe that the ascendance of the BJP will bolster India's military strength, they also see religious chauvinism as a factor of weakness rather than strength. A society increasingly divided along communal and social lines is viewed as internally weak and, therefore, incapable of being externally strong.

This study must be made compulsory reading for all of India's political parties. How many of our political leaders understand the long-term consequences of the short-term compromises they make? A corrupt, ineffective, parochial and bigoted political class can do far more damage to the nation and our CNP than any foreign enemy can ever hope to. Mercifully, these are neutralised to an extent by our democratic institutions, the upward social mobility they have enabled and the inherent secularism of the Indian people. If these strengths disappear, mere acceleration of economic growth is not going to do much for India's national power.

The coming of age of Korea Inc.

IT is a wonderful parable on the era of globalisation and I have told this tale before, but it is worth telling again to begin this column. When Saddam Hussein's troops marched into Kuwait in 1990, scores of South Korean nationals took refuge in their country's embassy. A Korean airline landed in Kuwait airport to fly them home but Saddam's men were on the streets already. Kuwaiti authorities threw their hands up and said they could not assure the safety of Korean nationals in the transit from embassy to airport.

"Never mind," a Hyundai official reportedly told his diplomats, "Our brand is very popular in Iraq, we'll fly the Hyundai flag on the buses and drive." And so they did, with Iraqi troops on the streets waving to them. Brand Hyundai had ensured the safety of the citizens of the Republic of Korea (ROK). The flag followed trade!

Someone in the United States State Department must have heard that story and recalled it back from memory before sending off a note to Seoul asking for Korean troops this time round in Iraq! The move has sparked a debate in this tiny peninsular nation in East Asia where relations with the US is a touchy issue. Can ROK continue to be shy flying its own national flag afar even as those of its brands fly so impressively around the world? It is a question that ROK will have to grapple with as Asia comes to terms with the links between trade, terrorism and national security.

Even as US President George Bush managed to convince his Asian interlocutors in the Asia-Pacific Economic Cooperation

(APEC) forum, in Bangkok earlier this week, to talk about trade and terrorism, diplomats, scholars and journalists from South Korea shied away from doing so at an India-ROK bilateral dialogue in New Delhi this week, hosted jointly by the Indian Council for Research on International Economic Relations (ICRIER) and the Seoul Forum. Yes, it is an issue we must discuss in the future, the Koreans conceded, but for now let us talk trade and economic cooperation.

Clearly this ostrich-like attitude will have to change sooner than later because the new form of terrorism that is raising its head across the APEC region will hurt Korea directly, now that its troops are in Iraq and Al-Qaeda is all over Asia. In dealing with this terrorist threat to trade in Asia, India will perforce be a key player. The manifest and immediate security threat that ROK must worry about here and now is high seas terrorism.

New Delhi is so far away from the waters of the Indian Ocean that few among Delhi's media and strategic analysts as yet give as much attention to the threat of piracy and high seas terrorism as they do to urban and air terrorism. This cannot go on for long. But the threat is even more imminent for ROK which now has its troops in Iraq, has scores of ships all over the waters between the Persian Gulf and the Korean coast.

Not only have incidents of piracy and ship hijacking in the waters between the Persian Gulf and the South China Sea increased, but they have become more technologically sophisticated, with helicopters and gunboats being used, and their link to Al-Qaeda groups is becoming increasingly manifest. The Indian Navy and Coast Guard are fully conversant with this threat and have been engaged in discussions and exercises with the navies of the United States, Australia, Japan, Singapore and others to deal with the emerging challenge.

Being an export dependent economy and one that is dependent on energy imports from the Persian Gulf, ROK cannot shy away for too long from discussing with India the potential for cooperation in the field of maritime security. The importance of India-ROK cooperation in maritime security was underscored by the thrust of the presentations made at the India-ROK dialogue.

India is emerging as a competitive destination for ROK's export-oriented foreign direct investment. There are three motives that have shaped Korean FDI, said an analyst from Seoul. Resource-seeking, market-seeking and efficiency-seeking. Initially Korean companies invested abroad in search of raw materials. This was followed by foreign market seeking FDI. In course of time and in some countries, Korean FDI sought local efficiencies in terms of labour productivity, infrastructure and so on to be able to then use such places as production bases for export to third markets.

Till recently only China met all three objectives and so has attracted huge Korean FDI, as it also has for similar reasons from Japan. However, more recently, India has also become an attractive FDI destination on all three counts for Korean companies, even though it still lags behind China in terms of the quality of infrastructure and productivity of investment. Hyundai, LG and Samsung find their India operations profitable, but more reform and better infrastructure can help.

If Korean FDI into India was only of the domestic market-seeking type, ROK need not engage India in a dialogue on high seas security. However, with both resource-seeking and efficiency-seeking (export-oriented) FDI coming to India, ROK must worry about the safety of ports, coastline and, more importantly, the sea lines of communication.

India does engage the APEC member nations in a dialogue on maritime security through the Council for Security Cooperation in Asia-Pacific (CSCAP) where ROK is also a member. However, ROK must directly engage India in a dialogue going beyond questions of economic reform and trade liberalisation and encompassing national and maritime security given the emerging terrorist challenge.

This also underscores the need for India to be actively engaged in APEC on economic issues. It is a pity that India was not present at APEC's Bangkok meeting this week. Sure, APEC membership entails the further pursuit of trade and investment liberalisation. A logical consequence of India's 'Look East' policy should be its greater integration into all forums of the APEC region. We must rediscover the forgotten history of this sub-continent's maritime links with the Indian Ocean and Pacific region, that reached out as far as the Korean peninsula!

State and market in foreign policy

INDIA and Russia are strategic allies. India and China are strategic competitors. Russia helps India feel more secure. China can't seem to help but make India less secure. So, you know who matters more for India. Right? Sorry. The world is not that simple.

Russia and India may be friends but neither is putting their money where their mouth is. China and India may badmouth each other but seem to be making good money nevertheless. Greater China (including Hong Kong) has emerged as India's second largest trade partner, next only to the United States of America. Russia is in danger of falling off India's trade map.

According to the most recent trade data available with the Union commerce ministry, Indian exports to the People's Republic of China (mainland excluding Hong Kong), in US dollar terms, increased at an unprecedented and unparalleled rate of growth of 86.1 per cent in the period April-December 2002 over April-December 2001. In the same period, India's exports to Russia declined by 10.26 per cent.

While exports to Hong Kong did not grow very much in this period, if India's total exports to PRC and HK are added up, then India's exports to what may be dubbed 'Greater China' stood at $ 2.9 billion, approximating 7.6 per cent of India's total exports during the period. This compares with a lowly $ 541 million exports to Russia, amounting to a share of 1.42 per cent in total exports. With such a low share of Indian export trade, Russia lags behind not just the Organisation of Economic Cooperation and

Development economies but also Sri Lanka, Indonesia, Malaysia, Singapore, and Thailand as an export destination.

In the late 1980s, just before the collapse of the Soviet Union, the USSR accounted for over 16 per cent of India's exports, compared to a share of just about 15 per cent of the US. By 1992-93, Russia's share came down precipitously to a lowly 3.28 per cent of India's exports, while that of the US was at an unprecedented 18.97 per cent—more than five times. The China market accounted in that year for a mere 0.76 per cent of Indian exports. Of course, with Hong Kong included, Greater China had a share of 4.89 per cent in Indian exports in 1992-93. By 1999-00, Russia's share was further down to 2.89 per cent, Greater China was up at 8.25 per cent and the US was on top with a 22.83 per cent share.

While China's share is marginally down in percentage terms, with exports booming this year its absolute level is up while that of Russia is in fact further down.

So who's to blame? There's a lot of finger-pointing going on. At a recent seminar on India-Russia bilateral economic cooperation, jointly organised by the Confederation of Indian Industry and the Department of Science and Technology of the Government of India (and therein lies a story), Russian diplomats were urging Indian businesspersons to let their animal spirits free and stop being so risk-averse. We are not risk-averse, their Indian interlocutors told them, but prefer steering clear of the Russian mafia's bear hug!

To be fair, neither side has in fact invested enough time and money in trying to do more business. Indian businessman Shiv Khemka of the Sun Group had loads of nice things to say about the business prospect in Russia and urged fellow Indians to go there and prosper. Dr. Reddy's Laboratories is another example of success in the Russian market. But there just aren't enough of them around.

The more important point is that in the case of Indo-Russian trade, both governments appear to be pro-active and are trying to get their businessmen off their haunches. When President Vladimir Putin visited New Delhi last year, external affairs minister Yashwant Sinha urged a CII-FICCI audience to "Go to Russia. Invest in Russia. Do business in Russia." There was no such official endorsement for China. If anything, the ministry of external affairs worried itself stiff about Chinese interest in the Indian information technology (IT) sector and took a close look at possible security issues in software trade.

Where the State has failed to deliver, as in India-Russia trade, the market is doing its job in India-China trade. But it is not as if the State has failed to try. In fact, the association of the GoI's department of S&T with the CII seminar is proof of the government's interest in pushing India-Russia economic cooperation. Much of the action remains in defence and defence-related areas. However, the ending of the rupee-rouble trading arrangement and the squeeze in the Indian defence budget in the 1990s, till Kargil, largely contributed to the State's inability to do much about trade.

On the other hand, China's relentless economic growth and the ease with which Indian companies have been able to establish production facilities in China, apart from trading networks, has helped push India-China trade.

The recent step-up in defence spending will certainly help increase India-Russia armaments trade, even though India has been diversifying the sources of its arms supplies. However, this alone will not suffice. There is a communication gap between India and Russia on the economic side. Unlike Chinese diplomats and business persons who have learnt the art of communicating their country's strengths, the Russians are still very wooden in their ways.

There is, however, an interesting dimension to Indian interaction with both Russia and China. It appears that both countries are reaching out to the Indian diaspora more readily than to resident Indian business persons. Indians in South-East Asia and North America, especially in IT, hospitality and financial sectors, are being courted by Chinese companies and institutions, maybe because they do not come under governmental scrutiny.

Interestingly, this is true in Russia as well where Europe-based Indians are more active than India-based companies. May be the already globalised Indians are less risk-averse and more market-savvy. However, this does underscore the relative role of the market in economic diplomacy.

59 | ESSAY

The economic consequences of the Kargil conflict for India and Pakistan

WHAT will be the impact of the conflict with Pakistan on the economy of India and Pakistan? Can the two South Asian economies afford a bigger war? What policy initiatives should the Indian government take, both at home and abroad, to deal with the economic and diplomatic challenges posed by the conflict with Pakistan? Even as the end-game has begun in the Kargil conflict, these questions are being raised and deserve to be answered.

At the outset it must be stated that economic considerations and the calculation of cost-benefit ratios are meaningless and dangerous in making any assessment of what our response should be to a willful act of aggression. Pakistan has occupied Indian territory and has questioned the sanctity of the Line of Control (LoC) that separates the Indian state of Jammu & Kashmir (J&K) from Pakistan-Occupied-Kashmir (PoK). Any government in India is duty-bound to respond to this act of aggression and illegality and the economic costs and consequences of military action can not be factored into the immediate response.

Having said this, it must also be clarified that the conflict in Kashmir has so far remained a limited border conflict in a limited, though difficult terrain, and neither Pakistan nor India have declared an all out war. India's response to Pakistani aggression has been sober and moderate and so far no attempt has been made to widen the conflict along the international border. However, it is necessary to consider the economic implications of a wider conflict, if not along the entire border, at least along the LoC and beyond the LoC, if and when necessary.

Defence analysts are convinced that even if a full-scale war is waged, it is unlikely to last for more than a few days, perhaps a fortnight at most, since any such widespread conflict is bound to set in motion diplomatic moves across the world aimed at an early resolution of conflict. Further, even earlier India-Pakistan wars have been brief affairs and in the current global and regional context a full-scale war may be of even shorter duration than in the past.

Defence expenditure and national income

To begin with, it is necessary to recognise that India is not a big defence spender and is capable of absorbing an increase in defence expenditure amounting to an additional one percentage of GDP over the course of two or three years without too much difficulty. Second, the costs of a limited military engagement are built into existing expenditure with funding for men and material already provided for. The only additionality is the cost of their transportation to forward border posts, and of ammunition.

There is a popular belief among social scientists and security analysts, in India and abroad, that India spends far too much on defence. While a case can be made that a poor country ought to spend more on education and health than defence, the fact is that given the security environment within which India lives, its defence expenditure is in fact in line with global trends and below par as far as the region itself is concerned. India's hostile neighbours, China and Pakistan, spend far more on defence and are out of line with global and regional trends (Table 59.1).

Moreover, some analysts believe India's defence spending is highly cost-effective and there is little margin for trimming. Not only is India one of the lowest spenders on defence, both in terms of share of GDP and per capita dollar income, but it has systematically reduced its defence spending in recent years (Table 59.2).

Table 59.1

Defence Spending: India and the World

Country	Defence Expenditure as Percentage of GDP		Per Capita Defence Expenditure (US$, 1995 prices)	
	1998	1996	1985	1995
India	3.4	2.5	11	9
China	5.1	3.9	26	26
Pakistan	6.9	5.3	29	28
Developing Countries	3.1	2.4	52	35
USA	6.5	3.8	1,473	1,056
Japan	1.0	1.1	243	401
Germany	2.9	1.7	634	509
Industrial Countries	3.6	2.3	742	526
World	4.0	2.4	185	143

Source: Human Development Report (various years), UNDP.

Table 59.2

India: Defence Expenditure Statistics (in Billions of Indian Rupees)

Year	Def. Exp. (Bn. Rs.)	GDP Current Market	Population (mns.)	Defence Forces '1000	Central Govt. Expenditure (CGE)	Defex/ GDP (%)	Defex/ CGE (%)
1961-62	2.8954	171.77	455.0	490	14.765	1.69	19.61
1962-63	4.7391	184.76	459.0	562	23.525	2.56	20.14
1963-64	8.1612	212.37	462.0	585	32.062	3.84	25.45
1964-65	8.0580	247.65	470.0	867	34.889	3.25	23.09
1965-66	8.8476	261.45	470.0	869	39.406	3.38	22.45
1966-67	9.0859	295.71	495.0	879	44.584	3.07	20.38
1967-68	9.6843	346.11	514.0	977	44.972	2.80	21.53
1968-69	10.3319	366.74	529.0	990	45.258	2.82	22.83
1969-70	11.0088	403.87	541.0	925	42.947	2.73	25.63
1970-71	11.9928	431.63	554.0	930	55.766	2.78	21.51
1971-72	15.2534	462.53	566.0	980	67.097	3.30	22.73
1972-73	6.5223	510.05	579.0	960	78.493	3.24	21.05
1973-74	16.8079	620.07	591.0	948	81.308	2.71	20.67
1974-75	21.1227	732.35	604.0	956	97.846	2.88	21.59

(contd. ...)

(... contd. ...)

Year	Def. Exp. (Bn. Rs.)	GDP Current Market	Population (mns.)	Defence Forces '1000	Central Govt. Expenditure (CGE)	Defex/ GDP (%)	Defex/ CGE (%)
1975-76	24.7229	787.61	617.0	956	120.36	3.14	20.54
1976-77	25.6253	848.94	630.0	1,055	131.500	3.02	19.49
1977-78	28.1300	960.67	643.0	1,096	149.856	2.93	18.77
1978-79	30.6000	1,041.90	61.0	1,096	177.172	2.94	17.27
1979-90	35.5000	1,143.56	674.0	1,096	185.042	3.10	19.18
1980-81	40.9100	1,360.13	689.0	1,104	224.948	3.01	18.19
1981-82	46.5180	1,597.60	704.0	1,104	254.012	2.91	18.31
1982-83	54.0830	1,781.32	720.0	1,120	304.937	3.04	17.74
1983-84	63.0917	2,075.89	736.0	1,250	359.877	3.04	17.53
1984-85	66.6057	2.313.43	752.0	1,380	438.789	2.88	15.18
1985-86	79.8749	2,622.43	768.0	1,515	531.124	3.05	15.04
1986-87	104.7745	2,929.49	784.0	1,492	640.231	3.58	16.37
1987-88	119.6749	3,332.01	800.0	1,502	703.046	3.59	17.02
1988-89	133.102	3,957.82	812.0	1,362	814.023	3.37	16.39
1989-90	144.1600	4,568.21	825.0	1,260	950.494	3.17	15.26
1990-91	154.2648	5,355.34	843.0	1,200	1,040.730	2.88	14.69
1991-92	163.4704	6,167.99	858.0	1,200	1,127.310	2.65	14.50
1992-93	175.8179	7,059.18	877.0	1,500	1,259.269	2.49	13.96
1993-94	218.4473	8,107.49	892.0	1,100	1,457.880	2.69	14.75
1994-95	232.523	9,634.92	910.0	1,100	1,669.984	2.41	13.92
1995-96	268.5629	11,189.64	934.2	1,145	1,916.182	2.40	14.01
1996-97	295.0508	12,769.74	950.6	1,145	2,173.184	2.31	13.58
1997-98	360.9900RE	14,592.30E	973.9	1,145	2,324.813	2.47	15.52
1998-99	412.0000BE	16,088.0IP	987.0	1,145	2,681.070	2.56	15.37

Sources: 1. Defence Expenditure (Defex) data of India: *Defence Service Estimate*, Union Budget 2. *Economic Survey,* Government of India, relevant years. 3. INDIA-A Reference Annual Ministry of Information and Broadcasting, Government of India of relevant years (for GDP figures 1961–1984). 4. Military Balance, (IIIS, London) various years. 5. World Military Expenditure & Arms Transfers, (ACDA US government, Washington DC) various years.

India's moderation in defence spending has finally come in for positive comment by western security analysts in recent years. Thus, a recent Regional Security Assessment by Jane's Information Group (UK, 1997) observed, "India's defence spending remains modest compared to other countries with major security concerns."

In a detailed analysis of Indian defence spending, a US analyst at the US National Defense University (NDU) has observed, "India's military expenditures are about 2.5 per cent of GDP, down from 4.0 per cent a decade ago. That is a low level of expenditure. It is difficult to see how much impact there would be on the Indian economy if the spending were cut by half."[1]

Reading a paper at a symposium on India at the NDU, Mr. Clawson said, "Part of the reason that there is such limited potential for a peace dividend in India in that spending is that the Indian military is remarkably cost-effective. That is, the Indian military is able to produce a considerable impact given the size of its budget. We economists usually argue that such cost-effectiveness comes from concentrating on one's comparative advantage, that is, doing what a country does best. It would appear that India has followed this prescription effective."

The data also show clearly that there has been a secular decline in Indian defence spending in the 1990s. Against a base year index of 100 in 1985 for the size of the armed forces, India's index value for 1997 was 91 compared to an index value of 122 for Pakistan. If the trend observed in India during the 1990s is corrected now, as a result of the Kargil conflict, India will still remain within a globally acceptable framework of defence spending so long as the net impact of defence modernisation and stock replenishment is around half to one percentage point of GDP. In short, available data suggests that India is a cost-effective defence spender and it retains the margin for increased spending over the next year without going seriously out of line with the long-term trend rate and world average of defence to GDP ratio.

For the limited purpose of assessing the impact of the present conflict on the economy, given the absence of actual cost data, one rule of thumb estimate can be derived by considering the economic and fiscal impact of a similar conflict in the past. The best parallel

---

1. Clawson Patrick, *The Relationship Between Security and Economics in South Asia,* Paper read at the India Symposium, Institute for National Strategic Studies, National Defense Univeristy, Washington DC, 1997.

to consider would be the cost of the operations of the India Peace-keeping Force in Sri Lanka in 1987-89. It is interesting to note that while India's defence expenditure was stepped up, as a proportion of GDP, in the mid-1980s, this happened before the IPKF operations were launched and not as a consequence of it. The ratio of defence expenditure (defex) to GDP went up from an average of 2.97 per cent in 1980-1985 to 3.41 per cent in 1985-1988, but came down to 3.37 per cent in 1988-89 and to 3.17 per cent in 1989-90. Subsequently, there was a secular decline to levels below 3.0 per cent of GDP. The 1980s bulge in defence spending was largely a catching up phenomenon, which took care of almost a decade of neglect of defence modernisation (Table 59.2).

Consider the impact of the IPKF operations on deficit management. While there was an undoubted deterioration in deficit management in the second half of the 1980s, with the fiscal deficit to GDP ratio going up from an average of 6.3 per cent in 1980-1985 to 8.2 per cent in 1985-1990, there was in fact an improvement in the situation in the late 1980s with the ratio peaking at 9.0 per cent in 1986-87 and gradually coming down in subsequent years. Even the revenue deficit to GDP ratio deteriorated sharply in 1984-1986, slipped again in 1986-1987, but remained stable in 1987-1990. In any case, much of this expenditure was incurred in rural development and domestic subsidies than on defence.

More importantly, during this entire period economic growth did not suffer and national income growth peaked in the year 1988-1989, with GDP growth registering a double-digit figure in that year of 10 per cent. NSS data also suggest that this period is associated with a decline in poverty and an increase in rural non-farm employment. It must also be borne in mind that during this entire period greater economic damage was inflicted by internal terrorism than the Sri Lankan operations. Despite substantial wasteful expenditure on internal and external security in the 1980s, there is no evidence to suggest that this hurt economic growth or industrial activity. If the government had taken appropriate action in keeping external debt, especially short-term debt, in check in the period 1988-90, the balance of payments crisis of 1991 may not even have occurred.

Going beyond this limited comparison, if we take a more long-term view of the role of defence expenditure in government expenditure and national income, it should be clear that barring the sudden jump in defence spending after the Chinese aggression in 1962, there has been no sustained increase in defence spending nor has there been any excessive episodic impact of specific wars on defence spending or GDP growth. While defence expenditure increased sharply in 1961-1963, as a percentage of GDP, it remained remarkably stable till 1986, when again it jumped for a two-year period. This was the phase of modernisation of the defence forces and was not a consequence of any specific conflict. Since 1989, there has been a secular decline in defence spending, as a ratio of GDP, and any expenditure this year, in response to the Kargil operations, can only bring this ratio in line with the long-term trend line. Thus, all concern about excessive defence spending in the wake of Kargil should be discounted and the problem viewed in a proper perspective.

The Indian economy today

While past trends are encouraging, the question remains if the Indian economy can afford a war today. There are two ways in which this question can be answered. First, by assessing the strengths and weaknesses of the economy today, compared to earlier periods when India was involved in a military operation. Perhaps, a more legitimate comparison in the present context would be to assess the strengths and weaknessess of the Indian economy compared to the Pakistan economy today. Between the two which country is better placed to sustain and absorb the economic impact of a conflict? We shall attempt to answer this question in this and the next section.

GDP growth and prices

After nearly two years of subdued economic growth and industrial recession, the Indian economy is on the recovery path this year. After the near zero-growth year of 1991-92, India recorded a five-year average rate of growth of over 7.0 per cent during 1992-1997. This slipped to 5.0 per cent in 1997-98 and improved to 6.0 per cent in 1998-99. In 1999-00, GDP growth is expected to climb above 6.0 per cent. Data for the fourth quarter of 1998-99 indicate a strong recovery in economic activity. The economy grew at the rate of 8.4 per cent in January-March 1999 over January-March 1998. This compares with a 1.5 per cent growth in the same quarter for the previous year. This is largely on account of an improvement in agricultural production and current indications point to a normal monsoon again this year.

Market analysts also point to signs of industrial recovery in the first quarter of 1999-00. Increase in cement sales, housing activity, steel demand and auto sales point to industrial recovery and increased household consumption. The IIP index of manufacturing recorded an increase of 7.8 per cent in April 1999 compared to 4.9 per cent last April. The general index of IIP recorded an increase of 6.8 per cent in April 1999 compared to 4.8 per cent last year. To push this recovery into double-digit levels, effective public policies are required and that will have to wait till after the elections. There is no doubt that political uncertainty and discontinuity has imposed a burden on the economy. For that reason, however, one can argue that the additional element of economic uncertainty introduced by the Kargil conflict can at best be marginal. If this conflict is resolved by the time a new government is in place, the overall impact of the Kargil conflict on investment decisions would have been marginal. In short, the timing of the Kargil conflict has helped minimise its negative impact on the investment climate.

On the macroeconomic front, inflation remains a concern despite the present low rate of point-to-point inflation based on WPI. If the impact of point-to-point comparisons is eliminated and annualised estimate is derived, the WPI rate of inflation works out to over 5.0 per cent. Even this is below the long-term average of 8.0 per cent. However, given fiscal and monetary pressures latent in the economy and the sentiment of scarcity that takes hold in a period of prolonged crisis, inflation can easily rear its head. More than a generalised inflation, commodity-specific scarcities can easily emerge, as it happened with onions last year. Unless the government is vigilant about such pressures and is prepared to use forex reserves to import scarce commodities the economy remains vulnerable to inflation.

Finally, in the medium term, war demand can have a positive impact on economic growth in a large economy, rather than in a small economy. Small economies, particularly Pakistan, are more import-dependent in general and with respect to war demand in particular, India's substantial domestic defence production potential can help internalise the multiplier effects of increased war-related spending. While the import demand for new equipment may increase after the war, in the course of the war much of the additional demand will be for local production and this demand can be more easily met in India than Pakistan.

External sector

The real contrast between India and Pakistan is in their external profile. India's external profile has been improving and is expected to improve further, while that of Pakistan has not only been deteriorating, but is expected to further deteriorate.

An important area of concern for India is the recent increase in oil prices, the burden of oil imports at a time when exports have not been doing well. After a spell of subdued and abnormally low prices, oil prices have shot up to around US $16 per bbl. While India can live with this level, any further escalation of oil prices can exert a pressure both on the external account and on domestic prices. However, an expected decline in gold imports and the recent boom in software exports are expected to balance this factor. After two years of stagnation there has been an upturn in export growth. Moreover, sustained capital inflows have kept the current account deficit very low and at extremely safe level of 1.0 per cent of GDP in 1998-99, with foreign exchange reserves (excluding gold) upwards of US$ 30 billion, compared to Pakistan's forex reserves of just one billion dollars, that too with support from a huge IMF loan.

While the post-Pokhran budget had a negative impact on the sentiment of foreign investors, the February 1999 budget helped bring external sector policies back on course and this has had a positive impact on FDI and FII sentiment. Thus, according to a Business Confidence Survey conducted among the CEOs and CFOs of the world's 1000 biggest firms, India's rating as an investment destination improved between December 1998 and June 1999. Interestingly, the June survey was conducted after the Kargil conflict broke out. Despite the heightened political tension in South Asia, India moved up from the 7th rank to the 6th, following USA, China, UK, Brazil and Mexico, and ahead of all South-East Asian and European economies. Even more reassuring is the fact that the increase in the pro-India sentiments among global CEOs was third fastest, after USA and South Korea, between end-'98 and mid-'99.

This shift in sentiment is reflected in sustained capital inflows into India. While the Kargil conflict temporarily disturbed this trend, with FIIs holding back new investments, the long-term sentiment remains buoyant. The AT Kearney study, however, emphasises the fact that FDI flows into India can easily be more if only India had a more transparent and consistent FDI policy. It is domestic policy rather than political uncertainty or conflict which is holding back more FDI into India. Post-Kargil diplomacy will be a new factor that any government will have to take into account in shaping India's external economic policies. The positive sentiment of the world community, especially the G-8, can be multiplied to India's advantage if the government pursues with renewed enthusiasm a more outward-oriented trade and investment policy. The sentiment in India's favour contrasts sharply with the negative sentiment on Pakistan, as we shall see below, and India must derive the full advantage of this positive environment by renewing her commitment to a policy of economic reform and liberalisation.

India's external debt profile has also improved. At $ 95 billion the total foreign debt is just 23 per cent of GDP, well within acceptable limits. At $ 3.6 billion, short-term debt is particularly low, being a mere 3.8 per cent of total debt. The debt-service ratio, which was around 35 per cent in the crisis year of 1991, is at an all-time low of 19 per cent.

Pakistan economy today

The thesis advanced by many security analysts that Pakistan's aggression along the Line of Control in the State of Jammu & Kashmir is more an act of desperation on the part of an increasingly

Table 59.3

Macroeconomic Indicators–India and Pakistan

Item	1997-98		1998-99		1999-00	
	India	Pakistan	India	Pakistan	India	Pakistan
Real GDP Growth	5.8	5.4	6.0	3.0	6.0	4.0
Agriculture	-1.0	5.9	5.3	4.5	3.0	4.5
Manufacturing	6.7	7.0	4.1	1.0	6.0	1.6
Services	8.3	5.3	6.8	4.0	7.0	4.2
Public Admn. & Defence	—	2.0	—	7.0	—	6.0
Domestic Demand	5.3	1.9	5.5	2.8	5.3	4.1
Real GNP Growth	5.0	5.6	5.7	2.9	5.4	4.2
Exports	1.5		0.4		2.5	
Imports	4.2		7.5		5.5	
Prices	6.8	7.8	5.0	11.0	—	8.0
Exchange Rate Rs./$	37.16	42.70	42.20	46.90	46.50	56.00
Forex Reserves	29.3	1.7	31.0	1.1	32.5	-
Fiscal Deficit (per cent of GDP)	6.1	5.4	5.8	5.3	5.2	6.0
Current A/c Deficit (per cent of GNP)	-1.5	3.3	1.0	4.5	1.3	4.7
Short-term External Debt Per Cent of Forex Reserves			$3.6 bn 12%	$2.3 bn 209%		

Source: For India: *Economic Survey* and CLSA Forecast.
For Pakistan: IMF & Credit Lyonnais Securities Asia (CLSA).

alienated government rather than an offensive launched by a confident regime is at least partly testified to by the fact that the Pakistani economy is in serious trouble and the present conflict can only make matters worse.

With the singular exception of the agriculture sector, Pakistan's economy is in a tailspin and all leading indicators suggest things can get worse before they get better. Apart from internal civic strife, Pakistan has been badly hurt by the post-Pokhran sanctions and the loss of investor confidence in its economy. While India has been able to recover from the negative impact of the sanctions and stabilise her external economy, Pakistan was forced to seek rescheduling of debts and a large package of assistance from the International

Monetary Fund (IMF) through the Fund's high-conditionality windows, namely, the extended Fund facility (EFF), enhanced structure adjustment facility (ESAF) and compensatory and contingency financing facility (CCFF).

Assessing the Pakistan economy, the IMF's PFP observes that, "Following the May 1998 developments, financial conditions have deteriorated as a result of loss of investor confidence, a decline in private capital inflows, imposition of economic sanctions, and the suspension of new official bilateral and multilateral disbursements for non-humanitarian purposes." Seeking to respond to this crisis, the Pakistan government hiked petrol and telephone rates and imposed a massive economic burden on the people. Says the Fund, "Notwithstanding these measures, the economy remained vulnerable."

The ESAF Policy Framework Paper (PFP), 1998/99-2000/01 states that Pakistan's total external financing requirements for the 3-year period are $ 19 bn. Given this demand, IMF expects private flows of not more than $ 1.3 bn. during the 3-year period, given the negative sentiment on Pakistan. The PFP states:

"After a relatively modest build-up of gross official reserves ($ 1.3 bn.), large residual financing gaps are projected. These gaps could be covered by official project loans amounting to US$ 4.0 bn. and grants ($ 400 mn.), which are linked to the public sector investment programme; and trade credits of about $ 680 mn. covering government-sponsored food imports. In addition, the government expects to mobilise $ 0.4 bn. of medium-term commercial loans and $ 1.3 bn. of short-term commercial loans. The residual financing needs, estimated at $ 12 bn. would be covered by expected financing over the programme period from the Fund ($ 1.6 bn.), the World Bank ($ 1.4 bn.), Asian Development Bank ($ 1.0 bn.), some potential bilateral creditors ($ 400 mn.), as well as large exceptional financing in 1998-2001 amounting to $ 7.7. billion. This exceptional financing would arise from a comprehensive rescheduling of public and publicly guaranteed debt owed to Paris Club and other bilateral creditors, as well as to commercial and private creditors—a restructuring or refinancing of government short-term debt; and the roll-over of short-term liabilities of financial institutions."[2]

In exchange for this large support programme, Pakistan has committed itself to a severe adjustment programme which includes hiking user charges, improved tax collection, privatisation of public enterprises and so on. The social and political consequences of such a deflationary adjustment programme, particularly in the context of a politically volatile Pakistan in the aftermath of its defeat in Kargil, could be serious.

Private investors have clearly factored this into their overall negative assessment of Pakistan. The response of the market to IMF's Pakistan programme has been very negative. In a hard-hitting assessment of the Pakistan economy the multinational financial firm, Credit Lyonnais Securities Asia (CLSA), has said:[3]

"The lack of political will to comply with tough IMF conditionality is well known. Our concern at the outset of the new Pakistan programme, is that the IMF may have lost sight of its objective which is to get the derailed Pakistan economy back on track (Criticism by some has gone further, suggesting that political expediency rather than economic considerations are driving the new programme)....IMF-Pakistan agreements have a low credibility status, not surprising following the repeated collapse of previous programme,.... Pakistan is personification of the IMF's Achilles' heel."

CLSA's second report for 1999 has warned that:

"If poor compliance (to IMF programme) leads to yet another breakdown of the IMF programme, the Sharif government will not survive. The country will plunge back into a debt crisis and suffer another bout of political destabilisation—an uncomfortable prospect with the military as ever, waiting in the wings."[4]

Making this assessment prior to the Kargil conflict CLSA adds that an improvement of India-Pakistan relations after Lahore could

---

2. "Pakistan: Enhanced Structured Adjustment Facility", *Policy Framework Paper*, 1998/99-2000/01, I.M.F., Washington DC, Dec. 1998.

3. Credit Lyonnais Securities Asia Ltd., *Eye on Asian Economies*, 1st Quarter, 1999.

4. *ibid.*, 2nd Quarter, 1999.

help improve Pakistan's economic prospects. By the same token, the deterioration of these relations following Kargil can have a serious negative impact on the Pakistan economy. In early 1999, CLSA in fact speculated that an economic downturn could trigger a military take-over in Pakistan. The military defeat in Kargil can only increase such prospects if the civilian leadership is unable to assert itself.

Finally, the impact of the macroeconomic downturn in Pakistan is already being felt on the country's human development indicators. Ever since the late Dr. Mahbub-ul Haq began computing the Human Development Index, which is a measure of well-being in terms of educational attainment, health status, longevity and per capita income, Pakistan has been one step ahead of India largely on account of a higher per capita income. This year's report places the Indian economy six steps ahead of Pakistan. While Pakistan's rank has slipped from 137 to 138. India's rank has moved six places forward from 138 to 132. This relative improvement is largely on account of the higher growth of national income during the 1990s. This simple figure captures the underlying reality about India and Pakistan. The Indian economy has been growing at unprecedented levels during the 1990s and is expected to continue to grow at an average rate of at least 6.0 per cent per annum over the next decade. The Pakistan economy, on the other hand, has been growing at a much slower pace and its external economic profile is extremely negative. For the first time since partition, the Pakistan economy is beginning to fall behind India.

Some South Asia observers have already recognised this trend and its implications for the region. An analyst at the US National Defense University, Washington DC, drew the appropriate conclusion that the acceleration of India's growth rate in the 1990s, and the relative stagnation of the Pakistan economy will increase India's economic, military and diplomatic profile both within the region and globally. To quote:

"The changed GDP ratio (between India and Pakistan) would have military implications. Given that India spends 2.5 per cent of its GDP on its military and that Pakistan's economy is 19 per cent the size of India's, Pakistan would have to spend 13 per cent of

GDP to match the Indian military budget in absolute size. In fact, Pakistan cannot afford to spend that much. Pakistan can only afford military spending that is little more than half the size of India's. That is, Pakistan can only afford to dedicate 6.5 per cent of its GDP to the military, because to do more would drain away the resources needed for the investment that sustains future growth. Already Pakistan faces the same quandary as the former USSR— the military spending necessary to keep pace with the historic foe would drain off so many resources that the economy would fall further behind that of the adversary. The problem will get much worse (when).... Pakistan's GDP slips relative to that of India. As India becomes richer, it will be able to afford to fund its military more generously. The ratio between the Pakistani military budget and that of India easily become one to three, rather than one or two. At that point, it would become less and less plausible to see Pakistan as in any way comparable in national power to India.

In short, the gap between Indian and Pakistani economic prospects could lead to a shift in the balance of power in the region. On present trends, India is likely to become the clearly pre-eminent regional power. Indeed, as the difference in economic growth rates becomes clearer, the trends in India's favour will affect perceptions— India will be seen as the power of the future, and that will in turn multiply its power in the present."[5]

This assessment of 1997 is even more valid today, particularly in the aftermath of Pokhran-II, the negative impact of sanctions on the Pakistan economy, and the loss of international confidence in the future of Pakistan given the growing 'Talibanisation' of the Pakistani polity and the inability of the urban elite to impose their vision of a modern Islamic state on an increasingly, fundamentalist and communalised people.

Economic policy options for India

The above analysis shows that the most important priority for India, on the economic front, in the wake of the Kargil crisis, is to

---

5. Clawson (1997), p.8.

continue to pursue the policies initiated in the 1990s to step up India's GDP growth rate within the framework of a more open and outward-oriented economy. If India can grow at even 6.0 per cent, hopefully the growth rate can be pushed even higher, and this growth increases the size of the home market as well as India's share of world trade, this will have a positive impact on her economic well-being as well as political influence. As China, Korea and some of the East and South-East Asian economies have shown, economic and political stability and influence are directly and positively linked to sustained economic growth and improved human development indicators. Hence, any policy that is growth-oriented and encourages trade-expansion is warranted both in the interests of well-being and national security.

Second, the government will have to take a closer look at its budgetary priorities, cutting down on wasteful expenditure and subsidies to the better-off sections of society and increasing public investment and social infrastructure, including defence and defence-related R&D. Productive public investment has suffered during the last decade of fiscal adjustment. This does not augur well for economic growth, well-being and security.

More than increasing defence spending, India's priority will have to be to restructure existing spending towards modernisation of the armed forces and their infrastructural support services. Government policy must be aimed at increasing public investment, both domestic and foreign. Public investment should be financed through increased public savings, higher revenue from improved collection of direct taxes and user charges for public services, privatisation of non-strategic public enterprises and diversion of funds from non-productive uses. A consistent, transparent and positive policy towards foreign direct investment is also necessary.

Third, in the short-term, day-to-day pressures may be generated by the course of events which get reflected in the response of the stock and money markets. Market operators must recognise that fluctuations in stock market indices and exchange rates are par for the course in a market economy and should not be viewed as symbols of national pride. A depreciation of the rupee can have both positive and negative consequences for the economy and should not be made a subject of national prestige at a time like this. At the same time, close watch must be kept on inflationary pressures and sound macroeconomic policies pursued so that adverse fiscal and monetary pressures are not generated on the price front.

Indians have generally welcomed the positive attitude of the global community towards India in the Kargil conflict. India must reciprocate this sentiment by becoming a more open economy. This will enable it to create relations of mutual benefit and inter-dependence so that the world has a greater stake in India's stability and prosperity.

Geography of business

Time, space and technology

AN enduring myth of the electronic age is that technology helps to telescope historical, geographical and social distance between nations. Almost three decades ago, the media *guru* of the television age, Marshal McLuhan, argued that modern media had made irrelevant the role of time and space in separating human experience and had, thereby, created the 'global village'. From this, rather simplistic, theorising about a developing common global experience has evolved the other enduring myth of modern industrial societies—that any business will have to be globally defined and competitive if it is to survive into the next century.

The reason why both these appealing ideas may in fact be myths as far as developing economies are concerned is because history and geography set us apart from post-industrial societies, making it that much more difficult for developing industrial economies to globalise freely. While technology may, in theory, have the potential of bridging the handicap of time and space, in practice developing economies are constrained by the unequal access to global technology. The technology gap is likely to be widened by the regime of intellectual property protection that is coming into existence.

The dominant role of electronic technology in the creation of a 'global village', the complex intermeshing of global corporate life and the pre-eminence of Western media in determining the creation and shaping of ideas have been three important pillars on which the notion of 'globalisation' has been built. The fourth pillar was the thesis that nationalism was an obsolete notion, that nation-states are an anachronism in the 'global village', and that geographical borders have lost all relevance in the satellite age.

The impact of these myths has been so profound on the Indian middle and business classes that policy makers and commentators in the media have uncritically accepted them as the defining elements of the paradigm of globalism and the intellectual bases of the 'new economic policy'.

It must, therefore, come as a rude shock to India's naively globalised elite that a publication with impeccable 'liberal' credentials such as *The Economist*, London, should warn multinational corporations that, "The weight on mankind of time and space, of physical surroundings and history—in short, of geography—is bigger than any earthbound technology is ever likely to lift."

History counts and so does geography, says *The Economist*, (July 30-August 5, 1994) in an editorial comment that must make Kenichi Ohmae (*The Borderless World*, 1990) and the ideologues of post-industrial globalism sit up and read on in disbelief. "The conceit that advanced technology can erase the contingencies of place and time ranges widely," says *The Economist*. "Many armchair strategists predicted during the Gulf War that ballistic missiles and smart weapons would make the task of capturing and holding territory irrelevant. They were as wrong as the earlier seers who predicted America could win the Vietnam War from the air.

"In business too, the efforts to break free of space and time have had qualified success at best. American multinationals going global have discovered that—for all their world products, world advertising, and world communications and control—an office, say, in New York cannot, except in the most general sense, manage the company's Asian operations. Global strengths must be matched by a local feel...."

This argument in itself is well-known to the global corporate person who has lived with the dictum 'think global, act local'.

Indeed, Indian businessmen can argue that they can teach the developed world a lesson or two in 'multi-culturalism' in business for, after all, major Indian companies have been 'multinationals' in a federal, sub-continental economy, selling goods, managing people and conducting business in diverse linguistic, cultural and social settings from Kerala to Kashmir and Calcutta to Bombay.

However, *The Economist* is concerned with more than the impediments that multiculturalism imposes on international business; it urges a respect for history in business strategy. For both 'ethno-enthusiasts' and 'neo-classical economists', says *The Economist*, "The world should tend towards a smooth dispersion of people, skills and economic competence, not towards their concentration....The reality is otherwise.... The main reason is that history counts; where you are depends very much on where you started from."

For the post-industrial society of North America, Western and Northern Europe and Japan, what Ohmae called the Triad, "where you are" is the product of the history and geography of advanced capitalism in the last 100 years, of where they started from and the process of how they got here.

An important instrumentality through which that journey was organised was the nation-state. The declaration of the death of the nation-state is essentially a West European idea in the 1980s. A continent that was at war with itself for centuries, culminating in the bloodiest battle it has ever witnessed barely half a century ago, has been going through the birth pangs of a nation-in-the-making, created through the dissolution of its many nationalities. When the English, Scottish, French, Germans, Italians and the many linguistic, ethnic, religious and political groups of Western Europe talk of the end of the nation-state, they are merely finding ways of facilitating the emotional unification of Europe—a phenomenon itself set into motion by the 'threat' of competition from the United States and Japan, and hastened by the anxiety with the unification of Germany.

The celebration of post-nationalism by the Japanese, best exemplified by Ohmae's *The Borderless World*, can in fact be interpreted as an attempt to build the intellectual edifice of an export-dependent society. For Japanese business, with a booming trade surplus and a saturated home market, it was necessary to delegitimise borders in trade and manufacturing.

If borders do not matter for trade and investment flows, how is it that they become so rigidly defined for technology and human flows? The persistent attempts by developed industrial economies to deny developing economies a free access to modern technology, even as they secure freedom of access to markets, can be understood only if we appreciate the 'telescopic' impact of technology on history and geography. The constraints of time and space can be overcome if access to technology is free. That is, indeed, the lesson of the last millennium.

By seeking a tougher regime for the transfer of technology, even as they seek a liberal regime for the movement of capital and goods and services, developed industrial economies are trying to ensure that time and space remain barriers so far as the developing world is concerned, even as the developed world itself uses technology to overcome them.

Advocates of unrestrained globalism who decry the so-called 'East India Company' syndrome have not addressed the vital question of what kind of a technology regime must go with genuine globalisation and free enterprise worldwide. India must not hesitate to be a global player, a participant in the global marketplace and an open economy if the freedom it gives to capital and trade flows can be matched by the freedom developed economies give to technology and skills flows. The latter is essential to enable India to bridge the time and space gaps in its development process.

Media multiplier

Soft power of Indian software

"INDIA has the potential to become a global media superpower," said Union finance minister Yashwant Sinha in this year's budget speech and proceeded to offer various tax benefits to the entertainment industry. This was part of a wider initiative to promote the information technology (IT) industry. It can be argued, though, that in India—media—both information and entertainment media—do not really require tax incentives to grow and globalise since they have been built over the years on the firm foundation of competitive skills and talent and increasing domestic and international demand. What they need instead is intellectual property protection and a world market that works according to multilateral rules of the game. Indeed, the Indian media must take a closer look at the emerging issues on trade in services in world trade negotiations.

From the days the Russians and the Chinese hummed *Awara Hoon*, through the years when Kishore Kumar and Amitabh Bachchan were folk heroes in such distant lands as Egypt, Somalia, Turkey and Central Asia and to the present day when the actors, actresses, singers, composers and musicians from 'Bollywood' and beyond are attracting a global audience thanks to satellite technology and cable television, India has always ranked next only to the United States and Britain as a 'global media player', if not a 'superpower'. However, India's recent success in the IT industry, the development of indigenous satellite and other electronic technologies, our ability to creatively use the Internet and the increasing success of Indian entertainment exports—film, TV and music—draw attention to India's competitive advantage in modern media.

The Indian media's self-confidence has been built in the face of decades of free competition in the cultural marketplace since India has remained an open society. Indigenous talent in the information and entertainment media has always been willing to benchmark itself against international competition and has not just survived but thrived. Bollywood's battles with Hollywood are an obvious example. Zee Television scoring over foreign channels is another. A.R. Rahman's greater appeal over Michael Jackson is a third. Surely, there are many more and each of us will have our favourite example. So far, the print media has shied away from such competition but there are enough potential global players in India who can make a mark in the world market if they so desire. The creative and technical skills exist, only the financial backing is required.

Indian entertainment exports have acquired a global market potential for several reasons. First, the increasing prosperity of the Indian diaspora across the world which offers a ready and growing market, as well as channels for trade for Indian entertainment exports. Second, the demand for Indian music and cinema has increased particularly in Islamic countries because cultural conservatism and religious fundamentalism have stifled the growth of indigenous talent in many of them and Indian media is able to cater to this demand. Third, the US entertainment industry is beginning to sub-contract creative work involving computer software and India has emerged as a competitive production base. Fourth, India's familiarity with new entertainment and information technology and with the English language is an asset. Fifth, the talent explosion in the news media, print and electronic, has created the basis for Indian news media going global, like BBC, CNN and *The Financial Times*. Finally, the Internet has created an affordable vehicle for the globalisation of Indian media talent.

It is not just Bollywood, which is exploiting all these opportunities, but also the technically more advanced entertainment industry in Chennai and Hyderabad and the nascent television industry in Mumbai, Delhi and the South. Low cost facilities for film production, computer animation and so on have come up in Hyderabad and Chennai, attracting business from Hollywood and Walt Disney. This kind of business rakes in the dollars, but it is the export of indigenous entertainment which is more important in projecting Indian images and India's image across the world. Surely, Hollywood has done more for US influence globally than the entire US diplomatic and military establishment put together.

It is important to recognise, however, that while governments can help by shaping sensible fiscal and industrial policies that facilitate the growth of domestic enterprise, and ensure a 'level playing field' against the unfair and predatory competition from multinational operators with deep pockets, like Mr. Rupert Murdoch, they have no other business than to get into the business of entertainment and news. The credibility of the media depends entirely on its perceived independence.

If the Pakistanis are today more concerned about the influence of Zee Television than they ever were about Doordarshan, or indeed we are about Pakistan TV, it is because an average viewer discounts propaganda very quickly and its influence is at best marginal and short-lived. Rather than block out Indian satellite TV programmes, the best way for Pakistan to deal with 'unacceptable foreign cultural influence', as one Pakistani politician put it to me, is to counter it with more acceptable domestic alternatives for the viewers. The indigenisation, some may complain 'hindigenisation', of foreign satellite TV channels bears eloquent testimony to the fact that viewer-friendly local programming can counter the craze for imported culture. The appeal of pure entertainment and open debate can potentially be far more persuasive, perhaps even subversive, than official propaganda.

The foreign policy dimension of entertainment and information export should be obvious to any observer. Both in news and entertainment, few major powers in the world, apart from the United States, can rival India's potential ability to acquire a global media presence. While there is no denying that India's role in international affairs will be shaped most importantly by rapid economic growth and the well-being of the Indian people, *a la* China, democratic and liberal India can make more effective use of various media than autocratic and insular China has been able to in winning friends and influencing people. While economists and strategic analysts emphasise the 'hard power' of economic growth and military strength, the influence of a modern power in today's world can also be projected through the 'soft power' of media software.

Widen that lens

WHEN Raj Kapoor sang, "*Mera joota hai Japani, yeh patloon Inglistani*," he was neither singing the virtues of globalisation nor was he reaching out to the hearts and minds of the Japanese and the English. Song-writer Shailendra's line about the 'red Russian hat' was, of course, an acknowledgement of Soviet Russia's ideological appeal at the time to newly independent India's film makers. The song was a poetic recognition of India's industrial backwardness and made a case for import-substituting industrialisation in an emergent nation.

It is a different matter that both this song as well as his famous '*Awara Hoon*' endeared Raj Kapoor and generations of Indians to audiences in China, the Soviet Union and large parts of the decolonising world. What Kapoor did with China and Russia, Kishore Kumar and Amitabh Bachchan managed to do in the Arab world. Even in distant Dakar, I was once asked by a Senegalese taxi driver whether I had seen *Sholay*, a movie he had seen at a local theatre several times!

Despite its global reach and appeal, even if largely confined to the so-called Indian 'diaspora', the people of Indian origin living overseas, Indian cinema has never really had a role in Indian foreign policy and has never consciously served any strategic objective. Perhaps Raj Kapoor was an exception. In his *Mera Naam Joker* he paid tribute to the Russian people for the love they so generously extended to him and to this nation. However, rarely has an Indian film been made to reach out to a different nation, a non-Indian audience, with an explicit foreign policy objective.

This reticence of the world's second largest film industry stands in contrast to the declared global interest of the world's largest film industry, Hollywood. Its willingness to use the medium of cinema to befriend nations or demonise them manifested itself across a wide range of movies from propagandist anti-communist thrillers to romantic entertainers. When Frank Sinatra sang Cole Porter's "I love Paris" in *Can Can* he was doing so at a time when Charles de Gaulle was making it difficult for Americans to say so officially!

If Hollywood was wooden in its anti-Soviet propaganda, blasé in its treatment of Latin Americans, it was more subtle in winning friends in Europe and Asia. Hollywood made films that enabled the United States to strike a chord with diverse nations, from Africans to Europeans, from Arabs to Japanese. American cinema played an explicit foreign policy role.

By contrast, the only interest that Indian cinema has shown in India's relations with the outside world has been largely confined to India's relations with Pakistan, through films devoted either to the heroism of our soldiers or the life of families touched by Partition. Film makers from among people of Indian origin have explored relations between Indians and non-Indians in such films as *Mississippi Masala* and *Bend It Like Beckham*, but these have not been conceived in the framework of any national foreign policy objective. Nagesh Kukunoor's *Hyderabad Blues* considers the angst of a non-resident Indian visiting home, but no one has looked at Indians interacting with foreigners abroad and creating bilateral relationships that can serve larger national policy objectives. Hollywood does it all the time. Bollywood never so far.

Is there a dearth of themes and contexts? Hardly. The life of the famous Indian doctor in China, Dr. Kotnis, the subject of a forgotten *Hindustani* movie, reminds us that there are stories to tell with possible implications for relations between nations. Consider the theme of the life story of Indians in South-East Asia, the restorers of *Angkor Wat*, a movie on a grand historical scale, or of Indian Americans who have made it big in the US. Consider the saga of Indians in the Persian Gulf and Africa and their positive contribution to these societies.

Why has Bollywood or Bengali cinema not made a film so far about Bangladesh's war of liberation? Hollywood used cinema to remind Europe in the 1960s about its contribution in the Second World War to European freedom and democracy, lest the French forget the role played by heroic Yankee troops! The world and South Asia must be reminded of what happened in 1970-72. It's as heroic a tale as *The Longest Day*, the Hollywood mega-movie that captured the heroism of Allied troops at Normandy.

Forget war and liberation, there is a tale of romance and adventure to be told, as there is of the influence of ideas and people. A movie about the travels of Huang Tsang or the Buddhist monks who walked to Bukhara. Consider the adventurous flying career of the late Biju Patnaik and his role in the naming of Indonesia's present President, Megawati Sukarnoputri. Can stories not be written around the role of our peacekeepers in Somalia, or our entrepreneurs in America. The Motel Patels and the Silicon Valley Andhras. Is their story of globalisation not worth telling so that attitudes at home to the outside world can change? So that attitudes abroad towards India can be moulded? Is this not an objective worth considering for Indian cinema makers?

Indian film makers use the world outside as a cute and colourful backdrop for frolicking and singing. Till recently foreigners made an appearance in an Indian film either to hold a glass of whisky and shake a leg at a smuggler's party or to stand amused on a roadside watching a young couple behaving like clowns. If the outside world ever enters an Indian film frame it is either in the form of a diasporic Indian, most often a Punjabi from a London suburb or a Tamil from Singapore. The globalisation of Indian cinema's audience has at best forced producers and story writers to incorporate people of Indian origin into their navel-gazing themes.

But the time has come for Indian cinema to take a larger view of its relevance to the nation. A globalising industry cannot remain a frog in the Indian, even diasporic, well. The world is a stage it must grandly straddle.

An India of Narayana Murthy or Sudarshan?

DURING his search for the soul of enslaved India in the 1930s, Mahatma Gandhi founded an *ashram* at Wardha, near Nagpur, because it was located in the centre of the Indian sub-continent. Half a century after Independence, the heart and mind of the Indian Republic is no longer to be found near Nagpur. It has moved further south.

The voice of new India no longer comes out of a city that is now better known as the headquarters of the Rashtriya Swayamsevak Sangh (RSS), but it comes more assuredly from a city like Bangalore, branded as the symbol of a new India because it is the home of people like the visionary founder-chairman of Infosys, N.R. Narayana Murthy.

This past week we have heard two views about our nation and our relationship with the outside world articulated by two very different south Indian *brahmins*. Mr. Narayana Murthy, on the one hand, and Mr. K.S. Sudarshan, head of the RSS, on the other. Mr. Narayana Murthy spoke with the self-confidence of a winner, Mr. Sudarshan spoke with the sullen anger of a loser. Mr. Murthy harped on the future, Mr. Sudarshan harked back to the past.

Delivering a lecture on "Role of Western Values in Contemporary Indian Society", under the auspices of the Lal Bahadur Shastri Institute of Management, Mr. Murthy chided us for our 'we know it all' intellectual arrogance. Addressing a gathering of RSS activists, Mr. Sudarshan bemoaned the growing love for English in the country and preferred the RSS version of bovine economics.

"No other society gloats so much about the past as we do, with as little current accomplishment," lamented Mr. Murthy, recounting the experience of Al Barouni, the famous Arabic logician and traveller of the 10th century. During his travels through India between 997 A.D. and 1027 A.D. Al Barouni was hard put to find a single *pundit* willing to engage him in a debate. When he did find one who was then impressed by Al Barouni's arguments, his interlocutor asked which Indian *pundit* had taught him these ideas!

"The most important attribute of a progressive society is respect for others who have accomplished more than they themselves have, and a willingness to learn from them," said Mr. Murthy. We Indians, on the other hand, pretend we know it all and have little to learn from others. Recalling Carlyle's dictum that "the greatest of faults is to be conscious of none," Mr Murthy observed, "If we have to progress, we have to change this attitude, listen to people who have performed better than us, learn from them and perform better than them."

We are not the world's only civilisational nation with a great past. We are not even Asia's only wise and ancient civilisation. We share our undoubted historical and cultural greatness with our civilisational neighbour, China, which today forges ahead economically fuelled by western technology and indigenous enterprise. At a time when the Chinese are learning English, not because it is the language of a former imperial power but because it is the language of global commerce and of the knowledge economy, the likes of Mr. Sudarshan bemoan that more Indians want to be so empowered!

Mr. Murthy alerts us to the positive aspects of western civilisation which can help deliver us from our backwardness even as he celebrates the unique and positive qualities of our own culture. His has been a story of the success of individual merit and enterprise unencumbered by social prejudice and political regimentation but enabled by public support and the cooperative spirit. It is these values of public good and cooperative enterprise that Mr. Murthy celebrates in his lecture.

But how can those who are steeped in exclusiveness and an inward-looking worldview appreciate these values? Therein lies the contradiction between the worldview of Mr. Murthy and Mr. Sudarshan. Both come from a similar social background, the world of a middle class south Indian *brahmin*. Yet, Mr. Murthy has grappled with the world as it exists, as any business leader and technocrat would. Mr. Sudarshan, on the other hand, wants to recreate the world in his mould. It is the Murthys of India who will take this nation forward, the Sudarshans will keep it pre-occupied with divisive and spent causes.

The empty hollowness of the RSS posturing on economic policy is brought out by the fact that in so many policy battles between merit and vested interest, the RSS has sided with vested interest over merit, betraying the cause of the professional middle class that men like Mr. Murthy symbolise. Recall the Sankhya Vahini project mooted by professionals like the distinguished scientist V.S. Arunachalam and the technocrat Raj Reddy. It is the RSS that sabotaged that project in the name of national security.

The most important aspect of Mr. Murthy's lecture, as indeed of many of his recent public speeches and writings, is the implicit point he is trying to make that modernism is not divisible. A nation cannot build a modern economy on the foundations of a backward social and political worldview. Modernism is not westernism and modernisation need not imply westernisation. However, there are certain basic building blocks of a modern society and those we must reinforce. Ideas like merit, dignity of labour, equity and equality, secularism, freedom of enterprise, freedom of thought and action, family values and a concern for the environment and public welfare and institutions. Such are the bricks that build a modern economy that Mr. Murthy has helped create in his entrepreneurial life and now celebrates in his intellectual forays. These are values that unite societies, not divide them.

Mr. Sudarshan, on the other hand, pursues a politics of negativism and an economics of defeatism. His anger against those who genuflect before the White Man is understandable, for many in this country are yet to rid themselves of their feudal and colonial mindset. However, his desire to hark back to a dead past and imagine external enemies betrays a lack of confidence. Confidence of the kind that Mr. Murthy has come to symbolise, having shown the world that Indians can do it. Mr. Murthy is the triumphant icon of our times. Mr. Sudarshan a tragic anachronism.

India's emergence in world affairs*

Jawaharlal Nehru

SIR, I welcome this occasion. Although we are discussing this subject of foreign affairs not directly but by way of a 'cut' motion, nevertheless, it is a novel occasion for this House and I think it is good that we realise what it conveys.

It means ultimately that we are entering the international field, not only by going into conferences and the like, but by really putting international questions before the country, before this House for its decision. There is no immediate question before the House today. But undoubtedly as time goes on, the major international questions will have to be decided by this House.

Listening to the debate, and to the speeches made by the Hon. Members, I find, as was perhaps natural, that there was no immediate issue, no particular question for discussion, but rather pious hopes, vague ideals and sometimes a measure of, let us say, denunciation of things that had happened in the world. It has been a vague debate, with nothing pointed about it to which one could attach oneself. Many of the Hon. Members have been good enough to speak gently and generously of what has been done in the realm of foreign affairs on behalf of the Government of India during the

---

* Speech in the Constituent Assembly (Legislative), New Delhi, December 4, 1947, in reply to Shri N.G. Ranga's 'cut' motion for the reduction of the demand under the head 'Ministry of External Affairs and Commonwealth Relations'.

past year. I am grateful to them, but may I say in reply that I am in complete disagreement with them?

I think the Government of India during the past year has not done what it should have done. That, perhaps, has not been really the fault of the Government of India as such, but rather of circumstances. Anyway, what we had envisaged that we ought to do, we have not been able to do, largely because other circumstances arose in this country which have prevented its being done. We are not yet out of those difficulties, internal and other. We have not had a free hand in our external relations, and, therefore, I would beg the House to be judge of this period in the context of what has been happening in this country, not only during the past unhappy three or four months, but in the course of the past year when we lived in the middle of internal conflict and confusion which drained away our energy and did not leave us time to attend to other matters.

That has been the dominant feature of our politics during the past year and undoubtedly that has affected our foreign policy in the sense of our not giving enough time and energy to it. Nevertheless, I think we have advanced in that field. Again, it is difficult to say how you measure advance in such a field. My Hon. friend, Dr. N.B. Khare, was critical of various things, as he has every right to be, and his criticism took the shape of a written speech to which your attention, Sir, was not drawn! I was glad of the Hon. Dr. Khare's intrusion in this debate, because the debate was getting rather heavy and he brought a touch of comedy and humour into it as well as unreality. When the Hon. Member represented the Government in the Legislature, it was a little difficult to attach much importance to what he said. I suppose now it is less difficult to do so, or a little more difficult to do so! So I will not venture to say anything in reply to what he said because it seems to me totally inconsequential and without any meaning.

But coming to other subjects, the main subject in foreign policy today is vaguely talked of in terms of "Do you belong to this group or that group?" That is an utter simplification of issues and it is all very well for the Hon. Maulana to hold forth that India will go to war under this banner or that banner. But that surely is not the way that a responsible House or a responsible Country views the situation.

We have proclaimed during this past year that we will not attach ourselves to any particular group. That has nothing to do with neutrality or passivity or anything else. If there is a big war, there is no particular reason why we should jump into it. Nevertheless, it is a little difficult nowadays in world wars to be neutral. Any person with any knowledge of international affairs knows that. The point is not what will happen when there is a war. Are we going to proclaim to the world, taking the advice of Maulana Hasrat Mohani, that when war comes, we stand by Russia? Is that his idea of foreign policy or any policy? That shows to me an amazing ignorance of how foreign affairs can be conducted. We are not going to join a war if we can help it—and we are going to join the side which is to our-interest when the time comes to make the choice. There the matter ends.

But talking about foreign policies, the House must remember that these are not just empty struggles on a chess board. Behind them lie all manner of things. Ultimately, foreign policy is the outcome of economic policy, and until India has properly evolved her economic policy, her foreign policy will be rather vague, rather inchoate, and will be groping. It is well for us to say that we stand for peace and freedom; and yet that does not convey much to anybody, except a pious hope. We do stand for peace and freedom. I think there is something to be said for it. There is some meaning when we say that we stand for the freedom of Asian countries and for the elimination of imperialistic control over them. There is some meaning in that. Undoubtedly it has some substance, but a vague statement that we stand for peace and freedom by itself has no particular meaning, because every country is prepared to say the same thing, whether it means it or not. What then do we stand for? Well, you have to develop this argument in the economic field. As it happens today, in spite of the fact that we have been for some time in authority as a Government, I regret that we have not produced any constructive economic scheme or economic policy so far. Again my excuse is that we have been going through such amazing times which have taken up all our energy and attention that it was difficult to do so. Nevertheless, we shall have to do so and when we do so, that will govern our foreign policy, more than all the speeches in this House.

We have sought to avoid foreign entanglements by not joining one bloc or the other. The natural result has been that neither of these big blocs looks on us with favour. They think that we are undependable, because we cannot be made to vote this way or that way.

Last year when our delegation went to the United Nations, it was the first time that a more or less independent delegation went from India. It was looked at a little askance. They did not know what it was going to do. When they found that we acted according to our own will, they did not like it. We were unpopular last year at the United Nations. I do not mean individually, but in regard to our policy. They could not quite make out what we were or what we were aiming at. There was a suspicion in the minds of the first group that we were really allied to the other group in secret though we were trying to hide the fact, and the other group thought that we were allied to the first group in secret though we were trying to hide the fact. This year there was a slight change in this attitude. We did many things which both the groups disliked, but the comprehension came to them that we were not really allied to either group, that we were trying to act according to our own lights and according to the merits of the dispute as they seemed to us. They did not like that, of course, because the position today is that there is so much passion and so much fear and suspicion of each other between these great rival Powers and groups that anybody who is not with them is considered against them. So they did not like what we did in many instances—nevertheless, they respected us much more, because they realised that we had an independent policy that we were not going to be dragooned this way or that, that we might make a mistake just like anyone else, nevertheless, we were going to stick to our own policy and programme, so that while possibly we irritated some of our friends even a little more than last year, we got on much better with everybody, because they understood that we did stand for something.

To give the House an instance of how we acted, take the Palestine affair which has given rise and will give rise to a great deal of trouble. We took up a certain attitude in regard to it which was roughly a federal state with autonomous parts. It was opposed to both the other attitudes which were before the United Nations. One was partition which has not been adopted—the other was a unitary state. We suggested a federal state with, naturally an Arab majority in charge of the federal state but with autonomy for the other regions—Jewish regions.

After a great deal of thought we decided that this was not only a fair and equitable solution of the problem, but the only real solution of the problem. Any other solution would have meant fighting and conflict. Nevertheless, our solution—which as the House will remember was the solution given in the minority report of the Palestine Committee—did not find favour with most people in the United Nations. Some of the major Powers were out for partition; they therefore, pressed for it and ultimately got it. Others were so keen on the unitary state idea and were so sure of preventing partition at any rate or preventing a two-thirds majority in favour of partition that they did not accept our suggestion.

When during the last few days somehow partition suddenly became inevitable and votes veered round to it, owing to the pressure of some of the great Powers, it was realised that the Indian solution was probably the best and an attempt was made in the last 48 hours to bring forward the Indian solution, not by us but by those who had wanted a unitary state.

It was then too late. There were procedural difficulties and many of the persons who might have accepted this solution had already pledged themselves to partition. And so ultimately partition was decided upon by a two-thirds majority, with a large number abstaining from voting, with the result again of trouble now and a great deal of trouble in the future in the Middle East.

I point this out to the House as an instance, that in spite of considerable difficulty and being told by many of our friends on either side that we must line up this way or that, we refused to do so and I have no doubt that the position we had taken was the right one and I still have no doubt that ours would have brought about the best solution.

This applies to many other things. But inevitably it means that to some extent we have to plough a lonely furrow in the United Nations and at international conferences of this type. Nonetheless, that is the only honourable and right position for us to take and I am quite sure that by adopting that position, we shall ultimately gain in national and international prestige, that is to say, when we take a long view of the situation, not a short view of getting immediately a vote here or there.

I have no doubt that fairly soon, in the course of two or three years, the world will find this attitude justified and that India will not only be respected by the major protagonists in the struggle for power, but a large number of the smaller nations which today are rather helpless will probably look to India more than to other countries for a lead in such matters.

May I in this connection say that during this last session of the United Nations General Assembly, many very difficult and very controversial issues were raised, and our delegation had to face extraordinarily intricate situations? I should like to pay a tribute to our delegation, especially to the leader of the delegation. Hon. Members often put questions about the appointment of ambassadors, members of delegations and the like and rightly so, because the House should be interested in such important appointments. May I say to the House that nothing is more difficult than to make these appointments, because they are not just appointments of able persons, but appointments of particular persons to particular places where they must fit in, which is an extraordinarily difficult thing?

In the key places of the world the ideal ambassador must be some kind of a superman. It is so difficult now not only to understand the intricacies—that is not difficult—but to remain friends with everybody and yet to advance your cause. After all we have in the past discussed foreign affairs from the outside, in other assemblies, or here perhaps, rather in an academic way, rather as in a college debating society. That is, we talked of high policies, but we did not come to grips with them when we had to say 'yes' or 'no' to a question and face the consequences.

If the House will forgive my saying so, even in today's debate many of the speeches were of an academic kind which did not take into account the vital questions which concern the world today, which may mean peace or war. But when the House does have to face the question and take a decision which may lead to war or peace, when one comes face to face, with realities, then one cannot rely merely on idealistic principles.

Foreign affairs are utterly realistic today. A false step, a false phrase, makes all the difference. The first thing that an ambassador of ours has to learn is to shut his mouth and give up public or even private speaking. It is not a habit which we have developed in our past careers—that of being completely silent. Yet this habit has to be developed, and in private one has to be silent lest what one says injures the cause of the nation or creates international ill-will.

It is in this background that I should like the House to consider international affairs. We have to get over the notion that it is merely some naughty men playing about and quarrelling with one another, some statesmen in America and the USSR or British imperialism lurking behind the curtain in the distance. We have talked so much about British imperialism that we cannot get rid of the habit.

To come to grips with the subject in its economic, political and various other aspects, try to understand it, is what ultimately matters. Whatever policy you may lay down, the art of conducting the foreign affairs of a country lies in finding out what is most advantageous to the country. We may talk about international goodwill and mean what we say. We may talk about peace and freedom and earnestly mean what we say. But in the ultimate analysis, a government functions for the good of the country it governs and no government dare do anything which in the short or long run is manifestly to the disadvantage of that country.

Therefore, whether a country is imperialistic or socialist or communist, its foreign minister thinks primarily of the interests of that country. But there is a difference, of course. Some people may think of the interests of their country regardless of other consequences, or take a short-distance view. Others may think that in the long-term policy the interest of another country is as important to them as that of their own country. The interest of peace is more important, because if war comes everyone suffers, so that in the long-distance view, self-interest may itself demand a policy of cooperation with other nations, goodwill for other nations, as indeed it does demand.

Every intelligent person can see that if you have a narrow national policy it may excite the multitude for the moment, just as the communal cry has done, but it is bad for the nation and it is bad internationally, because you lose sight of the ultimate good and thereby endanger your own good. Therefore, we propose to look after India's interests in the context of world cooperation and world peace, in so far as world peace can be preserved.

We propose to keep on the closest terms of friendship with other countries unless they themselves create difficulties. We shall be friends with America. We intend cooperating with the United States of America and we intend cooperating fully with the Soviet Union. We have had, as the House knows, a distinguished representative of the United States here for some time past. Within a week or two we shall have a distinguished representative of the Soviet Union here, in the Soviet Embassy which is being opened in New Delhi.

I do not want to say much more at this stage about foreign affairs partly for lack of time, partly because it is a little difficult to discuss these matters. Some of the Hon. Members might, perhaps, want to talk about what should be done in China, Japan, Siam and Peru, but I fear it would be a little irresponsible of me to talk about these various matters. Naturally, India is interested in Asian countries even more than the rest of the world. We have had an Asian Conference, and at this moment we have a distinguished visitor here, the Prime Minister of Burma.

May I say in this connection that some people are under a misapprehension? They think that we are conducting special negotiations with the Burmese delegation here. That is not quite true. It is primarily a visit of courtesy. At the same time, of course, we have broadly explored various questions, discussed various matters of common concern, not with the idea of instantly coming to decisions in regard to these intricate matters now, but rather with a view to laying the foundations for future talks. May I also say that the Prime Minister of Burma is interested, as many of us have been, in closer association, not only between Burma and India, but between various other countries of Asia also? We have discussed that also, again not with a view to coming suddenly to decisions, because these things take a little time to grow. It all indicates the new spirit of Asia which wants Asian countries to draw closer together in their own defence and to promote world peace.

Coming to another part of this 'cut' motion in regard to Indians in the British Commonwealth, this is an old subject and a painful subject. I entirely agree with any criticism that may be made that we have not been able to do anything substantial in this direction. Something has been done in Canada and elsewhere, but nothing substantial has yet been done. Now, the odd thing is that this subject becomes more and more difficult to deal with and not easier. Indians have gone to the British colonies and dominions in the past in various capacities, as merchants, traders, workers, indentured labourers and the rest.

The history of Indian emigration abroad, including that of the humblest of those who went from India, reads almost like a romance. How these Indians went abroad! Not even citizens of a free country, working under all possible disadvantages, yet they made good wherever they went. They worked hard for themselves, and for the country of their adoption. They made good themselves, and the country they had gone to also profited. It is a romance and it is something which India can be proud of, and may I say most of all of those poor indentured labourers who went out under unhappy conditions, through their labour, gradually worked their way up? It is also true that India is a country which in spite of everything has abounding vitality and spreads abroad. It rather frightens our neighbour countries, just as China which is also a country with abounding vitality and an abounding population. We spread. We tend to overwhelm others both by virtue of our numbers, and sometimes by virtue of the economic position we might develop there.

That naturally frightens others who may not have that vitality in them, and they want to protect themselves against it. Questions then arise of vested interests which India has developed or Indians have developed there. Such questions have arisen, and while on the one hand we are obviously intent on protecting the interests of Indians abroad, on the other hand we cannot protect any vested interests which injure the cause of the country they are in. There is that difficulty. Nevertheless, undoubtedly we shall try to do our best to protect all legitimate interests.

Now, one word more. I will not take more of the time of the House. An Hon. Member, Shri Kamath I think, referred to the expenditure incurred by the embassies. Now, first of all, one of the minor headaches I have had to suffer from is a relatively new tendency in old and new newspapers alike to publish without check or hindrance the most amazing lies. It is impossible to keep pace with it. It is undesirable always to go about contradicting every little thing they say. It just cannot be done and I have come across some new types of papers and journals which have been inflicted on us and which do not raise either the stature of Indian journalism or anything else. So many of these stories are untrue. I think I read somewhere in a Delhi paper about the UP Government presenting Rs. 20,000 and 200 *saris* to Mrs. Vijayalakshmi Pandit on her departure to Moscow. I read all manner of the most malicious and unfounded and false statements in these papers about Shri Asaf Ali.

Now, coming to the question of cost, the figure Shri Kamath mentioned, five lakhs, has of course no relation to fact. I do not know what the figure is. I suggest that if Shri Kamath makes any statements, he might investigate the facts before he makes them.

What I should like this House to remember is that these ambassadorial appointments have to keep up a certain dignity and a certain status. It is no good our sending an ambassador and not giving him a house to live in, not giving him furniture in the house, not providing him with the minimum wherewith he can meet and entertain other diplomats properly and decently. I doubt if any country, big or small, is conducting its ambassadorial establishments so cheaply as we are doing.

A great deal of criticism has been made about our Ambassador in Moscow getting furniture from Stockholm. Well, how a house has to be furnished in Moscow, of course Hon. Members do not realise. It just is not possible to furnish it easily in Moscow. You get an empty house. We thought of sending things from India, but it was almost a physical impossibility unless you spent vast sums on aeroplanes to carry chairs and tables from here. Of course, it could have been furnished alternatively with Russian furniture. The Russian people, and all credit to them for this, ever since the war, are so intent on doing what they consider to be the fundamental things, that they refuse to waste their time on the accessories of life. They have to rebuild their country after the most horrible suffering and damage suffered in the war and they are concentrating on major undertakings. They go about in patched-up clothes and worn-out shoes. It does not matter, but they are building dams, reservoirs and factories and the rest which they consider more important. So it is not easy to get any of these small accessories of life for the moment.

The only things you can get in Russia are antique pieces of Czarist days which are frightfully expensive. The result is that our Embassy in Moscow had to go to Stockholm for its chairs and tables, and as these were urgently required—office equipment, etc.—our Ambassador had to go there. But, of course, the visit to Stockholm was not merely, members of the House should realise, to buy furniture. When an Ambassador goes somewhere, that Ambassador does other work too, and any kind of shopping that might be done is incidental.

I am grateful to the House for their kind sentiments and their expressions of goodwill for our attempt to follow a certain rather vague policy in regard to foreign affairs. I wish it were a more definite policy. I think it is growing more definite, and in this connection may I say that at the present moment no country, including the Big Powers with their long traditions in foreign affairs, has anything which could be called a precise and definite foreign policy, because the world itself is in a fluid condition? Of course, if you call it a definite policy that one great country should look with bitter dislike upon another and suspect it, I would say that it is not a policy at all but mere passion and prejudice. Otherwise, there is hardly any very definite policy in any country and each country is trying to fit in its policy from day to day with the changing circumstances.

Sir, I have taken interest in the various suggestions and criticisms made. I think possibly, if I had been speaking not from my place here, but from somewhere else, I might have produced a longer list of criticisms. So I am grateful for the gentle way in which the Hon. Members have treated the External Affairs Department.

In criticising the foreign policy of the Government of India during the last year, I should like this House for an instant to turn its mind to any country today and think of its foreign policy — whether it is the USA, the United Kingdom, the USSR, China or France. These are supposed to be the great Powers. Let them think of their policy and tell me if they would say that the foreign policy of anyone of those countries has succeeded from any point of view, from the point of view of moving towards world peace or preventing world war, or succeeded even from the mere opportunist and individual point of view of that country.

I think if you will look at this question from this point of view, you will find that there has been a miserable failure in the foreign policy of every great Power and country.

Sources

The following chapters (essays/columns) comprising this volume have been reproduced with permission from their respective original source of publication mentioned alongside. Permissions granted are gratefully acknowledged.

CHAPTER NO./TITLE/SOURCE

1. The strategic consequences of India's economic performance
   Economic and Political Weekly, June 29, 2002.

2. The economic dimension of India's foreign policy
   World Affairs, Vol. 2, No. 2, April-June 1998.

3. Conceptualising economic security
   Satish Kumar (Edited), *India's National Security Annual Review, 2004*.
   India Research Press, New Delhi, 2005.

5. Stewing in our own juice
   Seminar, November, 2002.

6. India and the world
   The Times of India, December 25, 1995.

7. The economics of national security
   Business Standard, December 04, 1998.

8. The Bombay plea
   The Times of India, November 12, 1993.

9. Competitive advantage
   The Times of India, March 07, 1995.

10. The fruits of economic diplomacy
    Business Standard, 2000.

11. The Madrid impasse
    The Times of India, October 12, 1995.

12. Intimations of greatness
    The Indian Express, September 30, 2002.

13. Diplomatic business
    The Times of India, 1999.

14. The strategic imperative
    The Indian Express, December 29, 2000.

15. Brinkmanship blues
    The Indian Express, June 25, 2001.

16. Economic sanctions in war on terror
    The Financial Express, May 31, 2002.

17. Not an advisable advisory
    The Indian Express, June 03, 2002.

18. Who wants charity?
    The Indian Express, October 29, 2001.

19. Who is afraid of globalisation?
    The Financial Express, December 13, 2002.

20. Sizing up the competition
    The Financial Express, March 29, 2002.

21. Doing our own thing
    The Indian Express, March 31, 2003.

22. A Jaswant Singh doctrine on foreign aid
    The Financial Express, June 06, 2003.

23. India launches FTA spree before Cancun
    The Financial Express, June 20, 2003.

24. The business of foreign policy
    The Financial Express, August 01, 2003.

25. Slower track WTO *versus* fast track FTAs
    The Financial Express, September 05, 2003.

26. Foreign trade is also about imports
    The Financial Express, November 21, 2003.

27. An open market and an open society
    The Financial Express, March 19, 2004.

30. The Asian econmic crisis and India's external economic relations
    Money & Finance, ICRA Bulletin, Oct-Dec, 1998.

31. South Asian dialogue
    The Times of India, December, 1998.

32. Tackling trust, trade and terrorism
    The Financial Express, January 09, 2004.

33. A win-win race in South Asia
    The Financial Express, June 06, 2003.

34. South Asia can rise and shine together
    The Financial Express, December 05, 2003.

35. Economic consequences of J&K elections
    The Financial Express, October 11, 2002.

36. The business of other neighbours
    The Financial Express, June 14, 2002.

39. Mr. Rao goes to Washington
    The Times of India, April 29, 1995.

40. Beyond nuclear policy
    The Times of India, December 16, 1999.

41. Who's afraid of entities list?
    Business Standard, 1998.

42. Dotcom diaspora
    The Times of India, April 28, 2000.

43. Terms of engagement
    The Times of India, January, 1998.

44. Long and short of India-US relations
    The Financial Express, August 23, 2002.

45. The big deal about no big deal
    The Financial Express, April 19, 2002.

46. India and US
    The Financial Express, December 12, 2003.

47. Putin Russia in perspective
    The Financial Express, November 29, 2002.

48. G-8 Summit
    The Financial Express, May 23, 2003.

49. Business in command
    The Times of India, May 22, 1995.

50. Manhattan of the East
    The Indian Express, November 26, 2001.

51. Pacific blues
    The Indian Express, May 04, 2001.

52. The Chinese art of economic diplomacy
    Business Standard, 1997.

53. The new great game
    The Indian Express, November 24, 2003.

54. Business beyond borders
    The Financial Express, January 18, 2002.

55. An eagle's eye on the dragon
    The Financial Express, August 09, 2002.

56. Is India a paper tiger?
    The Indian Express, August 26, 2002.

57. The coming of age of Korea Inc.
    The Financial Express, October 24, 2003.

58. State and market in foreign policy
    The Financial Express, April 11, 2003.

60. Geography of business
    The Times of India, August 10, 1994.

61. Media multiplier
    The Times of India, April 05, 1999.

62. Widen that lens
    The Indian Express, August 04, 2003.

63. An India of Narayana Murthy or Sudarshan?
    The Financial Express, October 04, 2002.

Appendix:

India's emergence in world affairs
Speech by Jawaharlal Nehru in the Constituent Assembly (Legislative),
New Delhi, December 4, 1947.

Index

THE MANIAC'S CRYSTAL BALL

Many shopkeepers still don't get it. They think the Guide was written for them. They can't seem to wrap their heads around the idea that it's a SHOPPER's guide, written for SHOPPERS by a SHOPPER. "Why is it sooo critical?" "Why don't you only say nice things?" "Well, yes, I thought most of it was funny. Well, yes, it was all true. But why do you have to say anything negative? We're doing our best." That sort of thing.

From time to time, an owner or manager will call and ask me to consult. While I'd be happy to take their money, it just doesn't feel quite right. I can't be writing reviews one day, telling them how to go about running a bigger and better business the next (much as I'd like to). Sounds innocent enough at first, but think about it for a while. Will this mean that they can automatically expect a better review next time? more hangers?

O.K. For argument's sake, let's say I do agree to consult. Next Guide is printed. Then the ax falls: "Nancy, you told me to do such and such. I did. Why didn't I get four hangers this time?" Of course, follow-through is in the eye of the beholder. They might have done what I perceive to be only a 3 hanger job of it. Sooo, I decided I just can't ethically wear two hats at the same time.

BOTTOM LINE: REVIEWS AND RATINGS ARE NOT FOR SALE!!
(But The Guide is)

Someone, somewhere, will write the definitive manual on How To Run A Thrift, Resale, Secondhand And/Or Consignment Shop. Not me. Doesn't capture my interest. Besides, if they would only read The Guide through the eyes of a SHOPPER, not those of a defensive OWNER or MANAGER...Ah well, criticism is a toughie isn't it? Even if it is meant to be constructive.

What I decided I *can* do about all this is write...

THE MANIAC'S 36 COMMANDMENTS:

(God's got it down pat. She only needed 10.)

IF I HAD MY WAY, every secondhand shopkeeper would…

1. Say Hello!
2. Put hours on their cards and shop windows, and stick to 'em.
3. Print new cards and signs when hours do change.
4. Put inventory on card. Often, name only doesn't clue us to what is sold.
5. Put zip codes on business cards. (I use zip code maps, don't you?)
6. Make it so we can read the card, the name, the hours, the prices, etc.
7. Give out clear directions. Have a map by the phone.
8. Stop using New and Second in the name. It's been DONE.
9. Not claim to sell designer fashions if they carry gum-snapper duds.
10. Not gossip with each other or on the phone in front of customers.
11. Not gossip in front of customers about a customer who's just left.
12. Not turn down/accept a consignment in front of other customers.
13. Not help themselves to a consignment in front of customers.
14. Have a 50%-50% split and up, only (in the consignor's favor of course).
15. Forgo an annual fee, seasonal fee, per item fee, any fee of any kind fee.
16. Print and update a consignment or donation policy.
17. Give out the printed and updated consignment or donation policy.
18. Really donate the leftover stuff at the end of the year.
19. Stop playing insider-trading games with goods and prices.
20. Have EVERYTHING priced, somehow, somewhere.
21. Have younger and senior volunteers working at the same time.
22. Not eat in the shop in front of customers.
23. Abstain from smoking in the shop, even after hours.
24. Install good lighting, no-glare-you-in-the-eye stuff, no gloom and doom.
25. Make it so everyone can comfortably reach every rack, bin and shelf.
26. Have a public bathroom, especially if you sell kids' stuff .
27. Have a dressing room/area if you sell clothes.
28. Have a play area, especially if you sell kids' stuff.
29. Get rid of those 'We Sell Kids' signs.
30. Put vintage with vintage and sporting goods with sporting goods, etc.
31. Eliminate eau-de-old-clothes.
32. Refuse torn, stained, smelly clothing.
33. Not 'lose' our consignments.
34. Willingly direct customers to other secondhand stores when asked.
35. Buy, read and sell The Thrift Shop Maniac's Guide.
36. Say Goodbye!